W9-BYV-421

The Popular
Mood of
Pre-Civil War
America

Recent Titles in
Contributions in American Studies
Series Editor: Robert H. Walker

The Popular Mood of Pre-Civil War America

LEWIS O. SAUM

CONTRIBUTIONS IN AMERICAN STUDIES, NUMBER 46

GREENWOOD PRESS  Westport, Connecticut • London, England

Library of Congress Cataloging in Publication Data

Saum, Lewis O
    The popular mood of pre-Civil War America.

    (Contributions in American studies; no. 46 ISSN
0084–9227)
    Bibliography: p.
    Includes index.
    1.   United States—Civilization—1783–1865.
2.   Public opinion—United States—History.
I.   Title.
E164.S26   973   79–8281
ISBN   0–313–21056–X

Copyright © 1980 by Lewis O. Saum

All rights reserved. No portion of this book may be
reproduced, by any process or technique, without the
express written consent of the publisher.

Library of Congress Catalog Card Number: 79–8281
ISBN: 0–313–21056–X
ISSN: 0084–9227

First published in 1980

Greenwood Press
A division of Congressional Information Service, Inc.
88 Post Road West, Westport, Connecticut 06881

Printed in the United States of America

10   9   8   7   6   5   4   3   2   1

To my mother, Elsie Hunter Saum

CONTENTS

ACKNOWLEDGMENTS

The research phase of this work was made possible by grants from the University of Washington, the Henry E. Huntington Library and Art Gallery, and the National Endowment for the Humanities. The University of Washington Graduate School provided summer salary supplements; the award from the Huntington Library and Art Gallery in San Marino, California, allowed two months of research at that institution; and in turn, that institution has kindly given permission for use in this book of the various sources which I used there. A Younger Humanist Fellowship granted by the National Endowment for the Humanities sustained me through an academic leave during which I traveled to several manuscript repositories.

A myriad of individuals have encouraged me in this endeavor. I cannot here specify all of these people, and perhaps graciousness would dictate that I therefore specify none. But two individuals whose professional influence and encouragement have been of inestimable value to me must be mentioned: Lewis E. Atherton of the University of Missouri-Columbia who provided my graduate school direction and enduring inspiration, and Otis A. Pease of the University of Washington, my cordial colleague and thoughtful chairman when I was struggling to bring some order into this inordinately amorphous realm of popular thought. My thanks and gratefulness go to them, as well as to colleagues and acquaintances here and elsewhere and to those unfailingly helpful people in manuscript repositories from Portland, Maine, to San Marino, California, and from Columbia, South Carolina, to Seattle, Washington. Altered versions of two chapters have already appeared in print: one in *American Quarterly* and the other in *Indiana Magazine of History*. Chapter 4 appeared as "Death in the Popular Mind of Pre-Civil War America," *American Quarterly* 26 (December 1974), 477–95, Copyright 1974, Trustees of the University of Pennsylvania. Chapter 1 appeared as "Providence in the Popular Mind of Pre-Civil War America," in *Indiana Magazine of History*

72 (December 1976): 315–46. I appreciate the cooperation of those publications and their willingness to see the fuller versions in book form.

Finally I will note that I have not seen fit to ask colleagues or professional friends and acquaintances to read parts or all of the manuscript. Whether that be for good or for bad, I rest in the assurance that whatever credit might attach to this work will be no more than can be borne by one person, and, conversely, that whatever discredit might attach to it must not, in any way however indirect, be borne by any other than one person.

INTRODUCTION

This book attempts to portray the moods and beliefs of the ordinary American people of the pre-Civil War generation, roughly 1830 to 1860, based on their diaries, letters, and commonplace jottings. Such an approach might avoid the dangers one faces when trying to infer popular beliefs from parts of the popular culture such as novels, plays, songs, or poems. For those of scholarly or specialized interests, matters of method are discussed at some length in the appendix. But in general terms, this book seeks to convey and analyze what ordinary people themselves wrote about matters they deemed important. This book also seeks to relate the notions and persuasions of the common man to the views of some of his more sophisticated contemporaries. A secondary interest of this work is to indicate the degree to which the mood of the Age of the Common Man reflected the Puritan religious past and, conversely, the degree to which it foreshadowed secular modernity.

Examining common existence causes some to become uneasy. A half century ago, Joseph Wood Krutch saw in the modern temper a rejection of the heroic. Modern man, he contended, no longer believed in great men: "We do not write about kings because we do not believe that any man is worthy to be one and we do not write about courts because hovels seem to us to be dwellings more appropriate to the creatures who inhabit them." Human nature had come to be viewed as a trifling refinement of brute nature. In Krutch's portrayal, modern man turned his scrutiny away from the heroic toward "village politics," for example, or some other aspect of "the common man and his common life." Such things, Krutch dolefully concluded, were "small enough" for modern man "to be able to believe."[1]

Twenty-five years later, Krutch put a similar concern in terms of a question: "Is the Common Man Too Common?"[2] His answer gave little reassurance. In the book of essays which used Krutch's question for its title, D. W. Brogan ironically called attention to the "progress of popular culture." In doing so, he reminded his readers of the "cynical conservative who said that the only result of universal education in England was that rude words were written a foot or so lower on the walls than they used to be."[3] Another twentieth-century writer, Albert Jay Nock, put this concern in variant form in an essay titled "On Making Low People Interesting," a task which he presented as somewhere between challenging and impossible.[4] "Homely truth" may well be, as the creator of Tom Sawyer pronounced it, "unpalatable."[5] Perhaps that explains the churlish fromulation of another modern essayist, Philip Wylie: "Common Man: The Hero's Backside."[6] Such a sector hardly invites scrutiny, and one might better avoid what the poet William Cowper long ago called that "fond attempt to give a deathless lot / To names ignoble, born to be forgot!"[7]

But the attractions of investigating the common man's existence have come to outweigh the liabilities. In recent years, as will be discussed at some length later, various dimensions of that general subject have received the close attention of scholars and of more general investigators. And so those who have invested large amounts of time, frayed their patience and dimmed their eyesight by reading the diaries, letters and other jottings of farmers and clerks and housewives and schoolboys have the assurance that, at least potentially, their efforts may find approval.

The Tone of The Common Man's Writings

In 1935, the United States Weather Bureau station at Fort Wayne, Indiana, transcribed a nineteenth century diary kept by one Rapin Andrews.[8] For many years down to 1874, Andrews and someone else after him recorded the temperature three times daily, adding a note on general weather conditions. Theirs was nearly the quintessential weather diary. Some have supposed that common people confined themselves to such matters, and sometimes I received good-natured chiding for attempting a book on atmospheric conditions of pre-Civil War America. The weather reports of Andrews and his collaborator did not serve my purposes, but their spirit of earnest dedication did. We must not fault Andrews' successor for neglecting the weather on June 30, 1849, because that was the day that "Rapin Andrews Died." When Andrews and those like him wrote, they did so to a purpose, and they did so earnestly. More and more as my own research in such sources proceeded, it occurred to me that, as earnestness of tone departed, my suspicions rose. When a journal informed me that it would be more than a "record of facts," and would be as well "a book of fancies, whim-whams, and thoughts,"[9] I felt misgivings. It occurred to me that its author may have had more refinement than was allowable for my purposes. As I hope this study will show, the common people did not confine themselves to "facts," whether of the temperature or otherwise. They reveled in "thoughts," but only so long as those thoughts were to a point, generally a religious or moral point. Those sources that promise "fancies" or "whim-whams" should generally be avoided.

At one level, an earnest tone means hardly more than that people with little writing ability rarely wrote sportively; they wrote as they lived—prosaically, haltingly, unimaginatively, and, often, sadly. And at another level, a principle bordering upon the philosophical led them to avoid things pertaining to fancy. These people often harbored objectivist notions strongly suggestive of Isaac Watts, that religious moderator of "The Great Mr. Locke: America's Philosopher,"[10] as Merle Curti styled his position in the pre-Civil War years. Watts' urging to "take heed of a fanciful temper of mind"[11] resounded far more distinctly than most studies of that period would have us believe. The sober observation of fact and concrete detail laid heavy claim upon the ordinary people of that era.

"Some Carolinians out here," one North Carolinian who had moved to Illinois observed, "are so hard pressed for news that if a fellow were to f.f. fart they would send the report without delay."[12] His words have an uncharacteristic quality, a quality that is more in keeping with the Southern mood wherein earthiness, irreverence, and playfulness had fuller sway. The news conveyed by letter usually involved serious rather than jocular material: health, marriages, deaths, and the state of religion. That Tarheel in Illinois lived in a nation where most people sought "to be grave," as one young woman put it as she began a letter to her brother. Cheerfulness was one thing, she conceded, but "I know that levity is a besetting sin of men."[13] She readily participated in the dour vigilance that was yet upon the land, and she probably would have been quick to insist that that "besetting sin" was particularly pronounced among Southerners such as the aforementioned Tarheel. What one student of humor has called "the surrender of the James River to the Charles" was not as complete as some Northerners would have liked.[14]

By and large, it was not difficult to avoid levity, for the occasions for writing tended to be somber. These letters do not convey by their general spirit the much heralded optimism and assertiveness of that era. Letters, of course, derive from separation. Letters and loneliness are closely entwined. But there is far more involved here than the loneliness of the letter writer. There is a larger loneliness, the lasting loneliness of the Pilgrim, and an unprepossessing Pilgrim at that. In 1847, a young New Jersey woman made the move to Illinois with the man she had recently married. Like so many others, she kept a journal which, as promised, she sent to a sister. In a covering note she said that she regretted ever having made the agreement because the finished product seemed unworthy of the postage required; "maybe it will be more interesting to you but I cant bear to read it[;] it sounds so much like me."[15] All to whom the mirror gives an unflattering response can well appreciate Jane Lewis's rejection of what seemed "so much like me."

Beyond the matter of unshakable fact and reality, one must bear in mind yet other bases of the earnest, somber and restrained aura surrounding such writings. Many of these communications were family letters that were meant to be read to or by others than the receiver. That magnified the writer's effort to edify, and muted the frivolous. Parts of a letter would sometimes be specified for personal reading only, as when a San Francisco bartender conveyed an off-color story to his mother but asked that she not read it to his sisters.[16] Sometimes double letters were sent—one for general consumption and the other for personal consumption. For example, "two old letters" that Attorney J. H. Bankhead, Jr., came upon in settling an estate in Alabama in 1904 were in fact alternate versions of the same letter, both written on the same day.[17] The Mexican War volunteer who wrote them penned one version which his friend at home could read or show to one and all. The other version was not meant to be shown to others, particularly not to a certain woman because she might "turn a fool." According to the writer, "she is fol anof now." Surely, it would have served no good purpose to have this particular instruction regarding that woman (or perhaps another woman with whom the writer had been "so in timat") cast abroad: "I want you to wach that girl that I was so in tonite with when I left and wright to me For I think that she has got the wad stuct to her."[18]

That Alabama soldier notwithstanding, most of these sources contain very little of the spontaneous or the Rabellaisian. Discipline and dedication were more than postures assumed for the moment; they were practically the *raison d'être* of unsophisticated writings. "Having been a long while impressed with the importance of keeping a journal"[19]—thus a young man of Bowery Village launched upon an account which would reach print in book form over a century later. On August 11, 1859, Amelia Akehurst married Sylvester Lines, and six days later she wrote: "Have neglected my journal." Sylvester might well have taken it amiss if he had known that Amelia reproved herself again six days later: "Dear Journal[:] I am neglecting you without a cause."[20] Needless to say, irresolution and neglect occurred times without measure, but the failures were often noted and were apparently viewed seriously.

In 1942, the Editorial Department of the *Annals of Iowa* gave the urging, "Let's Keep a Diary!" At the outset, the writer bemoaned the low reputation which had come to diarists other than those in high places. Then, after noting the growing interest in "the common man and his society," the author contended that "second hand evidence" such as newspapers and books did not give sufficient testimony on important historical matters. And in a modern world vexed by urbanization and the breakdown of the family, "the gulfs between generations have widened." The family diary, it seemed to that writer, might do something to restore connections and to foster a sense of " 'belongingness.' " Oddly enough, though he urged his readers to go to old diaries to discern why people went west or what they "thought of Lincoln," he failed to note that our ancestors attached great importance to diaries and journals. Those documents represented far more than the idle prattle of the "immature" or of the "sentimentalists";[21] they partook of modest hope, of unblinkable reality, and sometimes of unutterable poignance as well.

With the passage of time, diaries and letters became mementos. Again and again, writers mentioned reading what had been penned long before, or they stated their intention of returning in years to come to what was being written or read at the moment. (And, *memento mori*, somewhere in America at the very infancy of photography in the early 1840s there came "a unique innovation— photographing the dead."[22]) A collection at the Huntington Library contains a tiny, fragile envelope yellowed by age. In it there is a card enfolding a lock of reddish-brown hair. The card bears the date of January 23, 1851, and a no- tation indicating that at a party on that date the lock of hair was clipped "as a relic of happy hours that are gone."[23] Here we have a sad and compelling story. The woman who wrote that note had meant to marry the youth from whose head she took that lock of hair, but a decade passed, war came, and she never married him.

Understated hurt and gentle melancholy suffuse much of what was thought and written in that era. As one of the most popular songs of the era put it,

> Oh, do you remember Sweet Alice, Ben Bolt,
> Sweet Alice with hair so brown?

To the modern taste, that has scant appeal for it smacks of what Charles L. Sanford called the "mawkish sentimentality common to the period."[24] The locks of hair and the other "relics" took written form in the letters that had been saved and in the diaries that had been started long before.

The earnestness surrounding the letters and diaries of the period approaches the devotional. In March 1855, a young Maine housewife entered the fol- lowing in her diary: "Reading over old letters of Samuel's and mine in the fore- noon, bringing old times to my mind and tears to my eyes." One wonders what sad reverie might have come to Samuel if his eyes fell upon that passage a year and a half later when he tearfully penned his adieu after the last words that his now dead wife had entered in her diary.[25]

And, of course, another motivation for letter-writing was the serious one of improving one's writing. "I have improved in writing a goodeal," Charles Dud- ley of Cheshire, Connecticut, happily asserted after three years of diary- keeping.[26] This intent is often mentioned in letters. Thus, a gold-seeker could commend his wife back in Pennsylvania for the fact that her letters were be- coming "better written and more interesting." As always, however, there was still room for improvement, and she was reminded that she should "never put a capital letter at the beginning of an unimportant word. . . ."[27]

The bent for improvement involved far more than mechanical facility with the language. As an upstate New York farmer noted at the outset of a diary, he sought not only to enhance his penmanship, but also "to exercise my judg- ment, so that nothing improper may enter" the diary that would "deface the pages within its lids."[28] This goal suggests much more than the stuffiness of one individual. It is the modern age, as F. L. Lucas put it rather shrilly, that "cares nothing if a writer is squalid or brutal, or grovelling, or imbecile, provided he is 'interesting' and leaves a new taste, however brassy, in the mouth."[29] "How peculiarly modern a preference it is," Lionel Trilling remarked, "to emphasize the disjunction between the life and the work, to find an especial value in a 'perfect' work that arises from an 'imperfect' life."[30] That farmer lived in a different era from our own, an era which found it hard to believe that an evil man could write good things. Simply put, form and substance were closely tied. While this farmer would never be a man of words, the words he did use and the sentiments they expressed had to be, as best he could manage, proper and dignified.

From that sort of fastidiousness it is only a step to another aspect of the common man's writing. Not only did his writings show attention to matters of discipline and dedication, but also to the religious and the spiritual. If only in vestigial form, the diary or journal of pre-Civil War America yet remained the Puritan confessional, prepared as "a daily record of the state of the writer's soul."[31] Thus, a student could revile himself in this fashion: "From coldness in religion I have neglected my journal. . . ."[32] The diary, the journal and, less systematically, the letter still recorded the Pilgrim's progress. On his twenty-sixth birthday, a farmer who had moved from New York to Minnesota Territory wrote the following:

A little more than a quarter of a century has passed over my head, and to what purpose have I lived? I want to live every day in such a manner that the night may reveal upon the pages of this book that I have not lived in vain; and while I trace all the little events that crowd upon my pathway, and which may interest me to reflect upon at some future period, this diary shall more completely speak of my life—shall be the mentor of my evil deeds; for I must fully portray, both what I have done through the day, and what I felt like doing.[33]

The writings of such people partake very little of the breezy, jocose, or earthy. That is a matter which gets further consideration, particularly in Chapters 5 and 7. Here it bears only a general mention as well as the reminder that the modern commentator should be cautious not to assume or inject such a tone.

Matters of Form in the Common Man's Writings

The tone of these writings was generally somber and the form frequently challenging. Whatever their content, they pose a problem of comprehension and analysis for the reader over a century later. There is, for example, the basic matter of definitions, a good illustration of which appears in a letter written by argonaut Andrew Cairns to the family in Orange County, New York. California's resources impressed this young man mightily, "but sosiety," he added by way of qualification, "is in an awful fix if sosiety i can call it were there is but one sect." Then he gave "a little history how we miners get along," an account that featured "blody noses and black eyes."[34]

The scholar who edited Cairns' letters for the *California Historical Society Quarterly* footnoted "one sect," explaining that usage as pertaining to social class, "the levelling influence of the mining camp on social rank and position." But that did not ring quite true, and at first, it struck me that by sect Cairns might have meant that in the moral degeneracy of the mining camp—where, for example, the "sactified profesor turns blasfemer"—there was indeed but one sect, the irreligious. In fact, he meant nothing more than its etymological relative, sex. This explanation is unmistakable a few lines later when he asserted that the devil would retain "univesel sway in californi . . . until we get more of the femingen gender to cool down the eavil pasions of man."[35] As we shall see, the very words "society" and "history," as used by this miner and others like him, bore meanings far removed from those we attach to them today.

While definitions in these writings can baffle, matters of presentation and substance can nearly overwhelm. One does not approach lightly the myriad of bizarre spellings or the dishearteningly woeful tune for which those spellings serve as off-key notes. "Old Sam Adams," his relative Elizabeth wrote to her sister, "is in the Caddis poor house." After that rather conventional pronouncement, Elizabeth Adams dismissed the niggling demands of orthography, as well as any rays of worldly hope. What Caddis for Cadiz foreshadowed in terms of form, the poor house foreshadowed in terms of substance. Someone named Joseph had again failed, this time in running a still, and he became so out of "hart" that he "imbraced infidillidy." Yet another relative or acquaintance of this Ohio woman had had his teeth extracted, resulting in the decay of the jawbone marrow. He was not "exspecked" to live long, and whatever the details, it was "verry sarton" that he would never recover. Old William Winters had "can sor" of the face and he too would die, but at least he was "resined" to God's will. Scarlet fever stalked that area of Ohio, and the crops were bad. But Elizabeth Adams noted, they still had their "Daly brea," and with that they must rest "contente." Not everyone spelled with such abandon as did this woman who referred to herself as a "Poor scoller,"[36] but reading generous amounts of such sources provides ample challenges to the eye and mind. Because the misspellings are so innumerable, I have trusted to the reader's faith and understanding, and have thereby dispensed with *sic* in nearly all cases. The only real emendation is the addition of punctuation in brackets. As the modern editor of a Gold Rush diary remarked, it seemed "almost sacrilegious" to correct such a "unique notion of English spelling."[37]

There are, of course, light and redeeming moments in the letters and diaries. On rare occasions one encounters a bit of humor, as when a young man told of a friend who was torn between a claim in Kansas and a sweetheart in New York, adding that the sweetheart was more "liable to be jumped in his absence" than

was the claim.³⁸ At times the very economy of language has a compelling quality. On a dreary Connecticut Monday in November 1846, thirty-year-old
George Lewis and the eighteen-year-old woman who had become his wife only
two months before stayed in because of rain. Lewis measured his diary words,
and he needed few to convey the tenor and progression of the day: "Rain[;] at
Home, *cross Helen*, (*Long evening*) (*a mistake*)."³⁹ And some things beguile
and entice. In 1858, Elijah Smith, a redoubtable carpenter and farmer of upstate New York, recalled what appears to have been the departure of his
second wife. Coming home of an evening, Smith found the house dark and the
wife and children retired.

I stept up to the side of the bead to undress and to my surprise she said to me mr Smith
you can not sleep here to night[.] [W]hat is the matter said I[?] [W]ell said she I have got
William in bead with me and there is no room[.] [W]ell said I put William in his own
bead[.] [N]o said she you cannot come here at all[.] I then lit a candle[.] I found hir
goods all packed up and a good many of my owne with them[.] I asked hir what this
packing of goods ment[.] [W]ell said she I am a going to leave you in the morning[.]
[Y]ou bee said I what for a cause[.] [S]aid she have not I used ⁴⁰

Regretfully, Smith's account breaks off at that point. Our disappointment perhaps justifies Ambrose Bierce's definition of historian in *The Devil's Dictionary* as "broad-gauge gossip."

Recalling the days when his father was a village postmaster, Charles Henry
Smith (Bill Arp) noted that he, as clerk for his father, often wrote letters for
those who were unable or disinclined.⁴¹ In the present study, I have not
troubled myself overmuch about the matter of amanuenses. A letter may occasionally suggest that it was written by someone other than the signer, and a
diary will sometimes show that the keeper of it did some writing for neighbors.
But it seemed needless and impossible to make separations where, if there were
an amanuensis, he was hardly more versed than the person for whom he wrote.

Bill Arp also recalled that "Nine out of ten of those country letters began, 'I
take my pen in my hand to let you know that I am well, and hope these few lines
will find you enjoying the same blessing.' "⁴² These wearyingly stylized usages
may indicate little more than unthinking ritual, but some might wonder about
the influence of the instructional letter-books of the period. Perhaps all of those
inconsequential people were writing in accord with what amounted to style
manuals. The sources covered in this study, as I have noted already and will
note again, made almost pathetic efforts to maintain form and propriety. These
people knew, as the wife of an unsuccessful "joyner" put it, that the pen "can
many times speak forth beautiful and Sublime things," but they also knew
that the pen did so only "where it has the strong and intellectual mind" guiding
it. We do not need the admission of this lady, or of the others, that the "strong
and intellectual mind" was not there.⁴³

The people studied in this work apparently did not bother with such contrivances as letter-books. A young South Carolina woman wrote the following: "Since fate interposed between us in the hour of prosperity, I cannot, in the bleak and chilling period of adversity, seek to unite your destiny with mine:–"[44] Was Rosannah McCullough getting pen and mind warmed and ordered for a letter which at that moment had to be written? Was she copying from a letter-book in the event that such a letter might sometime be needed? She may have resorted to a letter-book, but the only explicit mention of letter-books I encountered came in a complaint by a young man that the people at home did not write to him. He ironically surmised that, if what he wrote came from a "letter-book" rather than from him, it might be deemed worthy of response.[45]

Organizing and Presenting the Common Man's Writings

In a letter that went from western New York to Wisconsin, a woman urged her sister to respond soon and to "inform me with regard to your spiritual state as well as your temporal."[46] This, the fundamental duality of the age—spiritual and temporal—provides the general framework for this book. The spiritual category took precedence over the temporal. When Lewis E. Atherton, who directed my graduate studies some years ago, came upon me working on the early stages of this research in a manuscript repository, he noted the King James version of the Bible which I had near at hand. He made, as I recall it, some gentle remark about the pleasing intimation given by the presence of that book. That Bible, used so frequently to check sermon texts and other matters, testified to the degree that religious concerns informed the writings of our lesser ancestors. That Bible evokes the spirit which the poet Gray put this way in discussing the "mute inglorious Milton":

> And many a holy text around she strews,
> That teach the rustic moralist to die.[47]

Part One of this study treats things spiritual. Providence (Chapter 1) comes at the outset because the common people saw God ordering the cosmos and, directly or indirectly, all that was in it. Man's foremost obligation was to recognize that reality. In turn, religion (Chapter 2) equipped man to make emotional and spiritual accommodation with the reality that God imposed. Conversion and revival (Chapter 3) provided the means by which man achieved the reconciliation and resignation that religion offered. Notions regarding the millennium (Chapter 3) were apparently not very significant in giving direction to the Pilgrim's progress. The end of that progress lay, not in ecstatic expectations regarding the Second Coming, but in sober-eyed and resigned contemplation of and confrontation with death (Chapter 4). The "rustic moralist" was indeed taught "to die."

With regard to man's temporal existence, self and society (Chapter 5) came foremost, and the relation between them bears careful examination. Family, friends, church, and immediate community were construed as society, and society performed the salutary function of restraining and negating the self, that most imperfect aspect of man. The worldly forces inhering in politics and the nation (Chapter 6) made their claims upon and their erosions into the comforting microcosm of society. The nation was perceived as turning to the physical, geographical expanse that lay before it. That magnetic gravitation begot one of the more torturous dilemmas in the Common man's mood—the tension between nature and art (Chapter 7), the tension between what man had made or shaped and what he had not. However the debate over nature and art might be resolved, the temporal destiny, as perceived by the common people, lay in the West (Chapter 8), just as the individual, spiritual destiny lay in the grave. The parallel between death and the West is more apt than one might at first suppose. That destiny in the West posed some of the most formidable threats to the spiritually infused microcosm called society, to that delicate fabric which had somewhat shielded and comforted beleaguered man.

Frequently, modern scholars show secular inclinations, and they show impatience with what they deem unallowable amounts of religious expression. Sometimes, for example, they edit diaries in such a way as to leave the wheat of political or economic content while removing the chaff of religious fancies. Thus, even a scholar who ordinarily showed large regard for the integrity of humble writings explained of one of his editing projects that "a prolonged religious meditation has been eliminated in the interests of conservation of space." I strongly suspect that that was precisely the part of the journal that the writer of it would have most resented having excised; religious reflection was, as he himself noted, "the chief design" of his written efforts.[48]

The organization of this work reflects the separation of things spiritual from things temporal, and the presentation involves a synthesis of the writings of many people. Attempting such a synthesis poses some danger because writing intellectual history is, as William B. Hesseltine once remarked, "like trying to nail jelly to the wall."[49] Such a historical presentation not only involves one in the stickily unmanageable, but it also can seduce the scholar into grave errors of logic.

In an essay contrasting "History of the Elite and History of the Folk," Richard M. Dorson urges us to remedy the tendency to "ignore Everyman's history."[50] In Everyman, Dorson unintentionally presents an obscure formulation, for through it the individual, with all his crotchetiness and peculiarity, is lost in some overarching spirit. That woman on the farm in western New York disappears, as does her sister in Wisconsin, and in their stead comes forth some transcendent construct called Everyman. This verges upon a large philosophical issue, and here we can do little more than mention the problem. Speaking directly to the matter of depicting popular moods, George Boas briskly reminds us that "the common people are as diverse in their minds and lives as the upper classes. . . . It is about time that we recognized the existence of individuals and hence the irreducible heterogeneity of society."[51] Sound as that reminder may be, still one feels the urge to generalize, to get a bit beyond "irreducible heterogeneity." While I hope that the "rich particularity"[52] which Daniel Boorstin celebrated will be reflected in this study, still, this study involves an excursion into generalization. It involves an attempt to deduce what a sizable part of the American population believed from what a couple thousand individuals actually wrote.

Some historians have been accused of perpetrating the "idealist fallacy,"[53] and some dimensions of the present study may invite such suspicion. As just indicated, this book may be viewed as an effort to recreate a group mind. Some will insist that there is no such thing as a group mind, only individual minds. Whether that is true or not, when a majority of sources say roughly the same thing about the same concerns, the recreation is inevitable. An additional concern may be that I emphasize what these people said rather than what they did. If, as David Hackett Fischer sees it, Perry Miller went astray in depicting overmuch as *homo sapiens* those early Puritans who were genuinely astute,[54] what is to be said for an effort to recreate the reflections of the unreflective? Ought they not to be investigated in terms of, say, the total of their votes or the total value of their wheat crops? Perhaps so, but the informing precepts of this book are different. It is important to know what even humble people believed; what they wrote is the best, if not the only, key to what they believed.

One aspect of the presentation of what follows suggests a matter of conclusion or perhaps of interpretation. For purposes of comparison and contrast, some of the great writers of the period—especially, Emerson, Hawthorne, and Melville—have also been drawn into this study. I have used what I take to be some of the central and characteristic persuasions of those writers, and I do it for a particular purpose. I have not sought in any concerted way to match my findings with the perceptions of, say, foreign visitors of that era such as Alexis de Tocqueville, or Charles Dickens, or Domingo Sarmiento. Nor have I labored to determine, by way of another possibility, which of the popular writers—Timothy Shay Arthur, Harriet Beecher Stowe, Susan Warner or whoever—might have done best at describing or reflecting humble moods. The visitors, the novelists and so on provide subject matter for other books, a good many of which have already been written. The main purpose of this book is to reveal the beliefs of common people by studying what they wrote. But, as noted at the outset, there are some comparative dimensions also. One of them involves juxtaposing humble moods with certain forms of sophisticated expression.

Emerson on the one hand and Hawthorne and Melville on the other serve as spokesmen of lighter and darker moods. They were, of course, not only extraordinary men but also complicated men; but their names resonate aptly as shorthand terms for quite different basic perceptions of the human circumstance and destiny. In the pages that follow, those three, and occasionally others, serve as benchmarks. And in terms of general contention, I find Hawthorne and Melville more nearly in accord with common sentiments. In humble sources I do not find the self-assertion, the ebullience and the complacent sunniness so often ascribed to that period. Rather, I find an abiding moroseness.

This is not to say that the country was populated by mute inglorious Hawthornes and Melvilles, or that people in unprepossessing circumstances even showed any awareness of the existence of men named Hawthorne and Melville. Rather, the point is that a basic similarity of persuasion joins those two men with their lesser contemporaries. Puritanism provides the key to that affinity. Hawthorne, as is well known, was deeply preoccupied with his seventeenth-century ancestors, and Melville's fatalism partakes much of what Ernest Leisy called his "vestigial Puritanism."[55] These sources demonstrate that "vestigial Puritanism" exercised a far greater hold upon America than has often been contended.

In addition to that basic religious orientation, or perhaps as a reflection of it, the two authors are bound to their inconsequential fellows by an overwhelming sadness for man's condition. Man, the " 'poor player,' " Melville mused, "succeeds better in life's tragedy than comedy." That assertion came in *Israel Potter* just before an arresting depiction of poverty, a depiction broken for dramatic effect by reference to a "Plebeian Lear or Oedipus."[56] I suspect that there were more Plebeian Lears in America than many of our accounts have dreamed of. If a Lear is too much, an Abraham Lincoln is not. Almost beyond endurance he has been presented as a man of the people. Emerson's eulogy at Concord serves aptly: "a man of the people," "a plain man of the people," "the true history of the American people in his time."[57] Yet his sadness and melancholy, sometimes thinly veiled by jest, are often presented as quite uncommon. Some special effort seems necessary to explain those aspects of his character, even psychohistorical efforts. But there is a more commonsensical way of approaching the matter. One scholar's suggestion that Lincoln was "perhaps subconsciously"[58] a Puritan seems not at all farfetched to me, but it does seem somewhat roundabout. In describing his early life Lincoln borrowed a line from a poet: "The short and simple annals of the poor." In pre-Civil War America those annals were suffused with sadness and melancholy. Lincoln, it seems to me, was far more unique in ability than he was in temperament.

Lincoln, of course, had his mirthful moments, and Melville could depict the emblematic chanticleer sounding his triumphant call across the land. But the story "Cock-A-Doodle-Do!" has a very telling setting. When Melville's narrator succeeds in locating the source of that " 'glorious voice,' " he finds it trumpeting majestically amid forlornness, poverty and deathly illness. That narrator remarks that there seemed an incongruity between the magnificent bird—"more like a golden eagle than a cock"—and its pitiful surroundings, and that its calls—" 'so loud, so wonderfully clamorous' "—were hardly suited to its feeble auditors. In response its sickly owner poses questions: " 'Don't it do *you* good? Ain't it inspiring? don't it impart pluck? give stuff against despair? . . . Don't the cock . . . glorify this otherwise inglorious, lean, lantern-jawed land?' " The benighted Merrymusk family "seemed to sun themselves in the radiant plumage of the cock."[59] Melville's poignant little allegory tells us much that we sometimes overlook about America's heralded assertiveness, eagle-screaming and cock-crowing. The "aspect" of Hawthorne's "Old Apple-Dealer" conveys the tone of very much of the writing upon which the present study is based--"a patient, long-suffering, quiet, hopeless, shivering aspect."[60]

Putting it another way, the spirit of the ordinary American of the mid-nineteenth century more closely resembled his Puritan ancestors than his twentieth-century descendants. The "puritan catechism, with its emphasis on the deferral of gratifications and the avoidance of indulgence," Andrew Hacker has written, was devised for "an era of scarcity." That catechism had great influence throughout much of American history, but for the post-World War II generation it could act as hardly more than a psychic encumbrance. There is an immense separaton between the modern American and his pre-Civil War ancestor. The "new American," Hacker wrote, makes a "favorable" judgment of himself; "he can find no reason for diffidence or shame."[61] His ancestors found abundant reasons for diffidence, and even for shame.

> Full many a gem of purest ray serene
> The dark unfathom'd caves of ocean bear:
> Full many a flower is born to blush unseen,
> And waste its sweetness on the desert air.

When a boardinghouse keeper in Connecticut appropriated those lines from Gray's "Elegy Written in a Country Churchyard" (lines 53-56) and when a farmer in Arkansas attempted to do the same in a letter to his stepfather,[62] they may, in some pathetic way, have identified with the metonymous figure of the next verse, that "mute inglorious Milton" (line 59). They well knew that they were, in the general sense, mute, and, too, they knew it to be their lot to blush unseen. Those painfully transcribed lines, whatever they may have intimated about pitiful poetic ambition, underscored something about which their contemporaries, Hawthorne and Melville, wrote so well—the lasting loneliness and insignificance of the human circumstance. Nowhere, Paul Elmer More wrote, could one find so well expressed "this one truth of the penalty of solitude laid upon the human soul" as in the works of Hawthorne.[63] That farmer in Arkansas would never gain recognition, as the "Elegy" so well reminded him, but at least, from that "penalty of solitude" he and his fellow in Connecticut, and so many others like them, could pray for deliverance. A dreary and forlorn business, nearly all of it. The glum realities notwithstanding, the world did not weary of Gray's reminder, as it was written, for example, on the first page of a diary kept by a Detroit carpenter:

> Let not ambition mock their useful toil,
> Their homely joys and destiny obscure,
> Nor grandeur hear with disdainful smile
> The short and simple annals of the poor.[64]

PART ONE

THINGS SPIRITUAL

Providence 1

In popular thought of the pre-Civil War period, no theme was more pervasive or philosophically more fundamental than the providential view. Simply put, that view held that, directly or indirectly, God controlled all things. The people whose writings appear here were not theologians, but, sometimes tacitly and sometimes directly, they revealed the implications of that God-centered view. This chapter describes and analyzes various facets of the providential belief, focusing initially on the degree to which that providential sentiment pervaded the thought of the era.

The trip to California provided an almost stage setting for providential expression. A now unknown clerk aboard the brig *Belfast* in 1848, after writing of the "songs of the Christys on my banjo" and signing his doggerel "Pope," noted that, although there was "no Sunday off soundings," the Sabbath had a quieter tone. Spending the Sabbath on the sea tended to "impress one with the high power that rules the universe and wields supreme will."[1] Having left the farm and his wife and three children in Pontotoc County, Mississippi, another migrant to California, Jackson Thomason, developed second thoughts about his trek to "the land of golden dreams." He feared for his family, and he dreaded the cholera which was then ravaging the migrants. He hoped for word from home that would demand his return. When it did not come, he "cried like a child," but his was not a wail of desperation. "I believe ful concios," he wrote, that God "is a just being and that he controls & rules the destinies of us unworthy beings here in this world."[2] At roughly the same time, a New York State blacksmith suffered mentally and physically as his party moved across the desert country west of Tucson. "All things are known to God," he wrote, "& all that He does is right & we learn that not even a sparrow fallith to the ground without his notice, so I leave all in his hands."[3]

The providential view ruled the lives of the people at all times, and not just during the trials of migration. When the son of a New York City greenhouse-man began his long, introspective diary, he did so with "the help of God, who I trust is my wisdom and counsellor. . . ."[4] In upstate New York, the wife of an Auburn prison guard had to interrupt her diary at the time of her mother's death, thus failing to note "the dealings of God with me."[5] Letters of advice to children, marriage proposals, solemn or ritual recognition of approaching death—all contained references to or invocations of providence. In typical form, aged Sally Waters of the Spartanburg District of South Carolina opened a letter to her son in Alabama with the following: "thro. the goodness of a kind Providence I am still living."[6] "The Wheel of Providence," Julia Adams, a newly married Ohio farm wife wrote, "is constantly moving[;] nothing impedes its progress."[7] Among these common people, providence governed all.

Those with other views did hardly more than attest to the preponderance of providential assumptions. With some exceptions, which will be treated later, most cavillers spoke the language of youthful assertiveness. They had not yet faced the trials that make theodicy acceptable. "In youth," Emerson wrote in the essay "Fate," "we clothe ourselves in rainbows, and go as brave as the zodiac."[8] Eighteen-year-old William Hoffman, son of a Columbia County, New York, family and soon to be clerk in an Albany store, had a propensity for the flippant. Awakening one March morning in 1848 to find a thick cover of new snow and more falling, Hoffman wrote a pretentious vignette on nature, beginning with the word "Providence." After a bit of affected rhapsody, he revealed his disgust at having his plans for the day disrupted by God's disposition, "but we are to make no complaints as to the perfect course of Providence."[9] Another young man, Indiana flatboatman Josiah Campbell, wrote from downriver, whenever time allowed, to keep Miss Caroline Ward's recollection of him fresh. With the river high, spread "all over creation and a little piece of Texas," Campbell wrote, he worked up to twenty hours a day getting "this cursed old hay boat" to New Orleans. But, as he put it in a combination of personal ardor and gentle parody, he must look forward to the return to Indiana and days to come ("or rather nights to come"), and bear his present situation with "Christian fortitude and not murmer."[10]

The Standard Scholarly View

Because the providential view of reality is not the assumption of our time, it is necessary to investigate, in some detail, its intricacies and implications. For Ishmael, for example, the whaling voyage aboard the *Pequod* "formed part of the grand programme of Providence that was drawn up a long time ago" (Chapter 1). Few modern scholars, however, regard that renowned cruise, as providential.

Before discussing the providental view as revealed in the writings of the plain folk, we should first consider the standard scholarly treatments of the providential theme. The modern scholarly treatments, which are based on the speeches and writings of public figures, convey three general and interrelated motifs. First, our ancestors had a providential philosophy of history. Second, that providential philosophy of history was colored by optimism; thus, it was often focused on the future and came to be confused with the idea of progress. Third, providence was seen as being able to make itself evident, to become manifest. To a chosen nation destined for ever greater things, God vouchsafed his intentions. Believing its destiny had been determined and made manifest, an assertive and acquisitive people combined condoning word with muscular deed.

Historians understandably keep their attention on large themes and constructs—societies, cultures, nations, empires. The macro-providential workings which our ancestors perceived readily commend themselves to the historian, while the micro-providential ones have generally fallen into oblivion. Kenneth B. Murdock, for example, describes the view held among seventeenth-century Puritans as follows: "In the simplest terms it held that every event was manipulated by God. A man might make a fortune, a city might burn, someone might be saved from death, or a prince might fall—in each case God brought about the event."[11] Matters of definition having been settled, Murdock then focuses upon the larger, "historical" aspects of God's manipulation. And that is the general way modern scholars have treated the purported national and historical implications of the pre-Civil War mood. In one of the fullest descriptions of that mood, Robert P. Hay presents the early Americans as facing the task of "creating a usable past." Having struggled to understand their historical past, they created, as have various other societies, "the legend of providential protection for the nation."[12] Similarly, in *This Sacred Trust*, Paul Nagel tells the intellectual and emotional story of one hundred years of "American Nationality," dividing that story into three segments—the "Trust," the "Stewardship," and the "Vineyard"—that derive directly from or intimately involve God. Indeed, "as American doctrine looked to future accomplishment," Nagel claims, "the Union was Providence incarnate."[13]

As a social theory and a philosophy of history, the providential view not only explained the past but also rationalized the present and foretold the future. Indeed, it seems to have been more comfortable in the present and future dimensions than in the past. When it foretold the future, it did so in tones of trumpeting certitude. John W. Ward's *Andrew Jackson* has given us an influential depiction of the young republic's confidence. That society, Ward tells us, needed a faith equal to its "gigantic task," and such a faith it found. "In its optimism it firmly believed that God had foreordained its success and it therefore saw God's hand in the most unlikely places."[14] Sound doctrine would pronounce no place "unlikely," but sound doctrine, one gathers, was frequently eroded, prostituted, and replaced by notions of secular progress.

At the end of Fred Somkin's *Unquiet Eagle*, the contemporary historian George Bancroft attempted to still American uneasiness by pronouncing the "triumphant upward trend of history," doing so by turning Jonathan Edwards' "providentialism into a secular doctrine of progressivism."[15] In his study of the idea of progress, Arthur Ekirch tells of an "unquestioned reliance on the progressive purpose of a divine Providence." For the American, progress was both "a law of history and the will of a benign Providence."[16] As "benign Providence" received ever less emphasis following the emergence of evolutionary ideas, the progressive thrust found theoretical sustenance elsewhere. Hence, as Martin Marty, himself a student of religion, phrases it: "From Providence to Progress." With the new dispensations of the late nineteenth century, the hitherto operative "divine impetus" to American history seemed inadequate, but the shift to a new energy source was hardly more than semantic. Where the word "providence" had been used in an almost "habitual" way, "thoughtful people were neglecting it and speaking of 'Progress.' "[17]

The modern mind is quick to discern that sort of dissembling in the providential view, and J. B. Bury provides a good illustration of a modern historian warning against "the naive conception of a god in history to explain historical movements."[18] According to Bury, too frequently, transcendent laws and agents of change and progress invite human intervention and acceleration. What God has intended sometimes becomes subject to human prompting. During the pre-Civil War era, providence came to be part and parcel of assertive national policy. The Almighty, having entered a most-favored-nation relation with the United States, was harnessed to an imperial carriage. Having extended His favor and blessing, God did not apparently restrain that society which, for His benefactions, was drifting toward international antinomianism. A much-remarked imperial drive called manifest destiny became synonymous with providence, and John W. Ward concludes the following: "Since Andrew Jackson, as God's right-hand man, represents the rationalization of American imperialism, his own course of action might well stand for the unsavory reality that underlay the idealistic protestations of the United States as it extended westward."[19] "The expansionist," as Alfred K. Weinberg wrote in *Manifest Destiny*, "may have had the very devil in his blood, but he could not take or enjoy his land without saying grace to a manifest destiny identified with the will of God."[20]

Sources of the Standard Scholarly View

The preceding view of providence bears little resemblance to the informing precepts of the common man. In the writings of the common man, the providential emphasis is on the personal and the immediate, not on the national and the historical; on the pessimistic and the past, not on the optimistic and the future; on an unknown destiny, approached prayerfully and resignedly, not on a destiny rendered manifest and accompanied by assertive, guilt-relieving noises.

Scholars have employed certain sources too liberally in formulating that standard interpretation of the providential view. John L. O'Sullivan, who coined the term manifest destiny, and his *United States Magazine and Democratic Review* (*Democratic Review*) have done much to advance the scholars' concept of providence. Although the magazine appeared for only twenty years (between 1837 to 1859) and did little more than totter during several of them, Weinberg's *Manifest Destiny* has more index page references to it than to any other periodical or newspaper, more than double, for example, those to *North American Review*. It is only at great peril that the mood of the politico-literary clique at *Democratic Review*—brilliantly characterized in its isolation by Perry Miller—can be presented as the mood of America at large. "Despite the efforts of historians to tell what a great role he played in political journalism," Miller observed, O'Sullivan is known "mainly as the friend of Hawthorne."[21]

Just as O'Sullivan and the *Democratic Review* have been irresistibly attractive to historians, so have the speeches made on public occasions and at celebrations. Several years after his book on Andrew Jackson was published, John W. Ward described the work as "an attempt to get at the public mind . . . through a study of the themes implicit in the public celebration" of certain events.[22] Such attempts have led to the examination of eulogies and Fourth of July orations. Fred Somkin relied heavily on both, and Robert P. Hay used Fourth of July orations almost to the exclusion of other sources. To be sure, both forms have much to commend them, but, as with the *Democratic Review*, caution is in order. Funerals and July the Fourth celebrations were tailor-made settings for a mystical connection of the immediate and mundane with a transcendent God. Shabby would be the eulogist's performance if he were to usher the deceased into eternity with an equivocal injunction of the spiritual forces of the universe. Fourth of July orators also had obligations that went beyond speaking of prosaic reality. It was their lot to sweep the heavens and eternity for metaphors befitting the heroism of the nation's past, the grandeur of the present, and the sublimity just around the corner in the future. Providence was front and center extending a hand to Andrew Jackson or whomever. Given the setting, it would be unthinkable that, for at least one day of the year, providence would hesitate to make common cause with the United States of America.

The common man, however, when his imagination was not ignited by Fourth of July orators, exercised much caution in commandeering God's devices. The standard national version of the providential motif, while present in some of their writings, is very rare, and when found, it is generally expounded by the more prosperous. Men who had some control over their own destiny could more readily wax confident about God's intentions than those intimately acquainted with hardship and frustration. Thus, an example of national providentialism comes from New York City businessman Andrew Lester, who voted the Whig ticket for mayor and alderman in April 1843. With the election past and the Whigs defeated, he wrote that it was "All right for he that sitteth on high is ruler & all will be well."[23] William Williams, a small-town businessman in Tennessee, did not share Lester's politics, but he did share the apparently happy thought that God might shield America from disasters. While agonizing in 1834 over the possibility that the Bank of the United States might be rechartered, he quieted his fears with the conclusion that "there is an all-seeing Ruler of events that will not suffer such a calamity. . . ."[24]

Very few indulged in Williams' sort of divination. As is discussed later, a central part of the credo of providentialism held that to engage in such divination was futile, or worse. One could discern the workings of providence in the past, and one's present pain or exultation correlated to those workings, but, regarding the future there was hope and prayer, not pride or certainty. In 1844, the *Democratic Review* published part of Mark Hopkins' semicentennial address at Williams College and, in so doing, undermined its own futuristic propensities: ". . . it is safer and more becoming to ascertain what Divine Providence has done, and then presume it to be wise. . . ."[25] The common man was "far safer and more becoming" than the *Democratic Review*, for he knew that one could not anticipate. When Rhode Island appeared to face open insurrection in 1842, citizen William Hoppin could only hope and pray for the "merciful interposition of God."[26] Only after a potential disaster had been circumvented did one set about giving credit where credit was due. Thus, an Ellington, Connecticut, hatter active in Democratic politics dutifully waited until *after* the 1844 election to suggest God's help—"Thank God Clay is defeated and the Republic saved[.] Amen."[27]

In some of the instances in which the common man seemingly embraced a national interpretation of providence, it is clear that such an interpretation was not original to him. It appears that the average American of that era needed some prompting to record, let alone entertain, this version of providence. When Jackson Thomason, whom we last encountered preparing for the California trip, reached the Fort Hall area, he heard a sermon by a Cumberland preacher who took his text from Numbers 10:29. As was often done, Thomason noted the text, but he did not bother to give his reaction to the sermon, nor did he specify what that text was—Moses' statement unto Hobab: "We are journeying into the place of which the LORD said, I will give it to you."[28] We are free to infer that here Thomason was suggesting the manifest destiny theme, but to do so would be to infer too much.

For martial assertiveness, few could have matched one E.A.B. Phelps, a Mexican War private who wrote long and exultant letters to a Cincinnati brother. Once the American army had arrived at the City of Mexico, he thundered, it should press on to such places as Saint Petersburg and London. Yet, for all the ecstasy that prospect gave him, Phelps made only one reference to providence as manifest destiny. That was in a poem entitled "Chapultepec," which he pasted into a letter he wrote after returning to the United States. He had marked two lines treating the "proud flag" from the North:

That under its broad folds, to us was given
To spread o'er the earth, the destiny of heaven.[29]

But Phelps borrowed this manifest destiny sentiment from Mayne Reid, an Irish publicist, novelist, traveler, and Mexican War adventurer. Phelps' militant visions were of the United States Army liberating not only Mexicans but also Frenchmen, Englishmen, Russians—whoever suffered bondage. Not empire, but the end of monarchy, inspired this frenzied soldier, and the only reason the idea of manifest destiny appears in his writing is that he happened on Mayne Reid's poem in a newspaper.

Trembling Recognition of God's Limited Blessings

In the June 1857 issue of *Harper's*, the Editor's Table discussed the American mind. Providence, the article said, held the central position in the American outlook; ". . . it is the most general, pervasive, ineradicable feeling in the hearts of our countrymen. . . ." Like latter-day commentators, this writer sensed that the providential view could be prostituted.

It is sometimes shamefully abused; its significance perverted; its import falsified in the language of lust and licentiousness; its benevolence sacrificed to intensify a plea for piracy; its religion degraded into a superstition that talks of destiny as a Turk talks of fate or a Hindoo of relentless sovereignty, and whets a filibustering appetite for carnage and conquest.[30]

The Editor's Table returned to the subject in the October issue, once more condemning those who carried "the doctrine of a Providence in human affairs to a fatalistic conclusion, which they are pleased to call Manifest Destiny; a doctrine which baptizes robbery and murder as Providential phenomena. . . ."[31]

Harper's analysis separated what it called the American mind into three groups. The first included the vast majority of the citizenry, whose providential views were left, regrettably, more asserted than analyzed. Readers of *Harper's* were probably not surprised to find that segment of society depicted as "decent, orderly, respectable, intelligent, and productive." The second and third groups were in small and "diseased" opposition to the first as well as to each other. At one extreme were the "violent reformers" and " 'Come-outers.' " They had eschewed the seeming restraints of providence and made an obsession of "free-will and personal responsibility" to the point of accepting the "logic of anarchy." At the other extreme were the adherents of manifest destiny discussed above, people who had tortured providence into a fatalistic presentation of "national sins simply as necessary events in the nation's progress to glory."[32] The writings of the common folk suggest that this tripartite division was accurate.

Common folk most assuredly did not dismiss providence, nor did they harden it into ethical license. In particular, the much discussed notion of manifest destiny ran at fundamental cross-purpose to the popular credo. In this regard, one of Frederick Merk's general contentions is appropriate. The "national spirit," he writes, was "hopeful of divine favor for national aspirations, though not sure of it."[33] For example, when David Humphrey, a young New Englander who had permanently located in Minnesota, contemplated the future, he envisioned changes that would enable him to visit his native region, and he foresaw waves of exuberant westward migration—" 'Westward the star of empire takes its way.' " "All this and much more 'if,' as said the New England Pilgrims, '*if God prospers us.*' "[34] Humphrey was not sure of divine favor, and, in fact, the common man *never* seemed sure of it. That may account for my failure to find even one instance of the expression "manifest destiny" in their writings.

Traditionally, the American has been portrayed as smugly contemplating his own good fortune. But the American's sense of good fortune very likely derived from the *fact* of good fortune. When comparatively good conditions prevailed, the common man of the mid-nineteenth century ascribed them to God's purposes. It would have been wrong-headed not to recognize the good conditions, and it would have been inconsistent not to see them in providential terms. Thus, it is appropriate to treat briefly the common man's perception of God's seeming willingness to prosper us. Brevity is in order, for these humble occupants of a relatively smiling land had reservations, not about the sway of providence but about the proportions of its boons and exactions. Common men had ample reason not to embrace an ecstatic view of providence. For them, any coming together of God's intentions and man's well-being was only tentative.

The Editor's Table observed that "Providence teaches nations as well as individuals."[35] One infers that God's dealings with the individual were recognized by all, while matters of national condition and destiny had supplementary application. Simply put, plain people had constricted horizons. Wiley Vester, writing home to Nash County, North Carolina, to tell of his fortunes in Mississippi, illustrates the common man's tendency to see God's direct dealings with man. After giving gratifying word of himself—"on my fine hors with my gold watch in my pocket and my boots a glittering and my spir shining and my breast pin on my ruffled shirt"—Vester went on to suggest that his had been no vicarious acquaintance with those Nash County "men who plows bare footed." Then, sensing that the account of his Mississippi situation implied a hurtful comparison, he said that he meant only to give "the great God who presides over the destines of nations thanks for giving me sens spirit and resilution enogh to depart from the bounds" of Nash County. God may have presided over the destinies of nations, but more immediately and more importantly God had worked the removal of Wiley Vester from a land where "men plows bare footed."[36]

Most people were more restrained than Wiley Vester in seeing providential intervention in their lives. Even in their difficult lives, happy moments occurred, and the source of such moments required proper recognition. Thus, the untutored wife of a Buffalo nurseryman advised her son Lyman Hodge on how he should view the formal education he was receiving. Though her language is awkward, her central message is clear: ". . . improve remembering from whence all these blessings flow (it is from our Heavenly Father)."[37]

If Lyman Hodge did not remember, he was unusual. And here, the idea of remembering conveys the sense of the past which is central to providential celebration. Providence was all-dimensional, but the certitude necessary for celebration obtained only in the past. Each moment in time provided occasion for solemn and respectful retrospect. Letters frequently opened with thankfulness to God for granting the writer the opportunity to write: "it is through the goodness of God that our lives are spared to write you a few lines."[38]

While such an opening may have been unthinking ritual, it provided the backdrop against which life's happier moments appeared in their humble, providential unfolding. "The King Providence," a Massachusetts man wrote to his Connecticut brother, "has granted us a lovely daughter. . . ."[39] A New York City youth, whose diary is not as replete with prayerfulness as most, paused on a birthday to reflect that "the Lord in his goodness has spared me 16 years and has given me health and strength. . . ."[40] Young Tom Turner, writing uneasily to his mother that he had not reached the Alamo in time and might bear a coward's reputation, still saw God's intent in the fact that he and his brother were yet alive.[41] The much-harried wife of a small Virginia slaveowner counted less dramatic blessings. Having borne several children, not all of whom survived, she watched her "monthly courses" with concern, and in January 1850 confided in her diary that "my courses came on[.] I felt so thankful[.] God is good and kind to me a sinner." And the same lady was not, considering the era in which she lived, being obsessive in seeing "God in his infinite mercy" in the lifting of a siege of diarrhea.[42] For those people who survived to old age, God was to be thanked for the very fact that they still lived. Ira McCall of Delaware County, New York, having reached seventy, and, apparently, having just lost his wife, mused over all the friends now gone. All the others cut down, "yet I am left as a monument of God's mercy."[43]

"No Other Asistance But God"

Like others, Ira McCall well knew that "we live in a world of changes and disappointments," and the "lovely daughter" in Massachusetts, mentioned above, was yet unnamed, though a full two months old. One did not presume too much. "The Lord willing" was far more than a figure of speech. In December 1849, a company of Maine argonauts bade farewell to "the land of the Bible religion and truth," pledging themselves, as perhaps befitted their origin, to temperance during their voyage and their stay in California. Then, immediately after the name of their destination appeared the crucial and characteristic qualifier—"Should we be permitted by Kind Providence to arrive there."[44] A sense of tentativeness colored all.

That sense issued in the prayer, not that God would prosper them, but that God's will would be done. A visit to Auburn prison, for instance, made one sense keenly the fitness of a "thankful heart" and moved one to pray for perseverance in a path generally righteous.[45] When Mary Hodge reflected for the benefit of her youthful son on the imminent fate of Professor Webster of Harvard for the murder of Doctor Parkman, she was aroused to a dramatic reaffirmation of the truth "that it is the grace of God alone that can keep us from temptation."[46] Evil lurked in myriad forms. For one twelve-year-old girl, it took the shape of Maggie Hutton, who tickled her during school prayer. Maggie could control her laughter; the distraught diarist could not. "Oh!" she exclaimed, "what *can* I do?" Her evident answer was to trust in God and to recall His message: "My grace is sufficient for thee.' "[47] John Drake of New Hamburg, New York, got no torment from Maggie Hutton, but in closing a diary entry for a year he sought the same sort of assistance. He prayed "sincerely that Samuel W. Kelly and others may be preserved from persecuting me the ensuing year."[48] Levi Countryman of Minnesota bore greater burdens and, as he saw it, had greater wickedness to control. Town-builder Ignatius Donnelly owed him money; his wife was an unbeliever; he was too querulous to farm but unequipped to do anything else; and, perhaps most vexing of all, he had a vile and ungodly temper. "If I ever conquer it," he wrote in an anguish of self-deprecation following a particularly stormy outburst, "it will be through the mercies of God, and it will show what a great conquest can be made."[49] The man afflicted by that temper had little recourse other than hope of God's aid.

Countryman and countless, nameless others like him had little control over their circumstances—those "tyrannical circumstances" that even Emerson, the transcendentalist, could not ignore.[50] Countryman and his kind sent a call to God, there being no one else to whom they could appeal. Thus, a despondent miner on the Yuba River tried bravely to conceal his financial and physical condition from his wife, and then he attempted some reassurance in closing: "We will all be happy yet[—]please God."[51] Keziah Taylor of Vassalboro, Maine, whose family had been recently visited by death and was now fragmented, insisted there be no despair. "Oh Sister," she implored, "Dont feal discouraged for providence may open a Dore[.] I dearsiere to put my trust in the Lord. . . ." Three years later, addressing "Dea sister with disepointments," Keziah stated explicitly what was often a silent premise: "thare no other assistance But God."[52] In logical extension of Keziah's premise, Lovina

Smith of Water Valley, New York, asked her husband, "... why should we distrust Providence?"[53] Lovina Smith would not have confused trusting and knowing, and would not have denied the fact that trust involved things unseen, which by definition were unknown.

Having just learned of the death of his child and well aware that either his health or the elements could keep him from working in the diggings, argonaut John Brewster worried about the days and months ahead. His observation was that "the Lord only knoweth what will be in the future."[54] In *Redeemer Nation*, Ernest Lee Tuveson poses the question "When Did Destiny Become Manifest?"[55] The answer is that it never did, not even to those inflamed special pleaders who assumed the role of soothsayer. And even if John L. O'Sullivan succeeded in convincing himself, there is little reason to suppose that many others envisioned God in the guise of carnival pitchman giving intimations of delights just ahead under the sublunary tent. Angrily lecturing America about a particular abuse, Melville once spoke as if privy to God's design. It was a momentary lapse, and one to which we will soon turn. Far more commonly—almost obsessively—Melville spoke sound doctrine. Thus, the narrator in "Bartleby, the Scrivener" recognized the story's bizarre unfolding as "some mysterious purpose of an allwise Providence, which it was not for a mere mortal like me to fathom."[56] No fictive affliction moved John W. Bugg of Keene, New Hampshire, to pronounce this most characteristic sentiment. The God who had given him a child had five weeks later, "in the mystery of his providence," taken it away.[57] Fellow New Englander Horatio Chandler marked another death—William Henry Harrison's—and drew the same conclusion. "The ways and doings of Providence are inscrutable; it is not for anyone to say what were the designs in this instance of that infinite Power. . . ."[58]

Such sentiments were not limited to emotional occasions; they were nearly omnipresent. Where would one be a year hence? Would another be able to get out of California and back to a family? Why, as an exasperated young Georgian put it, should such a "low-life old wench"[59] as one Mrs. Irby be given God's license to exist? These and countless other questions were unanswerable—"inscrutable," "incomprehensible," "mysterious," "strange." Destiny did not manifest itself, and endlessly, Cowper's refrain bespoke that fact:

> God moves in a mysterious way
> His wonders to perform.

The Place for Human Initiative

Since God did not go about idly vouchsafing the details and intricacies of His absolute sway, it behooved man to be up and doing. At least from Augustine's time theologians and philosophers have tried to reconcile human action and divine intention. Logic suggests that providentialists and others with determinist ideas should appear in the garb of contemplative quietism. But Calvinists and others of determinist bent have been notorious activists. They act, as Crane Brinton observes, "as if their every moment were a portentous decision for the right and against the wrong."[60] New England Puritans of the colonial era worked out an articulate subdividing of activity whereby providence did not undo human initiative. God, though ordering all, allowed most everyday activities to operate "naturally." Human action and human initiative had spacious arena and powerful challenge—God's work to be done.

As Santayana once asserted, the nineteenth century had a habit of lisping its logic, and so the precision and articulateness of the early Puritans slipped by the way. However, the nineteenth-century descendants of the Puritans still attempted to reconcile providence with human actions. One of John Ward's larger challenges and accomplishments in the Andrew Jackson book was to bring providence and will into peaceful coexistence, if not full resolution. The inscrutability of providence did not perplex and overawe the common man; the universality of providence did not crush or lull him.

On a January day in 1853, Boston policeman Joseph Willard chatted with Judge Bishop. The judge contended that those who spent their money as they made it were quite as happy as others. When Willard countered this argument with the conventional insistence on putting money aside for hard times, the judge deftly resorted to a higher tribunal: " 'if sick God will take care of you.' "[61] Was Judge Bishop jesting or playing loose with the constable's credulity? Whether or not Judge Bishop was serious, the common man of America rarely assumed that sort of philosophical luxury. For example, Andrew Jackson Sterrett, a native of New York State who had survived cholera in Saint Louis, worked in a print shop while there, and saved enough money to engage in small-scale land speculation in unsettled areas to the west, wrote to his brother from Fort Dodge, Iowa, in 1855, informing him of the arrival of ne'er-do-well John Spotts with family and fever, but no clothes or money. Sterrett knew that Spotts intended to live off him, but "by George," he had better "bestir himself." "If the Lord don't take care of them & they don't take care of themselves & I haven't much confidence in either, they'll starve & freeze both in this country."[62] Though Sterrett was more sardonic than most of his peers, the message was standard.

Because of his belief that "God was in control," the American, John Ward writes somewhat unguardedly, had a license to indiscriminate action; man "was not responsible."[63] Although that may ultimately be true, it is actually and in specific instances quite wide of the mark, for the common man retained responsibility. Yes indeed, "God & the Constitution" had made John Tyler President, Stephen Goddard of Missouri angrily admitted, "but who made him Vice President?"[64] God and the Constitution could not bear full responsibility for that. To alter the setting, the Lord may have interceded in various January 8 and July 4 refightings of the battle of New Orleans, but the battle itself engaged *human* capacities. When Samuel Nichols visited the scene of the battle, he puzzled over the disparity in losses, and then concluded that it reflected the "great difference in judgment and tallent" between the two commanders.[65] A visit to a prison did not issue solely in the surmise that only God's will and grace kept the visitor from being a resident. Men's freedom—what a visitor to the penal institution in Columbus, Ohio, called their "folly and vice"[66]—was God's necessity. Or, as Emerson stated in "Fate," freedom is necessary.

When his brother died, young James Amsted Brown accepted his mother's source of solace—"a wise Providence." At the same time, however, there was no refutation or inconsistency in his writing that "I shall always feel as though he might have recovered had he been in the hands of *Competant* Doctors."[67] God was given to helping those who helped themselves. The effort was a joint one. "May Providence direct me," went the plea from Muncie, Indiana, "in the right paths and smile upon my honest and laudable efforts."[68]

"Honest and laudable" efforts did not always suffice. Human capacities have, in themselves, noteworthy deficiencies, and they could be undone by a "preventing providence." That usage frequently appears as a qualifier in the writings of the common people. For example, one Thomas S. Bennett wrote that he would be married in a week "if no preventing providence" interfered, an expression suggesting a more direct and personal divine intent than "act of God" would imply.[69] By the same token, Thomas à Kempis's axiom—"Man proposes but God disposes"—took on a particularly personal form among common people of the pre-Civil War era. Having been swept by enthusiasm to the Far West, Webster Abbott wrote his mother, brother, and sister regarding the vicissitudes of life in Nevada City, California, where many miners were "cursing" the place and leaving if they could. Abbott hoped he could soon return to his loved ones in New York, but, he noted, in a revision of à Kempis, " 'Man can [ap]point & God can disapoint.' "[70] The impersonality of *dispose* gave way to the immediacy of *disappoint*.

In *The Method of Divine Government*, James M'Cosh discussed the more negative aspects of divine providence, aspects which permeated popular thought. There are, M'Cosh wrote, "numberless restraints, corrections, medicaments, and penalties" awaiting man at every turn, "now with their bristling points to stop his career, and anon with their whips to punish."[71] When Webster Abbott wrote that letter from Nevada City on January 12, 1851, he told of the "bristling points." The "whips" that "punish" came on January 19 when he learned that his mother would not receive the letter he had so recently written her. She had been dead several months.

Providence and "Malignant Energy"

In his 1860 essay "Fate," Emerson treated that troublesome spectre which had so perplexed him as a transcendentalist. Although overall the essay reveals a more somber Emerson, in one place he made a twofold distinction which closely approximates the modern notion of providentialism. "The bulk of mankind," he wrote, "believe in two gods. . . . To a certain point, they believe themselves [in] the care of a Providence. But in a steamboat, in an epidemic, in war, they believe a malignant energy rules."[72] But based on the research materials used for this book, the "bulk of mankind" made no such separation. The steamboat, the epidemic, the war simply transformed the quietly pervasive providential tone into one of crescendo dimensions. It seems to me that Emerson erred in suggesting, as M'Cosh and the common man would not have done, a mutually exclusive relationship between providence and "malignant energy." Perhaps Emerson took so happy a view of God in order to disassociate Him from earthly untidiness. This premise raises the possibility that as a result of the modern emphasis upon the benignity of God some nineteenth-century views have been misconstrued. For example, if God is love, then those under God's control must enjoy a beloved and blessed condition. A later age would take our ancestors to task for the smugness of this view. They would have been quite bewildered by the charge; they had, most likely, read the twenty-second as well as the twenty-third Psalm.

In fact, there was no place for the providence-"malignant energy" distinction at the beginning of Emerson's essay, when the "way of Providence" came under specific scrutiny. There he expressed perfectly the sentiments of the "bulk of mankind." "Now and then," he noted, some "amiable parson" posits a "pistareen-Providence, which, whenever the good man wants a dinner, makes that somebody shall knock at his door and leave a half-dollar." But "the way of Providence is a little rude." The "snap of the tiger," the "crackle of the bones" in the coil of the python, the slaughterhouse just beyond the diner's view, the scurvy at sea, fever and ague on the western prairies, cholera, small-pox, the Lisbon earthquake, volcanoes, and intestinal parasites give evidence of that rudeness. "Providence has a wild, rough, incalculable road to its end, and it is of no use to try to whitewash its huge, mixed instrumentalities, or to dress up that terrific benefactor in a clean shirt and white neckcloth of a student in divinity."[73]

A "pistareen-Providence" would have been even more unlikely and unconvincing to Rose Spinney of Unity, Maine, than it was to the sage of Concord. Census figures indicate that Rose was a farm widow with small children and precious little else. On January 1, 1860, she told a niece that writing itself had become a burden—"the same old sad story to tell over & over again," there having been "a few days of sunshine," but "many nights of darkness." As she wrote to her parents on one of those nights of darkness in 1846, the storm outside evoked another kind of storm image to portray providence: "I hear the distant thunder which speaks the voice of Him who rides upon the s[t]ormy sky."[74] It would not have occurred to those who encountered what Emerson called the "huge, mixed instrumentalities" of providence, to whitewash them.

When Lizzie Robbins, with a seriously ill husband and at least one child already dead, confided in an old friend, she said that God had heeded her prayers, "though it has been in such a way, as almost drove me to despair."[75] When Augustine Holcomb of Sterling, Massachusetts, wrote to brother Milo about the departure of Milo's wife, he, too, indicated the rudeness and mixed instrumentalities that Emerson had in mind. Augustine hoped that the Almighty would now "heal the deep wound made in your affected bosom by the repeated strikes of his providence."[76]

Providence, being purposeful as well as all-encompassing, was seen as working not just trials, but, as it was frequently stated, "trials that are calculated." A specific answer to the question "calculated to do what?" would have been uncomfortably close to divination, and, as will be discussed shortly, divination was to be avoided. But the spiritual consequences of a past event could sometimes hardly be ignored; indeed, God occasionally became almost didactic. As indicated earlier, the common people generally gave the personal and immediate dimension their full attention, and it was in that dimension that they were most often led to do some rather hesitant calculating of suffering and hardship. Abigail Williams, for instance, concluded that the deaths of several members of her family ("not one of them professors of religion") were by no means coincidence and that those deaths represented a "loud call from God."[77] Unlike Abigail Williams, most people, while recognizing the possibility, had the good grace to resist attributing their neighbors' setbacks to God's punitive scourge.

Common people of the mid-nineteenth century portrayed God as jealous and as a deity not to be mocked by man's idolatrous love of his fellows. The popular didactic poet Martin Tupper, who was read widely both in America and in England, could warn in his poem "Of Marriage," "Take heed lest she love thee before God; that she be not an idolater."[78] Cordelia Randall of Norwich, New York, knew that "an all wise Providence" had worked the removal of her dearest friend, Emily Lewis. "I now feel that I thought to much of you. Ah! you were my idol. you robed my Parent above, of my affections, & he has seen fit to seperate us."[79] When the death of a small child was involved, this mechanism underscored an even greater dilemma. Thus, when Augustine Holcomb lost his child, he was forced to contemplate a sterner God than the God who had permitted his brother Milo's matrimonial sorrows. Writing to tell his father of his child's death, Augustine admitted that "we have loved him too much."[80] Mary Bunting of Cheraw County, South Carolina, was more explicit in portraying God as a jealous God. She informed her brother in Alabama that her love for her baby had seduced her soul into complacency. Obsessed with her child, she had ignored the source of her blessings. But "God would not be mocked," and He had taken Mary Bunting's child. Belatedly heeding her master's will, she felt that she richly "*deserved*" what she had received—"to be beaten with many stripes."[81]

Whatever other message might be inferred from the "loud calls," the least mistakable consisted in the warning most commonly stated as "be ye also ready." That theme was so fundamental and prevalent among the common men that had they stumbled upon the isolated expression "manifest destiny," they might well have pictured death and the grave.

God's Sway Over People and Nations

"Trials that were calculated" gave evidence, at the personal level, of providential retribution, jealousy, and warning. God's handling of larger matters fell into similar stern patterns, but, once again, the common man was less inclined to direct attention to them. In the spring of 1848, when "providential proceedings," as his preacher called them, took the form of heavy snow, William Hoffman, a clerk in Albany, wrote on the providential theme with both irony and irritation. This attitude would have been unseemly the summer before, for at that time providence had shown its wrath, allowing Albany to burn down. Writing on the evening of the fire, the young clerk attempted to describe the "indescribable": "Citizens thousands of them stood with frantic horor and gazed as if completely paralized with the astounding and frightful scenes of the raging element." Efforts to contain the fire were to no avail: "*Providence* it seemed ordained that such should be our destiny, & justly marked with her terrific *rod*, in destructive *flames of fire* that portion of our city meriting her awful sentence; wicked as I might suppose they were; received as a *lesson* & a *warning* to farther daily iniquity the striking down of their Dwellings— & Ware Houses. . . ."[82]

Similarly, in those infrequent instances when common people noted God's sway over the nation, the emphasis was on painful instruction. Writing from his Arkansas farm to his family in Kentucky, Jesse Owen told of the illness that had struck the Mexican War volunteers at Fort Gibson. He cautiously wondered if the epidemic, which had killed his son-in-law, had come as some general "scerge for wekidness."[83] In North Carolina, when Charles Peterson spoke of war measures for the Mexican War, he did so with the certainty that the United States would shortly receive its comeuppance, for when a nation tramples "justice under fot," providence has a "judgement awaiting."[84] This is not to say that most or even many people opposed the Mexican War. However, not one source covered ascribed to God any active guidance or support in the undertaking, and some agonized over the country's defiance of God. After all, tradition and orthodoxy had rarely showed God warmly and generously supplementing society's efforts. A man named Chapin at Bath, New York, probably did not strike an anachronistic note when he remarked on the meaning of the "*famine and pestilence*" he discerned in 1847. By such things, he wrote, "the Nations may know that the Lord has a controversy with the nation and that the Lord is at the Door in truth."[85] God's controversy was still more evident than His encouraging embrace.

Thus, it is difficult to explain the recent insistence that Americans viewed themselves as a "chosen people"—*God's New Israel*, to employ Conrad Cherry's title.[86] For this notion, Cherry and others have relied heavily on H. Richard Niebuhr's observation in *The Kingdom of God in America*: "The old idea of American Christians as a chosen people who had been called to a special task was turned into a notion of a chosen nation especially favored." Indeed, the "note of divine favoritism" increased as the nineteenth century advanced.[87] This may be so, but the common man of the pre-Civil War period would have regarded the idea of "divine favoritism" as blasphemy, drollery, or painful irony.

That "divine favoritism" is unabashedly elucidated by Herman Melville in *White Jacket*:

And we Americans are the peculiar, chosen people—the Israel of our time; We bear the ark of liberties of the world. Seventy years ago we escaped from thrall; and, besides our first birthright—embracing one continent of earth—God has given to us, for a future inheritance, the broad domains of the political pagans, that yet shall come and lie down under the shade of our ark, without bloody hands being lifted. God predestinated, mankind expects, great things from our race; and great things we feel in our souls.[88]

Yet time and again, throughout his works, Melville sketched a providence vastly removed from this godly underwriter of national intentions. In the chapter that contains the above quote, Melville was pleading against the use of flogging in the United States Navy, and he took liberty with providence for what he deemed a good cause, as, most likely, O'Sullivan did with regard to expansion. God, Melville contended, had "predestinated" us for things that transcended the brutal shabbiness of flogging derelict sailors. In that same chapter, Melville wrote an uncharacteristic chest-thumping paean to democracy worthy of Walt Whitman. We have long wondered, Melville blurted out in the heat of disquisition, whether the "political Messiah had come." Now we know; ". . . he has come in *us*. . . . Let us leave the Past, then, to dictate laws to immovable China; let us abandon it to the Chinese Legitimists of Europe." And let us straightway end flogging in the United States Navy.

Melville's outburst requires a more cautious use than it has hitherto received. In *The American Idea of Mission*, Edward McNall Burns, for example, employs the key sentence "And we Americans are the peculiar, chosen people" as a motif, placing it in emblazoned isolation on a frontispiece. However, Burns mentions Melville only once in the text itself; he tells us that, in regard to the American sense of mission, "only a few bilious critics like Herman Melville and Nathaniel Hawthorne expressed discordant notes."[89] Melville gets the same wrenching in Russell B. Nye's ironically titled *This Almost Chosen People*. The sentence from *White Jacket* stands dutifully at the head of the chapter entitled "The American Sense of Mission," but Nye's summary statement on that sense of mission reads in part: "It has sometimes been clothed with certain ambiguities and reservations (as in Cotton Mather, Melville, Hawthorne, Dreiser, or Faulkner). . . ."[90] Melville and Hawthorne hardly stood in bilious isolation; they had vast company in the common men of America.

The Effort to Attain "Sublime Repose"

Between the "diseased" extremes of manifest destiny, on the one hand, and "violent" reform, on the other, there resided, in *Harper's* charting of the American mind, a "sublime repose in the purposes of Providence."[91] Though a bit antiquated now, the editor's phrase neatly conveys the spirit in which unsophisticated America sought to meet the slings and arrows of providence. Man's final reflection on providence's harsh and awesome aspects consists in the nearly unbroken urging of resignation, meekness, and submission. Unsophisticated America developed an emotional and philosophical accommodation with a scheme of things that was not very solicitous of man's well-being. In *Manifest Destiny*, Albert K. Weinberg portrays an "anthropocentric theology, in which God himself served chiefly as a Providence watchful for mankind. . . ."[92] The sentiments in the poem "Providence" published in the *Democratic Review*, that vehicle of "anthropocentric theology," were far closer to the common view:

> Child in this fallen, blasted world,
>   From God and Truth so widely thrown,
> In Ruin's blackest vortex hurled,
>   We see thy form, we hear thy moan.[93]

In this "fallen, blasted world," man could hope for little more than spiritual peace, "sublime repose."

Some were not able to achieve that repose. Lawrence Parker's courtship of Fanny Barbour was stormy, largely because of Parker's unorthodox religious views. Fanny considered him perilously close to deism because of his failure to appreciate adequately God's immediate control over human destinies. She would have probably agreed with a later scholar's dictum: "Belief in Providence stands or falls with belief in a personal God."[94] How, she demanded to know on one occasion, could he doubt personal providence when he himself had so recently been raised from what appeared to be a deathbed.[95] The concern returned, not to Fanny but to Lawrence alone, in sadly intensified form. Some five years after their marriage, Fanny died after a long illness, and Lawrence was left to work out his repose for which he felt inadequate. This "dealing of Providence," he admitted to a brother-in-law, had never crossed his mind as a true possibility until his wife had grown quite ill. And now, this spiritually marginal man felt that he had "not lived enough like Christ to be prepaired" for

such a blow. "Like Christ" translates here as submissive and resigned, qualities that Parker could not assume. Fanny had been taken, he wrote, from a
supremely happy family "circle" in the midst of her "years of usefulness"—
"why this afflicting circumstance I cannot conceive." Then the heterodoxy
that Fanny had long before discerned surfaced again. "I do not feel right," he
complained. "I earnestly pray God to give me right views and feelings on this
matter, yet to say that I am reconciled to it would not be dealing truthfully with
myself."[96]

Lawrence Parker did not obey the period's central injunction to those in
"Ruin's blackest vortex": *mourn but do not murmur.* The intense and volumi-
nous shunning of the latter necessitates some definition. The word "murmur"
suggested a good deal more than a low noise of perhaps pleasant or poetic
nature. It denoted, far more than it would later, grumbling, complaint, and a
"sullen discontent" which the 1855 Webster's aptly illustrated with Exodus
17:3: "and the people murmured against Moses." Whatever came one's way,
it involved providential intent, and none must feel free to quarrel with that.
Thus, with another summer of cholera underway, a mother's advice to children
rephrased the enduring formula. Should it be "the will of heaven to afflict us let
us all endeavor to bow with meek submission to its holy will."[97] The inclusion
of "endeavor" suggests that some, like Lawrence Parker, would fall short of
the ideal of "sublime repose" and, of course, that advising came easier than
performing. The redundant and circular spiritual pleas—"I humbly ask for a
submissive spirit,"[98] "I do desire to feel willing to submit"[99]—underscore the
preeminence of that central urging to self and others. From God men sought
the temper not to murmur at His workings, however painful they might be.

In Woodstock, Connecticut, Lois Lillie, knowing she could no longer meet
the demands of common house work, thought of trying the "factory," but she
saw the poorhouse looming large before her. After a page detailing griefs,
ruined hopes, and the certainty of felicity's having eluded her, she concluded
by writing "but i am what i am so i will be content."[100] In 1859, a woman in
Cold Water, Wisconsin, wrote to a relative about how she and a son eked out a
living by needlework. A chronicle of recent events in their lives represented no
more than a litany of pain, but she concluded philosophically: "so it is and we
must bear it and not complain." Her son, George Henry, shared that view, perhaps in the face of greater anguish. He informed an aunt that he still had
wretched health; indeed, now he was suffering "fitts" at least three days in
every two weeks—"I must grin & bear them but I regret that I ever lived to see
this age."[101]

Even the more secular and, occasionally, irreverent reflections reveal a
people quite disinclined to take arms against a sea of ordained troubles. Beset
by physical afflictions, Andrew Jackson Sterrett, who was sometimes in waspish counterpoint to general views, assured his brother that "my philosophy has
never entirely deserted me."[102] A later age might inquire, which philosophy?

But in the popular thought of that era, in the absence of any qualifiers "philosophy" simply meant stoical bearing. A clerk aboard a California-bound vessel provided an almost definitive illustration when he translated "philosophy" as "making the *best* of the *worst*."[103]

Uncompensated Suffering

In part, this general spiritual quiescence can be explained in terms of simple, unadorned necessity. When young Thomas Hayter wrote from Oregon Territory, telling a sister of the death of their father and, apparently, a brother, he spoke in unanswerable terms: ". . . it has pleased the good Lord to Remove them and i Can but Submit and say His Will Be Done."[104] Here, there was literally no appeal. However, some would wonder about other situations where, at least in the modern view, there was appeal, and perhaps redress. Some might wonder if all that discussion of providence and the need to acquiesce in providence meant any more than manipulation of common people by their socioeconomic superiors. Unfortunately, it is very difficult to make a case either way from the humble sources themselves.

A rare instance of appeal for socioeconomic ills came from James Duffe, an employee of the marine hospital in Brooklyn. At the hospital Duffe experienced at first hand the horrors of that era's medical practice, as well as the putrid meat and wretched butter (stinking like a "sconk") that passed for food in institutions. Complaint was useless, he observed, because the "godly Superintendent" would coolly contend that "the Lord sent it and you must eat it you hireling."[105] Such items are quite uncommon, partly because of that period's lively belief in human responsibility. Stinking butter seems to have been a staple of the times, but very few had the ill-grace to make God accountable. The narcotizing aspect of the providential message was generally reserved for more unalterable problems than stinking butter.

Related to man's resignation to providential workings is the notion of compensation, the idea that the pain suffered in this world will redound to one's benefit in the hereafter. Emerson caricatured this belief at the beginning of "Compensation"; after dismissing it derisively, he replaced it with a view that itself has been scornfully dismissed. For all its apparent appeal, the compensatory idea received little attention from the people; perhaps, as Emerson suggested, "the people knew more than the preachers taught."[106] Clear assertions of the hardship-reward equation, of pie-in-the-sky payoff are uncommon. Robert Spinney of Boothbay, Maine, obliged posterity by putting it much as Emerson parodied it: we are taught that "our trials hear" work for a greater glory beyond.[107] And the children of aged and suffering Polly Tarble of Brookline, Vermont, urged her to remember that "our tribles and trials here will only make us richer their. . . ."[108]

That kind of certainty is rare in the writings of the common people. Afflictions abounded, but only some afflictions had a "sanctified" effect. Thus, Pauline Stratton offered the hope and prayer that someone visited by troubles might indeed gain spiritual benefit: "Oh that God would sanctify his afflictions unto him. . . ."[109] The spiritual benefit did not appear to be absolute; the word "sanctify," which was widely used in this context, suggests something preparatory. According to the 1855 Webster's, it involved "detaching the affections from the world and its defilements." Sanctification meant no cosmic *quid pro quo*, no street of gold for every painful step taken. The good lady Pauline Stratton prayed for something less than that; she prayed that, should her husband recover, he would get religion.

A Severely Qualified Form of Optimism

Perry Miller sees in the seventeenth-century Puritans a "cosmic optimism" that transcended their brooding sense of human shortcoming and godly vindictiveness. By "cosmic" Miller does not mean unbounded and unqualified—quite the contrary. Things of the moment were wretched, but things of eternity would be different. It was the optimism of intensely deferred gratification. Ultimately and necessarily, all things issued in good; in the meantime, man suffered but with indomitable spirit. The beleaguered and unfortunate endlessly took consolation in that article of faith during the nineteenth century—as indeed they perhaps have in all of recorded history. The providential view produced an attitude of resignation and the unanswerable conviction that everything worked for the best. What Miller calls "the indispensable premise of all Puritan belief"[110] still flourished in popular thought two hundred years later.

When Sarah Grimes insisted that a particular affliction "may be ominous of good," she seemed to combine the dimensions of immediate ill and ultimate good with an artful irony. But she was not as artful as it first appears; "ominous" (partaking of omens) had not yet been limited to the negative aspect. Sarah was no phrasemaker; rather, she was only a simple New Hampshire woman urging someone to see that "tis all right and just."[111] A school composition book kept by Mary Copp of Savannah listing the "Evidences of the Goodness of God" provides a conventional treatment. For her teacher's edification, Mary itemized and illustrated the many goods to be enjoyed in this world—the beauties of nature, abundant food, a "free country," and, of course, good parents and good teachers. But this young lady also had a strong glimmering of the kind of dilemma for which we have the word "theodicy." "The goodness of God," she made bold to continue, "is shown in another way by his afflictions—though they are not always so considered." Evidently, she was aware that some "murmured." For a bit, she struggled through thickets where even theologians would have been challenged to make their way. But suddenly she had the firm guidance and passage of a common-sense authority: William Cowper. Surely, as Mary's teacher sensed Cowper just ahead, there must have rushed to mind the mood, the meter, and then the serenity of that oft-used message:

> Judge not the Lord by feeble sense,
>   But trust him for his grace;
> Behind a frowning providence
>   He hides a smiling face.[112]

"Great men, great nations," Emerson reminded his countrymen in "Fate," "have not been boasters and buffoons, but perceivers of the terror of life, and have manned themselves to face it." He commented with regret that "Our America has a bad name for superficialness."[113] Coming in the particular context that it does, this assertion may well have intimated the sort of bluster to which Emerson's own transcendental individualism could have given rise. Now he cited some of the "heroic races" that were "proud believers in Destiny": "The Turk, the Arab, the Persian, accepts the foreordained fate. . . . The Hindoo, under the wheel, is as firm. Our Calvinists, in the last generation, had something of the same dignity. They felt that the weight of the Universe held them down to their place."[114] The "fatalist—whether providentialist or otherwise—steeled himself for "the terror of life." As Melville expressed it in *White Jacket*, such an outlook "relieves men from nervous anxieties."[115] Earlier in this chapter, a New York City man was shown taking comfort from the notion that God is our ruler "& all will be well," even as the Whig ticket which the writer supported met defeat in city elections. This attitude was not smugness; as the rest of his diary entry shows, it was the sort of "cosmic optimism" that may indeed have relieved him of "nervous anxieties." God, he insisted, works what is best, and "it may be best for the world that America yes our own beloved America shall fall & crumble to pieces." With that said, he again resolved to do right and work hard, leaving all else in God's hands.[116]

The wisdom and goodness of God's ways were customarily seen in things far closer to home than the downfall of the Whigs or of the nation. In 1833, Keziah Taylor delivered the incontestable judgment regarding a woman who had lost a son; ". . . for Her it is Duty to mourn but not to Murmur. . . ." Nine years later, Keziah lay "upon a bed of death" following a "grate operation" while loved ones were hastily summoned—"not fail not fail for your life." The Maine woman's last letter admitted great suffering from what likely was cancer, but she steadfastly maintained certain fundamental precepts. "I am willing to bair it because it is the hand of God."[117] The death of his horse Pep moved Emsley Burgess to melancholy reflection and then to a variant of Christian stoicism. To himself and anyone else who might be privy to his ruminations, he gave the assurance that "I do not wish to complain and murmur but at times I cannot help feeling rather discouraged and under the weather for the hand of misfortune has seemed to laid heavy on me." (The North Carolina farmer-mechanic garbled the tense here in rephrasing what seemed a bit of murmuring; he first wrote "has laid heavy" but then thought better of it and inserted "seemed to" above the line.) Pep was the sixteenth horse Burgess had owned and the eighth to die unexpectedly; over the years he had lost "a great number of fine hogs" and thus had often had difficulty providing meat for the family; and, in the past fifteen years, probably one of every seven days had been crossed off to "fever ague & sick headache." Where the dispensations of providence were concerned, Emsley Burgess had only a limited and inverted satisfaction—"to bear is to conquer."[118]

Conclusion

No "pistareen-Providence" came knocking for the Keziah Taylors and Emsley Burgesses. Such folk said little or nothing about being a chosen people, although, when near despair, they did occasionally remind themselves of Hebrews 12:6: "whom the Lord loveth he chasteneth." The question of Romans 8:31—"If God be for us, who can be against us?"—remained for them what it was in the stating—a double conjecture. They seemed rarely, if ever, to confuse providence with progress; indeed, they might have accepted James Malin's later contention that the two categories stood in "direct contradiction."[119] They would surely have agreed with one of the spokesmen of their own time, James M'Cosh, when he depicted providence throwing man "far back when he seemed to be making the most eager progress."[120] They would not have been astounded by a line from Bunyan: "That very Providence, whose face is death. . . ."[121] Someone somewhere may have domesticated God and put Him to the wheels of physical advancement, but the common man was notably hesitant to make the attempt. The common man's God was an inscrutable God, not a God who, by vouchsafing large and happy intentions, left "each citizen . . . bathed in a glorious optimism."[122] Indeed, one of the few sources of comfort derived from *not* knowing. Writing to an old friend in Savannah, Henry Hewes of Baltimore remarked on the political excitement of 1844 and observed that it was well that God alone knew the outcome; ". . . the future is wisely hid from our sight, if it were not so society would be in a much worse condition. . . ."[123] As the 1855 Webster's dictionary said of destiny, it was "happily concealed."

"As a general rule," Hawthorne mused in *House of the Seven Gables*, "Providence seldom vouchsafes to mortals any more than just that degree of encouragement which suffices to keep them at a reasonably full exertion of their powers."[124] Henry Hewes and his counterparts would have understood that as sound doctrine, as a gently stated way of explaining how Hepzibah, the "forlorn old maid," at her first doleful and inept day as a shopkeeper, was kept from "despondency." Melville put the same sentiment in grimmer terms, but the plain folk would have readily comprehended and appreciated it had they bothered to read. "Heaven," the gloomy mariner remarked in *Pierre*, had been at least "a little merciful." Perhaps for being "benevolently blinded to the larger arc of the circle which menacingly hems it in," the "soul of man" could never "confront the totality of its wretchedness." "The bitter drug is divided into separate draughts for him; to-day he takes a part of his woe; to-morrow he takes more; and so on, till the last drop is drunk."[125]

Time and again, when the mood of their age is under discussion, Hawthorne and Melville—those "Nay-sayers" who saw "shadows in the universe, and knew the power of blackness"[126]—appear as idiosyncratic counterpoints to the dominant confidence and assertiveness. However out of step they may have been with some optimism in higher circles, their dark brooding about fate and providence bore a powerful resemblance to the outlook of the common American. Like the "mute, inglorious Milton," they saw the workings of providence all about them and translated that perception, not into glib assertions of mundane ease, comfort, and accomplishment, but into dolorous pronouncements of mundane challenge, hazard, and defeat.

Religion 2

In the broadest sense, providence meant the way things were and would be; religion meant man's better efforts to accommodate to providence. Religion involved an undertaking in spiritual submission. Before examining some of the facets of that undertaking, it might be well to emphasize the submissiveness by recalling one of the most renowned religious statements of that era, Emerson's "Divinity School Address" of 1838. Whatever the importance of Emerson's views to refined contemporaries, his utterances were as alien to the common people as they were to his renowned adversary, Andrews Norton.

Emerson, of course, spoke in a comfortable and elevated setting, so much so that one was "constrained to respect the perfection of this world." In a world so indulgent, it must have come as no surprise to find that "Man is the wonder-worker." The "wonder-worker" should quite logically accept the admonition "to go alone; to refuse the good models," and the reminder that "that is always best which gives me to myself." God resided in the self. Indeed, "that which shows God out of me, makes me a wart and a wen." From that it was only a step to the theological finality: ".... a man is made the Providence to himself. . . ."[1] What Robert Elliot Fitch styled the "odyssey of the self-centered self" was entering its latter stages in such sentiments as Emerson's, and at the beginning of the 1960s Fitch saw about him essentially what Emerson had pronounced or prophesied: "The Self is god. The Self is the One True God."[2]

But a great gulf lay between the pre-Civil War common man and Ralph Waldo Emerson, a gulf almost as great as that which separates that common man from his late twentieth-century descendant. Emerson's was an assertive and autonomous view wherein religion consisted in the self-revelation issuing in the insistence that man is made the providence to himself. In contrast, the common man's view was a submissive and theonomous one. For him religion represented the means whereby man could become attuned with providence. Providence meant the givens, that "circumstance" which so fully aroused Emersonian defiance. It also meant "God out of me," and the corollary of being "a wart and a wen" was at least believable. For peace of mind here perhaps quite as much as for the Christian hope beyond, the common man could ill afford the luxury of rejecting that unengaging description and resorting to transcendental insurgency. Providence was the way things were, and religion allowed one to acquiesce with composure. For Emerson that was an old view, and "the old," he asserted, "is for slaves."[3] But the years would mute that disdain:

> It is time to be old,
> To take in sail:—[4]

In time, what Emerson called "the god of bounds" would whisper to him what for the common man was religious instinct.

"And What Is the State of Religion in That Quarter . . .?"

However far apart Emerson and his obscure contemporaries were theologically, they came fully together in their general concern for the religious condition. For orthodox Andrews Norton Emerson was a spiritual disturber of the peace, and many of the common people would have shared that opinion had they known of the "Divinity School Address." But in their prosaic way they endlessly raised the fundamental question posed by Emerson. "And what is the state of Religion in that Quarter. . . ?" Thus, Lyman Benson of Sharon, Vermont, made the inquiry of a relative over at Averys Gore. So it went around the country. Against the backdrop of apparent spiritual lassitude, Benson, like many of his fellows, was hopeful of some encouraging sign. Immediately after the question posed above, he conveyed the state of religion at Sharon: "It is a low time with us in that view."[5] Except in times of evident excitement, the situation at Sharon and Averys Gore—both dull, but hopeful of better conditions elsewhere—was representative of religion in America. In Wetumpka, Alabama, William Oliver may have been disappointed to learn that "Religion are verry dull" back in South Carolina,[6] but the news could not have come as a surprise. People obsessively probed and examined the state of religion, generally arriving at disquieting conclusions. One wonders what the common man and, for that matter, Ralph Waldo Emerson expected. For his part, Emerson apparently expected miracles. But could the spiritual underpinnings of human affairs actually have been endangered? Was the intense and ubiquitous concern for religion not only a sign of vitality but perhaps the vitality itself?

The "Divinity School Address" also focused on the question what is the state of religion? Emerson, of course, considered it wretched, stating that "a decaying church and a wasting unbelief" threatened "calamity." Irreligion drew "genius" from the "temple" and into the "senate" and the "market."

"Literature becomes frivolous. . . . Society lives to trifles, and when men die, we do not mention them." The ominous personification of this descent appeared in the figure of "the bold village blasphemer." This inherently craven fellow had now grown bold and threatening after seeing "fear in the face, form, and gait of the minister."[7]

William A. Clebsch contends that "if Emerson did not entirely describe contemporaneous America, he bespoke its immediate future."[8] But one wonders. One suspects that the village blasphemer was not all that bold and that he was unlikely to become so in the near future. Emerson may well have magnified the gravity of the situation in order to get a better hearing for his own form of spiritual cure—what Clebsch calls "transcendentalist modernness."[9] Except in one dimension of American life (which is treated later in this chapter), the common folk rarely depicted or reflected overt irreverence. Thus, the common man's writings of the period reflect a supremely religious society working feverishly to become even more so.

Nevertheless, some contrariness and even heterodoxy occasionally surfaced in these writings. A good illustration appears in the recollections written by Elijah Smith of New York State in 1858. Elijah recalled a host of setbacks, with his second marriage figuring prominently. In the same year that Emerson delivered the "Divinity School Address," carpenter-farmer Smith met and married a woman who, by her telling, had declined many offers of wedlock while waiting for a "good pius husband." But Elijah Smith had a surprise awaiting him. As husband Smith opened his Bible one morning for breakfast-table devotions, his new wife announced: "mr. Smith wee will omit reading and praying this morning." Smith acceded, but, when the same thing occurred the next morning, he insisted on "the duty I oed to my God." That duty involved a sore trial, for as Smith read, Mrs. Smith and her two children derisively accompanied him with a "continual groaning and saying glory amen."[10]

There were less serious deviations as well. On a warm spring day in 1852, young James Canfield berated himself for being party to "ridiculing or rather making light of religion."[11] Even this quite devout youth probably realized that "ridiculing" was too strong a word for what was very likely the levity of young people seeking to have a good time. "Making light of" could well have applied in Andrew Jackson Sterrett's innocuous story of the old lady at the prayer meeting who thankfully acknowledged God's presence, "*notwithstanding the inclemency of the weather!*"[12]

Spontaneous disparagement, whether like Mrs. Smith's malice or the young people's playfulness, posed a lesser challenge than those forms of concerted antipathy which Emerson depicted. The state of religion was a more worrisome concern when beset by hypocrisy and rigid institutionalism. Here again, these bases of disquietude, though far from pervasive, did surface in the writings of the common folk. When Abel Holton wrote back to New England from his new home in Illinois, he described himself in emphatic terms as "the same

old infadel." He considered it unlikely that he would ever change because, as
he put it, "I much dislike the hepocracy that I am obliged to witness among
those that stile themselves god's children." "You see," Abel's wife noted
resignedly in her part of the letter, he is "the same in sentiment as he ever
were."[13] Abel Holton may have kept very strict accounting where human professions and human performances were concerned. If so, he may have been
ahead of his time in a way other than his acerbic posture. The Romantics' insistence on genuineness and sincerity at any cost would bear fuller fruit in the
future, after, for example, Abel told the neighbors that he was moving to town
so that his wife could go to church without his needing to accompany her.

Fear of hypocrisy in religion has been a long-standing concern, as has been
clerical machination. In America, the work "priest" has had a powerful
impact, and not simply because of its Roman Catholic connotations. Doubters
and dissenters frequently employed it in a very broad way. Thus, Vermonter
Jonathan Parker told the folks back in Clarendon of the religious situation in
Davenport, Iowa, mentioning six "priests"—Methodist, Episcopal, Baptist,
Catholic, and two Presbyterians.[14] Such references as Parker's often seem no
more than matter-of-fact statements. In this regard, the 1854 Webster's recorded that the word "priest," though formally dropped by non-Episcopal
Protestants, was still used "either ignorantly or contemptuously" to apply to
any minister of the gospel. Parker's letter left no doubt; whatever his intelligence, his attitude was one of contempt. Regarding the clergy of Davenport
there could be no other conclusion, he opined, than that the "people are sufficiently Priest ridden."

A Kentuckian offered a similar sentiment in explaining his "long oposition
to relegion." He argued that his opposition arose not from hatred of hypocrisy, but from those "willing and anxious slaves of Sectarianism," people who,
for example, knew nothing of the Bible and "cannot cote one single verse." The
slavishness that he saw in others led this village storekeeper to dismiss all "sis-
tems," with, of course, the exception of the one formulated by Jesus and the
apostles.[15]

The Kentuckian's misgivings are carried a step further by a "poor factory
girl" in Clinton, Massachusetts, Lucy Ann. She provides one of the rare intimations that Emerson might have given some members of the lower class an
appreciation of his religion of nature. The girl evidently possessed some strong,
even abrasive, ideas on religion. On one occasion, she censured her cousin for
having written about churchly observation. Cousin Charlotte had apparently
mentioned the house of God, and that elicited the following outburst: "The
house of God, what do you mean? Our churches?" Poor Charlotte seems to
have stumbled onto an explosive situation, and now Lucy Ann was telling her
that "our churches" partook of "desecration" and "mockery"—indeed, so
much so that the "childish mummery" of Catholicism answered as well spiritually. Interestingly, the mill at Clinton stood some twenty miles from Con-

cord, not too far evidently to escape the subtle touch of Emersonian tranquility. Behind Lucy Ann's defiant condemnation of her own church one perceives
the shadow of the sage: "Mine is in the wild-woods." There, of course, no evil
could befall the Transcendentalist; indeed, some wondrous things occurred.
Lucy Ann probably did not become a transparent eyeball; hers was a less rapt
and powerful imagination. Still, her spiritual message to her cousin bore a
strong resemblance to Emerson's in "Nature." "I never walk alone amid
nature's solitudes without the same indescribable sensation of awe and
devotion. . . ."[16]

The One Thing Needful

Lucy Ann's religious ideas were quite far removed from those of most plain
folk. Hawthorne expressed the doubts which probably would have come from
the untutored had they been directly confronted with the spiritual elevation of
nature. In "Earth's Holocaust," Hawthorne portrayed and parodied the "zeal
for reform" that sought to destroy "the externals of religion," as well as a great
many other encumbrances upon human contentment. The impatience of those
like Lucy Ann appears in the ironic pronouncement: " 'The woodpaths shall be
the aisles of our cathedrals. . . .' " But at the conclusion of the story, with
churches and other impediments consigned to the purging flames, Hawthorne's "dark-visaged stranger, with a portentous grin" told the one thing yet
needing destruction, the one thing yet precluding felicity—" 'the human heart
itself.' "[17] To Hawthorne and his lesser counterparts, human evil could not be
escaped by venturing into nature. In fact, as will be discussed later, nature only
added loneliness and deprivation to man's inherent sinfulness.

Hawthorne might chide the Lucy Anns of the world for entertaining fond delusions, but by her own lights, her position was in no way areligious or irreligious. She and her Kentucky counterpart in heterodoxy—the storekeeper
much distressed by slavish sectarianism—were just as solicitous for religion,
though in different form, than most Americans. The endless inquiries about the
state of religion during these three pre-Civil War decades derived from the
conviction that, in some fundamental way, it was the one thing needful. Both by
vague intimation and by relentless explication, the parable of the sisters
Martha and Mary was advanced to express basic priorities. The storekeeper in
Ghent, Kentucky, evidently was well acquainted with the ways of the world,
for like Martha in Luke's account, he had been "troubled about many things,"
including visions of his "cuntry Drenched in human gore or tamely submitting
to a monied aristocracy." Still, the Kentuckian insisted on forswearing such
concerns and concentrating upon, in his terms, that "one thing needful." He
either heeded or unconsciously recalled Luke's version as he resolved to attend
"the better part."[18] Mary, according to the gospel account, "hath chosen that
good part, which shall not be taken away from her" (Luke 10:42). However

much common folk found themselves, like Martha, "cumbered about much serving" in their workaday setting, they continued to urge their fellows to emulate Mary's better part by ignoring the world to hear the word.

Emerson agonized over his suspicion that Americans were gravitating from the "temple" to the "senate" and "market." He seems to have been unaware of the degree to which his less intellectual fellows were uneasy about the same point. In popular thought, the Emersonian tension between the "temple" on the one hand and the "senate" and "market" on the other became the more prosaic imagery of, for example, Mary listening at the master's feet while Martha remained engrossed in mundane tasks. But the common folk were less worried about than resistant to the notion that America was on its way to the "senate," the "market," or the devil.

The people's repeated injunctions to self and others, of course, took forms other than those derived from Luke 10:42. Interestingly, the sentiment seems only rarely to have been couched in the well-known "treasures in heaven" terms. Perhaps these terms were avoided because for the common folk it was as alien a parallel as Emerson's "temple" and "senate." The same spiritual lesson could well be made without superfluous concerns about treasures in this world. Thus, Keziah Taylor, adept at putting large matters in succinct terms, advised a daughter to meditate upon that "which is more important than farther or mother."[19] Even when California laid siege to the soul of man, a topic regarding which more will come later, words of counsel did not instinctively adduce Matthew 6:20 and its words about laying up treasures.

The "one thing needful" found one means of expression that went at least a little beyond simple exhortation. Joseph McCool, writing in 1840 from Illinois back to Pennsylvania, commented on the variations in health conditions in the western country. One county of Illinois was, he stated, far preferable to another, and to give that fact additional weight he availed himself of an analogy: health "is to the temporal, what rel[igio]n is to the Spiritual life."[20] McCool reduced large matters to a standard formula, the spiritual-temporal duality. To him and others of his class, health meant the ability to respond to the demands of the world. But important as that was, religion took precedence. To these people religion meant proper response to spiritual challenges, the response to what providence imposed now and what eternity held in store.

Amarilly Lines of New Haven, Connecticut, when writing to a son and his new wife, glowingly remarked on the welcome news of their good health—"one of the greatest blessings that one can enjoy in this life." Far more emphatically, however, Amarilly "rejoysed to hear such good news from you that you have turned from the vain and transitory things of this life to something that is of greatest importance both to live and to die by[.] I could not have heard better news from you."[21] Her son Sylvanus had, as it was often expressed, come out on the Lord's side. His mother showed no deficiency in celebrating that above the marriage itself. She simply placed first things first.

As health was to the moment, so religion was to eternity. Religion demanded attention. Protestations to that effect were legion, and occasionally they are somewhat unconvincing. When a young man who had moved from Alabama to Waco, Texas, wrote to a friend at home, he told of the good fortune he enjoyed in the new location, now owning his own blacksmith shop and some other property. However, pleasing as that was, he professed to take greater satisfaction from the fact that he had become a "treu devoted cristan." Here, one might wonder if that religious profession might have been colored by guilty recollections of Alabama, where, as the blacksmith stated it, "i ware very wild" and where there yet lived a woman named Ann—"my consions hirts when i think of her."[22] And one might consider the case of a Carolina teacher who wrote to a young lady telling her that he feared for his eternal destiny if she ended their romance. Was this, one might well ask, a genuine concern for his spiritual well-being or was this rustic Byron trying to pressure the woman to continue a relationship by referring to the ruination of his "poor never dying soul?"[23] Even more doubts arise from a final instance. When Jesse Owen went to Arkansas he took two or three of the slaves from his stepfather's farm in Kentucky. In keeping with a promise to the slaves at home, Owen wrote letters that included news of the blacks who were with him, particularly a young boy named Tom. Owen did not confine himself to description of Tom's condition; he also included spiritual directions to Tom's parents. Some would darkly suspect religiously derived efforts at social control in Jesse Owen's message to them: "live religious Mary. . . . be religious harry[,] live for god."[24]

Perhaps these religious pronouncements of the Waco blacksmith, the Carolina teacher, and the Arkansas farmer were all quite sincere; but each invites some doubts. But surely, all of them attest to that era's capacity for talking in terms of the one thing needful, a capacity so great that, at least once in a while, someone asked for relief. When Lawrence Parker wrote "My dear lady" near the end of a letter to his fiancée, he was showing some weariness and impatience. He was attempting to mute some of her incessant concern with the one thing needful. "You have much to say," he wrote, "on that subject in all your communications to me. I suppose you think it is the most important subject that can be mentioned." His fiancée did indeed think that, and it would avail her suitor and others like him very little to urge that further "repitation" was unnecessary.[25]

A Prodigious Appetite for Religion

Over a century after he left Saxtons River, Vermont, to run a tin shop in Ohio City, Ohio, Oren Wiley's jottings reached print. His religious predilections, however, overburdened modern tolerance, and so some of what he had to say was excised. The tinsmith's description of the antics of the 1840 Whig campaign—a matter of "general historical interest"—passed muster, but what followed did not meet twentieth-century standards: Wiley's compositions had become "effusions" of an almost exclusively "religious and melancholy" tone. Indeed, we are left with the conjecture that the thirty-five-year-old tinsmith drifted in that inadmissible direction after having suffered an illness.[26] Perhaps he had, but those parts of his compositions that have been printed, as well as the editor's opening remarks, strongly suggest a consistently religious man. In his strength of religious conviction, Wiley resembled many others of that period. They had an awesome capacity for religious interest, inquiry, and exercise. That large capacity should be considered on its own grounds, in spite of the fact, as another editor put it, that "readers today" might well find the "religious idiom" of such writings an "embarassing or tedious feature."[27] As Joseph Haroutunian observed in 1932, "it is the secularized modern who must speak of the 'religious interpretation of life,' "[28] as if it were one of many rather than the only one.

One looks about uneasily for some means of presenting the dimensions of this spiritual propensity and at the same time avoiding the tedium of documenting the overzealousness. For example, a store clerk in Sharpsburg, Maryland, heard five sermons on one Sunday in 1833.[29] Even more impressive, though not unprecedented, is the record left by Nathan Parkhill of Weybridge Vermont. In a diary flysheet, Parkhill drew a graph with months intersecting years; in each square he entered the appropriate number—from 0 to 5 to indicate Sundays on which he attended meetings. For only one month of the decade that he recorded—1851 to 1861—did an ignominious cipher appear.[30] In rather denotative ways, the Maryland clerk and the Vermont farmer offer an intimation of the enormous religious appetite of the period.

Sermon texts had a large place in many diaries. Despite many gaps and errors, these entries represent minor monuments to man's search for enduring faith. By the mid-1850s, the intellectual intensity of the Puritan sermon of colonial New England—artfully expressed by Moses Coit Tyler and Perry Miller—had undergone changes. Only a few years remained before Tyler would dismiss his own time as "a grinning and a flabby age, an age hating effort, and requiring to be amused."[31] But attention was still being extended in pre-Civil War America. A sermon in Oswego County, New York, based on the last two words of Psalms 9:16—"Higgaion. Selah"—suggests that imaginative efforts, if not Perry Miller's "dialectial paces," still made occasional demands.[32] How the preacher brought those two words to bear upon general spiritual considerations would be difficult to say. More commonly, of course, didactic straightforwardness marked the citing of texts. Mary Nearing often ended diary entries with passages from her own Bible reading as well as from sermon texts. The illumination thus provided sometimes had a powerful effect. When a sleigh ride with her beau included a late-night spill and a frolicsome roll in the snow, Job 31:4 ended the account with the sobering question: "Doth not he see my ways, and count all my steps?"[33]

Steps were counted in a great many other settings than sleigh rides. A few days before his eighteenth birthday, William Hoffman answered his first call to "watch the *Dead*," in this case the daughter of a neighbor. According to his diary description of the night, he and two other watchers confined their conversation to "*Religion*."[34] The setting well explains the subject matter, but consider contexts that are less likely to elicit reflections on the infinite. Charles Dudley, a store employee in Cheshire, Connecticut, went to New York City for the long Fourth of July weekend in 1856, to take in the "fun." It was, of course, a celebrational moment, and we have no reason to suppose that young Dudley did not enjoy himself. But he improved his opportunity in a way which, though routine in his own time, would strike a later age as inveterately devotional. Dudley attended the Clinton Avenue Church in Brooklyn; he visited Greenwood Cemetery; and he heard Henry Ward Beecher address himself to what may have been Galatians 6:5: "For every man shall bear his own burden." Little wonder that on Dudley's return Cheshire, Connecticut, would seem the "dulest place" in the country.[35]

Sometime during his holiday in the city, Dudley went to Barnum's Museum. On another Fourth of July in New York City, another young store worker—at the moment a bakery-grocery employee, but shortly to be a bartender in Richmond, Virginia—went to Peale's Museum where he saw the standard array of freaks and panoramas. But he had by far the most to say about the " 'Infernal Regions,' " a theatrical intimation of hell itself. In this performance the "reverential awe and astonishment" had nothing to do with the nation's birth. In the foreground the figures of Beelzebub, Cerberus, Python, and Lucifer directed the tortured human traffic to the fiery gulf at the rear. "On a sudden the visiter is plunged into pithy darkness, whilst he is surrounded by the mournful shrieks of condemned spirits. The clashing of chains, and uproar of devils and imps complete the scene of horrors."[36]

Was there no escape then from the religious dimension and observance? It would be more accurate to say that few sought escape, as, for example, the visitors to New York City who considered it "fun" to go to the Clinton Avenue Church and the " 'Infernal Regions.' " Nor, as in William Hoffman's case, was a religious occasion the only pretext for religious sentiments. Hoffman practiced his religion almost to a fault, although some might see hypocritical tendencies in him. For example, on a September Sunday in 1850, he went to morning services at the Broadway Tabernacle, and he returned to his living quarters during the middle of the day. There he had an unforeseen "pleasure": through a hole in the door of an adjoining room he witnessed "the perfect female form of the two Miss Whitings, young girls or ladies about 17 & 19 years old . . . for about 20 minutes with every part of their bodies exposed. . . ." If this young man felt any remorse afterwards, he failed to reveal it. Indeed, he had enjoyed what he called "a fine view."[37] That evening, he again attended the Broadway Tabernacle. Such a juxtaposition of activities would probably have horrified Abel Holton in Illinois, for it would have represented unanswerable evidence of "hepocracy." But young Hoffman and others might well have imagined worse places for him to have spent that evening than at the Broadway Tabernacle.

The Indiscriminate Fascination of Religion

William A. Clebsch's *From Sacred to Profane America* has particular significance for this study in that he sought to discover the religious temper of "many social strata." That quest led him to some representatives of the common folk. In treating the moral and ethical dislocation which these people encountered on the frontier, Clebsch showed that some remained sedate and inhibited. "And then there was Horace Muzzy of Maine. . . ." On a Sunday in "wicked" San Francisco, Horace Muzzy attended a Methodist service, sermon, baptism, and communion. He spent the evening at a Presbyterian church hearing a lecture on the life of Solomon. "This ecumenical harbinger," Clebsch observed, "was no doubt lonely and homesick. . . ."[38]

Here, the unwary might come to a wrong conclusion. Being lonely and homesick may have driven Horace Muzzy to religious excess, but many of his contemporaries showed similar propensities, and they did so regardless of loneliness and the like. Charles Dudley on his holiday in New York City probably did not suffer emotional pain for being away from Cheshire, Connecticut. In turn, the "ecumenical" aspects of Horace's San Francisco Sunday are less unique than one might at first suppose. Indeed, Horace's actions were probably more a reflection of the indiscriminate religious fascination of his own time than a foretaste of later religious tolerance.

In a small-town or western setting, the religious observer attended whatever service was available. Thus, on an April Sunday in 1848, Josiah Chaney, another native of Maine and a newcomer to the Illinois-Wisconsin region, went to a Catholic church in the day, and in the evening he attended a Swedenborgian meeting where he "liked the sermon well."[39] Chaney may have had no choice, but others were motivated to attend services other than their own out of curiosity. Testy John Drake, a man of intense religious convictions, tried the modestly different spiritual fare of a Lutheran church while on a visit to New York City. Nor did he allow his recent excommunication to keep him from attending Presbyterian services on the same day.[40] The diaries indicate that many varied their religious observance, participation, or sightseeing from Sunday to Sunday, or from Sunday morning to Sunday afternoon to Sunday evening.

In simplest terms, excitement continued to inhere in the religious dimension. "What could be more full of meaning?" Melville asked regarding the "seataste" of Father Mapple's Boston chapel for sailors. Mapple moved in full harmony with the true church setting:

for the pulpit is ever this earth's foremost part; all the rest comes in its rear; the pulpit leads the world. From thence it is the storm of God's quick wrath is first descried, and the bow must bear the earliest brunt. From thence it is the God of breezes fair or foul is first invoked for favorable winds. Yes, the world's a ship on its passage out, and not a voyage complete; and the pulpit is its prow.[41]

F. O. Matthiessen contended that Father Mapple's sermon on the story of Jonah broke down "the arid divisions between learning and ordinary existence." It allowed Melville, through his partly fictive Father Mapple, to combine "the locutions of everday speech with a vocabulary that does not scant the resources of complex philosophical diction. . . ."[42] Artistry aside, Melville's era equated the spirit of the "pulpit" and the spirit of the "prow."

Whether one sought reverence or the sideshow ridiculous in religion, it provided both. For example, late in the troubled year of 1854, Daniel Hunt heard Theodore Parker preach from Galatians 6:7: "Be not deceived; God is not mocked: for whatsoever a man soweth, that shall he also reap." Four days later, Thanksgiving Day, he again heard Parker, and this time Hunt described "a great surmon."[43] When Parker addressed himself to the proposition that " 'God hath not dealt such with any other nation,' " he did not, as the previous chapter suggests, deal in amiable congratulations. As Hunt understood it, the reformist preacher's contention was that his recent arrest in a fugitive slave case constituted his greatest pride; thus, the sermon was more nearly sombre than celebrational in mood.

Three days after the Thanksgiving sermon, Hunt beheld another of the spiritual fixtures of Boston, Father Edward Taylor. (This ex-seaman turned Methodist preacher to north-end sailors probably served as the model for Melville's Mapple.) Hunt could be even more latitudinarian, for in Boston he also responded to the enticement of Mrs. Sprague, "the great Spiritual Medium," as well as the Spiritualist songstresses, "the Misses Hall." In Bangor, Maine, a fortune-teller made him privy to larger designs: soon he would be 1200 miles away and henceforth he would not need to work for others. In spirit some of these attractions were not far from other things that Daniel Hunt enjoyed, hearing the rape trial and life sentence of Barney Healey, or watching Edwin Forrest do a seething rendition of "The Gladiator."[44]

For the common people of America, the sublime and the ridiculous were not always far apart. For example, Northerners traveling in the South reconciled the infinite and the bizarre when they made the standard visit to a "nigger" meeting. Most seemed to share the reaction of a New Englander doing repair work on ships at Savannah: he was "well paid" for the trouble.[45] A man from Michigan on his way to the gold fields had a brief stay in New York City before boarding ship, and a few days later he wrote of his activities in the metropolis. He went to church twice and to the "musium," probably the American. "Great sights there," he noted, but he mentioned only one particular: "our Saviour in full stature with a plate of thorns on his head."[46] Young Cyrus Sanders, lately of Ohio but now of Iowa, enjoyed a similar combination of cultural offerings on a trip to Saint Louis in 1840. At the "Museum," Miss Hayden's magic particularly impressed him; then he "went to the Catholic Church & C."[47] "The feats of the monkeys, the feats of the lady in the lion's den," and the "light farce" titled " 'I Prefer the Widow' "[48] did not, as noted earlier, preempt all of Charles Dudley's attention. Similarly, the bakery worker on his way to being a Richmond bartender probably got his twenty-five cents' worth at Peale's. He may have witnessed with "wonderment and delight," as the *Evening Post* put it, the wizardry of "Monsieur Adrien," and he probably beheld that "facetious Lilliputian Major Stevens."[49] But he wrote about " 'The Infernal Regions.' "

In *From Sacred to Profane America*, Clebsch found "the aspirations of Americans sacred in origin and their achievements profane in fruition."[50] Emerson's discernment of a movement from temple to market is a symbol of this larger movement. A drift to the market had not gone nearly as far in pre-Civil War America as is often supposed, however; the temple surrendered its hold only slowly. Its influence still radiated in a myriad of direct, subtle, and even prostituted ways throughout that society. People paid it homage within their own sects, in the sanctuaries of variant creeds, and in shamelessly contrived commercial spectacles. They were inveterate churchgoers; they were less the "willing and anxious slaves of sectarianism" than the Kentucky storekeeper and others have supposed; and they had few qualms about combining religion with what others might adjudge downright entertainment. The "Steps to the Temple," as Carl Bode called them, were far more complex and various than his neat combination of tracts, Bibles, and biblical novels.[51]

Theological and Religious Tensions

Emerson identified "theological problems" as "the soul's mumps and measles and whooping-coughs," but in "Spiritual Laws" he took some satisfaction from the fact that "a simple mind will not know these enemies."[52] The simple mind does seem to have encountered these enemies but maintained only a passing acquaintance with them. Doctrinal matters did not have a large place in the writings of common men. It could hardly have been otherwise, for in the presence of "theological problems" the "simple mind" almost necessarily becomes shy and circumspect, if not mute. And common men occasionally expressed forthright appreciation for being spared "the soul's mumps." When Hiram Peck of New York City took "Emma N" to hear a sermon on the "fall of man" with the text from Genesis 3:1–7, he came away pleased that there had been no "medling with intricate points."[53] He did not say it, but he likely would have felt that verse seven ("And the eyes of them both were opened . . .") adumbrated quite enough of the results of eating from the tree of knowledge. In Boston, Constable Willard recorded his reaction to a sermon from Isaiah 28:10: "Not much pleased."[54] The upshot at verse thirteen conveyed an acceptable lack of doctrine, but 28:10 itself may have had a forbidding cast even in Boston: "For precept must be upon precept, precept upon precept."

Though comparatively immune to "mumps and measles," the simple mind experienced some spiritual afflictions. Pre-Civil War America, an age of overt and sometimes violent religious antagonisms, had unlovely aspects fully as bad as "theological problems." However, as recorded in the writings of the common people, religious hostilities seemed to have been considerably less intense than one might suppose. Given the personal nature of those sources, their comparative lack of testiness or malice toward other sects cannot be attributed to dissembling. To be sure, some concerned person might offer prayers for the Methodists, "these poor blind deluded creatures,"[55] but bigotry is generally muted, though certainly not absent.

During the pre-Civil War era, there was already a proliferation of creeds in America. Thus, the people, with their vital interest in religion, had a wide variety available. One of these was Quakerism which had been an important part of the religious landscape since America's early years. By the mid-nineteenth century, however, its abrasively exciting edges had been smoothed. Distinctness of identity waned and withdrew into "thee's" and "thou's" and the numbering of the days of the week and the months of the year. "Quakers are not what they once were," the son of a Brooklyn greenhouseman wrote in the 1830s.[56] While Quaker spokesmen, like other religionists, still received attention, that attention was now rather perfunctory. In January 1848, Hoosier Josiah Hickman traveled to Newcastle to hear a Quaker woman preach. It was doubly a curiosity, but the attention of this religious young man went to the matter of justifying "a woman speaking in public."[57]

What Quakers lacked in excitement, the Shakers lacked in numbers. Common writings treated them both perfunctorily. Given the occasion, many would probably have done what Seth Willard did. In July 1859, this farmer improved the opportunity to hear a Shaker "preacher"; in November, he heard a Quaker. To him, those trips to the schoolhouse to behold the visitors may have been as rewarding as going to the village to hear John P. Emerson "take the poor debtors oat."[58]

By the 1850s, the Quakers and Shakers were curiosities, but there were even more eccentric forms than these. Some, such as Mormonism, Catholicism, and Universalism, served as catalysts of rancor, and one, Spiritualism, proved enticing to many in the ranks of the humble.

During that era Mormonism aroused such hostility that violence sometimes erupted, but with the exception of letters from the Missouri-Illinois area, there are few emotional observations regarding it. The letters simply make matter-of-fact comments on Mormonism. For example, Eben Weld, a native of New Hampshire, showed little uneasiness when his brother went to live at Nauvoo.

Early in 1846, when Eben worked as a government farmer for Little Crow's Sioux near Fort Snelling, he wrote that, by a letter of July 1845, he had learned of his brother's marriage to a Mormon in the Mormon City. Eben knew nothing of his brother's wife except that she was sufficiently "impertinent" to inquire through her husband "how many papposes I had and wives."[59] Eben admitted elsewhere in the same letter that the Indians were urging him to marry Little Crow's daughter; but he seems to have felt that Mormon women, be they ever so worthy, had small call to pry into the domestic relations of others.

Common people such as Eben Weld did much observing and sampling of variant religious forms, and when Eben went down the Mississippi on his way to the Far West, he stopped at Nauvoo to inquire of his brother and, as well, to view the former city of the Saints. And a young man from Mobile took advantage of the Salt Lake City stop on the California trip in order to attend a Mormon service. His hope of hearing a good sermon went unrealized, however; instead he heard too much about "their suffering and tithes."[60] While not downplaying the tension and resentment many felt in crossing Mormon country, even here, it should be emphasized that a wide-eyed curiosity about the spiritual remained. Perhaps the fury of some of the orthodox clergy can be accounted for by the fact that the laity had an inclination to stray.

The "Mummery" of Catholicism

While the Mormons were still at Nauvoo, an Illinois woman, a Mrs. Aiton, wrote to her missionary husband in the Minnesota country telling of exciting things on the religious scene. The Saints had completed their "splendid" temple, and now, as the lady understood the matter, the edifice had by some chicanery passed into the control of Catholicism.

Now methinks were I an inhabitant of Hancock County I would much rather the Mormons would have possession than the Catholics. Doubtless they have deep designing well laid plans and when once they get a foothold there is no telling what they may do connected as they are with a foreign power.[61]

Here, in abbreviated form is the Protestant's standard image of the Catholic Church as a sinister threat, insidiously ensconcing itself in the heartland. She neglected some of the more unlovely characteristics of the standard portrait—depravity and prurient abominations. Her Catholics are simply crafty and manipulative, and masters of political intrigue. Some of her lapses were remedied by a Yankee schoolma'am who stopped at Bardstown for a few days while traveling across Kentucky. She described one of the Catholic functionaries of that community as follows: "Fat bishop disgusting object, taking snuff with fingers full or [*sic*] rings."[62]

However much the run of Americans mistrusted Catholicism, they seldom expressed that feeling in their private diaries and personal letters. Perhaps scholars have placed too much emphasis on the official pronouncements of Protestant spokesmen, especially the Protestant publicists and clerics. To be sure, there had to be soldiers as well as leaders in what Ray Allen Billington designated *The Protestant Crusade*, but one senses that the ranks may have filled with less haste and with less antipathy than might be inferred.

In *The Rise of the Common Man*, Carl Russell Fish considers the religious tensions of that era. He states: "This was hardly an atmosphere in which one would expect tolerance, and yet, except in the Eastern cities where religious differences were emphasized by those of race[,] and riots occurred between a rather rowdy type of Protestants and Catholics, intolerance did not often run to violence."[63] Billington's study *The Protestant Crusade* carefully portrays the factors, especially class and economic disparities, which hastened the transition from religious antagonism into violence. It would appear that the potential for violence was low until other volatile elements such as Fish·and Billington mention were introduced.

The suspicions which the common folk harbored about Catholicism bore little relation to the lurid sensationalism spread by members of the upper classes. Billington somewhat inguardedly describes the "lower classes" of Boston at the time of the burning of the Ursuline convent as "peculiarly susceptible to the propaganda being circulated against the Catholic church and especially against nunneries, for their natural American curiosity made them read all disclosures concerning the building on Mount Benedict and to believe racy of this statement can hardly be demonstrated. We know very little about what such people read, if they read anything. My research, for example, disclosed only one mention of Maria Monk's salacious sensationalism titled *Awful Disclosures*, and that was a peremptory dismissal by a devout New York City Methodist.[65]

The average man's misgivings about Catholicism involved two major elements, neither of which was very mysterious or had anything to do with unspeakable horrors. The first centered on an almost timeless cliche, but one that may have had greater impact in that era than others. From Ralph Waldo Emerson to the most obscure scratcher of an occasional letter, the age obsessedly exorcized spiritual deadness. It did not stand the Catholic in good stead to appear, however accurately or inaccurately, as participant in "mummery," in cold unthinking ritual. The other element had to do with what to the Protestant mind was the offensive contrast between the wealth of the Catholic Church and the misery of its communicants. After reading Joseph Holt Ingraham's *Beatrice, The Goldsmith's Daughter*, a young Pennsylvanian derived greater satisfaction from living in a "free and happy land" far removed from the conditions suffered by that "very miserable set of beings [the poor Catholics]."[66] Both elements appear in a diary entry made by a Forty-niner to record his attendance at Catholic services in Santa Fe. For him, the participants in "mummery" became, simply, "mummies," in this case, "poor miserable looking creatures

kneeling alongside a beautiful senorita."[67] Perceptions of "mummery" and
proverty seemed to suffice. And so perhaps the common people could leave the
much-remarked salaciousness to their purported spokesmen, people described by Sidney Ahlstrom as "religious and political adventurers, profit
seekers, publicity hounds, fanatics, opportunists, 'joiners' of all kinds, and
some men who in retrospect seem almost mad."[68]

When Frederick Marryat was in Boston, not long after the burning of the
convent, a native explained the affair in terms of *"curiosity."* A dozen planks,
the Bostonian insisted, nailed up in some fashion on the commons, with notices
to the public to keep their distance, would attract a mob within twenty-four
hours that would storm the place to unravel the mystery. The Englishman
wavered a bit. He viewed that contention as a "dextrous" effort to "palliate
one of the grossest outrages" ever committed in America, but he did not doubt
the new nation's high curiosity quotient. Americans, he noted, "cannot bear
anything like a secret,—that's *unconstitutional.*"[69]

Curiosity took more than the idle form suggested by the above anecdote.
Things spiritual held an intrinsic interest for the people of that era. Certainly
where Catholicism was concerned, some went to a Catholic church to gape
and others to sneer; still others went for the sober purpose of witnessing the
transcendent dimension as it might be shown in another setting. In that age of
religious experimentalism, some people would go far afield, sometimes as far
as a Catholic church. And as noted earlier, people frequently had to make do
with what was available. They often employed the term "privilege" in
connection with things religious, a term basically meaning the opportunity to
participate in formal, organized spiritual functions. When non-Catholic
Americans appeared at Catholic churches, they generally had something in
mind other than burning.

Caroline Poole, the Yankee schoolma'am visiting in Bardstown, had occasion to see the "fat bishop" who aroused her disgust because, having no
Presbyterian services available, she went to Catholic services. A few days
later, she enjoyed meeting some of the teachers at Saint Joseph's College, "&
could we divest ourselves of prejudice I should think them very aggreeable
men." Indeed, she found them so agreeable that she spent an hour in Reverend
Spalding's room "looking at paintings and engravings" that he had brought
from Rome. And in this, the year of Maria Monk's greatest influence, this inveterate Protestant visited the nunnery at nearby Nazareth. The spirit of
Caroline Poole's reaction to the nunnery bears almost no resemblance to the
spirit of Monk's *Awful Disclosures*, though there may have been some innu-
endo in this observation by the schoolma'am: "Spin & knit their *own* stockings
and perhaps a pair for a priest now & then." By and large, however, the nunnery impressed her very favorably. Everyone there treated her "very graciously," and the aura was one of order, simplicity, cleanliness, and tranquility. Caroline Poole admitted her unfriendly idea of Catholicism—"the idea of

a 'snake in the grass.' " She may have been prejudiced but that did not prevent her from indulging a curiosity that was well above the idle, and of deriving whatever spiritual benefit she could from this alien religion, however faulty it might appear to her.[70]

Caroline Poole and her contemporaries—even Mexican War soldiers who had some basis for hostility—were most reluctant to represent Roman Catholicism in terms of lust and violence. Indeed, the era's general feelings toward Catholicism might be reevaluated. In particular, the Protestants' fear of Roman conspiracy may not have run as deep as some scholars have contended. David Brion Davis, for example, has presented the lurid "nativist literature" as "a medium for articulating common values." Common values having readily been established, they then bear explanation. "Why," Davis asked, ". . . did nativist literature dwell so persistently on themes of brutal sadism and sexual immorality." According to Davis, those themes arose from an "increasing anxiety and uncertainty over sexual values and the proper role of woman." Thus, the period exhibited "deep-rooted feelings of fear and guilt"; nativists sought to "escape from guilt," and psychologically they worked a "projection of guilt as well as desire." "The sins of individuals, or of the nation as a whole," Davis contended, "could be pushed off upon the shoulders of the enemy and there punished in righteous anger."[71]

In order to answer questions about the prevalence of "themes of brutal sadism and sexual immorality" in a contemptible literary genre, we would do well to consider the source, those cranks and charlatans referred to by Sidney Ahlstrom. It is possible that a violent, salacious, and aberrant propaganda form had only a limited relation to common values. There were, of course, consumers, and Maria Monk's *Awful Disclosures* has been called the "Uncle Tom's Cabin of Know Nothingism."[72] Still, one might recall that the indulging of prurient interests has often been done with some larger rationale. Perhaps popish plots, however unlikely, gave a patina of redeeming social value to otherwise shameful literature.

John Higham once observed that "the modern mind dwells on the unconscious savagery lurking in its own dark corners." In the same essay dealing with nativism, he urged his readers to stop neglecting "the less spectacular but more steadily sustained contentions" that informed such things as anti-Catholicism.[73] Earlier, Oscar Handlin did something of that order in treating the upheaval in Boston. Handlin, providing even more explanatory (even exculpatory) context than Billington, noted, for example, that Protestant fears transcended the merely chimerical because the Catholic Church was, at the time, a "church militant."[74] Another scholar, John R. Bodo, offers the simple contention that "the basic insights of the Protestant 'crusaders' were altogether correct"; they had "every reason to look upon the coming of large numbers of Catholics with alarm."[75] To venture into the "less spectacular," common perceptions containing anti-Catholicism derived not so much from fictions such as that surrounding the Hotel-Dieu nunnery, or from the horrific realm of libidinal fancies as from the lackluster notion that a predominantly Protestant nation would be best served by remaining so. The apprehensive perception of Catholicism centered, almost stodgily, on "mummery" and on the seeming contrast between opulence in Catholic church and indigence in Catholic society.

The Infidelity of Universalism

Catholic Americans could often be identified as such by their language, custom, class, and origin. For anti-Catholics, strictly doctrinal matters were rarely the greatest sources of concern. But the social sources of denominationalism and interdenominational hostilities are not the only ones. Indeed, according to A. Leland Jamison, ". . . some eclectic interpretation of the Bible has, in final analysis, been the bedrock on which every dissident movement has sought to justify its own separate existence."[76] Doctrinal matters, as distinguished from the practical application of doctrine or attributes coincidental to doctrine, exercized many Americans. The shame or the glory of American religion has often been seen as that unfolding in which interest begot discussion of fine points, and discussion of fine points begot the disagreement necessary to the formation of new sects and denominations. Those staying in the mainstream spread their sour appraisals of renegades fairly indiscriminately. Surprisingly, a great deal of disdain was shown Universalism—a disdain which excelled that shown Mormonism and rivaled that shown Catholicism. And here, matters of language, custom, class, or whatever played very little part; "mumps and measles"—matters of theology and theodicy—did.

In writing about "popular freethought" in that era, Albert Post contends that Universalists sometimes bore greater censure than that meted out to professed infidels.[77] In fact, common folk made very little effort to separate infidelity and Universalism. Often, the word "Universalism" served merely as a vague indicator of forces to be resisted and ultimately to be overcome.

"Vary discouraging," Stephen Humphrey wrote about the state of religious affairs around Goshen, New York, in 1834: ". . . iniquity seems to be pouring in upon us like a flood[.] [T]he universalists seem to be gaining ground."[78] When the tide of battle went the other way around Woodstock, Connecticut, a lady of that area marked the triumph by the fact that "the unerverselers are coming into the fold almost every day."[79] One senses that such usages make of Universalism a metaphorical device, a linguistic measure of light and darkness not closely deriving from articulated creeds. Catholicism might be disparaged as "mummery," but Universalism suffered the worse fate of becoming a synonym for infidelity.

Here it might be noted that Unitarianism apparently came almost not at all to the attention of the common people. Henry Miller, a young plasterer and builder from Pennsylvania, described the religious spectrum of Saint Louis, putting Unitarianism into likely context. Miller seems quintessentially American—young, Democrat, builder. Like so many others, he was a religious shopper, but he gravitated towards Baptist and Methodist functions. Vitality and curiosity inform his remarks about various aspects of Saint Louis life; and, when he described the churchly dimension, he enjoyed a dual perspective—structural as well as spiritual. Perhaps because Saint Louis was "the strongest hold for Catholics in the Western Country," his first and lengthiest attention went to that religion. But he avoided entirely the fretful ruminations of, say, Lyman Beecher's *A Plea for the West*. Indeed, not even the fact that "His Holiness at Rome" had sent presents to adorn the Saint Louis edifice moved Miller beyond straight description or open approval. The hospital kept by the Sisters of Charity, for example, respresented a "blessing to this City." With the mason's eye for physical detail, Miller noted a succession of churches—the Episcopal, Presbyterian, Methodist, Baptist, and on to a "quite neat edifice built with considerable tast" standing at the corner of Fourth and Pine. There, William Greenleaf Eliot presided over "quite a respectable congregation" at the Unitarian church. Miller, of course, made a point of attending there one Sunday, and he heard a "very good sermon."[80] He learned why Missourians were coming to have a high regard for Eliot, and why, though dead a year when his grandson Thomas Stearns Eliot was born, he remained ruler "*in absentia*" of that family.[81]

Miller had one other occasion to see Eliot in action. The young visitor went to the Presbyterian church to hear a debate pertaining to the use of the Bible as a "reading Book" in the common schools of the city. The issue proved so "warmly debated" that "unfortunate sectarian prejudices" became quite apparent. With Protestants generally favoring such use of the Bible, and Catholics almost entirely opposed, Eliot rose to urge that the matter be debated no more.[82] That apparently ended the debate. This small episode suggests why A. Leland Jamison emphasizes the importance of the question "what does the group do with—or without—the Bible."[83] Eliot may have felt that the "social sources" of denominational problems were sufficient and that the doctrinal vexations that would emerge from debating what was to be done with or without the Bible would merely compound them.

The doctrines of Universalism could be taken seriously by other churches, as Eveline Ostrander learned in April 1835. The Second Presbyterian Church of Bath, New York, having had Eveline admit a Universalist position, formally called on her to attend a meeting "to answer the charge of heresy." Mrs. Ostrander emerged with a suspension and a warning about her "most inconsistent and futile" notion.[84] Unlike Eveline Ostrander, Elam Slagle of Macon County, North Carolina, encountered Universalism but rejected it. In 1854, young Slagle's employer in the tanning business sent him to Baltimore to learn the newer refinements of the trade. Slagle wrote his wife Amanda that he attended various churches, and he discussed religious affairs in the larger world. When fire struck an Episcopal church, he noted that "Irish Catholics" were warmly suspected and that there would be a "bad time here" if those suspicions were borne out. In the same letter, he told of attending a Presbyterian church where he heard a sermon from First Corinthians 16:2, and the "best vocal music I ever hird[,] all new tunes." On another occasion Elam heard something he considered far less pleasant; he "hird what I never hird before a universalist preach or at least what they call preaching." The Universalist had contended that no man was so "mean" as to be unfit for church membership, and "a great many other things that is as bad."[85]

Young Slagle did not specify those other things that "is as bad"; nor did Mary Covey of Hopkinton, New York, when she invited Lucetta Abbott to come for a visit. Lucetta should come on a Saturday, Mary suggested, and then they could go to meeting the next day. Next the sprightly Mary wrote: "I think it will not defile you to hear a wicked Universalist Preacher once, as you will not need to imbibe the sentiments you hear held forth." But she never specified what Lucetta might find "wicked" in the sentiments expressed by a Universalist preacher. She playfully added the following postscript: "Burn this as soon as you have read it for fear some pious soul may find it."[86]

Hence, as Eveline Ostrander, Elam Slagle, and Mary Covey well knew, Universalism did have doctrinal content, and that content managed to offend people other than church officials. On a Sunday aboard ship, an Alabama argonaut heard a Universalist preacher deliver a sermon, "which every one looked on as a burlesque."[87] Albert Post contends that "Universalists were regarded as worse than infidels because they hid their unbelief under the cloak of Christianity."[88] True infidels, he thought, occasionally found it expedient to masquerade as believers in a variant creed. But there was another, larger issue involved here.

Tom Hayter, a youthful migrant to Polk County, Oregon Territory, had tried to embrace Universalism's notion that God "would not send anyone to Hell," but the words of a dying friend had caused him to reconsider. Now, as he informed his mother back in Missouri, he could see that "there was something for man to do. . . ."[89] The potential antinomianism of the doctrine of universal salvation caught the attention of the common law as well as the common man. "It was argued," Albert Post writes, "that the rejection of the idea of a state of rewards and punishments freed one from the fear of certain retribution, and therefore opened the way to the falsifying of testimony."[90] Tom Hayter was moving in accord with the common law; he was forswearing what now appeared to him as the worldly license of the Universalist position: "i saw i had lived a Sinful life and had Tried to Belive that the Universalist was right. . . ."[91] Tom Hayter's position, like that of the common law, involved secular and human considerations; important as those considerations were, however, matters of theology and theodicy took precedence.

Universalism's most fundamental affront to orthodoxy—its claim to have definite knowledge—is shown in the writings of two members of that sect, Oren Lee and John Brown. Oren Lee, a seventy-year-old farmer and former black-

smith in Connecticut, took pleasure in ridiculing the orthodox; their missionary efforts, Lee felt, ended in ruin, and their revivals left a wake of madness and
suicide. Although his attitude towards death was the orthodox Christian one—
at the death of an acquaintance, he observed that "Gods ways and his footsteps are not known"—he possessed a certainty which his orthodox counterparts did not allow themselves. "God is love," he insisted, and so salvation
would be universal. When his third wife died, Lee wrote that she remained a
Methodist to the end, but she had confided in him that her greatest "Sattisfaction and Comfort" came from hearing Universalist preachers.[92]

In February 1833, John Brown had extraordinarily sorrowful news for his
sister Lucy in Roxbury, New Hampshire. A sister-in-law and his father had
died, and shortly thereafter, after posting a letter to his brother Oliver, Brown
picked up a Concord, New Hampshire, newspaper and read in the death list:
"Oliver Brown[,] Feby 12th." "Good God, I exclaimed can this be possible."
To this point in his letter to his sister, Brown had expressed orthodox sentiments. His father's death was "this stroke of divine providence," and the compounded tragedy represented "so many afflictions as kind providence hath afflicted us with." But then, like Mrs. Lee's finding "Sattisfaction and Comfort," Brown presented the "balm" for these "many afflictions." He took his
text from First Thessalonians 5:9 and 10, a text which allowed him to see in
God's purposes "that mankind Universally" shall be saved.[93] At this point,
John addressed his sister Lucy somewhat uneasily, and he assured her that he
broached the subject only for their mutual consolation. Her brother's caution
suggests that Lucy may not have cared to be consoled in that way, and that she
may have preferred verse 5 of that chapter where Saint Paul seemed to be dis-
tinguishing the "children of light" from the children of "darkness."

Though the usage was listed as obsolete in the 1855 Webster's dictionary,
the word Universalist had a second meaning: "One who affects to understand
all particulars." For the orthodox Christian, John Brown and Oren Lee violated generally held precepts by claiming to have fathomed an ultimate purpose of God and, in turn, by finding that ultimate purpose a pleasing one to
man. In these ultimate matters, certainly was a rare commodity, one more
nearly reviled than cherished. Those with unduly large claims in understanding
"all particulars" appeared, not only as credulous, but also as dangerous.
Gray's epitaph to the "mute, inglorious Milton" made guarded mention of nothing more than "trembling hope." Writing to Hawthorne, Melville allowed
himself some hyperbole in noting that "we incline to think that God cannot
explain his own secrets, and that He would like a little information on some
points Himself."[94]

Spiritualism

Orthodox Christians of the pre-Civil War era considered Spiritualism to be
more heretical than Universalism. Whereas Universalism somewhat shyly

spoke of well-removed eternal destinies, Spiritualism, taking those destinies for granted, summoned the past, present, and future from the vasty deep with which the orthodox felt so uneasy. Here, the theism of the older order gave way to the pantheism of the newer persuasion. In the orthodox theist view, mortals, with proper care, could catch fleeting glimpses of the ultimate and infinite; under the enticing dispensation of Spiritualism, the infinite was easily visible to all. That enticement shows quite frequently in humble sources.

On an August Sunday in 1851, Francis Squires, a thirty-year-old farmer in Oswego County, New York, heard two sermons, one of which was directed against "*Spiritual Knockings*." The preacher aptly chose Deuteronomy 18:9–14, and we suppose that he had stern things to say about the "abominations" of a "consulter with familiar spirits." Squires made terse diary entries, and he did not always separate clearly what he personally attended from what he had heard. For that reason, we cannot know whether, on that same August Sunday, he attended or merely knew about a "*Spiritual meeting at Nichols.*"[95] Certainly, spirits were assuming an impressively "familiar" way, and some people, stunned by that familiarity, resorted to less subtle but more efficacious methods than Deuteronomy 18. In 1860, a former New York State woman recalled vividly a spiritualist experience she had had years before. At 2:00 A.M. near the window of the north bedroom, there began "a raping very low," and, before long, that "raping" was at the door itself. At this point her husband Horatio asked his wife to hand him the double-barrel shotgun, and then he called out loudly: "Depart you cusard into outard darkness and scamper of with your self." The spirits may have respected that kind of forthrightness, for they "never rapt more."[96]

The varying methods of exorcism were not always effective. Early in 1852, the inhabitants of Shaftsbury, Vermont, had such "a very great excitement about here at present regarding the rappings" that "there is scarcely anything else to be thought of."[97] The immediate catalyst of this outburst came in December 1847, at the Fox farm in Hydesville, New York. "Soon throughout the entire nation, from Maine to the westernmost reaches of Wisconsin, in the houses of travelers recently returned from New York the joists were jumping from the game of Puss-in-the-corner being played incessantly by the spirited furniture."[98]

There are two errors in this quotation. First, the western limits of spiritual familiarity went even beyond farthest Wisconsin. Second and more important, the "entire nation" was not affected, for the South remained aloof. The frequency of content or curiosity regarding Spiritualism in the writings of the common people was suprisingly high, but my research revealed not one clearly discernible instance at the South. In 1855, a New Englander wrote from Portsmouth, Virginia, that two New Yorkers were attempting to induce rappings in that neighborhood but were not taken seriously.[99] What is implicit by its absence becomes explicit in the letters of a Hoosier who spent the winter of

1851–1852 at Memphis. In February, having learned that the folks back in Wayne County, Indiana, had succumbed to the Spiritualist craze, Lewis Macy chided them for their delusions: "Well I did think the good people of old Wayne too sober minded to be led away after strange things." A month and a half later, he returned to the subject, this time with a direct and invidious comparison between North and South. "I almost begin to think," Macy wrote archly, "that the people of the north are more easily humbugged than those of the south. . . . I believe I have never heard of a 'spiritual manifestation' in the south yet."[100]

If the joists did not jump at the South, they certainly did elsewhere. On June 19, 1857, Lewis Campbell of Washington County, Iowa, received his copy of Andrew Jackson Davis's autobiographical work, *The Magic Staff*. As God had spoken to Swedenborg, so Swedenborg, though long dead, spoke to Davis, and now Davis, one of the foremost prophets of modern Spiritualism, spoke to Iowa farmer Lewis Campbell. Soon, the "Harmonial Philosophy" was on a rampage among the Washington County farm folk. The tables tipped brazenly, and spirits laid hold of mediums with abandon. Other interests were ignored during this period, as when a scheduled debate on the slavery controversy folded in April 1858 "for want of a sufficient audience." Political concerns received only bare election-day mention. Lewis Campbell at midterm in 1858 stated simply that he "went to election," but he gave a full description of the "Spiritual meeting in Swire's grove" where the "audience benefited" by hearing the Harmonial Philosophy "set forth with a reasonable degree of clearness & force."[101]

An almost endless succession of Spiritualist circles began at this time. However harmonial the philosophy, the action at these circles often partook of spiritual rough-and-rumble. At one session reported by participant Campbell, the circle called on a contacted spirit to have yet other spirits take control of the medium. The spirit took the suggestion not at all "good naturedly," "making a good deal of complaint in his valedictory address." And there could be worse things than a lecture by a peevish shade. Two weeks later, a Mrs. Fritchen came under the influence of a spirit who caused her to write in German (elsewhere in Campbell's diary the name appears as Friedschen). This spirit not only failed to cooperate linguistically (except perhaps with Mrs. Friedschen), but it also distressed the circle by revealing that "the Catholic religion was the true religion."[102]

The circles were not always entirely helpless in problematic situations. Tom Paine and Voltaire became renowned for their zealous grasping of available mediums, perhaps hoping thereby to redeem themselves for materialist errors. Even though they were favorites, they could be called to account. Thus, at one of the Washington County circles in October 1858, Tom Paine controlled Frank Noble but obstinately refused "tests of his identity." In response to Tom Paine's contrariness, yet another spirit took control of Mrs. Woolly and, speaking through her mediumship, dismissed the godfather of the nation as a spirit "two physical for any high and very useful mission." Spiritual splenetics often gave way to straightforward signs of what lay ahead. Zachary Taylor had been dead several years now, but he evidently kept abreast of national affairs and cared about the nation's future. "Old Rough and Ready" had never stood on formalities, and he certainly did not do so on September 19, 1858:

The medium was about eating a piece of pie when he was instantly taken possession of by what purported to be General Taylor. . . . The speaking was very enthusiastic and vigorous. . . . General Taylor purported to controll the medium & spoke of war as being iminent between whites & indians & that in less than 20 years this country would have to encounter Great Britain in another war. Insisted on perpetuating the union of the states as the only means of national safety & the next war we would be involved in would be with Mexico.[103]

Spiritualism and Reform

James R. Stewart, a Pennsylvania saddler who arrived in Kansas in the mid-1850s, said little about politics, drank frequently, worked rarely, built "castles in the air," and read widely. In the summer and fall of 1855, the new Jay-hawker read the Bible, Emma Willard's *System of Universal History in Perspective*, James Thomson's *The Seasons, Paradise Lost*, Edward Young's *Night Thoughts, Gertrude of Wyoming*, some Pope, and Tom Paine's *Age of Reason*. But another work pertaining to Paine kept the young saddler occupied for a time—"Tom Paine, in the spirit world." Indeed, when he began his Kansas diary, Stewart was reading Andrew Jackson Davis's *The Great Harmonia*.[104] Unfortunately, in his diary he rarely commented on his reading. One might suppose that Stewart read whatever came to hand and that *The Great Harmonia* had as much intrinsic interest as *Gertrude of Wyoming*. Spiritualism had, of course, a large fascination, and it became a frequent point of reference in letters and diaries whether or not the writers took it seriously. Writing to his mother in the East, an ex-sailor turned San Franciso bartender remarked, only half playfully, that "I pass an evening occasionally with *circles* investigating *Spiritualism*,—In fact I investigate it all day in the *Bar Room*.— It amuses me some."[105]

It amused a good many, but, as Sidney Ahlstrom observes, Spiritualism "was not merely commercialized entertainment"; it was a "religious force," and, for some, "it was a religion."[106] The component parts of that religious force, as outlined by Ahlstrom and others, appear fairly clearly in the common folk's writings of the late 1840s and the 1850s. Perhaps the desire of the aggrieved and remorseful to make contact with departed loved ones came foremost. Lewis Campbell's descriptions of the circles in Washington County, Iowa, frequently mention otherworldly word from relatives and friends. One "Frances" who was probably the writer's deceased wife had greatest interest for Campbell, but others such as "Silas Jackson who died on Wednesday last, of a rattlesnake bite" made themselves known.[107] In a letter to her family in Ohio, Clara Day of Minnesota brooded painfully about a sister now lying in the "dark cold grave." She next posed the question: "do you hear from her often?" Clara would not believe the preacher from Northfield; man does not die "much as the brutes do" thus to remain until the "trump shall sound." "I believe it is most as sure," another family member wrote, "that the spirit of man can come back after death. . . ." The departed sister, Arodine, had hardly gone to that unconfining grave before yet another sister "felt the influence of spirrits." "I think," mother Day now wrote encouragingly, "we shall hear from our dear Arodine before long. . . ."[108]

There was a good deal more to Spiritualism than the often imprecise, invariably questionable, and nebulous contacts with the deceased. From the Spiritualists' point of view, some aspects of their endeavors had very manifest and immediate qualities. In the large philosophical sense, they genuinely believed that theirs was a scientific approach of reality. They acted, R. Lawrence Moore has written, "as adamant champions of empiricism." Illustrative of the general posture, Moore contends, was the prominent Spiritualist of the 1850s who "worshipped devoutly at the shrine of reason erected by Tom Paine who, not incidentally, became a favorite spirit voice."[109] Spiritualists called on others to recognize the empirical facts of the matter, phenomena such as rappings, table-tippings, and messages. When their fellow mortals failed in that recognition, messages of reassurance and condolence came to Spiritualists from those who would understand—Franklin, Newton, Bacon, Paine.

Not surprisingly, the subtle relationship between scientific thought and religious thought receives little illumination in the common people's writings. These writings make almost no explicit reference to the scientific nature of Spiritualism. With regard to the spiritual return of the dead, to Alfred Day of Geauga County, Ohio, it made good sense that "if there is power to carry them one way the same power will bring them back again."[110] But such people *practiced* Spiritualism; they probably did not theorize about it. One of their spokesmen in the larger society might "worship devoutly" at Tom Paine's shrine, but humbler Spiritualists would readily allow another spirit to dismiss Tom Paine as "two physical" if he failed to cooperate in the "tests of identity."

Contrary to the general supposition, Spiritualism involved this worldly quite as much as otherworldly matters. For example, Andrew Jackson Davis had conferred with Galen even before he had conferred with Swedenborg. The "magic staff" served not just as an emblem of the autobiography; it was also that instrument which Galen gave him to work the physical betterment of mankind.

To be sure, some prostituted the message of Spiritualism. When ailing Nancy Williams in Oregon, Illinois, wrote to a "spiritualest" doctor in Syracuse, New York, she received, in return for her dollar and the lock of her hair, some "Restoreative," some "Lung Syup," and a bill for eight dollars. Nancy persevered and tried again, this time receiving a bill for five dollars, more medicine, the directive to bathe her affected parts in "Brandy or good whiskey," and some relief for her distress.[111] Spiritualist diagnostics ordinarily tended to be more abstruse. When Lydia Day wrote that someone was ill, she expressed the hope that "sary's indian" would be able to advise the cure.[112] This comes in a sentence replete with allusions to mesmerism and mediumship, and it is not clear whether Geauga County, Ohio, had a mortal Indian somehow involved in therapeutics, or whether this is a reference to the spiritually standard Gate Keeper,[113] an American Indian who directed the spiritual traffic, ensuring that only pertinent spirits would approach those attuned and susceptible people such as Sarah. Elsewhere, Spiritualist medicine seemed to be commendably straightforward. In Washington County, Iowa, the circles contacted the spirit of a deceased doctor, perhaps on the assumption that his existence in a new dimension had powerfully enlarged his talents. Through the medium of a Mr. Prindle, Lewis Campbell received a "physiological examination" from the departed Dr. White. Campbell learned that, though his lungs and stomach were sound, his "liver was out of order." (The Spiritualist doctor in Syracuse informed Nancy Williams that her liver was "sorpid.") The prescription for Campbell's condition strikes one as no more fraught with disaster than many of that era—mustard plaster and a tea containing ergot and spearmint.[114] Whatever the particulars of the method involved, Spiritualism meant to enhance the physical being.

It was not just the ills of the body that came within the bounds of these new views. Whether Andrew Jackson Davis or Lewis Campbell, the confirmed Spiritualist appeared in the ranks of those seeking a larger felicity for mankind. At one level, this was expressed in Universalism, which promised eternal felicity for all. At another level, it surfaced in the relation between Spiritualism and the reform causes of the time. James R. Stewart, the interested observer in Kansas who seemed only to read about Spiritualism, had no interest in this relation. Indeed, he could debate against both woman suffrage and Universalism.[115] But a believer such as Lewis Campbell combined Spiritualism, particularly the open sessions at a schoolhouse or at a meeting grove, with such concerns as woman's rights, tax relief, and railroad control.

When such high purposes were frustrated, the Spiritualist had no difficulty locating the cause. Placing Davis among the " 'radicals' " of his time, one scholar has written as follows: "For him every enlightened cause hastened the approach of the new dispensation; the greatest deterrent to the realization of this happy estate was the traditional church."[116] Those common people who embraced Spiritualism had less certainty because they often maintained some ties with that "traditional church." Still, they strongly suggest that tension, if not antagonism. James Jones, the San Francisco bartender and man of the world, did more than flirt with Spiritualism for its entertainment value; he, too, could earnestly repeat the standard Spiritualist contention that "there is no such thing as dying, it is merely a change. . . ."[117]

Having been a sailor and now tending bar for Sam Brannan, Jones felt that he could spot a "humbug," and there were more "humbugs" than "crazy" reports of gold strikes on the Fraser River. "So Bill has been washed," he archly observed in apparent reference to a friend's joining an orthodox church. Immediately thereafter this man, gravitating toward Spiritualism, delivered the following aspersion upon orthodox religion: "I am sorry to hear of Mrs. Patch,—they are careful to mention whenever spiritualism makes a weak minded person crazy, but when what is called *religion* does it, it is not mentioned."[118] That same summer of 1858, at a grove meeting back in Washington County, Iowa, Mrs. Jay, with the spirits "discoursing" through her, held an audience enrapt for an hour. Earlier in the session, "monopoly of all kinds" had come in for severe treatment, but now, through Mrs. Jay, "the harmonial philosophy was sustained," and "the old theology was repudiated."[119]

Conclusion

The "old theology" represented, to use Emerson's phrase, "God out of me." It portrayed God and man as quite separate, man being the creature of God. God ordered things obsolutely as he saw fit, rarely vouchsafing his intentions to imperfect mortals. To embrace the sanguine certainties of Universalism was to gull oneself, as well as to diminish and blaspheme God. And however intriguing and attractive Spiritualism may have been to a large number, in the view of society at large, it involved a further extension of the gnostic impertinence. Spiritualism directly undermined providential resignation. It professed a divination revealing ultimate spiritual secrets, and it represented a motive force for redoing the fundamentals of human affairs. Alice Felt Tyler long ago noted "a connection between Spiritualism and social reform," and she explained that connection in terms of Spiritualism's "optimism" and "its vision of a glorious future."[120] She was probably quite correct in ascribing such attributes to Spiritualism, but doubts arise as to whether that "optimism" and that "vision of a glorious future" were, as Tyler put it, "truly American."[121]

The present work depicts a "truly American" spirit at quite some remove from such. In his letter to Hawthorne regarding *The House of the Seven Gables*, Melville allowed himself another exaggeration. He wrote of Hawthorne's "No! in thunder," when in fact it was a very quiet "no." But, whatever the volume, that abiding negation, that resignation bordering on fatalism, made Hawthorne and Melville much more attuned to their society than is frequently supposed. In an old but influential work, Raymond M. Weaver told of their pessimism and judged them "quite out of sympathy with their time and its tendencies."[122] But it is just the traits that Weaver mentioned in this context that made them at one with their time. Thus, "scowling, poor, dim-sighted"

Hepzibah of *The House of the Seven Gables* bears strong resemblance to her real counterparts. Sensing disaster ahead she

strove hard to send up a prayer through the dense gray pavement of clouds. Those mists had gathered, as if to symbolize a great, brooding mass of human trouble, doubt, confusion, and chill indifference, between earth and the better regions. Her faith was too weak; the prayer too heavy to be thus uplifted. It fell back, a lump of lead, upon her heart. It smote her with the wretched conviction that providence intermeddled not in these petty wrongs of one individual to his fellow, nor had any balm for these little agonies of a solitary soul; but shed its justice, and its mercy, in a broad, sunlike sweep, over half the universe at once. Its vastness made it nothing.[123]

The assertive views of a compartively small group in pre-Civil War America have too frequently been mistaken for the attitude of the nation at large. Russel B. Nye, for example, summarizes the drift from the mid-eighteenth century to the Civil War as a "complete change"—"from Mather's distrust of man, to Jefferson's qualified confidence in him, to Emerson's and Jackson's deep and abiding faith in his capacity to find and act upon divine truth."[124] What we have at the end of this progression may have been Emersonian and Jacksonian, but it was not pervasive and popular. In Melville's *Pierre*, one of the Prometheans in pursuit of the "Ultimate Transcendentals" entertains the delicious thought of " 'coming boldly out . . . stumping the State, and preaching our philosophy to the masses.' "[125] All the enthusiasms of the time notwithstanding, Apostle Charlie Millthorpe showed a sense of the possible when he dropped that fond prospect and turned the conversation to cold cuts, hoping that Pierre had a shilling to pay for them.

Charlie Millthorpe's opportunities lay yet in the future. The docile mood was waning, and, a generation after Hawthorne's dolorous depiction of Hepzibah, W. D. Howells discerned the passing of that "grim antique Yankee submission."[126] In the riot of assertiveness of our own age, such a view seems a caricature bordering upon the incredible. Our own age may or may not be what Andrew Hacker has called a "Time of Decline," but certainly religion today has vastly less power to forbid "acts and ideas deemed injurious or immoral."[127] For a vastly smaller proportion of the population can religion serve as it once did, as spiritual vehicle for acquiescence in the slings and arrows of whatever outrageous fortune; submission has now given way to assertion and liberation. The spirit of Hepzibah yet appears in our own time, but with increasing infrequency and ever diminishing force. The Charlie Millthorpes of the world need not now settle for cold cuts.

Conversion, Revival, and Millennium 3

For the pre-Civil War American, religion prepared man for the circumstances which providence ordained and involved some preparatory measures or conditions. There were three dimensions of spiritual preparation: conversion, revival, and millennium. Conversion involved the individual, while revival involved the community. The radically ecstatic extension of these two dimensions was called millennialism. Millennialism does not figure in this discussion as prominently as conversion and revival because the letters and diaries of the common folk yield very little evidence of that concept. The reason may be that the submissive nature of the common people left little room for the sanguine expectations of millennialism.

In August 1842, James Tuthill wrote to his sister, telling her of his imminent marriage and inviting her to the wedding. He then turned his attention to another important matter. Although his sister might "think it very strange," James had some things to say about his religious conversion. The "Spirit of God," he remarked, "has been for months striving mightily with me." During this time, he had known the "deepest trouble and distress," but now comfort had come.[1] The depth and genuineness of Tuthill's experience would be exceedingly hard to assess, for his account is too scant and, like others of his class, he left the close scrutiny of the conversion process to the divines. For Tuthill conversion simply represented "a mysterious & simple thing."

An Ithaca, New York, woman, upon receiving word that an acquaintance had experienced religion, stated that it did not seem "possible." It was, to be sure, welcome news, "but how happened it?"[2] One senses that the question was rhetorical. Even the religionist Robert Baird left the matter of conversion largely unresolved. For him, the necessary ingredients in conversion were "*activity* and *dependence*," things "which are so commonly felt to be subversive of each other. . . ."[3] Whatever riddle resided in that combination, fruits more than process were involved; conversion was known by what it effected. By and large, that consisted, as it had for ages, in willing submission to the ways of providence. It involved the attainment of that state of mind wherein "sublime repose" could be enjoyed. Perhaps aware that her question was unanswerable, the lady in Ithaca gave it this context: "But how happened it? speaking after the manner of men—" Speaking after the manner of men, it may have sufficed to denote that quality that allowed the converted to make the best of the worst.

A Submissive Spirit

Philip Greven has recently shown the degree to which submissiveness permeated the thought of the evangelicals of the seventeenth and eighteenth centuries.[4] That spirit evidently lived on and thrived in their nineteenth-century descendants, the people whose writings provide the subject matter for the present study. As a North Carolinian put it regarding his "pious and plain Methodis" wife, she had that Christian hope "which teaches us to be humble."[5] Victories achieved were victories over the world's aspirations more than over the world's frustrations. A Thanksgiving Day sermon in New York City in 1847 elaborated that theme by adducing such things as the barriers to the working of the holy spirit, "political party feelings," slavery, and the Mexican War. Mary Harris, who heard the sermon, could only echo its Thanksgiving Day moral in a hackneyed manner: "in a world like this how can we rejoice except with trembling?"[6] Crossing the Mississippi to a new home in Missouri, another woman felt her soul fill with "awe and reverence" at the mightiness of the river. Such sights, Martha Woods wrote, "conspire to make us remember our own feebleness" and our utter reliance on God's mercy.[7]

Marriage, too, reflected providential workings. Apparently, whatever subservience characterized marital affairs involved the man-God relation as well as the man-woman relation. Zach Burnett, in describing his "pious and plain Methodis" wife, offered the awkward observation that "what ever I tell her She as much believes as if she knew it." What Zach had told her about the brother to whom he was writing was that "you and Mary is very plain" and that, in turn, sister-in-law Mary "need not put herself to much trouble" preparing for Zach and his "Methodis" wife when they visited. Zach and his wife were only plain Christian folk, notwithstanding the fact that "her farther is got a heep of property and money." Letters from one woman to another at the time of marriage reflected a mood of sober resignation. Writing from Mississippi to a friend in her native Ohio, Mary Nutt assumed a characteristic pensiveness regarding the marriage her friend approached. Mary rejoiced at the prospect of happiness, but more philosophically than joyously, she advised: "I would caution you not to expect too much felicity, in the state in which you are about to enter . . . depend upon it, you will find there are bounds to human enjoyments." Mary would offer various prayers for her friend's well-being in marriage, especially that God would "breathe into her soul, a spirit of love to himself, and entire dependence upon his power, in whose favor is not only present peace, but life eternal."[8]

Writing to a newly married sister, Matilda Drew, whose family was moving to the Minnesota area, commented on the painful breaking of old, comfortable associations that marriage necessitated. Matilda had preceded her sister in marriage, and now she confided that she had had "in sailing on lifes rough sea . . . as much comfort as mortals can look for in this imperfect state of being." Then came hope, injunction, and afterthought:

May your sailing and steering be much better than mine for affiction will come, if we live long we shall certainly lose our friends[,] we shall often have to meet a cold and heart-less world, many times frowns instead of thanks[.] May it be yours to be meek and of a lowly mind that if the rough waves of adversity sweep over your bark you may have a hiding place out of sight of the wicked world[.] If these lines are preserved they will stand here in bold relief when this heart will throb no more and this hand is mouldering back to dust.[9]

Those lines may stand in bold relief against other, later persuasions; but they register well and powerfully the moods of Matilda Drew's time.

The effort to be "meek and lowly" applied to all things, and not just to marriage. Imprisoned in Perote castle after the Dawson raid on the Texas-Mexico border, Norman Woods wrote to his wife that he had little expected such a fate, "but it is the will of the Almighty."[10] Shortly before expiring in the Mexican prison, Woods received a letter from a brother urging acquiescence in whatever befell him: "You must bare your imprisonment with philosophic resignation & the mildness of Christian fortitude[.] I have no more to rite at presant."[11] Though Southerners generally expressed themselves less piously than Northerners, a despairing Alabaman conveyed much of the general spirit of this time in telling his mother of his outrageous fortune. "I earnestly seek & desire that humble submission to all events of life as will make the worst condition tolerable & even a subject of gratitude & in this way only do I expect to triumph over misfortune—"[12]

The pervasive mood of "humble submission" may be illuminated further by contrasting it with the sentiments of an eccentric young man who sought to cir-cumvent it. As a private soldier in the forces occupying the City of Mexico, E.A.B. Phelps exulted in the good work of the invasion. He sought directly to counter the narcotizing creeds of his society:

Pursue the path of duty and leave the results to God. That may do. But I am much mis-taken if these things are not in the hands of men. As much as it may shock our good old women, as much as it may shock our good old men—I believe that every man should make himself a *God*—[13]

Phelps attempted to forestall some worry by saying that his position did not "remove one jot of the humility that should bow every head." But his appro-priation of the Napoleon motif (apparently inspired by the innumerable busts of the emperor that he saw in the occupied city) seems quite inconsistent with that qualifier. As John Cawelti has shown, Emerson stopped short of full acceptance of Napoleon's willful drive to success.[14] And his knowing or unknowing acolyte in Mexico may have hedged his celebration of Napoleon's personal "energy of purpose" by adding, "as far as action is concerned." In his own time, Emerson seems to have made scant few of those "hundred million American godlets" of which D. H. Lawrence would later accuse him.[15] But his general philosophical position seems to have nurtured at least one, E.A.B. Phelps, a man standing in this regard as fully isolated from common views as did the sage whose notions he echoed. Pre-Civil War America yet had a long way to go to reach that "pervasive popular faith in the individual's adequacy to fulfill all his aims and functions."[16]

"And Happy We Are"

"Think not that a Christian life is a dreary, low spirited life."[17] Sarah Russell of Maine was sincere in that urging, and very likely young William Houlton read the urging respectfully when he received it in Minnesota. But "Willie" Houlton and others must occasionally have had doubts. If not a "dreary, low spirited" condition, to some it must have appeared suspiciously close to it. Perhaps religion is ever thus for the common people—not the vehicle to bliss, but the "reality capable of sustaining them through adversities and tragedies that could shatter many men."[18] In an anguished letter telling of her brother's death, a New York woman told of experiencing "a deeper work of grace." In part, that consisted in the sense of her brother's spirit hovering about her. "O how happy I have been while all alone. . . . O sister in these happy hours I have been made to praise God aloud, with my heart melted to tenderness and eyes full of tears. . . ." Sarah Smith had never before realized "that there was so much enjoyment in religion."[19] Her loss had been sanctified to her. In addition to the wake of immediate personal affliction, wherein people, in anaesthetic frenzy, "got happy," there was joy at softly accepting the world's circumstances. In 1854, Susan Seymour, a Covington, New York, woman, counseled her daughter-in-law in Wisconsin as to how to face loneliness and frustration in her new area. Susan, who was soon to die a worn-out "old woman 56 years of age," knew well the toll that would be taken. But she urged her to "keep up courage," keep your husband "as good-natured as possible," and "hope for the best." And finally, ". . . if we trusted that the Lord is gracious, and cast our cares upon him, we go on our way rejoicing, and happy we are —"[20] That advice can seem hardly more than a sad antiquity to what Paul Carter has called "a pleasure-loving modern America trying to shake off the last of what it calls the 'Protestant work-ethic' in favor of a 'fun morality.' "[21]

By later standards, outward signs of an inward joy seem pitiably few and strenuously repressed. With some few exceptions, the inward ecstasy did not lend itself readily to translation into outward form. A well-known facet of this reluctance involved Sunday observance. Philip Schaff, the German-American theologian, saw "strict observance" as a hallmark of the American religious scene; his contention is upheld in the writings studied here.[22] For example, Connecticut clock peddler Milo Holcomb took typical advantage of the day that "our God and our country renders sacred" by writing from southwestern Pennsylvania back to his home in Granby.[23] Some felt uneasy about using the Sabbath in this manner, but letter-writing and diary-keeping were so close to spiritual exercise as to be deemed acceptable Sunday endeavor by most. Writing on another Sunday, Jennie Akehurst of New Hartford, New York, upbraided herself for her abuse of the Sabbath while attending a teachers' institute at Norwich. To be sure, she attended church twice, but at her residence she had "laughed and talked with the girls all the time." "I am glad," she concluded, "that I am not going to spend every sabbath here with so many young people."[24] Jennie would not have needed Max Eastman's dictum that "Humor is of all things most unlike religion."[25]

Milo Holcomb and Jennie Akehurst probably illustrate what Schaff discerned as the radiating influence of Puritanism throughout American society.[26] Seeming diversions such as singing schools and donation parties derived from religious concerns, but that probably indicated little more than that religion colored the lives of all. Christmas usually received short shrift. Though there were intimations of what Daniel Boorstin called "ingenious ways to elide religious issues in order to share in the national Festival of Consumption,"[27] the Puritan misgiving about Christmas still dominated.

The extent and duration of the Puritan influence pose one of the most fundamental questions about American religion. The Puritans had great staying power, as is evident by the nineteenth century's emphasis on personal retrospect, and the Sabbath-day hearkening back to the comfort of childhood, home, and the past. William A. Clebsch notes that religion changed "from a rejuvenating to an archaizing element in American life." In the letters and diaries of the pre-Civil War period, Clebsch found "repeatedly the twin peals of religion and nostaligia."[28] An amen would not be out of order. The common people had few pleasures other than those of melancholy, in this case nostalgic melancholy. As they made their way to a land sale at Paola on a summer Sunday in 1857, some new Kansans sounded the "twin peals": "O for a thousand tongues to sing Alass and did my savior Bleed. . . . We sang just as we felt and I need not tell that we all thought of home."[29]

An Interesting Condition

The very words and usages of the pre-Civil War era were often freighted with meanings pertaining to man's spiritual condition, meanings to which a later, secular age may be insensitive. Time and again, terms referring to thought and inner mood revolved distinctly about the religious condition. Such terms often served as indicators of spiritual progress, and they frequently infused discussions of conversion and revival.

In the turmoil at the camp meeting in the wake of Sut Lovingood's sending the lizards up Parson Bullen's trouser leg, a fat woman stood, fainted, rolled down a slope, " 'tangled her laigs an' garters in the top ove a huckilberry bush, wif her heard in the branch an' jis' lay still.' " To the inimitable Sut, author George W. Harris gave this line of general description: " 'She wer interestin, she wer. . . .' "[30] One must be cautious of F.O. Matthiessen's contention that Harris "brings us closer than any other writer to the indigenous and undistilled resources of the American language, to the tastes of the common man himself."[31] In this instance, however, the creator of Sut Lovingood chose his language with a care and purpose that might be lost on later Americans. That simple assessment—" 'She wer interestin' "—partakes of the comic not because it is an understatement but because it is ironic. In that age, as in others, the word "interesting" could apply to a host of things, but most of all it connoted the working of the soul and spirit. Harris's fat woman—" 'es big es a skin'd hoss, an ni ontu es ugly' "—sought an "interesting" condition at the camp meeting. With the help of Sut Lovingood and his lizards, she realized her wish in an outrageously unanticipated way.

Harris achieved hilarity by leaving the word "interesting" in the accustomed religious setting while dissociating it from its conventional meaning. Common folk used the language in a conventional way; thus, when one judged a minister to be "not very interesting," one judged him, in effect, to be "not spiritual enough for the holy calling."[32] A "very interesting and intelligent Christian" combined reflectiveness with intensity.[33] When it was said of a dying child that "he never was so interesting as now," the assessment was made not from a morbid but a spiritual perception.[34]

As in the case of the word "interesting," certain modes of expression which at first glance have a blithely general quality in fact are strikingly exact. Unless otherwise qualified, the word "thoughtful," for example, betokened things spiritual. When her hushand "seemed unusually thoughtful," Mrs. Andrew Adams foresaw the possibility of his achieving "the comfort of knowing himself the child of God."[35] In Milo, Maine, when Hector Sargent lapsed into "a thoughtful state of mind," a decidedly spiritual issue hung in the balance. When Hector announced that he wanted no one to speak to him of his soul, his neighbor Albina Rich pitied him. But she also noted an inadequacy in the thoughtful one's wife, notwithstanding that it was her own sister. That lady did not seem to have the ability to bring contentment and fulfillment to her husband. "I feel," Albina wrote, "that if he had a different wife he would be a different man."[36] Expressions pertaining to mind and thought derived so fully from religious concerns that an old man, taking up the pen after forty-five years, could state: "the chief design of these writings is to keep in mind the exercises of mind in Religion."[37] John Clark knew that mind could be exercised by other things, but he, too, put first things first, leaving almost no place even for the war for independence.

The religious person avoided a "dreary, low spirited" existence because his enjoyment was firmly predicated upon inward peace rather than outward action. Indeed, the language of enjoyment as well as thought gravitated inevitably to religion, spirit, and mind. Inquiries and descriptions about the state of one's mind resounded across the land, nearly always addressed to religious considerations. "*My Dear Husband*," Albina Rich wrote, "wont you write to me what your feelings have been since you went from home?"[38] Here one would imagine that she is referring to secular feelings, but not so. To be sure, Albina wanted her Charles back, and she found some importunate and even passionate ways of stating a longing that Charles evidently shared. But the "feelings" she asked after here were those pertaining to the eternal soul. Similarly, Mercy Spinney of Ohio wrote east to a relative requesting information "concerning the state of your mind."[39] It could go without saying that "the state of your mind" pertained to things spiritual. The language of thought was the language of spirit.

Enjoyment, or at least contentment, came from a state of mind properly attuned to providential dispensations, and enjoyment pertained directly to the converted condition. Young Sid Smith, who had moved to the Saint Anthony, Minnesota, area, from Maine reported that the new home was a good place "for young folks to enjoy them silves," a view which he substantiated by itemizing his religious activities.[40] A pioneer Iowa schoolma'am would endure many trials of body and soul, but at the outset she could happily observe that she stayed with "a very fine pious family, and I enjoy myself very much."[41] At the end of the definitions of the word "enjoy," the 1855 Webster's dictionary appended: "*To enjoy one's self*, is to feel pleasure or satisfaction in one's own mind, or to relish the pleasures in which one partakes. . . ." The first of the two definitions reflects the mood of the time, and the second foreshadowed more modern persuasions.

"Pleasure or satisfaction in one's own mind" meant the enhancing of spiritual sensibilities. When a Vermont woman went to the New Hampshire shore for health purposes, she wrote home that "I have enjoyed my mind a good part of the time since I left home."[42] The details of her enjoyment came in overwhelmingly religious terms. In letters that passed each other in transit, a Vermont couple, separated by the three thousand miles lying between home and gold fields, enunciated in stark precision the centrality of religious spirit to enjoyment. Nineteen-year-old Mathilda Roberts called upon her husband, Andrew, to write of fundamentals: "I want you to write how you enjoy your mind." Her next two sentences left no doubt as to what she had in mind: "I hope, my dear Husband, you will not give your religion up. Give up everything of an earthly nature but cling to that." In a letter incorporating some workaday realities, Andrew had already spoken to his Mathilda's imperative concern: "I enjoy myself the best in retiring to a little cabin where I stay, and there I read a few chapters and a Hymn and now and then in reflecting upon seasons of prayer that I have enjoyed in Vermont where I hope to end my days." The key to "pleasure or satisfaction in one's own mind" came in Mathilda's urging: "Pray on, dear Husband, never stop praying till death summons you to eternity."[43]

The most basic tension in the pre-Civil War world view had to do with the juxtaposition between the spiritual and temporal. A Vermont woman, for example, wanted to know how relatives were "enjoying their minds and how you prosper in the world."[44] The dry season and the rainy season worked their tempos upon Andrew Roberts in the California mines, but "seasons of prayer" remained fully in memory, if not fully in performance. There was indeed a season to all things. But the spiritual had the higher priority, for the word "seasons" was used much as young argonaut Roberts used it. The world's reaping and sowing went on, but a "profitable season" often came from a private exercise of mind, as, say, when an Ithaca, New York, schoolteacher put to spiritual benefit some unexpected calm and quiet.[45] Although Americans often seemed active and self-assertive, their values and ideals were at some remove. A young man who was on his way to subdue the Iowa frontier expressed these values and ideals in poetic form for his fiancée:

> O! loved one, when thou kneelest
> In secret and silent prayer,
> And offerest up thy homage,
> So free from worldly care,
> When in they secret chamber,
> Is heard no voice of glee,
> And when each thought is holy,
> Sweet Gusta, pray for me.[46]

Augusta Hallock's prayers proved futile; but there is no reason to suppose that she did not offer them generously for the man she was fated not to marry.

"Meetings" Reform "Society"

What prayer and "season" meant to the individual, "meeting" and "society" meant to the group. Of course, meetings were convened for many reasons, but "meeting" per se represented a spiritual privilege. In the absence of a specific qualifier, "meeting" meant religious exercise. In Brigham Nims' succinct "Account of My Time," "meetings" were in serial, seven-day procession. On a trip into upstate New York, a spiritual and emotional hiatus occurred: "no meeting rather lonesome." Nims had forearmed himself for such an eventuality by having "bot Testament" on the day he left his New Hampshire home.[47] Writing to tell a brother in Maine of the attractions of Minnesota, Horatio Houlton emphasized the abundance of "Ministers Deacons and class leaders." "We have," he noted, "metings and Sabath school every Sunday."[48]

The word "society" designated a less formally arranged contact among Christians than "meetings." To the modern mind, the word denotes macrocosmic entities—nation, culture, even mankind. As is discussed more fully in Chapter 5, pre-Civil War America gave it a constricted application. In general, it could denote a circle of acquaintances or simply company. However, it was not, in common language, a general designation for things removed from the working of the spirit, for things secular.

Whitney Cross suggested that separation in his reading of how ministers used the expression "the church and society"—those attendant upon the word in contrast to those in various postures of estrangement.[49] Whatever clerical usage may have been, common folk inclined to make "church" and "society" more nearly interchangeable than distinct entities alienated one from another. Indeed, one senses that they would have had difficulty conceiving of society apart from the religious format. For example, in what was probably a studied effort to render common discourse accurately, Augustus Longstreet Baldwin presented three women in "A Sage Conversation" as one of his *Georgia Scenes.* In their colloquy, when someone was referred to as having "joined society," it meant simply that that person had gotten religion or had joined a church.[50] Thus, when a revival came to her New York community and various churches cooperated, a woman there remarked that she had never witnessed such good feeling among the "different societies,"[51] that is, among the different churches. To gauge the condition of society was, almost by definition, to gauge the condition of religion.

The common people generally had an eye to religious tenor when they made assessments of society. Thus, when word came from Lisbon, Connecticut, that the "state of our Society affairs is very unpleasant," the details revealed growing tensions between the "new" and the "old" elements within that religious community.[52] More frequently, however, the condition of society involved the tension between godliness and ungodliness rather than sectarian divisiveness. An Iowa woman writing to a relative in Kentucky took a broader view than that of Lisbon, Connecticut, by noting the existence of "good society[;] we have all Denominations."[53] And when nineteen-year-old Sally Rice of Vermont took housework at Union Village, New York, she congratulated herself on having a good home and good "society" rather than the "profane Sabbath breaking set" she would have had to suffer back in Vermont.[54]

For the more ecstatically inclined such as an Auburn, New York, woman, the longing for "pure society" meant the "conversion of the world," a project to which "all my energies shall be put forth." Susan Fox's longing for "pure society" could also take the form of "panting for immortality" and "longing to

be freed of the prison house that holds me to earth." Here she worked a somewhat noteworthy transformation of metaphor. The much overworked expression "clay tabernacle" gave way to "prison house." Susan's husband was a
prison guard, and perhaps there was something about him that prompted his
wife to draw him and his activity into her metaphorical depiction of worldly
error and irreverence. Susan's diary—by the conspicuous absence of her husband from it—suggests that the spiritual work she envisioned might well have
started at home. Apparently, her husband had a sense of humor, an attribute
which might have caused him to look with some wryness upon Susan's
"panting for immortality" and with some testiness upon her cosmic longing for
"pure society."[55] Whatever the case here, most took the constricted view
which an Alabaman did in adjudging his new home in Texas to have as "Fine
school & society" as any place.[56]

When "society" was not that fine, heroic measures were in order. The fall of
1858 found Levi Countryman, a twenty-six-year-old farmer of Dakota
County, Minnesota, in an anguished frame of mine. He wanted to get away
from the farm but he had no option. The conventional wisdom indicating that
"this scramble for gold will send our souls into the pit" may have eased distress
in that regard, but other vexations loomed even larger. On August 10 he reproved himself for having committed some "dastardly, cowardly, sinful act."
Two weeks later, in the absence of his wife, he was up all night with year-old
Theophilus who "squalles like a fury." In that setting, little wonder that "Satan
disturbed me to wicked thoughts and deeds." Worst of all, his spouse, Alte,
had the supreme shortcoming. Though she was a skillful housekeeper (and "I
need fear no rival in her love"), she had "no religion at heart . . . and lacks but
that to make her a complete wife."

Relief for the sad plight of these ex-New Yorkers began on November 21,
1858, with the unanimous vote at conference meeting to hold a "protracted
meeting." Four days later the "revival effort" began, and one senses the
mellowing of Levi. To be sure, as late as November 28 he could still slip into
one of his fits of temper while trying to get a calf back into a pen. But by December 2 a somewhat transformed Levi was giving thought to governing his
class at the district school "entirely by love," thus avoiding such things as a
shouting match with a student over a point of grammar only the day before the
revival began. On December 7 when he went into the cowyard to pray "and
struck my head against a post which hurt very much," he quelled his usually
unmanageable temper. The folk around Nininger were indeed enjoying a profitable season, and for the Countrymans the consummate day was December
8. "Bless the Lord Oh my soul," Levi exulted; Alte was among those who
"came forward." Pilgrims, of course, have ever known setbacks, and within
three days the new Alte accused her husband of hypocrisy for using twenty
cents of "society" money. But the next day, Levi wrote, she "fell weeping
upon me confessing her fault desiring me to show her how to be a Christian."
The blissful dismissal of such things of the world reached its apogee the night of

December 12: ". . . we had the happiest meeting of all. Royal got happy and Oc, and Alte spoke, some shouted and we had a good season."[57]

In pre-Civil War America, there was almost obsessive concern with exorcising spiritual deadness. When an Indiana farmer wrote that "the State of Society here is rather dull at preasant," he meant that religion lagged.[58] Other standard descriptors for religious decline were "dead," "stupid," "cold," "formal," and "prone to cling to earth." The Countrymans and others around Nininger launched a frontal attack on apathy and worldliness in the late fall of 1858, and it seemed to bear fruit. As a New York City businessman mused after hearing of the conversion of an aunt in a Newburgh revival, "Nothing to hard for the Lord."[59] Still, the challenge was great and the struggle unending. When Susan Fox, the panter for immortality and "pure society," saw that the preparations for revival in her neighborhood had collapsed, she withdrew into her closet and enjoyed her own "sweet seasons."[60] Things of the spirit ebbed and flowed. Those periodic spiritual invigorations and relapses have captured as much scholarly attention as almost any other facet of pre-Civil War America. Perry Miller calls revivalism the "dominant theme in America from 1800 to 1860." Indeed,

We can hardly understand Emerson, Thoreau, Whitman, Melville, unless we comprehend that for them this [revivalism] was the one clearly given truth of their society. By its basic premise, revivalism required—indeed demanded—that between outbursts there come lulls, which would shortly thereafter be denounced as "declensions." This was the accepted assumption, and for the mass of American democracy, the decades after 1800 were a continuing, even though intermittent, revival.[61]

In January 1843, an Ohio woman, Julia Adams, sensed that the meetings getting under way in her area might result in a "plentiful shower." In general commentary on what was developing and on the "stubborn," sinful "habbits" of the world, she contended that "our cold hearts require the preached word."[62] The "preached word" provided the stage setting for the spiritual renovation and represented the preparatory move for bringing such "interesting" and "thoughtful" things as "society," "meetings," and "seasons" to fruition.

The Revival as Arminian and Transcendental

In juxtaposing "plentiful shower" and "preached word," Julia Adams wandered, quite unwarily, into a central theological difficulty. This juxtaposition suggested what Robert Baird saw at the personal level as the seemingly unmanageable combination of *dependence* (God's agency) and *activity* (human agency). Since the time of Solomon Stoddard in the Connecticut River Valley (1680 to 1720), the metaphor of shower had been widely used to indicate God's free grace. Surely, it remained in wide use in the mid-1800s. When Mathilda Roberts informed her California husband of the conversion of the Oliver sisters, she could add the hope that "this will be but a few drops before a more plentiful shower."[63] A New York City student who felt uneasy with the word "Arminian" provides an even better illustration of the mixing of *dependence* and *activity*. In describing his spiritual quest from age eight onward, he wrote of having been caught up in the good work at a time "when the churches received plentifully of the shower of Grace from the Almighty." But even though he could deride himself for having been "Arminian in sentiment," he chronicled the "Holland protracted meeting" as the next high mark in his religious course.[64] How could one show a becoming *dependence* suggestive of resignation and at the same time the seemingly needful *activity* or enlargement of human agency in the conversion process that often bore the worrisome label of "Arminianism"? The question was much easier asked than answered.

Since Stoddard's time, the element of "calcuation" and purposive human agency had entered fully into the revival equation. Thus, a Rochester woman could write in the fall of 1830 that she had never heard a man "so well calculated" as Charles Grandison Finney "to call up the attention of the thoughtless and wicked sinner." One of the foremost "devices" used by "revival engineers," as Whitney Cross called them, was the protracted meeting. He stated that such devices were invariably accompanied by "apparently sincere statements that all came from God." Cross concluded that both lay and clerical minds ignored the "contradiction."[65] Certainly, unsophisticated lay people did; as always, they showed little inclination to ponder providential imponderables. Whatever the misgivings of those such as the New York City student, an "operational Arminianism," to use Perry Miller's term, was abroad in the land.[66] However tacitly or inconsistently arrived at, it involved an enlargement of the human agency. Given the severe and explicit delimitations placed upon human agency in other facets of his thought, the common man may have come closest to the exuberant assertiveness ascribed to him when he was at the protracted meeting, the camp-ground, or the revival.

It has been frequently contended that untidy revivalism in some way intersected rarefied Transcendentalism. Timothy Smith describes revivalism as "a kind of plain man's transcendentalism,"[67] and one has little difficulty finding passages in Emerson that demonstrate the compatibility. In "The Over-Soul," for example, Emerson described the enthusiasm (that "certain tendency to insanity") attendant upon "the influx of the divine mind into our mind." In this work, Emerson's illustrations progress from major historical figures to the more common men of his own time and very near his own place.

What was in the case of these remarkable persons a ravishment, has, in innumerable instances in common life, been exhibited in less striking manner. Everywhere the history of religion betrays a tendency to enthusiasm. The rapture of the Moravian and Quietist; the opening of the internal sense of the Word, in the language of the New Jerusalem Church; the *revival* of the Calvinistic churches; the *experiences* of the Methodists, are varying forms of that shudder of awe and delight with which the individual soul mingles with the universal soul.[68]

Here it could be suggested that the parallel between Transcendentalism and revivalism does not hinge merely upon emotion or enthusiasm. Insofar as the Transcendental war on circumstance had any reflection at all in the common man's thought, it appeared, not in the unleashing of the human will or in the empowering crucible of nature or in the comforting solicitude of providence, but in the potential for personal reworking afforded by society, meeting, protracted meeting, and revival. Such a setting could produce remade men, though not precisely self-made men.

Quite aside from differing levels of sophistication, the equation between Transcendentalism and revivalism must be approached with caution. There are indeed certain resemblances between the two, and Emerson saw the resemblances. The element that ineradicably separates the two is a disparity in sense of potential. Whatever triumph and assertion the revival proclaimed had a hedged quality compared to the omnicompetence proclaimed by the egoistic Transcendentalists. Perhaps that is why Timothy Smith's contention that this "kind of plain man's transcendentalism . . . geared ancient creeds to the drive shaft of social reform"[69] seems so ill-focused when the common man's writings are considered. It may be that the expansive pronouncements and actions of leaders could lend themselves to such conclusions, but such conclusions seem quite out of keeping with the quests of the lowly. For the ordinary folk, triumph came almost solely over self, not over circumstances.

Ralph Henry Gabriel's contention that there was a nexus between evangelical religion and the Romantic movement in pre-Civil War America has much to commend it, but like Timothy Smith's thesis it ultimately fails. It claims too much—too much assertiveness, too much confidence, too much competence. For example, the revival "shout" takes on questionable implications in Gabriel's analysis. It becomes too much the echo of "Brobdingnagian yarns," as Gabriel puts it, of "extravagant and earthy narratives of the bunkhouse, the flatboat and the tap room." Mike Fink, Davy Crockett, and Paul Bunyan get religion, and the "aggressive individualism" of the "exuberant, optimistic, and undisciplined frontier" sets up a shouting clamor of ecstasy and triumph. A far safer contention would be that, whatever such "mythical heroes" and unwashed Transcendentalists as Fink, Crockett, and Bunyan represented, it was not the inner spirit of those "untutored men and women" suffering "the drabness and squalor, the pains and sorrows, of poor and isolated communities."[70] These humble folk did not aim lower, but they did aim finer. Simply put, they had a singlemindedness that kept the aim on personal peace and hope of the hereafter. They left comprehensive conquests to the Emersons and the Finks.

The Revival as Submission

One can hardly argue with Perry Miller's assertion that "The Revival was a romantic phenomenon," but immediately afterwards he announces that the revival "nowhere better showed its inner nature . . . than by arraying the pious against their seventeenth- and eighteenth-century heritages."[71] But which parts of those seventeenth- and eighteenth-century "heritages" came under assault? The internal and personal language of the revival had little of Transcendental hubris or of tall-tale bluster; the upshot of the revival, rather, was abasement and resignation. In this regard, the quite articulate, self-professed commoner Michael Floy is a tempting source. As his conversion account indicates, the decibel level went high in Brooklyn, as well as in Gabriel's frontier settlements. His own "cries," Floy wrote, "could be heard all over the church."[72] However, the tone was quite different from that presented by Gabriel; Floy probably did not view "Heaven as a place where the shout continued."[73] In fact, Floy's shout was a "groaning and agonizing" that came amid "sweat and tears." After the agony came the quiescent ecstasy. Young Floy became "dumb in silence"; he "felt like a child in every respect, helpless, innocent, docile, without guile."[74] Fink, Crockett, and Bunyan would have been inappropriate guides in this progression.

Time and again, the language of conversion and revival hinged upon metaphors of submission. When a "refformation" swept the Woodstock, Connecticut, area in the winter of 1841-1842, a native marked the alteration in standard imagery: "the stout hart and stubborn knee has bin brought to bow."[75] The stout heart and the stubborn knee routinely symbolized the fundamental foe. Reporting that a relative seemed not fully receptive to the "pleasing work" in the Galena, Illinois, region, caused one writer to say that "he appeared tender but his stubborn heart was not willing to bow."[76] When Horatio Chandler of New Hampshire went to work in a store in Montrose, Pennsylvania, he came under the revival influence that seemed to move across that area each winter. George Catlin's family, some members of which young Chandler knew, lived thereabout, and their letters reveal something of the workings of spirit in northeastern Pennsylvania. Early in 1840, George's father, Putnam Catlin, mentioned an aspect of the protracted meeting-revival progression that perhaps deserves more attention: the fortuitous acceleration which untimely deaths gave to the good work. Within about a month, he wrote, "several young people" had died, and the "result" was a "singular stir of Religion"—"all the young Lawyers of that Place, merchants, clerks, students, and all the young women came forward to join the good Cause."[77]

Horatio Chandler joined the ranks of Montrose clerks shortly after Putnam Catlin wrote the above, and in December of the same year he told of renewed activity on the religious front. On December 20, he recorded the death of a fifteen-year-old girl, and two days later all appeared "solemn & interesting." With death as harbinger, the clerk from New Hampshire set down the central features of the appropriate posture. "Be perfectly submissive," it was urged upon him, "letting go of everything connected with this wicked world, & casting yourself wholly upon the mercy & will of our Heavenly Father, you must be humbled freely to submit, and come as sinner beging for mercy. . . ."[78]

This then was the process that begot the new man. As a rural New Yorker concluded in noting "quite a change" in himself, "truely hope is the daughter of despair."[79] This was little more than the age-old inducing of an emotionally smitten condition from which could come a repose shorn of worldly expectations. Writing to one brother in Chapel Hill, Carolinian Zachariah Burnett told of the transformation in yet another brother. At the end of a "revival of religion," that brother had gone home with a "broaken hart" but with the all-important work yet unconsummated. However, the proper coordination of man's agency and God's agency—Robert Baird's *activity* and *dependence*—tipped the balance. Though the revival had ended, brother Addison continued to "wresle Jacob like" with his soul, and, at the same time, "we ought to prayes and love god" for working the conversion. From the joint effort came a new Addison Burnett. "I think he is as much changed," Zachariah wrote, "as ever I saw any person in my life. [H]e dont look like the same man."[80]

Addison "took up the cross," to use his brother's expression. That way of putting it richly signifies sacrifice rather than assertion. All of this involved a spiritual and, in turn, a heavenly quest rather than a worldly one—"a fresh start to try to get to heaven," Zachariah called it in that same letter. As is shown in the next chapter, simple people showed much hesitance in envisioning heaven, but, insofar as revival religion helped them accommodate to the world, it did so by drawing them from the world and by muting their aspirations in it. Frances Lea McCurdy's generalization about the rhetoric of ministers in general and revivalists in particular probably has accuracy for more than the Missouri area that she studied: "The people expected the minister to concern himself with heavenly matters and to leave worldly things alone."[81] Sally Rice, whom we saw taking housework at Union Village, New York, illustrates this idea well by complaining of the references to slavery that she heard in the sermons there. She did not specify the nature of those references, but she did register her disgust. "I swallowed so many it made me sick," she wrote, "but I went out and puked them up and felt better. . . ."[82]

Camp Meeting and Protracted Meeting

"When I go to camp meeting," another of the Burnetts wrote, "I feel as if [I] never want to leave, that I would be willing to live and die there." This pronouncement came in the context of sound doctrine to the effect that people vainly sought their happiness in "worldly things" when "religion is the only source of happiness."[83] The camp meeting, however, did not offer as full refuge from the world as this woman supposed. Whether invited or not, the world came skulking along. Almost inevitably, things of the spirit were compromised, and it would appear that people sought as vainly to escape the world as to find their happiness in it. As Charles A. Johnson states in his sympathetic account of "Sociability in the Tented Grove," "the worst as well as the best people of the community were drawn there by the longing for a spectacle, and they brought their morals with them."[84] Politicians, whiskey peddlars, bootblacks, dentists, daguerreotypists—these and many more arrived to do what business they could.

William Hoffman, the upstate New York farmer's son and future store clerk, had a reverence of a desultory nature. At the end of August 1847, we find him preparing to go to a camp meeting, but his eye was not to the skies but to the pies which he intended to sell. This entrepreneurial excursion entailed even grosser deviations, for William and his companions were "obliged to pilfer corn & oats" for their horse on the way. Once arrived, they had a good time, even though "there were more pedlars than I ever before have seen" and they "did not do very stiff business" in the pie line.[85] It would require an exquisitely fine discernment to assess the motives of those who had no pies or the like to sell. Scrutinizing motives with too much rigor can be hazardous. But, even re-calling that Sut Lovingood was a fictive and highly tendential figure, one occasionally perceives his resemblance to those of flesh and blood. For example, when an acquaintance wrote that sluggard John Spotts went "pro-specting" to an Iowa camp meeting, we must suspect that this man, whose "best game," according to the same source, "was played in bed," may have had an eye to other forms of contentment.[86] For opportunists to have avoided camp meetings would have been a harsh denial of human nature.

Overall, the camp meeting dimension of the religious excitement of that era probably looms too large, both in popular imagination and in historical litera-ture. As Johnson's study indicates, the camp meeting was being phased out by around 1840, and after that date more and more it persisted mainly in one region. The early fall camp meeting would remain a fairly common feature of northern life, but it would endure longest in the South where weather and worldly necessities were more inviting. The South also seemed more willing to allow the compromise which the camp meeting offered: the combination of the social and religious. Put another way, the common man in the South was less spiritually oriented. Certainly, the South seemed to accept more readily the extraspiritual aspects of religion. When, for example, young Bryant Redding who was working at Whitesville, Georgia, wrote to a cousin at home, he in-sisted upon a return letter as soon as the camp meeting ended—to tell "what for times you had." Be sure, he added, to give regards to "all the young Ladies about the camp ground."[87] This reference appears to be a frank recognition of the social dimension of religion.

In the nation at large, the proper focus would probably be upon the pro-tracted meeting (often rendered "distracted" meeting by those inclined to satire). As Robert Baird noted in *Religion in America* (1844), camp meetings "had better give place to 'Protracted Meetings,' which is the course, I believe, they are now taking."[88] Ironically, what Whitney Cross called "the village counterpart of the camp meeting"[89] had much less exposure to diverting and questionable influences. These gatherings, held in churches, meetinghouses, private residences, barns, and public buildings, could far more effectively exclude those who sought to prey upon the prayerful. The protracted meeting—"as much a product of an urban environment," Charles A. Johnson wrote, "as the open-air revival had been of the frontier"[90]—had greater potential for escape from the world than did its forerunner. That the camp meeting was better remembered than the protracted meeting does little more than evidence that fact.

The protracted meeting offered a fuller escape from the world because it had greater cohesion and even privacy than the camp meeting. The protracted meeting also was better attuned to the seasonal ebb and flow: it was usually held in the winter months when a predominantly agricultural society was freest from worldly demands. The winter season not only freed a larger percentage of people for devotions, but it also sent them to devotions with a more appropriate religious attitude than was possible during balmier seasons. This thesis can well be illuminated by examining the contrast of Transcendentalism, and even Perry Miller's sometimes waspish treatment of it.

For the New Englanders of this era, Miller wrote, "the governing concern in every walk of life" was "to get through the winter." Emerson might lyricize that season into gentle acquiescence, but for others it must have seemed the "god of bounds"—time indeed "to be old, to take in sail." Thus, to use one of Miller's illustrations, an anonymous "widow" gave the theme this form in the sole issue of the *Aesthetic Papers*:

> Winter, dread Undertaker, thou art come!
> And how unique are thy official deeds!
> The living and the dead, uncoffined, both
> Live in our meanest traversings concealed.

The crux of the Transcendental problem was as follows: "Openly to admit that life in New England was in danger of extinction every January would be to concede that circumstances shape man's purpose. . . ." According to Miller, the stratagem for circumventing circumstances consisted in "anticipation." Thus, *Walden* became "an adroitly suspended anticipaton of the climax of thawing sand and clay in the railroad cut. . . ."[91] All men looked with hope and longing to the arrival of spring, but simpler folk did not have a philosophical stake in denying this existential manifestation of circumstances. They were too prosaic and too providentially fatalistic. Winter only intensified their almost innate sense of relentless providential workings. It elicited from them a heightened submissiveness and a greater awe of the forces over which they had no control. Emotionally and psychologically, winter prepared them, as other seasons could not, for the prayerful and penitent humbling that came in the protracted meeting.

When a Tennessee woman complained that a fall camp meeting had failed, she explained it by saying that "it was to early entirely, the farmers had not half their grain taken care of."[92] In a few more weeks, one supposes, those farmers could have more effectively withdrawn from the world, and had some sobering weather come upon them, they would have withdrawn all the more readily. As Thoreau stated in a Concord December, " 'You come near eating your heart now.' " In winter the Transcendentalist made, as Miller noted, the "retirement to prepared positions" in the self, mind, and journal.[93] His humbler counterparts retired to the prepared positions of the protracted meeting.

When winter gave way to spring, the spiritual working waned. The diary of young J. W. Canfield of Orange County, New York, reveals the typical pattern. Yet in winter's icy grip on February 3, 1852, he felt, as it was often put, "quite a change" come over him. A day later he concluded that "truly hope is the daughter of despair." But as late as February 24, the personal spiritual issue remained unresolved: ". . .the devil is carrying on a war with my soul. . . . Oh may the Lord's cause succeed." Soon thereafter, the "Lord's cause" ran afoul of the weather. On February 26, Canfield felt "more cool," and he feared that "pride is much the cause." The next day he felt "quite dull," indeed diverted by "fancyful humors." On March 3 and again on March 14, deaths gave momentary restoration to the proper frame of mind, but those "cool" and "dull" prefigurings were about to be realized in spring. Soon, much as Thoreau's premonitory nuthatch, the "sweet notes" of the robin and the peeping of frogs came to J. W. Canfield. For the time being he moved away from his quest for holiness in order to go fishing, to shoot robins, and to plan for a study of surveying. May 17 was a "Beautiful day," and "the music of warbling songsters is everwhere heard." "Warbling songsters" ended that entry and began a hiatus in Canfield's diary. He made no further entries until November, another month that Thoreau judged suitable for a man to "eat his heart."[94]

The general pattern seems unmistakable; whether in Montrose, Pennsylvania, or Nininger, Minnesota, or Orange County, New York, winter was the revival season. As temperature and hopes dropped, spiritual fervor rose. The obverse—such things as those "fancyful humors" dulcetly calling one back to the world—would be seen and warned against as marks of coolness and dullness. The religious excitements of the prewar generation involved not so much a summery equation of camp meeting-revival as a wintery progression of protracted meeting-revival. That was more in keeping with seasonal demands and with the psychology of the enduring Puritanism yet abroad in the land.

Less than the Millennium

To a later, naturalistic age, the pre-Civil War period frequently appears a phantasmagoria of religious frenzy. The people of that time, however, took much satisfaction from the "interesting" times and bemoaned the fact that those times were sporadic and transient. Indeed, they were ever alert to spiritual deadness. As a Pennsylvania farmer Jesse Beaver routinely wrote in January 1846, "as regards religion in this place it is tolerable low."[95] The folk in that area had recently had a two-day meeting, but that was not enough to avert the description of "tolerable low." As Timothy Smith observes regarding one of the revival leaders in the "annus mirabilis" of 1858, "to a modern observer" his "hopes seem to have been amply fulfilled," but "perhaps his generation was disappointed."[96] As a matter of fact, his generation was very often disappointed, but unpretentious people had ample familiarity with disappointments. If the Jesse Beavers of America had inordinate expectations, it is well to keep in mind that those expectations were not as inordinate as some latter-day scholarship would lead us to believe.

The recurrent mood of failure and disappointment is an apt preface for a consideration of the merging of conversion and revival into millennial notions. For this to get any more than very abrupt treatment here requires some mention of the propensity of modern scholarship to discern millennial notions, not only in the airier meditations of divines and visionaries but also in the mood of American mankind generally. As one essay puts it, ". . . recent cultural historians have found the idea a compelling one."[97]

The prototype for much of the modern writing came in 1937 in H. Richard Niebuhr's *The Kingdom of God in America*. In this work, the notion expressed by the title became a basic impulse of American religious and social thought. Niebuhr's panoramic depiction involved what he saw as a gravitation from "sovereignty of God" in early America to the gentler perception of "reign of Christ" and on to the discernment of an imminent "kingdom on earth."[98] This construction has proved so compelling that Ernest Sandeen has written of an early nineteenth-century America that was "drunk on the millennium." "Americans seemed unable to avoid—seemed bound to utilize—the vocabulary of Christian eschatology," a mode that reflected "their brimming optimism and hope."[99] As something of an historiographical finality, one can cite Sidney Ahlstrom's elaborately conceived and awesomely woven *A Religious History of the American People*. Here again we encounter that "almost universal American conviction that the United States had a mission to extend its influence throughout the world. To mainstream Protestants, a denial of America's manifest destiny bordered on treason. Translated into theological categories, this meant that the American was characteristically a 'postmillennialist.' "[100] The postmillennial notion held that the Second Coming would follow rather than precede the thousand years of felicity. That was indeed a comfortable view of things, a view which was much more in keeping with the earthly kingdom than with a kingdom eternal and removed.

At the conclusion of what he considers "at least an intimation" of how the "everyday American" viewed millennial matters, Ernest Tuveson notes how attention has shifted from "the heavenly life which had so long inspired the

Christian world" toward an earthly "holy utopia."[101] Here again, the writings of the common people are not of great help to us. The "mute inglorious Milton" evidently possessed a good deal of ardor for religion and religious expression, but he seems rarely to have hazarded divinations about a thousand years of earthly paradise. The almost endlessly discussed conversions and revivals had imminent, discernible, and attainable qualities. Simple people doted on such matters, but only very rarely did the headier millennial subject enter their writings. Perhaps they knew better, or perhaps they showed what Tuveson recognizes as "a kind of common-sense impatience"[102] with the more ecstatic visions. As a churchgoing mechanic in Detroit phrased it when someone referred to a local revival as a visit of Christ, "Maybe so, hope it is, he will find us a hard lot of beings."[103] This laconic skepticism does not smack of irreverence; rather, it reflects some "common-sense impatience" with the delvings of overheated imaginations.

When millennial intimations surfaced in the writings of the common folk, they often did so as little more than predictions of cataclysmic retribution. They involved perceptions of prosperity and wickedness grown to such dimensions as to presage or demand destruction and final accounting. Thus, in 1852 aged Asher Freeman viewed the passing times in cause and effect terms that would appeal to an uncomplicated understanding.

People seem to have grown remarkable proud and extravagant in these days of prosperity, but I think according to all accounts that when a nation gets so proud, extravagant and wasteful the Almighty will send judgments upon them for their sins, either by wars, pestilence or famine.[104]

When the perception emerged in the intensified form of the utter and final undoing of evil, it did so, not as the end of evil by gentle melioration, but by direct and immediate destruction. Bemoaning his own "unlikeness to Christ" as well as "the increasing wickedness of the people," C. H. Sherman of Fairfield, Vermont, stood ready to "cry in the anguish of my soul, O let the wickedness of the wicked come to an end." Indeed, to him that prospect seemed not only meet but likely, "for the time is short[.] [T]he signs are thickening around us declaring the end is near."[105]

A quick perusal of the world's shortcomings has often led to such utterances, and some can be found in the common writings of the pre-Civil War period. Still, given the interpretive framework discussed above, two points bear noting. First, as the illustrations of the preceding paragraph might suggest, such outbursts often came as little more than unadorned and unimaginative judgments. Wishing disaster upon the wayward is not, of itself, a demanding task. Second, insofar as those expressions partake of millennialism (some notion, however vague, predicated upon a thousand years of felicity), it is more nearly premillennialism than postmillennialism. To appropriate one scholar's descriptives, though not his conclusions, these simple people anticipated a "future marked by tribulation" much more than a "future of hope."[106] For the ordinary American, the sternness of "God's sovereignty" probably seemed far more plausible than did an imminent beginning of a thousand years of progress and felicity capped by the Second Coming. A Connecticut farmer luxuriating in Universalism's optimism might see, despite current "Tirony and Oppression," that the "Kingdom of Jesus shall become a universal Kingdom."[107] For most people, however, that "future marked by tribulation" yet bore a lively cast. When, for example, "the warning voice that is going through the length and bredth of the land" was heard in Montgomery, Vermont, in 1855, the listener sensed that "if time continuws a year or to we shall wittness such times of trouble as we have ever seen."[108]

In turn, expressions of worldly betterment couched in religious metaphor translate much less as comfortable postmillennialism than as prosaic urgings to perseverance, as common reflections of the instinctual wisdom of pluck and faith. Apparently writing to bolster the spirit of a young relative in Oregon, Jabez Whiting availed himself of the arsenal of encouragement. He specifically urged the young man to hope "of meeting in a better world where we shall have neither Slavery nor Intemperance." The aged native of Connecticut recognized evils that stood beyond remedy, but he also urged the recognition that the "world is getting better and better." For a moment he approached the ecstatic as he imagined a time when "War and Oppression and every evil thing shall be done away with." Not so visionary as that, but perhaps all the more resonant of hope, was the reminder that, before long, railroads would connect Oregon with Indiana.[109] Surely, the comparative good was likely to precede the absolute. Simple people frequently employed the expression "good time coming," a term popularized by Stephen Foster's 1846 song of that title, but a millennial construction of that song or of the usages inspired by it would be strained. Indeed, the song itself has at best an ambiguity where the workings of spirit are concerned; in that good time coming, "Religion shall be shorn of pride . . . wait a little longer."

Writing to console the wife he had left behind on the Maine farm, Charles Rich, who was at work on a terrestrial railroad in Illinois, told his Albina "to *pluck* up the more courage & resolution and bear up with the more energy & firmness & persevere looking forward with confidence to the 'good time a coming.' " This master of didactic redundancy seems to have been as thoroughly religious as his wife, but the good time coming probably had a more immediate meaning than concern with millennialism would allow. Charles Rich did not hesitate to disdain his temporary accommodations in "Suckerdom" and to relish the prospect of a return to his "own good bed & *bed fellow*."[110] But, as the refrain had it, "wait a little longer." In this imperfect temporal realm, one did one's best and waited a little longer, and that waiting involved a righteous and submissive erasing of the gap between birth and death. During that secular interim, one worked for and occasionally gained the comparatively better—a good bedfellow, a railroad to Oregon, as well as spiritual preparation in the form of conversion and revival.

Conclusion

In early winter 1858, the Countrymans at Nininger made, as Levi put it, "a new start for the kingdom of Heaven."[111] That inept farmer employed phrasing so standard as to lead to the conclusion that, with few exceptions, ideas of kingdom pertained only to the otherworldly realm. The writings of the common people contain only rare glimmerings of what that kingdom would be like. In nearly all cases, it sufficed to envision the ultimate good in terms of a kingdom where the wicked would cease to have power and parting would be no more. In a highly mobile society where the normal rate of separation and estrangement was greatly increased, that seemed promise enough, promise which, it was constantly urged, must not be relinquished. If distances or simple contrariness sundered the bonds of family, friends, and lovers, Heaven held the hope of reunion. Jesse Owen of Arkansas had left the family home in Kentucky, and that separation was compounded over his stepfather's handling of his mother's property at her death. "And now dear father Perhaps I take final leaf of you," Jesse wrote in 1851. "I have been unfortunate," he noted, and am poor, "and could not law and you knew it," so "you keep my just Rites, who are full and have plenty." By his second to last letter to his stepfather, Owen's bitterness had abated, and he ended with "May God blesse you. . . . I do trust that we will for give each other and at Last meet in heaven. . . ."[112] Far away in Oregon, Wellborn Beeson received consoling words from John Clayton, a friend from his schooldays. Clayton opened and closed a poem, "Can we e're forget," in trite but unanswerable fashion:

> Oh can we e're forget Wellborn
> the pleasant days of yore
> Though save in memory's treasured dream
> They come to us no more
>
> . . . .
>
> But Oh what joy twill be to meet
> Where ties are never riven
> Though parted here to meet no more
> Oh may we meet in heaven[113]

John Clayton's hopes would not be painfully and endlessly deferred, as visionary notions would. So "be ye also ready" resonated across the land—ready not for the Second Coming or for some illusionary version of it, but for death, that quiet usher of the weary over Jordan or into the nameless void. A century earlier, a poet of larger renown than John Clayton ended the "Elegy" with an epitaph. There, "in trembling hope" reposed the "merits" and the "frailties" of the "mute inglorious Milton."

> Large was his bounty, and his soul sincere
> Heav'n did a recompense as largely send:
> He gave to Mis'ry all he had, a tear,
> He gain'd from Heav'n ('twas all he wish'd) a friend.

Death 4

"... And when men die, we do not mention them." With those words Emerson concluded his gloomy forecast for a society suffering a "decaying church and a wasting unbelief."[1] In time, cultural commentators saw something resembling Emerson's contention. Over a century later, the Spanish scholar Julián Marías wrote that in the United States death assumes "the air of an undesirable alien and has therefore made no progress towards citizenship."[2] Neither philosopher spoke quite accurately, however. Marías allowed a faulty inference. Death had once had full citizenship, but it had suffered exile probably with the rise of naturalism and materialism in the late nineteenth century. As suggested in another context, in 1838 Emerson played Jeremiah with too much intensity. As forecast, his observation was precise, but as description, it fell very wide of the mark. In fact, his society was overconcerned with death and fastidious to a fault in observances pertaining to it. Carl Bode in *The Anatomy of American Popular Culture, 1840–1861* concluded with "A Trio for Columbia," three themes on which American culture of that era might be focused. Two of the three themes—love and success—involved aspiration and possibility. The third—death—had certainly and universality.

Interestingly, however, Bode showed some impatience in his handling of the death theme in poetry, plays, and novels. Aspects of that theme seemed to impress Bode as fulsome and, perhaps, emotionally exploitative. Bode's readers have difficulty forgetting that, after Little Mary Morgan of *Ten Nights in a Bar-Room* fell at the strike of a hurled whiskey glass, author Timothy Shay Arthur devoted "most of the next sixty pages to her lingering, pathetic demise." Nor can one readily dissociate the fact that Mrs. Sigourney was "a classical example of an extremely popular bad poet" from the fact that "her favorite single subject" was death.[3] Kenneth S. Lynn more abruptly shows a later age's misgiving about the presentation of death in pre-Civil War culture. In an essay praising the artistry of *Uncle Tom's Cabin*, Lynn speaks of Harriet Beecher Stowe's characters as "shockingly believable." But, he allows, Stowe did employ some "factitious" dramatic situations, most notably the death of Augustine St. Clare. To Lynn, it was an exercise in "saccharine phoniness," one that "strikes us today as hackneyed from beginning to end."[4] It would not do justice to Bode and Lynn to suggest that their artistic and cultural criticisms illustrate what Geoffrey Gorer calls "an unremarked shift in prudery" in the twentieth century, from sex to death. There seems to be little danger in suggesting, as Gorer did, that deathly dramatics gave a lot of theatrical, poetical, and literary mileage because death was among the relatively few situations "that an author could be fairly sure would have been shared by the vast majority of his readers."[5]

A Full Familiarity

At the end of a diary, Connecticut cook and sailor William Sprague inscribed a toast:

> Here is to the world that goes
> round on wheels
> Death is a thing that all
> man feels
> If death was a thing that
> the rich could buy
> The rich would live and
> the poor would die[6]

Death was indeed that thing "that all man feels," and it behooved all men to give that fact sober consideration. A great many assiduously fulfilled their obligation, giving almost ceaseless advice to self and others to keep death firmly in mind. Here again we encounter a persuasion and an appetite that by later standards would seem to be a blend of the gargantuan and the pathological. Thus, a New Yorker's diary page titled "Needful Counsel" had, centered at the left, the injunctive opening, "let your." To the right of that came a vertical series of subjects—conduct, diet, and sleep, among others—followed, in turn, by the single verb "be." At the right came an appropriately arranged, vertical series of compound predicates, thus giving, for example, "let your Diet be temperate, wholesome sober." Appropriately, this diagrammatic didacticism concluded with: "let your Reflection be of death and future state."[7]

In Alabama, schoolboy Isaac Barr filled entire pages of his penmanship book with reminders, most of which have a more solemn tone than the following: "School expires Isaac on the 8th day of May 1852." Whatever his exact age, young Isaac had ample years to contemplate sobering ultimates and, thus, outnumbering such notices as the end of school, came reminders of the end of life. "Death takes the young as well as the old"; "Remember this life is not long"; or simply "Remember you must die."[8] In Cheshire, Connecticut, Maria Durand, friend of young Charles Dudley whom we encountered on a holiday in New York City, did not ignore fundamental matters when she composed an acrostic on Dudley's name. With the second "D" of Dudley she opened this line: "Death the grim monster soon will come to close your vile career."[9] It seems a bit heavyhanded to a later generation, but Dudley dutifully entered it in his own diary. He probably realized that Maria was willing to sacrifice artfulness and delicacy to assure that there be no confusion in the elementary matter of personal destiny.

The end of the year almost demanded the contemplation of such themes, and even those comparatively disinclined from such exercises marked the calendar change as did Pennsylvania farmer John R. Cummins. His diary yields far less of religious and spiritual concerns and far more of political and secular ones than do most. But the meditative tug of December 31 could not be denied. The reflective mind, Cummins wrote, senses in the end of a year "something solemn," something "suggestive of a nearing to an . . ." Here, illegibility intrudes, but the sense is unmistakable. Man must now wonder "whether he shall again behold another year. . . . Tempus Fugit: and so will the next year, and so to the end."[10] What Cummins committed to paper once a year, others did with far less cause and far greater frequency. It was not just the aged who could muse in an evening entry that they were one day nearer eternity. In turn, words did not elude the laconic and the prosaic when the cycles of time required reflection on death. When Melville's fictive philosopher Babbalanja burst into soliloquy on death at the banquet table, one partaker of the feast wished to eject him. But the voice of thoughtful moderation urged otherwise: "No, no, my lord. Let him sit there as of old the Death's head graced the feasts of the pharaohs—let him sit—let him sit—for death but imparts a flavor to life."[11] Though he might have stated it differently, the less sophisticated American would have arrived at the same practical conclusion.

The risk of idle supererogation or even impertinence looms large in any effort to explain the superabundant musings and dotings on death. Accepting the hazard, one must note first that death was an ever-present fact of life. A normally unreflective Maine farmer cited the conventional wisdom: " 'in life we are in the midst of death.' "[12] Few cultural commentaries on that era fail to remark the intimacy most people had with death. Theirs was an immediate, not a derivative or vicarious, awareness. Thus, in the context of melancholy poetry Carl Bode reminds his readers of the "somber story" told by mortality statistics.[13] In this case, Bode mentions figures from New York City, but the condition was general, not particular. As Perry Miller remarks about Concord, "the supreme fact was death."[14] Others, however, have shown puzzlement and even impatience when treating the popular inclination to dwell on death at the expense of what a later age would deem more important. One editor of the writings of common people, though he took satisfaction from the "few references to political and social events" that appeared in his material, had to admit that, of such, there were "not as many as one might hope for." That illness and death should receive so much attention he guardedly ascribed to "the uncertainty of individual life."[15] In that conclusion he was at least partly correct.

When upstate New York common schoolteacher Sophronia Beebe opened a letter to an old friend, she did so in this way:

The grim messenger has been at work all over the land calling for his thousands. The lovely child has been taken from its sports; the youth has been taken from its circle of loved ones; the teacher from his arduous duties, the lawyer from the bar, the doctor from his office, the statesman from the senate chamber. . . .[16]

This doleful overture left matters in the abstract, as perhaps befit the lady's calling. Far more commonly, the immediacy took on almost awesome proportions. In the fall of 1841, Alabama planter LeRoy Upshaw was "exerting every nerve to make a living." He had a good stand of cotton, but the best it could do would still fall short of clearing his debts. At midpage in this letter to his brother, different pen and ink suggest that some time had passed, and now, with the hope that there would be no rain, came an indication of the toll his exertions had taken: "I am failing very fast indeed. . . ." LeRoy Upshaw did not finish his letter. Son James, whatever he did with his father's cotton and debts, completed his father's letter and did so by telling the demise of the man who started it.[17] Far to the north, farm woman Annis Pierce sent what consolation she could to a daughter who had lost an infant child. Mother Pierce expressed herself awkwardly, but she was not as callous as one might infer from the following: "I wast not any disappointed when we heard of the death of little Emma[.] I was very sure that I would hear of the death of some one of those dear little ones. . . ."[18] People routinely specified what proportion their living offspring bore to the total. If Little Eva and Little Mary Morgan were accorded so much time and attention in dying, it probably had much to do with the fact that childhood mortality was staggering.

> My brothers (and) sister kind & dear
> How soon youve passed away
> Your friendly faces now I hear
> Are mowldren in the clay

This Indiana youngster can well be forgiven his or her contribution, "On the death of my 2 brothers & sister," to the melancholy poetry of the period.[19]

The immediacy reflected in mortality rates (and that without resorting to the ravages of the cholera years) conjoined with the comparative lack of professional or institutional services for handling the dying and the dead. Ineluctable realities brought people to most direct contact with fundamentals. In February 1846, Brigham Nims of New Hampshire recorded what may have been his first full participation in handling the dying and the dead, and he did so in a way very strongly suggesting that the function was a routine one for such people. On the night of February 10, he "watched with Seth Towns[.] [H]e was very wild the fore part of the night[;] more calm toward morning." Nims visited Seth again on February 11, and, when word came that all was over, he returned to prepare the deceased for burial: "I went and helped Lay him out, and shaved him[,] the first person that I tried to shave."[20] Late in 1834, a young Maryland store clerk did such duty at the end of September, in the middle of November, and again on the last day of the year. In one case it was a friend, in another it was the daughter of a friend, and the third a cousin. In the case of the dying friend, he sat by the deathbed for several nights consecutively. The end came at 11:40 at night. "I then shaved & washed him," the clerk wrote, "& Marker assisted me in dressing him (*he died hard*)."[21]

Letters, being a central means of communication of the period, often tended to be obituary notices, reporting the death of friends and relatives. Writing to her brother-in-law from Mason, Tennessee, in 1855, Dily Richards recorded an awesome death list:

Your Brother Jon is ded[;] he Died the 11 of Septenber last I am her by A lone. . . .Jon dident live but five days[.] [S]uppose he died with the fluks. . . . Ammy Richards is dead[,] Rebecah Richards is dead [,] Henison is Dead[.] [M]y yongest child About Twenty too years old an my our step son died in Mexico[.] Burrels oldest son is dead[;] he was About twenty years old[.] [H]is dagter is dead[;] she was About five years old.[22]

Quite understandably, such letters would elicit reflections such as the following: "I dread mail days . . . the sight of a letter makes me so nervous."[23]

It did not always suffice to tell who had died; the manner of their going also received a good deal of attention. There is so much physiological detail in the letters as to suggest a purposive eye to medical or therapeutic concerns. Nearly all common people had reservations about the medical profession, and frequently they were openly hostile. Given the state of medical knowledge and practice at that time, it could hardly have been otherwise. An Alabaman's assessment of his doctor's level of care during a nearly fatal illness was, unfortunately, not an atypical one: "he tended on me till he had liked to a kild me."[24]

Left to their own devices, common folk recorded and conveyed, not gratuitous morbidity, but the information of pathology. Her daughter "little Lydia," an Ohio woman wrote in an account of her child's death, "did not swell as much as some." This is only a sample of the graphic description of the course of Lydia's trials—measles in January, then the whooping cough, then smallpox, and finally, death in May.[25] On his way west to work as foreman of a carpenter crew on the Illinois Central construction, Charles Rich wrote from Bangor,

Maine, to his wife back on the farm at Milo. At the very outset of his long, revealing correspondence, the forty-five-year-old husband wrote of death. One
Gilman, a man who had started with Rich on the way to the West, had fallen ill
almost immediately and had died in a tavern at Waterville. Charles did not
spare his twenty-six-year-old wife, Albina, the details. The deceased carpenter had been constipated for several days, Rich noted, and the pills and the
oil had worked no relief. At the tavern, when Gilman had become incapacitated, some others "took hold and helped" Rich administer enemas. Lobelia
and thoroughwort in two or three applications yielded a half-pint "of what appeared more like sheep manure only in larger rolls and very black." The pathological particulars changed when a doctor arrived with the predictable calomel,
the almost murderous mercurous chloride. The dead carpenter was soon on his
way back to Milo.[26]

Gilman would build no more houses, Albina mused as she wrote late in the
night after the funeral. At the service itself "while looking at his dead bodie,"
she had entertained other questions and other associations: "I thought who
heard his last words, who laid him out, it was my own *dear husband*." With
that dead body before her, she felt "as if I wanted to see you and ask many
questions."[27] Since the details of a person's death were routinely given, it
appears that here Albina had in mind some spiritual concerns. It would be fair
to assume that Charles Rich had sought to share his knowledge of a particular
path from vitality to death. In more than the ultimate sense, death was ines-
capable. People knew it by its existential proximity as well as by its actuarial
prevalence.

A Certain Impassiveness

If there was a powerful intimacy with death and a fascination with the spiritual aspects of death, the writings of the common people also show a capacity
to accept without questioning. At one level, that capacity was no more than an
extension of the providential resignation discussed earlier, and at another
level, it may have been little more than an inevitable inuring to life's realities.
"Not simply as a matter of rhetoric," Fred Somkin writes, "but in frightening
actuality, Americans seemed strangely able to accept the possibility of violent
death on a mass scale." That most indiscriminate killer, the steamboat, appeared as no more than the "most recent embodiment of the elemental
power."[28] Mark Twain provided an illustration that Somkin might well have
used. Writing of antebellum America, and assuring us in footnote that he was
not fictionalizing, Twain told in *The Gilded Age* of the race between the
Boreas and the *Amaranth*. There was pride, "hurrah," juvenile swagger, a
"nigger roosting on the safety-valve," and "then there was a booming roar."
When the horror and the screams of the dying subsided, thirty-nine were in-
jured, twenty-two dead, and ninety-six missing. The head engineer of the

Amaranth took off his ring, peeling off steam-eaten flesh with it, and handed it and his eternal curse to the man who had been in command at the time. But the court of inquiry returned "the inevitable American verdict which has been so familiar to our ears all the days of our lives—'NOBODY TO BLAME.' "29

In his indictment of "the inevitable American verdict," Mark Twain did more than indulge an intense and mordant irony. Far to the north on the same river, Daniel Hunt, a young brickmaker from Maine, rode the *North Star* as it raced the *H.M. Rice* to Saint Cloud. When the *North Star* tried to pass, the *H.M. Rice* "run her bows across our track and ran us ashore." Hunt's boat extricated itself quickly, and then mile after mile, while the *H.M. Rice* "was burning tar or rosin to a great extent and carrying so much steam that the engineer put his hat over the gage to hide it from the passengers," the boats battled the river and each other. In brief form, this is the prescription for disaster that Twain presented. Fortunately, it issued differently. When the *North Star* became incapacitated and pulled to shore, Hunt stepped off with some ladies to pick flowers and play cards.30

Hunt said nothing in his account to indicate that he meant the hat-covered gauge and the flower-picking as ironic juxtaposition. With a hat covering the gauge and a "nigger roosting on the safety-valve," Americans raced to fate's embrace. Mark Twain's court of inquiry differed from Hunt's America only in bothering to raise the question at all; it troubled itself to give official statement to the self-evident. Only the argumentative, like Mark Twain, went beyond description. Andrew Jackson Sterrett seemed to have such temperament. In 1859, when this arch and skeptical fellow boarded the *Sky-Lark* at Leavenworth for the trip to Saint Louis, the *Meteor* pulled away at the same time. The boats raced through the daylight hours but, for insurance purposes, tied up at night. However, when the boats reached Jefferson City together with the race yet unresolved, insurance and all other considerations went by the board. After an evening stop at Jefferson City, the *Meteor* and the *Sky-Lark* raced through the night to Saint Louis. The *Sky-Lark* won by fifteen minutes, and Sterrett slipped quickly into mention of what may have been Ambrose Bierce's theatrical brother playing to a thin house.31 Sterrett saved his grumbling and archness for things other than steamboat racing on a darkened and hazardous river.

On the same treacherous Missouri, a student at Lexington, Thomas Coleman, described the fate of the *Saluda* in 1852. According to this youth, the captain had openly resolved that, despite the strong current, "he would turn that bend just above Lexington or Blow his Boat into Hell." The *Saluda* had barely cleared its moorings when the boiler burst. "Such shrieking and moaning I never heard before," the young man informed his father. Even though he understood the captain's culpability in the disaster, Coleman did not ask what might seem to others the inevitable questions. His description of the horrors gave way directly to a plea for money.32 Days later, a Vermont woman on her way to California with her family saw the "fine little town" of Lexington and the remains of the "ill fated Saluda." "Eyes, finger & toes of the poor unfortunate sufferers were found on shore and quite a distance," she learned. But "ill fated" seemed sufficient explanation, and, shortly thereafter, she was near Saint Joseph fretting about the dangers of sleeping outdoors with nothing but "a canvas to protect us from the dews of Heaven."[33]

On his way from Saint Louis to Glasgow, Missouri, in 1842, New Englander Walter B. Foster's boat, the *Satan*, tied up for the night at the mouth of the Missouri. As the *Satan* pulled away in the morning, another boat nearby, the *Edna of the Platte*, exploded. Writing a few days later in Glasgow, Foster took some care to describe the ghastly scenes that unfolded as the *Satan* went to assist. For explicit horror, his account far exceeds the *Amaranth* episode in *The Gilded Age*. There were "screams and groans, curses and prayers" that "resounded from all sides." Some victims begged in "piteous accents" to be killed forthwith; others lay perfectly still and quiet; those who had inhaled steam screeched hideously; a "respectable looking" man with a demolished hand and various scald wounds graciously accepted a glass of wine; a German woman pleaded with Foster to remove the skin of her arm and hand that now hung from her nails like a rolled-off glove, and he did so. Clearly, Foster had an eye for clinical detail. Some of the sound aided as they could; some shrank back in horror; some suffered such shock as to be rendered "incapable of attending to anything"; and some "drank, smoke, and laughed." Some did worse. A German man who had been killed and denuded by the blast and the steam had a "belt of sovereigns" around his waist; "an Irishman standing by pocketed it." Almost at the end of his account, Foster found it "strange" that anyone "could be so depraved!" "But enough," he concluded, not bothering to ask how or why the *Edna of the Platte* had taken so many to such a dreadful end.[34]

As is evident from these examples, the facts of death were obsessively marked, but the whys were rarely probed. When an overloaded building in New York City collapsed killing a friend and several others, one dutifully recorded the tragic event. When the *Lexington* blew up in Long Island Sound or the *Pearl* did likewise on the Sacramento River, one contemplated death, not cause.[35] The modern reader might ponder the pioneers' staggering propensity to draw weapons muzzle foremost from the backs of wagons. On May 4, 1859, a Pike's Peaker, for example, told unreflectingly of a comrade's stumbling on this way—"musle foremost"—of propelling himself into the great majority. In the next two weeks, this diary reveals two or three similar occurrences.[36]

In 1845, young Josiah Chaney of Maine took a trip into the White Mountain country of New Hampshire where twenty years before the Willey family was engulfed and killed in an avalanche. Chaney wrote of "their fate" and of that religion by which the Willeys had met and accepted their fate: "A Bible was also found open, indicating that they had been perusing its sacred pages for consolation in their trial hour."[37] Chaney's account coincides exactly with generally held beliefs as to the function of religion, that of bringing people into submissive accommodation with providence.

Ten years before Chaney wrote his account of the Willey story, Hawthorne published "The Ambitious Guest," a short story based on the Willey tragedy. The fictional guest, arriving at the Willey home in the notch on the fateful evening, tells the simple family of his "high and abstracted ambition." Before death takes him, he insists he must leave some monument. The Willeys, impressed by their young visitor's sincerity, begin to reveal their own inner hopes. The grandmother's wish concerns the preparation of her dress at the time of her burial, and she now seeks a promise regarding that matter. A child urges that they turn to livelier prospects, but the ambitious stranger muses that "old and young, we dream of graves and monuments . . ." "For a moment, the old woman's ghastly conception so engrossed the minds of her hearers that a sound abroad in the night, rising like the roar of a blast, had grown broad, deep, and terrible, before the fated group were conscious of it." Then they "fled right into the pathway of destruction." While Hawthorne saw these people as "fated,"[38] he also presented them as so absorbed by the thought of death, so entranced by its prospect, as to allow it in its real form to steal a march in overtaking them.

It has been common to see ambition—though generally not the form veiled in Hawthorne's ironic complexity—as much of the causal context for the seeming heedlessness of American society. Fred Somkin's previously quoted observation about the American ability to accept violent death came, for example, in a chapter titled "Prosperity the Riddle." One finds intimations of that theme in humble writing. When Andrew Jackson Sterrett completed his account of the *Sky-Lark-Meteor* night race to St. Louis, he mentioned a contemporaneous event, John Wise's balloon flight from Saint Louis to upstate New York. "What next?" he asked in probably an approving tone. A man in Smith County, Texas, conveyed more precisely the often-remarked ability to ignore human hardship while contemplating physical achievement. As did so many others, A. P. Moss related in an 1853 letter "some quite melancholly" news. In this regard, he recounted the ravages of the flux in his area, but then, "laying aside mortality," he stated that Smith County was prospering. It was "live with enterprise," and "Railroads is all the go."[39] Here, of course, we are edging into Colonel Beriah Sellers' neighborhood. But however inviting, the idea of progress and its various concomitants do not fit very well with common views of that era. If people showed a seeming indifference to death or a stoic equanimity, it probably stemmed far more from enforced intimacy with death and from what they would have considered a Christian, providential resignation.

Christian Resignation

Hawthorne's "ambitious guest" lured the Willeys into an untoward contemplation of worldly hopes; only the grandmother retained her common sense by keeping her eye fixed on the grave. By deftly interchanging "graves" and "monuments," Hawthorne moved from monuments construed as worldly accomplishment to that monument that would in a moment cover them in unintended graves and immortalize them. The "ambitious guest" realized his ambition. Whether or not the Willeys of Hawthorne's tale tempted the gods, their real counterparts took almost obsessed pains to avoid tempting God. Writing to friends in the East after the first three years of their life in the West, a Michigan couple noted assuringly that it had not been "very dying" in their locale recently. But they did not move off-guard for that fact and shortly they made note of the "very good place for a burying ground" that was on their land. With help from the neighbors, they were putting first things first by getting the graveyard ready; ". . . as we are very exposed to death it is necessary we be altogether prepaired for it."[40]

Fatalism reigned supreme during the pre-Civil War era. After the New Hampshire tour that took him by the Willey house, Josiah Chaney gave a typical expression of this mood. He thought he would probably travel again one day—if he lived.[41] Similarly, Walter Foster had a birthday while at New Orleans which he announced in his diary as follows: "Tomorrow I'm twenty-three if I live. . . ."[42] That grim reservation—if life is spared—was endlessly expressed in pre-Civil War America. It applied both to the self and to others—to the old who required least reminder, to the sound and active who might forget, and to the very young who might not understand.

In *White Jacket*, Melville mentioned the "very prudent caution" which American naval officers showed in preventing smoking while gun powder was brought aboard. He began to contrast that caution with the practice of "Fatalists" such as Turkish sailors who would nonchalantly smoke "while kegs of powder are being rolled under their ignited pipe-bowls." Melville suddenly withdrew the disparity, however. Turkish sailors were not the only "Fatalists," Melville asserted:

We are all Fatalists at bottom. Nor need we so much marvel at the heroism of that army officer who challenged his personal foe to bestride a barrel of powder with him—the match to be placed between them—and be blown up in good company, for it is pretty certain that the whole earth is a vast hogshead, full of inflammable materials, and which we are always bestriding: at the same time, that all good Christians believe that at any minute the last day may come, and the terrible combustion of the entire planet ensue.[43]

Christian doctrine joined with hard fact to emphasize the emotional desirability of a tentative, almost interrogative approach to life. Such a posture could yield that "great comfort" enjoyed by Melville's Turkish "Fatalists." Melville probably saw Emerson as one of those "amiable philosophers of either the 'Compensation' or 'Optimist' school,"[44] but in "Fate" Emerson brought together in mood the Turk, the Arab, the Hindoo, and "our Calvinists" "in the last generation."[45] Because he saw the *persisting* similarity, Melville came nearer the truth. Emerson saw American fatalists in the past but not in the present; had he looked more closely, he may well have shared Melville's conviction that they were all about him.

One of the more compelling evidences that the pre-Civil War mood was a blend of caution and resignation can be seen in writings regarding children. As discussed earlier, orthodox Christians had a great fear of idolatrous relationships, especially with children. For example, a Vermont woman wrote her gold-prospector husband that their baby was ill with a cold. "The most I am afraid," she admitted, "is that I shall love him too well and the Lord will take him from me."[46] She set about repressing hope. This fear of idolatry is also reflected in a letter Albina Rich wrote to her husband, Charles. They had been separated a long time now, and life without him on the Maine farm intensified her loneliness: "My Dear Charles my whole heart is *yours* . . ." and "I sometimes fear that you are to preashious to me."[47] "I hope," a Connecticut farmer stated at the birth of a new daughter, "we may not love her too much."[48]

The frailty of hope can be seen in the census files of the period. In the censuses, infant children were very frequently identified as "anonymous," "not named," or "unnamed." Infants so designated were sometimes several months old and sometimes over a year of age. Upstate New York farmer Francis Squires made frequent diary references to a son born in July 1852, but only after weathering a severe illness in March 1853 did "bub" assume full identity in his father's writings. In an entry that probably marked the naming, Squires wrote: "*Clarence Augustine Pierce Squires* weighs 20 lbs."[49]

On the occasion of the birth of a daughter, Josiah Crosby of Westernville, New York, received a letter of congratulations and hope that the child would be a great blessing. "But don't," came the ritual warning, "set too mutch by it."[50] George and Fidelia Baldwin of New York were overjoyed at the birth of their healthy new baby, "but how long we shal be allowed to keep him is inknown to us." This same letter referred to a previous child they had lost; hence, it was that they used what was a fairly common designation for the new arrival—the "little stranger."[51] A letter from Carrolton, Alabama, to a grieving brother and sister urged them to turn to their remaining children for comfort.

But do not O do not I beseech you lean too much on this fond hope lest in a moment you least suspect it shall be torn away *forever*. . . . O how heart-rending it is for us to be told that we must call off our affections from these dear second selves and yet if we do not in some degree turn our affections away from them we sharpen the arrow that is to pierce our vitals.[52]

In the full despondence that ensued—"the heart withers and joy sickens & dies and existence becomes a troubled dream"—this Alabaman went beyond that quiet resignation counseled and sought by most. But a situation incorporating "little strangers" and involving the self-preservative need to "in some degree turn our affections away from them" tells much about childhood, life, and death in pre-Civil War America.

Learning to Die

Philosophy has been described as the learning how to die, and insofar as the common man philosophized he did indeed learn how to die. Countering the assertive optimism of the Emersonian position, Melville bespoke that older re-signed mood. *Pierre* becomes an almost angry rejection of the specious felicity of the Transcendentalists' war on circumstances. Pierre Glendinning's in-surgency leads only to "conclusive proof that he has no power over his con-dition." Pierre comes to "deep-down, unutterable mournfulness": " 'Away, ye chattering apes of a sophomorean Spinoza and Plato, who once didst all but delude me that night was day, and pain only a tickle.' " Here, young Pierre "is fitting himself for the highest life, by thinning his blood and collapsing his heart. He is learning how to live, by rehearsing the part of death."[53] The common man arrived at that position somewhat more readily for having no " 'chattering apes' " to circumvent.

The American drift to comfortable worldliness had not run its course by the pre-Civil War period. Cyclone Covey has given us a brief and imaginative account of the move away from a world-view centered on "a symbolic pilgrim-age through the wilderness of this world to an ultimate home-town in the next." At the outset of our history, the mood appeared in the Augustinian equation "Destination: Death." By the end of a century in the New World, the Pilgrim found himself in "Vanity Fair," and, a moment later, "The Big Switch" had been completed. With this eighteenth-century "revolution to modernity," Covey wrote, ". . . death has been the subject to be most avoided of most con-sidered."[54] The conspiracy of silence settled in, and Abraham Lincoln's mel-ancholia assumes the guise of atavistic epilogue. But the move to "modernity" probably came far slower than such an overview indicates. What Covey calls "The Psychology of Bereavement" took expression in ever-lessening elo-quence and intensity, but the mid-nineteenth century writings of common peo-ple are powerfully similar in thrust to the sophisticated writings of three centuries before.

When Francis Squires' wife died in March 1860, the minister chose Romans 13:12 to instruct the survivors: "The night is far spent, the day is at hand: let us therefore cast off the works of darkness, and let us put on the armor of light." "I am very lonesome today," the forty-year-old widower wrote, "& feel that the world is not our home."[55] Death came to be looked on as a warning to prepare for the next life. A dying man in Sterling, Massachusetts, asked his wife to "Tell them [the family] that my being about to be cut off in the midst of my years may prove a warning to my dear friends to be ready."[56] The bride-groom cometh, and lamps must be kept trimmed. The metaphor of Matthew 25 informed the mood of the period. God's purpose was, of course, never clear, but the death of a loved one prepared the survivors by weaning them from worldly attachments. When Lawrence Parker's baby died, relatives did what they could to explain: "You have now one less object to attach you to the earth, and one more to draw you towards heaven. Undoubtedly this was God's design in taking the *Dear Babe*."[57] To be sure, the "Pilgrim" was indeed in "Vanity Far," and "the ties of nature are strong."[58] People resisted the allurements and did what they could to keep the ties loose. As was pointed out to young Wellborn Beeson, not even Oregon should be allowed to capture his fondness so that he would not be ready to leave.[59] Lincoln's poetic statement captures the spirit of his lesser counterparts and the degree to which thoughts of death pervaded their existence.

> I hear the loved survivors tell
>   How nought from death could save,
> Till every sound appears a knell,
>   And every spot a grave.
>
> I range the fields with pensive tread,
>   And pace the hollow rooms,
> And feel (companion of the dead)
>   I'm living in the tombs.[60]

With every spot becoming a grave, the death motif became part of a new and voguish cult. In *The Sentimental Years*, E. Douglas Branch tells of the popularity of Edward Young's *Night Thoughts*. Indeed, the lugubrious "Night I." ("On Life, Death, and Immortality") "probably invoked more imitative poetry in this country than any other one item of English literature—with the exception of 'The Graves of a Household' by Mrs. Felicia Dorothea Hemans." The land was swept by "the gentle delight of melancholia," and "the greatest enticement into romantic melancholy was probably the graveyard."[61] Literary publications developed a near-obsession with the grave. A *Knickerbocker* poem entitled "Lines on Greenwood Cemetery" opened with the contrast of "the gorgeous pomp of summer day."

> But sunshine, verdure, song and bloom,
> Charm not my soul from thoughts of gloom;
> One only feeling thrills me here—
> The dead, th' unheeding dead, are near![62]

For the Transcendental *Dial*, the younger William Ellery Channing set "The Friends" in the "village grave-yard," and he assured his readers that "This watch o'er human bones fatigues not us."[63]

For people with few pretensions, however, the graveyard represented a spiritual nexus that stood at some remove from popularized forms of what Mario Praz called "The Romantic Agony." For devastatingly good reason melancholy abounded, and pleasure derived from it as it had from "The Psychology of Bereavement." For the simple man, the pleasure of melancholy consisted in something more or other than "gentle delight" in mordant or titillating self-indulgence.

People relentlessly visited final resting places, whosoever they were. In the dismal expanse of the prairie crossing, as one argonaut noted in his diary, each wayside grave "had a well beaten path, as if it had been travelled by a great number of people."[64] In a school composition entitled "Things that I Love" a Georgia girl wrote as follows:

I love to walk in the graveyard, and read the inscriptions on the tombstones, the weeping willows fall so gracefully over the silent dead; here and there you may see a rosebush, or a bed of violets, planted and trained by some gentle hand over a dead friend.[65]

In Savannah or on the Great Plains, they probably reacted as did a visitor in Rochester who had "nothing particular to see except Mount Hope Cemetery." He "enjoyed it much."[66]

The graveyard served as a symbol of past associations and of fond hopes which were now only a memory or perhaps in ruin. "Sweet Alice, Ben Bolt," an immensely popular song of the 1850s, seems an almost too precise lyrical statement of that mood. The questions put to Ben Bolt regarding the departed Sweet Alice were couched in terms of "do you remember." James Bell left upstate New York and the woman he meant to marry in order to establish himself in the West. In 1855, not yet fully victimized by the circumstances which were working separate fates for him and his Augusta, Bell wrote to conjure images of those better days they had known together. "Do you remember walking in the Burying Ground one Sunday afternoon. . . ?" Whatever particular associations it may have had, that walk in the graveyard represented a "sigh for the good old times."[67]

A fundamental aspect of the power of the grave appears in a letter written by a Plattsburgh, New York, woman to friends or relatives in her native area around Houlton, Maine. Sarah Ames asked that they visit that "sacred, dear and interesting spot" where resided "the remains of my dear husband."[68] The word "interesting" merits some attention here. As noted earlier, when that word appeared without specific or contextual qualification, it connoted things spiritual and religious. An "interesting spot," like the pulpit, was invested with religious importance and excitement. The grave, whether a solitary and anonymous one in an uncharted vastness, or one in the tailored serenity of a fashionable cemetery, offered some vague but compelling token of things ultimate and infinite. The rural cemetery movement, represented especially by Mount Auburn in Boston and Greenwood in Brooklyn, demonstrated more than the aesthetic and sanitary avoidance of the charnel house and the stacked grave. Though enjoyed directly by the affluent, nearly all appreciated the enhancing of burial sites. It gave further dignity and solemnity to those "sacred, dear and interesting" places.

The graveyard became a focal part of the American landscape for three reasons. First, a weepy melancholy became fashionable in poetry and in other cultural forms, and the graveyard became a prime setting for it. In her treatment of the rural cemetery movement, Barbara Rotundo writes that "the development of rural cemeteries seems to have put new vigor into Romantic melancholy. The poems written about Mount Auburn alone would fill a book, though hardly a book congenial to twentieth-century poetic standards and tastes."[69] Second, the graveyard served as a vehicle of recollection, the meeting ground of past and present, of the quick and the dead. Lesser, individualized tokens of the same motive can be seen in the photos of the dead which came into great vogue among those who could afford them, in the locks of hair taken from the deceased and often worked into such things as brooches, and in the swatches of cloth cut from burial garments.[70] Finally and most fundamentally, the graveyard was "interesting" because it was invested with religious and spiritual intensity. Whether at Mount Auburn, at a prairie grave, or at Fairlee, Vermont, where "a part of the yard is planted to potatoes,"[71] people gathered to observe and reflect.

Death as Didactic Spectacle

On learning of the death of a relative, Mary Ann Haile of Vermont instructed one who had been in attendance: "I want you should write the perticulars."[72] Bereaved witnesses did what they could to oblige the Mary Ann Hailes. "I shall now give you," Samuel Nichols wrote to his father regarding the death of his own son from cholera, "the full particulars of the sickness and death of George."[73] The witnesses to death did not participate as idle observers, though in later times their curiosity might be considered morbid. In most general terms, even the lives of the poor took on importance at the moment of death. There were many inequities in the "Man-of-war world" depicted by Melville. "But there is something in death that ennobles even a pauper's corpse; and the captain himself stood bareheaded before the remains of a man whom, with his hat on, he had sentenced to the ignominious gratings when alive." And the "snow-white, solitary fowl, which—whence coming no one could tell—had been hovering over the mainmast during the service, and was now sailing far up into the depths of the sky" attested to the spiritual source of the solemnity at the death of Shenly, a common sailor.[74]

Here some *obiter dicta* regarding public executions may be allowable. Though such spectacles represent a shameful part of America's past, closer attention to the moods and values of the time might alter the focus somewhat.

Seeking the "psychological implications" of such episodes, David Brion Davis describes "a ritual demonstrating a united hatred of evil" and providing reassurance to "normal, virtuous men."

At the same time, a public hanging provided an approved outlet for collective revenge. The death of a criminal was a sacrifice which assured the virtue of society, justified mankind in the eyes of God and all other paternal authorities, and allowed each frustrated individual to fortify his own antibodies against private aggression by a vicarious act of murder.[75]

Without discounting such factors, it might be contended that other impulses entered in. Given the decree of death, people may well have foregathered to do other than revel in self-satisfying "hatred of evil" and to participate in "collective revenge." Death itself had far greater significance here then "hatred of evil" or "collective revenge," and in the public execution, death came in a setting where all could attend and profit. However powerful emotionally, death was not to be approached furtively or guiltily, but rather with eye steadfastly fixed on the very vortex of the most fundamental of matters. It could be a privilege to be in attendance.

Given the decree of death, the public execution may not have been so great and ghastly a demeaning of humanity as is commonly supposed. Some misfit or outcast to whom no attention had hitherto been paid, unless it was disdain and horror when his hand grasped a dirk, was now the central figure in the most solemn rite. For one moment in a misspent life he had the awed and undivided attention of his fellow men. As Bower Aly has written in a treatment of gallows oratory, the condemned received three things: a favorite last meal, the ministering of the gospel in accord with his wishes, and a forum for a gallows speech.[76] Surely, the Sysyphean war against evil went on; but it took more forms than acts of "collective revenge." The condemned himself might prevail over evil by attesting in his last moments to the pitfalls of a wayward life. The worst of men could thus be redeemed. Annihilation faced him, but not ostracism. Restoration to civil and spiritual communion might come through the ritual of the gallows, particularly the gallows speech. Bower Aly has remarked some "irony" in a persuasion

. . . that judges twentieth-century Americans, who have viewed with equanimity, if not with pride, the death of one hundred thousand men, women, and children from an atomic blow struck in a distant land, to be incompetent to witness in person, as did their forebears, the farewell speech of some lone man condemned to die on the gallows.[77]

Whatever the accuracy of the foregoing paragraphs, they smack of the sort of inferential construction that this study has meant, by and large, to avoid. The written sentiments of those who had witnessed an execution are too few to allow any but tentative conclusions. Assuredly, crimes and their punishment elicited great interest; but that, in itself, says woefully little. Many noted executions; but probably few had occasion to attend. Many diaries, for example, recorded the date of the hanging of Professor John White Webster for the Harvard murder of Doctor George Parkman, and nearly all withheld comment. Surely, a goodly crowd would have been in attendance had that execution been public. But, as perhaps befit his scientific calling, Webster went to his death in "socially antiseptic" seclusion. A New York State store clerk's reaction to the Webster hanging was the common one. On the day before the execution, he stated that it "seems to be the public theme of the day." "This," he remarked the next day, "will for a long time remain fresh in the memories of many."[78]

The Deathbed

Participation in the ritual of dying centered, of course, on the deathbed. To an almost unnerving degree, the imagination and emotion and memory of humble America hovered about that sacrosanct spot. Small wonder that literary and dramatic creators gravitated to it, or that, when the muse moved the pen of the less intellectual, it might seek to express the poetic perception of "the Death Bed of my friend."[79]

While there were individual variations, the writings about death show that certain preparations were standard. Generally, three veiled hopes informed these preparations: (1) the hope of providing solicitude, emotional comfort, and some reassurance for the departing; (2) for the gathered circle, the hope of receiving inspiration by witnessing a calm and clear-eyed death; and (3) the guarded hope for the soul of the deceased that derived from a demonstration of Christian fortitude and resignation. Death could be a powerful lesson and reassurance for the living, as well as a final outward sign of the departed's inward grace.

A preliminary ingredient in the death setting involved the gathering of family and intimate friends. In the vernacular of that era, the dying person was said to be "among friends," the word here designating more intense connections than the indiscriminate host it would later come to cover. One figure whose presence was not at all crucial was the clergyman. Fictive deaths such as those of Little Mary Morgan and Little Eva went thus unattended, and common writings indicate that the preacher or minister had no necessary place at the deathbed. Of course, the cast varied, but some bond of friendship at this ultimate moment had nearly unutterable importance. White Jacket Melville began the death vigil over sailor Shenly; and at the 4:00 A.M. bell a man from the other watch came to relieve him. Melville allowed himself none of the accustomed hyperbole in closing the chapter titled "How Man-Of-War's Men Die at Sea:" ". . . I told him I chose to remain where I was till daylight came."[80]

An unattended death sparked terror and signified a great spiritual and emotional loss. Surely, part of the fear about going west centered on the fear of dying alone in the wilderness. At the end of his trek, Forty-niner E. D. Perkins perceived the "grim monster" now grown "doubly" ominous; "the grave has more terrors than I ever before felt."[81] Perkins had had ghastly preparation for this sentiment: some four months earlier he had seen the remains of the Donner party. Not long after Perkins saw that "most melancholy" spot, an Ohio saddler's son who had spent time as a sailor in the Texas navy reflected on the same point as his party crossed the arid waste west of El Paso. Now on the southern route to California, he spontaneously lapsed into a eulogy for a "very worthy" young Englishman who had died from hydrophobia:

It is ever hard to die, but to die thus, far from home and friends amidst strangers in a strange land, with no mothers prayer or sisters tear to sooth the wretched heart in this last but fleeting hour, and finally go down to the grave in this wild desolate plain. Oh how terrible it is—but there he lies, with nothing to mark the spot save the simple cross upon which his future hope depends.[82]

In the country beyond El Paso, the triumphant rhetoric of "O Death, where is thy sting?" may have had a hollow ring.

Here we might comment on the Hawthorne story "Roger Malvin's Burial" which treats death and the "rites of sepulture" in the setting of the wilderness. In this tale, the dying Roger Malvin persuades young Reuben Bourne to leave him and to press on alone toward the settlements, thus preserving what chances he has for survival. Bourne's soul-wrenching decision is made with the recognition of the "ghastly fate to be left expiring in the wilderness": " 'How terrible to wait the slow approach of death in this solitude!' exclaimed he. 'A brave man does not shrink in the battle; and, when friends stand round the bed, even women may die composedly; but here—' "[83] Edwin Fussell has suggested the centrality of the Indian in this story. Indeed, the Indian and death merge into a single identity; "Death is an Indian slaughtered by the white man."[84] But the Indian, and the Indian wars from which the story stemmed, provides little more than general background; the Indian serves an anonymous and incidental purpose. The story treats death and the "rites of sepulture" in the excruciating setting of the wilderness.

In emphasizing the East-West, frontier-settlement, Red-White tensions of the story, Fussell noted the connotation of the name Bourne "('limit,' 'boundary')."[85] But another aptness would have occurred far more quickly to pre-Civil War America. "Bourn" had an almost ineluctable association with death. "That undiscovered country, from whose bourn no traveler returns" was Hamlet's metaphorical identification of "not to be."[86] Time and again, "from whose bourn no traveler returns" (or some variant or corruption) would appear in cliche-like representation of death. And in Hawthorne's depiction, as in the imagery of so many common people, death wore the guise of the "grim monster." "Roger Malvin's Burial" shows that "grim monster" assuming doubly horrific proportions for lack of the comforting context that could have been had "among friends." Before exacting the promise upon which the rest of the tale hinges, the dying Malvin confers upon Reuben a blessing that ends with these words: " '. . . and may your children's children stand round your death bed!' "[87]

To be beyond the reach of "friends" was a fearsome prospect for Elizabeth Cooley of Virginia. Following the New Orleans-Red River route, she lapsed into a "deep shade of desponding melancholy." Writing during a painful delay in a village in east Texas, she verged on incoherence.

A sick husband here in this nastly warehouse and nastly sickly alligator river, before us a sickly southern clime to contend with . . . a long and sickly dangerous road before us and no home nor friends. . . . I fear to die here and my grave tramped over by strangers.[88]

But, as White Jacket sat with Shenly, so there could be the surcease of proxy friendship. In the summer of 1843, common schoolteacher Sarah Smith agonized over her brother Silas in Michigan. "Do O do write," she implored a sister who might know more about him. Sarah had heard nothing from Silas for months; another brother had sought him and failed; and, finally, the first lake boat of the spring arrived without the Silas who was to have been aboard. "I feare," Sarah concluded, "he has fallen the victim of the hand of death among strangers[.] [N]o one to follow his remaines to the tomb." Months later, when the fatal intelligence regarding Silas had arrived, Sarah took particular care to pass on the particulars of his demise. An important comforting word had come by letter from a committee of the Jackson, Michigan, Guard, of which Silas had been a member. Two officers of the company had kept the death watch over Sarah's brother, one of them holding his hand as he expired.[89]

Writing from the same east Texas county that Elizabeth Cooley found so "nastly" and "sickly," Mary Cole wrote home inquiring into the particulars of her sister's death. Mary wanted especially to know "if sister wose in her senses . . . and if she read enny thing about d[y]ing."[90] Such questions were standard concerns about death. To play out life properly necessitated awareness on the part of all concerned. Visiting a sick friend or relative who had been married only three weeks, Minerva Bacon of Odgensburgh, New York, found her "pale as death." In conversing with this woman who had but one week to live, Minerva evidently gave delicacy and tact low priority: "I told her thene she was worse of than she had a ware of."[91] When a friend was dying there were considerations far larger than tact. Just who performed Minerva's function generally is difficult to ascertain; but evidently someone did. Time and again, it would be marked as a source of satisfaction that the dying person was "sensible" of the situation. Indeed, those who were unwilling or unable to recognize their condition, might be described as "very stupid,"[92] as was a man in Pawlet, Vermont.

Gratification came even from a child's being "sensible." "Little Lydia" suffered delirium much of the time, but in a lucid moment she asked to have read to her a tract treating "poor Joe the Collier." That request, her mother hopefully inferred, indicated that Lydia had "reflected with understanding."[93] On July 4, 1856, James Bell's fiancée, Augusta, wrote him about the death of a child named Homer. She said that the child suffered more than she had believed possible. Still, those around him had taken comfort from the fact that "he talked of dying while he had reason. . . ."[94] In a rare instance where a preacher had a central part in the ritual of dying (he may have been a relative as well as minister), he asserted that a "perfectly delirious" child would become sensible before dying, and "sure enough all at once he became so." This Lumpkin, Georgia, boy gave profound satisfaction by showing full awareness of the fate that lay only hours ahead.[95]

Death by consumption was particularly compelling because of its side-effects. Consumption became a hallmark of the Romantic sensibility grown morbid, and it may have left an enduring mark on cosmetology. In *The Romantic Agony*, Mario Praz noted the "Romantic fashion for consumptive ladies," a fashion that he evidenced in part by "the American 'Ode to Consumption.' "[96] A young woman so afflicted grew doubly "interesting": she was a knowing witness to the inexorable approach of death, and her beauty was heightened as the disease progressed. Bodily deterioration lent alabaster pallor to the skin, and fever gave luminous intensity to the eyes and brightly contrasting red spots on the cheekbones. Amelia Akehurst, a New York State common schoolteacher who moved to Georgia and who was in self-appraisal "a pennyless unattractive girl," gave a precise description of the physical effects of consumption. In reporting the death of her nineteen-year-old sister by consumption, she wrote that

the broad snowy brow grew more and more fair[,] her eyes beamed with almost unearthly lustre & the bright crimson spot upon her cheek rendered her even more beautiful than when in her usual health[.] [C]onsumption *seems to delight to deck* its victims just as they are to be hid in the tomb[.][97]

This description is strikingly close to Catherine Sedgewick's treatment of the death of Lucretia Maria Davidson. Lucretia was an incredibly necrophiliac poet who died of consumption in 1825 at the age of seventeen. At nine years of age, whe wrote "an elegy on a dead robin" and then elaborated on the theme of death.[98] In 1838, her sister Margaret also succumbed to consumption, and the two poets received much attention in pre-Civil War America, including biographical treatments by Sedgewick, Samuel F.B. Morse, and Washington Irving. The "pennyless unattractive" Georgia schoolteacher may have borrowed from Sedgewick's description of the dying Lucretia Davidson: "She shrunk painfully from the gaze her beauty inevitably attracted, heightened as it was by that disease which *seems to delight to deck the victim* for its triumph."[99]

Nothing could have commended Lucretia Davidson more to her society than her unfinished deathbed poem, "Fear of Madness."

> There is something which I dread;
>   It is a dark, and fearful thing;
> It steals along with withering tread,
>   Or sweeps on wild destruction's wing
>
> That thought comes o'er me in the hour
>   Of grief, of sickness, or of sadness;
> 'Tis not the dread of death; 'tis more,—
>   It is the dread of madness.[100]

Death stopped her pen as she reached the words: ". . . let not dark delirium steal . . ." Hers was no abstract and removed weighing of death and madness; she sought to exorcize the latter that it might not detract from fundamental perception. In the same 1846 poetry that compellingly caught the concern with death, Lincoln compared that with the worry about madness much as Davidson had done.

> But here's an object of more dread
>   Than ought the grave contains—
> A human form with reason fled,
>   While wretched life remains.[101]

For a Columbus, Ohio, man, Christmas of 1842 was a time of "melancholy." "What is there so hard," he asked, "as to lose a Kind beloved and Affectionate *Mother*." His sorrow was compounded by the fact that he had not been at her deathbed: "Perhaps she would have knew me and gave me a *mothers* blessing before she died." But, more important, "If dear *Mother* could only have spoken, her death would not have went so hard with any of us."[102] With the circle gathered, it was important that all be resigned to the workings of providence. It was very desirable that the dying person give an explicit statement of submission to God's will. Such a statement was, of course, not always forthcoming. In the fictional ideal, Harriet Beecher Stowe and Timothy Shay Arthur gave famous illustrations in Little Eva and Little Mary Morgan. And Parson Weems' Washington, one might suggest, endeared himself to the two succeeding generations quite as much for his deathbed patience and submission as for his inability to tell a lie. Melville, who was greatly concerned with death in his works, concluded a disquisition on the subject in this way: "To expire mild-eyed in one's bed transcends the death of Epaminondas."[103]

"To expire mild-eyed" was indeed the ideal. Mrs. Andrew Adams took large satisfaction from knowing that a dead neighbor had departed conscious and resigned: "Am rejoiced to know these facts."[104] And A. J. Hayter of Saline

County, Missouri, wrote to his mother to get the details of the death of "dear old pappy":

Mother i should have liked to have node whither he was resined to gow[.] Joseph could not tell me exackly whither or not[.] [Y]ou must tell A to rite to me and let me now all about that gives me eas if he was perfectly resined to gow mother in that triing ower if he was prepared to gow what sweet thoughts to himself and all of his children.[105]

Two recurring expressions—"great sufferer" and "died hard"—seem to have served as shorthand descriptions of how the deceased had faced death. To describe one as a "great sufferer" indicated not only that the deceased had suffered great physical anguish, but also that the approach of death had been borne submissively. Thus, one woman described a recently deceased friend as a "grait sufferer in this world & a patient one to."[106] The combination—"grait sufferer" and "patient one"—borders on redundance, but the writer probably did not fear the emphasis of repetition. The contrary could be suggested in the cryptic phrase "*died hard*." Here again it is apparent that more was involved than a quotient of bodily suffering. The Maryland store clerk, who earlier was shown busily watching the dying, had instructive contrast in that fall and winter of 1834. He used the term "great sufferer" to describe one of the departed. But in reluctant, parenthetical reference to a close friend who had attempted to cut short his agony by stabbing himself, the clerk wrote, "*died hard*."[107]

Survivors occasionally engaged in sorrowful conjecture about the spiritual condition of those who "died hard." A North Carolina woman, writing about a friend fatally stricken when married only three months, described her as "not willing to die": "she was very much opposed to dying[.] [S]he prayed as long as she could speak, and the last thing she said was tell me if I am dying. Lord have mercy on me have mercy on me, but whether or not she obtained mercy is not for me to say. . . ."[108] In the spring of 1848, John Barber borrowed money to make the short trip to Oswego to see his dying daughter, Mrs. Lawrence (Fanny) Parker. Her father wanted the "great satisfaction . . . to talk with her about leaving the world."[109] Perhaps it was as well that he could not be there, as her husband was. In humble setting, Lawrence Parker approximated Augustine St. Clare. Stowe's perhaps Byronic Louisiana planter would not accept the condition of his dying daughter, Eva: " 'I *cannot*,' said St. Clare rising, I *cannot* have it so! . . . 'Papa, you break my heart!' said Eva, rising and throwing herself into his arms; 'you must not feel so!' "[110] And in time St. Clare did not. Real life was not as obliging. Lawrence Parker, himself not a spiritual man, had his own doubts about God compounded when the woman who had sought to guide him in life failed him in death. To Fanny's brother who solicited the details of her demise, Parker wrote that his wife had refused to hear any "discouraging word" and had insisted to the end, comsumption and the doctor's candor notwithstanding, that she would live. Parker could only write: "she died

very hard and strugled much after her sight failed, all of which I will not distress you to read of. . . ."[111]

Evidently there were deviations in the path from time to eternity. Not all
died to expectations. But the passing of a fellow mortal always had instructive
quality. If all went well it could be a privilege to behold the death. At one level
this could involve a celebration of man in humanist terms—the witnessing of a
person's calmly putting the things of the world into order, and unflinchingly
accepting the bodily change. Mark Twain, in emphasizing the "privilege" it
was to Laura to attend her dying father, left matters at that. Indeed, Si Hawkins
expired with dimming eye and halting tongue still on the chimerical Tennessee
land grant.[112] Large wisdom held, with Shakespeare, that "More are men's
ends mark'd than their lives before." And if life were properly concluded, it
could be said of a man, as it was of Cawdor, that "Nothing in his life became
him like the leaving of it."[113]

Mark Twain did not seek to be either ironic or macabre in presenting Laura's
death watch as a "privilege." The term itself, and the sentiment behind it, frequently appear in the writings of the common man. Not to be able to attend at
the deathbed was routinely set down as a striking deprivation. Six years after
leaving Nicholville, New York, a Wisconsin couple wrote back to express grief
at the death of a mother, grief in this case compounded by absence: "if I could
have had the privilege of being with her in her sickness & have felt her loss, it
would have been a great satisfaction. . . ."[114]

Only rarely did one deliberately forego that privilege. One such example
appears in the diary kept by the wife of a small Virginia slaveowner. Driven to
her emotional and physical limits by sickness and death among her children,
and suffering the endless vexation of directing four or five slave women,
Pauline Stratton could not react properly when her mother-in-law seemed
mortally ill. Relations between the two had long been strained, and now, when
Pauline made soup for the apparently dying woman, her effort brought only
complaint. Much given to self-recrimination, Pauline assumed yet another
emotional burden by becoming "so hardened that I felt . . . I did not want to see
her die. . . ."[115] The more usual attitude was that of New Englander Lizzie
Robbins who ministered endlessly to her dying husband. Although the expiring
man was a "great sufferer," Lizzie felt the toll and began to speak of her "task."
But immediately she caught herself: " 'task,' indeed *it is not*"; it is "not only my
duty but my great privilege."[116]

A Triumphant Death

The highest privilege came in witnessing a "triumphant" death. In one
sense, "holy dying," to use Jeremy Taylor's famous usage of the seventeenth
century, represented the logical finality of "holy living." Moved by a northeast
Pennsylvania revival to contemplate general matters, visitor Horatio Chandler

of New Hampshire put it this way: "The last act, on earth, of our gratitude to our dear Redeemer, to set the example of *holy dying*, as well as *holy living*; surely in proportion do we glorify God; & do a real blessing to those around us. May we be prepared to say with martyrs,—'Welcome death.' "[117] Chandler's expression of the Christian mood was unimpeachable, but generally, common folk were more cautious in their choice of words. To describe a death as "holy" was somewhat of a presumption. "Holy" dying remained an ideal; "triumphant" or "happy" dying often occurred in fact.

Of course, there were many gradations between a "very stupid" death and a "triumphant" one. Here it is well to recognize that, in letters particularly and in diaries to a lesser degree, prevarication or omission might occur. Lawrence Parker, for example, gave differing accounts of his wife's death, depending upon who the recipient was. The spiritually devastating account described earlier went directly from Parker to his wife's brother. But her sister evidently gained a different impression. She reported that Fanny's husband had been "so much affected that he could not give us any particulars of her last moments," but the particulars he finally did give her bore little resemblance to those sent to the brother. The dying woman, as sister Fidelia understood it, had shown much "fortitude" and had had "sufficient... hope in Christ." Shortly before Fanny's death, the circle of friends sang "Rock of Ages," and "it seemed she more than entered into the spirit of it."[118]

Thus, it would appear that Parker thoughtfully tailored his accounts to his audience. Other correspondents simply avoided mentioning unsettling particulars. In his diary, a New York City man observed that his brother retained reason until the end and that he showed "an interest in Christ—though his death was not attended by any particularly striking ————"[119] That line of omission has eloquence. But common folk probably were fully prepared to accept the fact that, in death as in life, high hopes came reluctantly to realization. An Ohio man, writing to family in Connecticut regarding a grandmother's death, noted the "pleasing evidence of her interest in the L. Jesus Christ. This is all we could have expected & nearly all we could have wished. We should indeed have been glad if her departure had been of the more extatic and triumphant cast...."[120]

That "extatic and triumphant cast" came as the final intensification of the knowing acquiescence in God's will. Grief, fatigue, pain, and spiritual awe supplied the context for ecstasy, that last emotional balm which served to ease the living past a profoundly unnerving moment and the departing from time to eternity.

Late in 1838, John and Rachel Ricketts of Franklin County, Indiana, conveyed to a brother the details of the mother's death. With the letter went a lock of her hair, "some of the grave clothese," and the urging to "till all the purtikler about the death of our Old Mother." In this case, the "purtikler" were worth relating:

I feel gratified to inform you that she left the wourld in the triumfs of faith, in her dying moments Jesse and myself Sung a Cupple of favorite hyms and She Slapt her hands and shouted and give glory to god and retained her senses while she had breath which gave us all a great deel of Satisfaction to See her leave[.] Such a great witness that she went happy out of the wourld[.][121]

When a fifteen-year-old Pennsylvania woman died a "very triumph" death after great suffering, it was, as Catherine Beaver wrote, "quite a privilege to be there."[122] She had departed happy, as had David Slagle of North Carolina. David, his brother Elam informed the rest of the family, went "in the full triumph of a living faith. . . . he got very happy and remained so until he got so weak that he could not controll his mind."[123] The word "happy" pertained especially to things religious. It indicated spiritual transportation, in this case the salving ecstasy that allowed at least the Pyrrhic victory over death itself. For simple people, accomplishments and victories came only infrequently, but everyone—not just movers and shakers—had the chance for a final conquest. "And to yield the ghost proudly," Melville mused, "and march out of your fortress with all the honors of war is not a thing of sinew and bone."[124] The weakest and lowest could do that. They could draw the fangs of the "grim monster" itself, the witnessing of which "triumphant" spectacle was a "privilege" indeed.

Although happiness and triumph could well intimate a Christian hereafter, the letter and diary reflections on death almost totally omit explicit references to otherworldly rewards or even to the assurance that a particular person would enjoy them. Certainly, people died "happy" in a prospect, or in the "triumph" of the faith, or with the consolation of a Christian hope, but these people, like Gray's paradigm possessed only "trembling hope." However fraught with otherworldly implications and intimations, deathbed writings resolutely maintained a general and allusive quality where the most profound matter was concerned. Even when a striking portent occurred, common people were cautious about interpreting its meaning. For example, when a Missouri man was laid out in a back room, a dove flew onto an open windowsill near where his body lay. That bird, like the one in Melville's account of the burial of Shenly, betokened things ultimate. "Pore John," a sister wrote, "could not talk to nun of us[;] if he could he would have told us he was agowing home whare christians are at rest." But her letter stopped well short of heavenly visions; indeed, she shifted abruptly to immediate realities. Whatever "pore John's" immortal destiny, "that dove came to console us." In a world where "i have nothing to write to you but greaf and trouble," no more could be asked of the delicate harbinger on the windowsill. People with intense awareness of "the trouble in this world for humane beaings to gow through"[125] left matters of eternity to those who purported to have greater discernment.

When twenty-four-year-old Halbert Stryker of Brownstown, Indiana, lay moments from death, he informed his parents that "he was goeing to Jesus and Exhorted us all to try to meet him in heaven." A burst of illumination allowed the dying man to say that the path "from Earth to Haven looked clear to him."[126] Characteristically, the path and not the destination became manifest. The writings of the common people contain almost no heavenly imagery. They seem to have left "microscopic viewings of a much inflated afterlife"[127] to their cultural and literary superiors. Their imagery for death is more prosaic and immediate, centering far more on what was to be escaped than on what was to be realized. Whatever "trembling hope" of heaven may have informed their deepest longings, these people more often spoke of death as a release from whatever had plagued them. Of course, the woes to which they sought an end had many forms. In 1848, the Thompsons of Mount Meigs, Alabama, seem to have fallen on evil days. John killed his uncle Solomon, and Nancy, having been "to frindly" with someone, appeared to be in a "family way." In the midst of such unfoldings, Mary, another member of the family, took mortally ill and professed to be quite ready to go. "All she wanted," a neighbor wrote of her death, "was ease." With "the Devil . . . turned loose amongst the Thompsons," Mary may have felt the quite ample attraction of unadorned withdrawal.[128] Given the conditions of this world, it was not engaging in ecstatic visions to say that someone had been "cald to try the realities of a better world."[129]

The only specific, rapturous images of the hereafter which these people used involved children. In the spring of 1852, Charles Riddick of Yalobusha County, Mississippi, received the details regarding the death of a woman named Ginnie. Twelve months earlier she had lost a child, and now, following the birth of another, she was on her deathbed. The stricken woman was not "affread" to die, and near the end she told of hearing children singing, among them her departed little Willie. Ginnie's husband, perhaps hoping to bring her back to earthly realities, suggested that she heard children in the yard, but the dying woman perceived what was beyond her spouse. Evidently, Ginnie, with a "sweet smile" on her countenance, gently demurred.[130] Similarly, when Annis Pierce of New York State attempted to comfort her daughter Emily, she did awkward rhapsody on the departed child's now singing "the song of Moses and the Saints."[131] Typically, the person who described Ginnie's death offered no thought about Ginnie's hereafter. It was enough to express the ritual trust that she was now beyond the cares and vexations with which mortality had burdened her. Or, as a Pennsylvania woman put it, there was the hope of a "wresting place . . . whare the wicked shall for ever ceace to trouble us."[132]

Conclusion

For the common man, death represented an escape from the world's sadness, an end to the "pilgrimage" through spiritual and bodily hostility. It meant the passage to that realm "where parting is no more." Years earlier, Keziah Herrick and her sister Eunice parted on Lake Seneca's shores, and now in 1854, having neither seen nor heard from her sister since then, Keziah thought that whatever hope for reunion yet remained centered on "fairer climes than these where the fears of parting will no more trouble us."[133] Therein resided the anticipation of an end to earthly separation and, as an Ogdensburg, New York, man put it, the place "where monster [death] will part us no more."[134] While this was a qualified, even a negative vision, for people who could expect few earthly delights, it seems to have been heaven enough. The headier prospect of limitless bliss and glory remained an abstraction for them, perhaps humbly to be accepted should providence see fit to bestow it.

PART TWO

THINGS
TEMPORAL

Self and Society 5

In seeking to set forth the attitudes of the common people toward the affairs of the world, we begin with their views of the self (the internal dimension) and the relation of the self to those surrounding it—family, friends, and community (the external dimension).

An Interpretive Framework

While visiting in Providence, Rhode Island, in September and October 1850, Vermonter H. N. Rhodes took in the standard attractions. On two consecutive evenings, he went to the "Musium" to see a "horse drama entitled Kit Carson, or the California Robber Chief." Two days later, he walked along the docks to India Point. He sat for a while with his back against a once busy but now decaying building and made a diary entry. As he wrote, a wood train left the station area and left him in solitude. "And as the Bible says, 'tis not good, for man to be alone!' I too will depart for the busy haunts of man in the heart of the city."[1] There was probably some irony in that remark, and surely some conviction as well.

From India Point to downtown Providence symbolized the often-considered tension between self and solitude on the one hand and society on the other. Back in the "haunts of man" one could, as Rhodes did, read about an imminent hanging and perhaps bring to mind the very recent Boston execution of Professor John White Webster for the murder of Doctor George Parkman. If the "horse drama" about Kit Carson lost its lure, one had ready access to other delights. Soon, Rhodes suffered a "slight attack of the Jenny Lind *fever*" when the Swedish singer arrived in the city. He could not afford four dollars for a performance, but he could stand in the throng outside the singer's hotel and get a precious glimpse of her. If the urge to solitary contemplation arose, it took him, as it did so many others, on a visit to a burying ground.[2] As the confidence man in one of his guises aboard the *Fidèle* told the student reading Tacitus, " '. . . if to know human nature is your object, drop Tacitus and go north to the cemeteries of Auburn and Greenwood.' "[3] Such a suggestion would have been far less startling and sardonic then than it would now.

In one of the most forceful statements of the alteration of mentality that accompanied the Romantic movement, and particularly its Transcendental epicenter, Richard D. Mosier feels moved to write of the "Great God Self." "This new theology of Selfhood" developed in America most notably from Emerson, and it would be echoed more stridently by acolytes such as Thoreau and Whitman. Modern scholar Mosier, in language redolent of Whitmanesque unrestraint, concludes his section on the "Great God Self" with a statement of its unbroachable "first commandment": "Thou shalt have no other gods before me."[4] That formulation has a compelling quality, but it is by no means a singular assessment. Indeed, whatever the degree of accuracy, such assessments have been very common. Emerson, however much he may have qualified at the time or reconsidered later, set the tone with pronouncements regarding "the great and crescive self," with postulates such as "I who alone am," and with commands to get hands off "this kingdom of me."[5]

Although the headier views were confined largely to the pages of the *Dial* or to Bronson Alcott's backyard, those views are frequently presented as having worked subtle but forceful permutations within society at large. The pre-Civil War period, perceived by Emerson as "the age of the first person singular,"[6] obligingly assumes cultural identity as the age of the self-made man, of self-assertion, of will, of individualism, an age wherein the lone man gained or assumed sufficiency to his own needs. In fact, when the contrary theme of "individual powerlessness" surfaces in an Emerson essay, when the sage of Concord pronounces that "you shall have everything as a member, nothing for yourself," a modern scholar offers this observation: "A strange encouragement to offer a still Jacksonian America!"[7]

The present study contends that such a sentiment would not have been at all strange and that a suggestion to make an ego-stifling visit to a graveyard would not have been taken amiss. In simplest terms, the common view did not construe the self as a spiritual category but as a temporal one. The self stood as no accommodating channel to enhancement or perfection; it stood rather as an endlessly frustrating, dark-hued impediment. "The townsmen of Concord may not have apprehended much about the Romantic Agony; however, when Thoreau confronted them with his rustic caricature of the Byronic egotist, they, remembering their Puritan heritage, could recognize a limb of Satan when they saw one."[8] Perry Miller's aside about microcosmic Concord and its "Puritan heritage" ought to be kept in mind when larger realms of American society come under attention. Those townsmen of Concord had vast company throughout America. Insofar as their untutored jottings reveal them, the average Americans warned as insistently, if not as eloquently, as did their un-recognized spokesmen Hawthorne and Melville against the unleashing of the self. Or, to put it another way, "The Invention of the Self,"[9] in its modern ac-ceptation, had not yet occurred in their realm.

As a comparative point of departure, it would be difficult to concoct a state-ment of the relation between self and society more alien than parts of Emer-son's "Self-Reliance" to the precepts of the common people:

Check this lying hospitality and lying affection. Live no longer to the expectation of these deceived and deceiving people with whom we converse. Say to them, "O father, O mother, O wife, O brother, O friend, I have lived with you after appearances hitherto. Henceforward I am the truth's. Be it known unto you that henceforward I obey no law less than eternal law. . . . I must be myself. I cannot break myself any longer for you, or you."

Emerson knew that that outburst violated the beliefs of "the populace."[10] To them, comprehensive ultimatums directed at father, mother, wife, and others within earshot would have defied all instincts and training, and would have seemed unadorned ventures into callousness. "The populace" held few fears indeed about the dispelling of solitude. And those less intellectual sorts did al-most no brooding about intrusions upon the self. They applauded the intru-sions of society in its various forms and dimensions. They could not applaud the hurtful intrusions upon and deflations of self worked by circumstances and experience, but they tried to respond with unmurmuring resignation to those tyrannies.

Here as in other ways, "the populace" of Emerson's time bore much resem-blance to "The Evangelicals" of the seventeenth and eighteenth century dis-cussed by Philip Greven. Their perception was "That Monster, Self"; their goal was "The Self Suppressed."[11] Emerson did not echo the views of his own age; he anticipated those of a later age. As Andrew Hacker asserts, in spite of the fact that "philosophers have been locating 'the individual' at the center of their systems for several centuries, it is only recently that this emphasis has entered the vernacular." Now "virtually everyone looks upon himself as an 'individual.' " Now that that has been perceived, these "individuals" "explore their egos" intensely, "invest their personalities with potentialities ripe for lib-eration," bemoan "individual 'powerlessness,' " vilify whatever thwarts "self-discovery and self-development," and relentlessly ask "Who am I?"[12] Some have espied other than an interrogatory tone. In making the impish but earnest conjunction of "The Me Decade and the Third Great Awakening," Tom Wolfe depicts a modern egomania that is almost literally trumpeting in its certitude. Now we have "the mightiest, holiest roll of all, the beat that goes . . . *Me . . . Me . . . Me . . . Me . . .*" Those "dreary little bastards," now rendered comfortable, assertive, and self-indulgent, put attitudinal light years between themselves and their pre-Civil War ancestors when "they discovered and started doting on me!"[13]

Love, Marriage, and Companionship

The most basic dimension of society revolved about love, marriage, and companionship, and in terms of definition, society had a far more constricted use than would later be the case. "Society and solitude are deceptive names,"[14] Emerson wrote, but in one sense they had far more directness than they were destined to have. Emerson and "the populace" disagreed strongly about how one reacted to society, but they were quite at one as to what society was. The word "society" was not commonly used to designate a nation or some other comprehensive entity such as The Great Society or The Affluent Society. Society meant the approach of another person, hardly more than what is now called company. Emerson used it that way in "Solitude and Society," and his less intellectual counterparts used it that way too.

Writing from a village near Binghamton, New York, a mother happily informed another member of the family that her son Dan was "very steady, and appears to enjoy the society of his family."[15] That Dan remained "very steady" gave reassurance, but this period had many forces drawing people such as Dan from the society of their families. Plain people were not only aware of such forces but were also disheartened by them. In their language, "society" suffered. In anguished diary entries written at New Diggings, Wisconsin, early in 1850, forty-year-old Abner Goddard bemoaned the absence of the "Sweet Society of my Dear family." But at least Abner could thank providence for having kept him from the greater error of going on to California, that "land of gold and distress."[16] A mere allusion to that theme and locale will suffice here. In the purview of common people, whatever movement did to "society," it did to wife and family.

Society ringed, curbed, and comforted the self. As the ancient wisdom had it, it was not good to be alone, and the most fundamental avenue of escape from that state consisted in love between man and woman. In the Transcendental counterpoint to common moods, "we come now," Alfred Kazin and Daniel Aaron have written, "to the comic and even farcical" part of that persuasion.[17] "Armed all over by subtle antagonisms," that group did appear at times as a blend of the silly and the abrasive. Outside of Concord and its circle, however, there was precious little that was subtle, though antagonisms assuredly occurred. And, as is perhaps ever the case with the written language of love, the comic and the farcical intruded. Love letters often have pitifully little appeal to others than the particular couple, and sometimes not even to both of them. One should not undertake lightly to read the amorous writings of the common people. If one has a whimsical taste for wretched poetry, that will help, but even unintended drollery becomes wearying. Whatever the lack of subtleties and whatever the hazards to artistic sensibilities, however, common people expressed some basic and important notions in their language of love.

In a youthful and vital nation, romantic attachments often came early, and, as has been frequently noted, they tended quickly to issue in marriage. But the dynamics of that era sometimes had far differing results. The story of James Bell and Augusta Hallock, an upstate New York couple who appear in other contexts in Part One, illustrates some contrary implications for people in a society on the move. Just when their emotional attachment began is beyond determination now, but by mid-1854 it showed some depth of involvement. The couple exchanged valentines and breezy notes early in the year, and on June 1 Augusta invited James to attend a party with her, a "donation" party where the delights of "society" entailed small money gifts for religious causes. Augusta pointed out that a buggy would leave her area for the party and that there would be ample room for "*you and I*." The two following sentences could suggest the badly stated coyness of a romance not yet well under way, or they could suggest that the relation had already involved some antagonisms: "Do as you like best about it. It makes no difference to me either way."

If it did not make a difference then, it certainly would later. The fall worked separations, and Augusta lapsed into the characteristic pensiveness of associations riven by change. "Yes," she wrote from Norton Hill in October, "they *were* good times," but now little more than "memory pictures" remained. "What a volume of meaning there is in those two short words—*Scattered—gone*. Distance separates us from some, and Eternity from others. But we can *think* of them if they *are* never again to be realized." A poetic snowbird then informed her revery. When all others had gone with the change of season, that delicate reminder stayed:

> Love, like that bird, when friendship's throng,
> With fortune's sun depart,
> Still lingers with its cheerful song,
> And nestles on the heart,
>
> from
A. snowbird

The captialized "A" could be taken for Augusta, but, whether her own composition or merely a transcription, it spoke her feelings.

That letter does not indicate how far her James had wandered by then, but in the spring of 1855 he appears in the correspondence near Kaneville, Illinois, now in pursuit of the needed competence for marriage. Augusta remained at Norton Hill to enter the "Bedlam" of common schoolteaching. Soon, the vexation of separation told. Some of it involved the "forever scratch, scratch, scratching with a pen"; some of it involved her feeling of being so "*neglected, cooly neglected*" as to feel ashamed to continue her futile enquiries after mail

at the post office. As time wore on, the efforts at humor degenerated into churl-
ishness and pointed irony.

Each wondered about the other's spiritual condition and whether they were
sufficiently sincere Christians to make a go of marriage. Early in 1856,
Augusta brooded over their youth and inexperience. She insisted that they
must be cautious, but in the same letter she could state her opposition to long
engagements. These were trying times, and it is at least understandable that
Augusta could resort to some artfulness. An April 1856 letter which Augusta
described as being "just as I would talk, to you if you was here"—its self-con-
tradictory careful draft notwithstanding— conveyed her resolve to end her correspondence with Ansell Elliott. Possibly with that fellow in mind, James returned that winter, only to be gone again shortly for the Illinois-Iowa area.
Early in 1857, Augusta renewed the Ansell Elliott leverage by again expressing determination to end that correspondence; she did not specify if
Elliott was that sole fellow she had kissed since James had left. In response
from a farm near Iowa City, James surmounted the temptation to be abrupt by
noting his trust in her good sense where Elliott was concerned.

The separation and the correspondence continued over the ensuing years,
but that winter visit apparently provided the next to last opportunity for James
and Augusta to see each other. In November 1863, the woman from the north
slopes of the Catskills wandered down the rows of cots in a Washington, D.C.,
military hospital looking for the man she had so long hoped to marry, the man
who had gone west to make their future in farming and who had refused a clerk-
ship in an Iowa City store because he felt that it partook of the dishonest. In an
exquisitely poignant letter, Augusta told her brother that she at first did not recognize the man she sought, but James could still recognize her, and at her approach a "beautiful smile" eased his haggard features. "Oh Eddy, *that
meeting*, for long weary years almost seven we had hoped and prayed that we
might meet again Oh *once more*." Augusta had arrived in time.[18] Nine years
earlier when she had written to James as "A. Snowbird." Augusta identified
"Distance" and "Eternity" as the great agents of separation. The two worked
together with devastating effectiveness upon this couple, and now Augusta
leaves our consideration to go on to become Mrs. Ansell Elliott, in which
capacity one would hope she found happiness.

When Maria Louisa Smith moved with her family to Henderson, Texas, in
the mid-1840s she evidently left several forlorn young men in the north
Georgia-western North Carolina area. She could be excused for taking some
satisfaction from that, but it was not an unmixed blessing. To leave smitten
ones in the wake opened one to the sort of romantic and poetic onslaught as that
launched by Jesse M. Huckabee of Union County, Georgia. What the
sprightly Miss Smith thought of this opening is perhaps better unknown: "I
raise my pen and look around mee[;] that Beutiful sun that surveys the Meriden
is now behind the western hills and I am still promited to in joy that Beautiful

Bespoken moon light." Fortunately, others had a more prosaic than poetic bent. R. A. Moss of Cherokee County, North Carolina, who himself moved to Texas but not to marry the much-sought Maria, used a direct approach. With the Mexican War underway he announced his intention of enlisting as a volunteer and his hope of combining a venture into the martial realm with one into the domestic. "My object for Righting you," he told the desirable Miss Smith, "is to let you know that I am a candydate for matrimony and that you are the object of my choice. . . ."

It may be that Maria overplayed her hand. Letters from the adoring continued for a while, both in east Texas and when Maria's father brought the family temporarily back to Georgia at the beginning of the 1850s. In time "candydates" dropped out. A distant cousin who clerked in Buncombe County, North Carolina, and who once addressed Maria as "my dear and affectionate lover" finally "grode werry." What the letters suggest as by the far likeliest fellow married someone else in the home area while Maria was in Texas. Relatives replaced suitors in Maria Louisa Smith's correspondence, and those relatives had ways of broaching sad realities. A decade after the original Texas move, the now twenty-eight-year-old woman received a letter from her cousin Eliza who told Maria that she had married a man with children and was, by that fact, already a grandmother. "But dont let that," she advised Maria, "skeer you from marring *even an old widower*."[19]

Even "*an old widower*" was a better shield against self than nothing, and an isolate and eccentric could attest to that fact. Rinaldo Parker of Vermont wandered in the West and the South a lonely, strange, and embittered man. By his own telling, he was "self-willed," and in moments that seem pathologically troubled he could intone a question characteristic of a much later time: "Oh Heaven, where & what am I!" Parker insisted that he had himself chosen the solitary existence which went on "silently & sullenly" and which had issued only in "tragedy." More sullenness than silence entered the same letter home when he suggested that someone else in the family, perhaps his sister, contemplated a life similar to his own. "You all must have outgrown my knowledge As I hear Rozilla talking about living in a state of celibacy." That sentence does not readily yield its meaning but the purpose is apparent. One "self-willed" person in the family was quite enough. Having tasted the "tragedy" of isolation himself, Rinaldo could all the more tellingly warn Rozilla against it.[20]

Inhabiting this bleak world alone had scant attractions, and Thomas Moore's lines on the last rose of summer were occasionally cited to make the point.[21] Those who suddenly found themselves in that condition set about changing it with deliberate speed. Before he was anathematized in the South as "Spoons," Ben Butler came to be known as "Widow" Butler in Massachusetts politics. He would, he let it be known, forswear the routine flummery about letting the office seek him. Butler openly acknowleged that he would seek

office, not as a shy maiden seeking a husband, but with the direct purposeful-
ness of a widow at the same task. If Ben Butler invoked the haste to escape
loneliness in explaining his haste to get office, it surely would have been understandable to a nation that had ample experience with both phenomena.

For calculated forthrightness, Brigham Nims, a forty-two-year-old farmer
of Cheshire County, New Hampshire, probably would have aroused Ben
Butler's admiration. He went about things with an almost blunt directness, but
he also prepared carefully, as can be shown by the three different drafts of an
important letter he sent to Susan Selina Gould. What is probably the first was
done in pencil, and it bore no date; the two penned versions were dated March
5 and June 28, 1853. The context suggests that the last came under the eyes of

Miss S. S. Gould:
   You will not consider it intrusion to receive these lines from one who is almost a
stranger. Your appearance and the limited acquaintance, with the representation of
friends, respecting you, has awakened the desire to have further acquaintance, should
you be disposed to continue it on your part.

All of this smacks of the tentativeness of overture, but the remainder of the letter speeds on, as might Ben Butler, to basic matters.

An interest has been awakened in my own mind for sometime and further acquaintance
is desired with the understanding, should both parties be suited, and it seem to be the
will of Providence to enter upon that relation in life, than which there is no other more
important, as regards this life certainly, and having great influence in forming character
for eternity; a relation where the parties shall share each others joys and sorrows in this
world of chance and tumult and which not only affects the parties for good or ill but has a
great influence upon the families with which they are connected and the community
where they dwell. . . .

Comparative analysis of this segment reveals a couple of slight changes. Most
importantly, Nims apparently deleted a later section of the March 5 version
wherein he had mentioned that Selina could expect the company of his mother
"as long as Mother shall live certainly." No reason, Nims might have mused,
to open the campaign in a defensive position.

Selina responded on July 15, noting that Brigham's letter came "quite unexpected to me," but she left no doubt that she would be happy to hear more in
the same vein, coyly employing the language of acquaintanceship while apparently leaving larger matters to time. Two months sufficed; exactly two
months from the date of her response, Selina and Brigham entered marriage.
Romance would have been better served had Brigham not kept a diary through
that same summer. The dozen miles between Nelson and South Stoddard separated the two. Selina's crucial letter of July 15 came to Brigham on July 23 by
the hand of his brother Rufus. That evening the day's developments went into

Brigham's diary as follows: "Mowed the Island &c[,] get in 2 loads & 2 loads of Rye[,] 40 stooks[,] Rufus & Wife come out tonight." Given Brigham's practice, they probably had arrived when he wrote this entry. And from this entry to the marriage seven weeks later, Selina merited only three diary allusions. On September 15, Brigham penned this matter-of-fact account: "Rainy[,] went to South Stoddard[,] brot Susan S[elina] Gould and Mariah Gould home with me[,] eve about 7 0 Clock was married to Susan S. Gould[,] Mr Townsend officiated & paid him $5.00[,] had about 48 persons and 11 children were present at the time &c[,] did not rain much after noon."[22]

In this item, as in most others like it, romantic abandon had almost no place. As is suggested later in this chapter, even the effusive poetry probably ought not to be seen in that light. Painstaking care went into the composition of love letters; if passion moved the pen, it did so after coming under rough-draft discipline. That drafts were prepared and retained probably meant that nothing short of one's best efforts would answer in such important matters, that both parties ought to have at hand the points of reference of what had gone before, and, of course, that these sensitive modes of expression had and would continue to have large sentimental value. As love letters began to touch upon marriage, another consideration entered. People such as Augusta Hallock and Brigham Nims knew well that the change and tumult of the world could work alterations in feelings and in personnel. For emotional, ethical, and legal reasons, a fair copy just might be worth having.

The Romantics, Morton Hunt wrote in *The Natural History of Love*, "delighted in being demonstratively sentimental, melancholic, tempestuous or tearful, according to the occasion."[23] Common folk at times slipped into all of these postures, but, by and large, they managed to keep at least one foot on the ground. To have done otherwise would have been self-abandon, an error against which they stood vigilant guard. An upstate New York girl who would later go to Georgia as a schoolteacher broached the subject in writing to the man she would marry. She mused for a moment over the benefits of a condition which she had never known before, the condition called *"being in love."* Then, almost fiercely, she set about making a distinction; she did not mean lovesick. "Such weakness of our mental faculties," she fumed; of "all the diseases of the mind that to me appears the most horrible."[24] A man who later gained notoriety in another arena provides an illustration. In a gossipy letter from New Lisbon, Ohio, in 1841, James Armstrong told of the visit to that community of two attractive young ladies. One of them, he continued, took with her "the *heart* of one of our young gentlemen, (Mr. C. L. Vallandigham.) he is a smart fellow, but he is too deeply in love—it makes a fool of him, I dislike to see *anyone* let his feelings which are the offspring of a *day* be so apparent to all—*they may last and they may not.*"[25]

Five years after heatedly making the distinction between *"being in love"* and lovesick, Amelia Akehurst married the man whom she had informed in that regard. Twelve days after the wedding, she could note in her diary that "Nothing yet has occurred to mar our happiness."[26] People entered marriage with few illusions. As a Georgian put it to a cousin who would soon move into that sometimes troubled state, "take kear[,] Jordans a hard rode to travel."[27] An Indiana woman who evidently had known marriage before noted her intention to stay at her Lafayette teaching job "untill I get married or die, yes, and I cares not which, for one is about as good as the other."[28] As always, sentiment was divided as to which was better, and a neighborhood debating society in Orange County, New York, even put the matter to formal consideration. One would like to know how the issue was settled, but unfortunately the farm laborer who kept the records failed to make the result clear. Whatever the outcome, it probably provided a livelier session than going over the well-trod ground of determining whether Washington was a greater man for saving America than Columbus was for discovering it.[29]

Whatever the general misgivings, people selected their own companions and then made the best of their choice. "Heare I bee," Levina Lilly happily wrote to granite worker Jacob Stevens, "and you may come and git me when you are a mind to."[30] Her parents, the young Vermont woman stated, had no objections, though they felt bad because they were too "poore" to be of much assistance to the couple. From the south shore of Lake Oneida, Charlotte Whipple sent word to the man who would marry her and would take her to the banks of the Columbia, reporting that her parents felt uneasiness because they had never met him. Charlotte's mother wondered whether he was a temperance man, how religious he was, and if he had property. She showed little concern that suitor Samuel was "poor," but she did wonder aloud if his "piety" might be "put on to suit the occasion." But Charlotte, by her own telling, was "perfectly willing to spend my days with you in the West," and, that being evident, her parents "do not wish to interfere with my choice." The Oregon country was a bit farther away than the Illinois for which Charlotte originally supposed she was destined. But, however long the road, she had chosen her companion. It would be Samuel and not the rich widower "(who came ten miles to see me but who *cannot* stay to tea)."[31]

At the end of the letter in which she announced "heare I bee," Levina Lilly signed "your lover . . . to my only lover." Without the modulation of the spoken language, perhaps such usages ought not to be dissected at all, but it is apparent that the word "lover" was readily applied to those in chaste relationship. During the course of the romance leading to their marriage, Lawrence Parker and Fanny Barber suffered long separations, especially when Lawrence went on clock-selling expeditions through the South. Early in September 1834, he summarized his account of their relationship by noting that "this matter between you and myself has gone to far to meane nothing." He closed the letter in this way: "I am with much respect your Sincere friend & Lover." A letter written two months later clarifies their relationship. True happiness can be found, Lawrence wrote in the characteristic fashion, only in the "sosiety of females." He very promptly qualified that statement by adding that Fanny alone possessed his affections. "And Fanny," the young man wrote, "rest satisfied that that love is directed by chastity, and I hope to retain the same conduct that gave that love its rise[;] be not flattered but pardon me for saying that I think I find that blessing in you."[32]

Both before and after marriage, the words "friend" and "lover" became nearly synonymous. In the writings of the New England literati, too, Perry Miller remarks, "love and friendship are interchangeable terms."[33] However, the "interchangeable terms" had vastly different implications for the sophisticated. In the ethereal "Transcendental search of meaning on the plane of 'Reason', the object of devotion may indifferently be of the same sex or of the other. . . ." Much as the simple people revered nonromantic friendship, no such merging could have occurred. Time and again, they specified priorities, always placing love of spouse at the pinnacle of earthly allegiances. Even more alien to their moods was the egocentric propensity in Transcendentalism of devoting, as Miller sardonically notes, "a dismaying portion of their energies to attesting the paradox that the more they loved each other, the more they could do without each other."[34]

As common sense so readily suggests, the common people gave no thought to the notion of the inviolate self. Indeed, the expression "better half" may represent no more than a handy foreshortening of "better half of self." When Albina Rich, a farm wife in Maine, referred to her absent husband as "the better half of myself,"[35] she did so without attenuation and without jocularity. Through marriage, the "friend" or "lover" became the better half of that which was inherently none too good, the self. Marriage did not obliterate the self, but it did mute its force by preempting its territory, or at least half its territory. The other use of the expression "better half" was to designate the soul as distinguished from the body, things spiritual as distinguished from things temporal. The "better half" stopped short of the self. After a visit with Selina midway in their short courtship, Brigham Nims took encouragement from her seeming willingness to "come live with me at this place, and be that better half which has been and is needed to make life move sweetly along."[36]

Brigham's experience with self had been none too inspiring. He had, he revealed to Selina, "a temper and a disposition" that were "not so easily governed," causing him to forswear thoughts of marriage while trying to improve. "But as I grow no better," he now mused, "there seems to be no alternative than a *gentler hand* to smooth the path of life." Brigham expressed his hope that Selina would become his "counsellor & friend," his "friend and companion," his "companion through life's toilsome journey."[37] The word "companion" was the fondest and most frequent term for spouse. Lonely Abner Goddard at New Diggings, Wisconsin, rhapsodized on the theme while his wife was in Pennsylvania bringing yet another Goddard into the world: "O 'tis

delightful to dwell upon this heaven born principle—love.—Love to God first.
Love to my chosen companion. Love to my children."[38] On the pilgrimage
through this lower world, it was necessary to have a chosen companion.
Regarding her absent husband, Albina Rich said: "I have chosen to share with
one all the joys and sorrows which this life is heir too"—"my *Companion*."[39]
Not everyone was fortunate enough to have made a wise choice. In 1855,
words of loving counsel came to twenty-eight-year-old Edward B. Drew from
his "very decriped" mother whose time, she felt, was "most run out." Putting
first things first, she stated her hope that Edward would be among the "useful
christains"—"how I wish that of you[;] if you had a good wife to help you along
in spiritual and temperal matters it would be fine." Matilda Drew then reinforced that hope about a companion with lines which she fairly accurately
appropriated from Thomas Campbell's "The Pleasures of Hope":

> 'The world was sad the garden was wild
> Man the hermit sighed till woman smiled'

With things "spiritual" and things "temperal" firmly in order of priority,
Mother Drew pressed on to the matter of choice, beginning with the notion that
"the wisest men are most apt to err" where wives are concerned. "Above all
things," she emphatically concluded, "never seek property with a wife. . . ."[40]
Given all the references to "speculations," this injunction may have been as
fully honored in the breaking as in the keeping. Be that as it may, few items of
marital advice were as frequently and as painstakingly imparted as those given
by Mother Drew.

In distressing succession, Amelia Akehurst recounted the deaths in her
family during the 1840s. Last in the long list was the mother who expired with
the entire family and a select group of friends circling the deathbed in the still-
dark hours of the morning. Attention soon shifted to the father, a man whose
"cup of sorrow" was now full. To be sure, he had lost mother, father, brothers,
and children, but all of that stood as "light affliction compared with the present
bereavement." Death had done its fullest; it had taken the "choice of his youth,
his bosom friend, his affectionate wife, the fond Mother of his children, the
chief charm of his home." James Akehurst, the tanner of Hartford, New York,
had, at least for the time being, no "bosom companion."[41]

The emphasis upon the notion of companion seems to have involved the
need for mutual spiritual aid and the inhibiting of the self, that ominous repository of worldly inclinations. It may provide a latter-day reflection of the
Puritan reordering of marriage priorities. Taking their inspiration from
Genesis 2:18 (just as H. N. Rhodes did when he found himself alone at India
Point outside Providence), the Puritans, as James T. Johnson has shown,
emphasized companionship over procreation as the fundamental rationale for
the marriage bond.[42] That bond, for the Puritans and for the common people in

pre-Civil War America, partook of the temporal realm, but it paralleled and foreshadowed things spiritual. On a late summer day in the 1850s, an aggrieved husband closed the diary which, until an abrupt end five months earlier, had been kept by the woman he now prayerfully addressed:

1856   Aug 26   Dear Wife
Your work of love is done. God has called you to a higher sphere of action. He has tried you as with fire. The dross has dropped to the dust. The gold he has taken.
May God so guide me by his spirit that we may *Together* praise him through the cycles of eternity. S. W. Furber [43]

As paraphrased by Johnson, the seventeenth-century views of Thomas Gataker and John Milton strongly resemble the utterances two centuries later regarding the "primacy of companionship." "A good marriage," Johnson has written in summary of Gataker's views, "is the highest of gifts for this life because it provides a companion for life. The gift of a good mate compares in this life to the gift of salvation for the next, and both gifts are sought in the same way: through prayer, humility, and exercise of religion." Human agency entered into such matters, and the likes of Brigham Nims took care to do their parts, but the result was the same for them as it had been for Milton: "the prevention of loneliness to the mind and soul of man."[44] The lesser sorts would leave it to a fugitive from society, Thoreau, to insist that "I never found the companion that was so companionable as solitude."[45]

Education as Society

Ten months before her husband lovingly addressed her at the end of her interrupted diary, Lucy Furber set down some disquieting thoughts about her child. While playing with another boy, he showed some clearly aggressive tendencies, and his mother now noted that "I am distressed to see so much evil & depravity in Peirce." Still, as she resignedly mused in that same entry, it was better to know what was in the boy, the better "that I may *combat* it." "O what a work," she sighed in language derivative of Proverbs, "to *train up a child*!"[46] The twenty-nine-year-old Maine woman did not live to "*train up*" Peirce Furber, but she had had ample time to make a standard judgment of human nature and a standard commentary on the challenge faced by those who would mold or "*combat*" it. The sunnier pedagogical sentiments of an Alcott or an Emerson evidently had very few echoes in society at large. The zeal of reform may have pushed some educators to think in terms of "the dignity of the human personality" and of the "infinite perfectibility of mankind," as Lawrence A. Cremin has contended.[47] Common people were of a different mind. When, for example, Lewis Campbell attended a neighborhood debate in Washington County, Iowa, the participants turned their energies to the proposition "Ignorance, the Source of all Evil." The young farmer gave no attention to argumentative details, but he did record that the issue was "decided in the negative by the audience."[48]

In fact, the common people seem to have spent no great amount of time reflecting on education, although they sought and respected it. The gospel of education probably went abroad in the land at least among a few, but for a common expression of it one has to rely on such items as a youthful and flippant essay written at Houlton, Maine, in 1843. Some of the young folk there evidently composed a script miscellany sheet for distribution within the group. One essay meant to treat education, and it read in part as follows: "Education is a good thing—It is very *nice* to have an education—It is better than gold or silver—But after all, to write on this subject ant so nice as I thought it was."[49] Most likely, this irresolute essayist meant to spoof well-worn platitudes, but the platitudes themselves seem surprisingly rare among the lower classes. Of course, few if any would have quarreled with the idea of education as a refinement of capacities, but little rapture appeared. Parental admonitions to diligence and discipline abounded, but what rewards these virtues would lead to were not emphasized. Education simply was said to give people the ability to read and write, and perhaps a bit more, particularly, as Westerners knew, if it could be channeled into surveying. A young Pennsylvania farmer, more utilitarian than most, expounded after a hot June day working in the woods: "What an immense benefit an education is to one; it is a help every way in shortening work often, and a thousand other ways."[50] Few, if any, ventured closer than that to panegyric.

Perhaps as a result of the economic upheaval of the 1930s, the common people often spoke of education as something "they can't take away from you." By that time, a sizable shift in values had taken place. A hundred years earlier, education was depicted as an "immense benefit" or, playfully, as better than silver or gold, but it was very much of this world and, therefore, its value was never unqualified. In that earlier era, something other was that which "they can't take away from you."

Exercising its large propensity to moralizing, the 1855 Webster's gave the following definition of education: "To give children a good *education* in manners, arts, and science, is important; to give them a religious *education* is indispensable. . . ." In an essay entitled "Spring," schoolgirl Fidelia Hunt elaborated on that theme: "as the farmer sows his seeds in the Spring so we should sow good seeds in the spring of our life that they may spring and flourish and bear fruit an hundred fold." Then she specified the good seeds: "good habits and principles, truth, knowledge and above all the better part which cannot be taken from us." Here again came the formula regarding the better part: spiritual over temporal, soul over body, society over self. It probably did not bother Fidelia's teacher that "knowledge" ranked distinctly behind that "better part which cannot be taken from us." That a doctrine militating against the supremacy of the school should appear in a laboriously tailored school essay probably indicates that schoolteachers themselves accepted that scale of values. However, Fidelia was not so thoughtless as to overlook the place of the teacher in that "better" work. He might prepare us only for this world rather than for the next, but in delimiting the self his role had significance for higher things. "To honour and obey our parents and teachers in all things" was, she stated, one of the ways "to get this better part."[51]

The educators who outlined "The Uses of Pedagogy" in Michael Katz's *The Irony of Early American School Reform* had particular interest in erecting "restraints" that would result in "the control of the passions." In that regard, their "key words" are very similar to the constructions and expressions of the people studied here. However, by Katz's telling, those Massachusetts educators emphasized the development of "an inner sense of right" as distinguished from the "dictates of society"; they urged reliance upon "internal standards" rather than upon the "opinions of others, of a venal and shallow society."[52] This latter persuasion varies substantially from the notions of plain folk. They had far less faith in "internal standards," and, by the same token, they had much less inclination to take a disparaging view of society. For them, education represented an extended version of "society," and thus yet another vehicle for inhibiting the self. Education so readily became an enlargement of the family circle in part because so many participated, not only as receivers but also as conveyors of fundamental knowledge. Except at the higher levels, what a later age would think of as professional educators were rare indeed. By common practice, people who had little attainment beyond bare literacy taught school in the winter. A Lebanon, Connecticut, farmer of "common education and experience" specified in 1837 "those regular Lebanon employments such as hoeing, milking, and making Cider in the Summer and fall, and teaching school in the Winter."[53]

And so an unusually high proportion of the passably literate had some occasion or another to use the following lines from James Thomson's *The Seasons*:

> Delightful task! to rear the tender thought,
> To teach the young idea how to shoot.

In a wide variety of serious and playful forms, this passage served as a poetic designation of pedagogy. Rather more so than some would suppose, that task involved putting a curb on the students' self and the will. If the "good seeds" were to "spring and flourish," if those "young ideas" were to "shoot," all available energies were to be directed to assuring that they sprang and shot to a predetermined, socially sanctioned mark. Always the emphasis rested on the preceptive agency of the teacher and the self-less and will-less obedience of the student. Georgiana Espy's effort to describe "A Good Scholar" opened with the conventional idea that "A good scholar is known by his obedience to the rules of the school and the directions of his teacher."[54] Georgiana expressed a secular analogue of the standard spiritual message pronounced by an older woman: "it is my prayer that I have no will of my one but be wroled up in the will of God."[55]

An item from the hand of another student (written "Ma the 9[,] 1837 to day our Chool Closes") incorporates two significant usages, the first coming in the doubly doleful poetic overture.

> Fair will my frind & teacher to
> I am sorry that you must bid us adiu
> I am sorry that we must take the parten hand
> I am sorry that we must be seperated from this Sotial band

However awkward and misspelled, this poem embodies a typically somber progression running from "frind & teacher" to "bid us adiu" to "the parten hand" and so on, to "seperated from this Sotial band." That "Sotial band" had restrained and comforted the self of "your Chollar S Ross." Now, scholar Ross noted in the straightforward prayerful prose that followed, "freedom fils my mind with sorrow."[56] The part-time teacher of Bath, Maine, who received this end-of-term salutation may have wondered about the sad effect the thought of freedom had upon S. Ross in early May. Still, his "Chollar" had hit upon a standard sentiment. "Sotial bands," however construed, protected one from self. Freedom, in the personal sense, aroused no outburst of fond contemplation.

Of course, teaching those "young ideas how to shoot" was seldom easy, as Edward Eggleston's *The Hoosier School-Master* so well suggests in fictional form. The nature of the nineteenth-century schoolhouse has received much scholarly attention, but one illustration indicates that its social control purpose was both understandable and not always realized. A young newcomer from Maine described an interesting day at his Missouri school in this way:

A big fellow spoke saucily to me. As he had been a bad boy I undertook to flay him[;] he drew back and struck at me[.] I grappled him and a *tall* scuffle commenced. The boys parted us. I got another hickory and marched of to the attack once more[.] [H]e put his hand in his pocket for a knife. I took up a stool and told him to go on. The result was I beat him like *hell*.[57]

An exhausted John B. Orton stated regarding his Niagara County, New York scholars: ". . . it is hard to induce them to improve their time."[58] Fifty years later, Edward Bellamy referred to " 'improve the time' " as an "old-fashioned prayer-meeting phrase," but it was not at all confined to the religious setting.[59] Orton, whose health was inadequate for the physical demands of this especially bad school, spoke of improving "time" or of improving an "opportunity." It had not yet occurred to people such as him to improve the self. Generally, common folk of the pre-Civil War era did not employ the language of self-improvement. Even the tedious list of self compounds in the 1855 Webster's failed to include self-improvement. "No brief account," Merle Curti remarks in his assessment of that period, "can convey any adequate impression of the hold of the cult of self-improvement."[60] One ought not to quarrel with that assertion, except to note that the central mode of expression is that of an Emerson and of a later age. Standard usage of the time centered upon improving something other—time or opportunity. As a Yankee working in the South sighed on his twenty-fifth birthday, "O that time were improved to the best possible purpose."[61]

Other Modes of Enhancing Society

Two days out of Westport in early May 1850, the wagon train in which Elias Daggy of Indiana traveled suffered the vexation of begging Kaw Indians, and at the end of the day camped on a hill near the grave of "S. Hough I.O.O.F."[62] Since de Tocqueville's pronouncements, the tendency of the American people to form associations has been probed unceasingly. Those associations which so impressed de Tocqueville and the others represented further extensions of society, further hedges against the self. According to Daniel Boorstin, from the outset "*communities* existed here before there were governments. . . ."[63] Perhaps an extension of this notion is in order: where "society" lagged "associations" began.

The marker over the remains of S. Hough showed that he died with one of the bands of society—the Odd Fellows—still holding him. Ralph Henry Gabriel's use of the lonely death of mountain man Bill Williams as an impressionistic point of departure for a discussion of American individualism may be far more striking than accurate.[64] From such an existence, and especially from such a death, ordinary Americans would have turned with shock and horror. Whatever Bill Williams meant, fraternal orders such as the IOOF probably owed much of their vitality to the instinctive need to combat the forces eroding the social fabric of a people turned loose upon a continent. As was suggested earlier, one of the most fearsome prospects of the westward movement was that of dying unattended. Carpenter George Magoon, stranded at San Juan del Sur, Nicaragua, while on his way to California in 1852, witnessed an almost total absence of the comforts of society he had known in Massachusetts and in Muscatine, Iowa. He rushed to the judgment that the place was "one of the most god forsaken towns" in the world, one where "every vices that man can do" abounded. But, however bad the setting, something of society remained. When a brother Odd Fellow died, Magoon and others saw him to eternity by "the rights and ceremonies of the Order."[65]

Where the restraints and cushions of natural society weakened or ended, institutional surrogates began. The Sons of Temperance, a variant of which de Tocqueville first took to be a joke, served more than the ostensible reform purpose. It had the appurtenances of society. It had a slight aura of the arcane and the mysterious, though not enough to arouse vestiges of the anti-Masonic sentiment. "I think it an excellent society," a young man in Maine wrote, "it has signs & Pass Words &c.,—no initiation fee."[66] A Pennsylvania woman writing to her sister in Missouri reasserted her opposition to secret societies, but then, after describing the lodge rooms in Milton, she had to admit that the Sons of Temperance "have the preference."[67] Temperance "houses" served as homes away from home for those of like mind, and many of the common people traveled from one such establishment to the next. The Sons of Temperance, as did the Odd Fellows, also had funerary functions. The Sons offered many advantages. An Indiana Quaker youth noted, after going to a nearby town to witness the Sons in parade, that he also ate "some of their cake and pie and came home very well satisfied with my trip."[68] Or, as a new arrival in San Francisco remarked candidly to his mother, "my connection with the I.O.O.F. is going to be an advantage to me."[69] He did not specify the advantage, but one takes it to have been in the area of the main chance. There were other benefits, and unlike Bill Williams, the simple American wished neither to live alone nor to die alone. Associations provided another shield against self and solitude.

In the remoteness at Fort Vancouver on the Columbia, solitude could be nearly overpowering, and that condition probably gave rise to another form of association and society. In October 1850, a civilian carpenter who had arrived there shortly before recorded the formation of a "Macanics Liceum" or "debating clubb."[70] What Benjamin Dore had learned in Maine he brought with him to the farthest frontier. The countless debating groups throughout the nation, even unto Fort Vancouver, embodied and sustained "society" in yet another way. Evidently, debates, lectures, performances, sermons, and the like were very attractive to folk of that period.

The end-of-term school "exhibitions" were similar to debating societies, and Mark Twain's description of one in *Tom Sawyer* has a good deal of accuracy. The progression was routine: the very small boy doing "You'd scarce expect one of my age to speak in public on the stage"; his female counterpart lisping "Mary had a little lamb"; Tom himself soaring into "the unquenchable and indestructible 'Give me liberty or give me death' speech"; then the always serviceable "The boy stood on the burning deck"; then reading exercises and "spelling-fights"; and then young ladies reading their own compositions. Mark Twain offered some general commentary on the culture of the period in describing a couple of these compositions. A "slim, melancholy girl, whose face had the 'interesting' paleness that comes of pills and indigestion" read a sad poem on separation. That performance gave way to a lugubrious exercise that "wound up with a sermon so destructive of all hope to non-Presbyterians that it took the first prize" (Chapter 21). Earlier in the exhibition, Tom had made his unsuccessful attempt to master the words of Patrick

Henry with "fine fury and frantic gesticulation," that apparently being his translation of the discipline called elocution. However rendered, the contrived delivery prohibited naturalness. At about the time that Sam Clemens suffered what he described in *Tom Sawyer*, Herman Melville recorded an equally sour reflection on "that great American bulwark and bore—elocution," a training whereby "the sons of the most indigent day-laborers were wont to drawl out the fiery revolutionary rhetoric of Patrick Henry. . . ."[71]

As the exhibition neared, pressure mounted, and Tom's teacher became a tyrant. But that teacher, his many counterparts, and their numberless students bore sizable social pressures. The diary of John Savage, who taught during the winter months in southeast Iowa, has provided more sustenance for mice than for historians, and so, for the absence of corners, one has to rely somewhat upon inference. But there is no doubt as to the purport of the entry of March 2, 1860, the last day of Savage's school term: "I have not ——— for the last 2 nights thinking of ———." Happily, the next entry shows that his exhibition was "very good." Eli Beard, a fellow teacher nearby, had not fared as well at the end of his school a week earlier. Beard started his exhibition at 10:00 A.M. and continued it until dark. The plan called for a full evening session as well, "but there were several rowdies out from near Salem who were so disorderly" that Beard gave up and closed early.[72] Like revivals, exhibitions drew all kinds of participants.

Like the school exhibitions, debates were sometimes not completed because of disorder from the audience, especially when the issues involved were controversial. Andrew Jackson Sterrett wrote to his brother about the effort of a local group near Erie, Pennsylvania, to resolve the matter of woman suffrage. After noting that the meeting place was packed, the sardonic printer turned small-time land speculator concluded: "Spoke once around amidst great disorder & then broke up in a row without decision."[73] In cases where debating failed to spark sufficient interest, surrogates such as singing schools were brought in as replacements. When his son moved to Canton, Mississippi, farmer Joseph Workman of Ohio was concerned about "whether debating societies are in fashion or not" in that location. Later in the same letter, he grumbled that a singing school had been formed in his vicinity some months earlier, and "wee then had nothing but faw, sol, law, night & morning all winter" instead of more rewarding endeavors such as debates.[74]

Some descriptive illustrations of undertakings in debate may be allowable. On December 23, 1840, the "Alder creek Paulemic" of Bainbridge Township, Dubois County, Indiana, held its first meeting. The minutes show that this interestingly styled association came into being to further "ealocution and usful knowlededge." The first meeting addressed itself to the "fowling query": "which is the most butiful to the eye Art for the one part or nature for the other." The "Alder creek Paulemic" did not last long, perhaps because too much time went to levying fines—candles or sheets of paper—upon "criminals for mischief making and laughing." The "Alder creek Paulemic" was a very youthful organization, and the four members whom I located in census records had, at the time the debating society started, reached ages thirteen, thirteen, fourteen, and nineteen, thus possibly accounting for mischief making and demise of the organization.[75]

The Mount Hope Debating Society of Orange County, New York, was founded in December 1856 "in order to improve the understanding, and cultivate the social faculties of the mind, with which we are endowed by the Creator." Mostly mature men joined this effort to "cultivate the social faculties of the mind"; according to census records, their ages ranged from nineteen to sixty-three. Before adjourning sine die in April 1857, this group held over two dozen debates. Here, as at Alder Creek and elsewhere, they argued the comparative merits of Columbus and Washington, and, of course, the question of nature versus art. The men at Mount Hope also focused on more practical matters. For example, the opening session considered this question: "Has the New York & Erie Rail Road been a general benefit to Orange County?"

During 1856–1857, issues of the day had some place on the Mount Hope society's agenda. The society deemed slavery unjustified in all cases, but it upheld the Fugitive Slave Law as well as capital punishment and tax-supported education. One matter that occupied the men of Mount Hope on January 26, 1857 was "Does wealth exert more influence than knowledge?" Some of those scheduled to speak in the negative could not attend, and, perhaps for that reason, the presiding officer for the week "delivered himself" of a speech to the negative. That necessitated a suspension of the rules and the removal of President Alex Borland from the arbiter's position. In lieu of his judgment, the audience voted on the performance, giving the nod to the negative. Alex Borland, who according to the 1860 census was then a forty-four-year-old day laborer with four hundred dollars in personal property and no real estate, helped carry the day for knowledge. Two weeks later, a more critical question was considered: "Are Debating Societies beneficial?" That debate was decided in the negative. The minutes kept by a twenty-one-year-old farm laborer and teacher suggest that parliamentary rules were suspended, allowing people to speak from the floor.

Most notably, Reverend Littell made some "very pertinent remarks."[76] The record does not show what this thirty-year-old Methodist minister said, but he may well have spoken about those "social faculties of the mind, with which we are endowed by the Creator." The desirability of social bonds was an attractive theme to folk such as those at Mount Hope, and a man in Littell's position may have offered some reminders. Orange County bore little resemblance to Fort Vancouver, but the mobility of the American order made existence solitary and transient. Reverend Littell could have spoken along lines suggested by a before-and-after census check—1850 and 1860—for those participating in the debating society in 1856–1857. A fairly thorough search of those censuses for Mount Hope township for twenty-two names that appeared fully and distinctly in the minutes yielded less than half of those sought, and in terms of definite identification, substantially less than half. Where "society" was that tenuous, all reputable reflections of it deserved nurturing, even in the face of overly effective devil's advocacy.

Such a person as Reverend Littell might have remarked on the need of disciplining the mind, of curbing the rash spontaneity that Emerson sometimes seemed to encourage. Improvement of the mind entailed the inhibiting of one's own sentiments. Hypocrisy, about which the Romantics would rail so relentlessly, had not yet assumed a frightening mien to lesser sorts. Writing from a Wisconsin village, a young man informed his mother in Massachusetts that a "lyceum" had been formed; the first issue before it centered on the sale of alcoholic "lickors." He had been assigned to the positive side, but, his "principles" notwithstanding, he would "try and make a bold defense for the whiskey seller."[77] And if a debating society blundered into considering the value of its own existence, it ought not to commit the folly of being hoist by its own petard. Associations strengthened "society" and confirmed the discipline necessary to it.

Social Control of Pen and Mind

At the end of a poem entitled "The Passions," Henry Atwater of Connecticut wrote "Selected Sept 11, 1837," thus indicating that it was not his own creation. The twenty-two-year-old stone mason who would later keep a boarding house here struck upon a standard statement of the persuasions of his time.

> The passions are a numerous crowd
> Imperious positive and loud
> Curb those licentious sons of strife
> Hence chiefly use the storms of life
> If they grow mutinous and rave
> They are the master, thou their slave[78]

Perhaps order had ceased to be heaven's first law for this age which, as someone observed, was everything that Pope's was not. But standard treatments of the period have exaggerated the drift away from Pope and his precept. Various analyses emphasize that it was an emotional, frenetic, and disorderly society. Carl Russell Fish's formative work, *The Rise of the Common Man*, describes a "riotous generation," one that was "so much more inclined to believe and feel than to think."[79] A more extreme assessment appears in Fred Lewis Pattee's *The Feminine Fifties* where we encounter "emotionalism in the saddle," indeed an "emotional explosion." "No era was it for thinking, all was feeling."[80] But Fish does qualify his analysis: "Some of the decorum of colonial life remained on the surface" of that "riotous generation." And when he refers to "the power of ratiocination," Fish adds an ironically understated qualifier—"of which this generation was not devoid."[81]

The "decorum" of the age, if not its "power of ratiocination," deserves more attention than it has gotten thus far. "Society," whether in the fundamental dimensions of spouse, family and friends, or in the ramifications of education, association, debate or whatever, imposed regularity. By the same token, the timeless and ubiquitous capacity to emote notwithstanding, expression came under an ordering and disciplining too.

Whether or not America at large had any appreciation of true poetry, it most certainly had a lively penchant for rhyming and versifying. Farmers, housewives, teachers, students, flatboatment, Forty-niners—all turned an occasional hand to poetry, often, of course, with distressing results. What this poetic epidemic meant does not admit of ready answer. In part it was a matter of fashion involving such things as the Byron cult and the tedious aping of other bards of the Romantic era. But perhaps as well, if only in some half-conscious way, these lesser sorts sought simply to create. The occasional use of pertinent lines from Gray's "Elegy" attest to that.

Whether they wrote original poems or cribbed the lines of others, the people turned to poetry to best express their feelings and attitudes. In March 1846, Indiana flatboatman Josiah Campbell composed (or perhaps appropriated) some "Lines to Miss C." Though the expressions of love have been considered earlier in this chapter, this item has sufficient elevation to be bearable and perhaps rather good, as may be attested by the fact that "Miss C" married the young man who subscribed his initials to it.

> Ive mused on thee oh lovely one
> At evenings gentle hour
> Till on my thoughts thy loveliness
> Has left its spell of power
> Thine is a brow and thine an eye
> The wildest heart to tame
> For lightning like each glance of thine
> Can thrill through soul and frame.[82]

Josiah wrote well and effectively, but his effort lacks the pervasive melancholy and the drift to otherworldliness which were so characteristic of the poetry of his time. A six-stanza poem addressed "To My Dear Charlotte" by her husband conveys those attributes nicely, and it incorporates the theme of wife as salvation. At the beginning of the poem, the newly married man used conventional means of expressing that sentiment "Which visiteth my heart when at thy side," a sentiment that would endure until that heart "Takes up its death march to the spirit shore." At that key juncture, the poem shifts to ultimates: "Then as thy lips shall kiss me to my slumber / As on lifes verge I say the long good night. . . ." The final quatrain reads as follows:

> Yet in that distant bourne where broken hearted
> Thou shalt deem haply that my soul hath rest
> Can I but meet thee when life hath departed
> My sin sick spirit shall be doubly blest.[83]

For this Bath, New York, couple separation was death. Separation, whether caused by distance or by eternity, was a constant theme in the poetry of that period. Before leaving Alleghany City for the Far West in 1853, young Agnes Stewart received a diary in which she could record the trip. In the front of that book, she inscribed words of heartbreak "To Martha."

> Thou wert my first and only friend, the heart's best treasure thou;
> Yet in the shades of trouble sleep, my mind can see you now,

"Oh Martha, my heart yearns for you," she wrote in an entry some ten days out of Saint Joseph, but only in the mind's eye would Martha Hay ever again appear to Agnes Stewart. As did others, the two little girls chose a star on which to reflect, and only a handful of letters and the gentler communions by that star eased the hurtful chasm between Pennsylvania and Oregon.[84]

> He left his own beloved home
>   Ohio's pleasant shores
> Far in the western wiles to roam
>   Where Mississippi roars

These sorrowful lines were "Composed by a young Friend at Mountpleasant School on reading the letter that Joseph Hoag sent to Ephraim Beeson's parents concerning his death," thereby attesting to the fact that the doleful virtuosity Mark Twain presented in a fictional Emmeline Grangerford had real-life counterparts. In the fall of 1843, "Chills and Fever" overtook young Ephraim in Iowa Territory; his death outside the family circle elicited some notoriously standard imagery.

> But if no parents near him stand
>   To raise the drooping head
> If no kind sister lend a hand
>   To smooth the sufferers bed
>
> Oh then let pitty more and more
>   Tears of affection shed

For him who on the strangers shore
Now sleeps among the dead[85]

Love, separation, and death evoked the more intense creative efforts, but playful themes were also employed. Having written an especially long entry during the voyage to the gold region, a young clerk chided himself for the effort in this way: "I can now say with the poet

'My task is done, my tale is wrote
Ive sketched from life as we do float
Upon the ocean from day to day
On our passage to California—
                                          Pope'[86]

Even postmen occasionally benefitted from the poetic urge of that time. An 1856 letter made its way from Lafayette to Columbus, Indiana, bearing this address:

To Columbus go,
In Bartholomew Co.
To Mrs Mary J. Bass,
I have come at last;
And without any doubt;
You may please take me out.
Care T. Bass   State   Indiana[87]

A New York to Michigan letter gave even more intricate iambic directions, half of which read as follows;

If you please, Mr. Postmaster, to send me straight through,
To Mr. James Harris of Kalamazoo (Michigan)
And in Galesburgh post office, please let me stay
Till the said Mr. Harris shall take me away.[88]

And then there was Nathan Parkhill of Weybridge, Vermont. Ordinarily, this farmer personified the laconic, but poetry (or doggerel) unlimbered him. It would arouse suspicion to suggest that Calliope or Euterpe murmured promptings to this unwordy man; but something occasionally moved him.

Amelia P. has left
She's left us here alone
How sad to be bereft
Of such a lovely one

Things other than the departure of Amelia P. intruded upon the succession of prosaic one-liners ending in letter designations of weather conditions. The August 11, 1857, entry reads in this sprightly fashion:

> We cut an acre and a half
> Of wheat this very day
> Now Sir! my friend you need not laugh
> At what I'm going to say
> We had bad luck and no mistake
> As you will shortly see
> For Niels cradle Bill did break
> And father cut his knee

August 11 seems to have been a day for bad luck at the Parkhill farm. On August 11 in the previous year, a storm had occurred, and an epical treatment was rendered.

> This storm of damage did a sight
> I can't begin to tell
> Of oats and wheat that was full ripe
> The best half of it did shell
>
> The corn leaves are all split in two
> The tasels are broke off
> The pumpkins vines are hurt a few
> Perhaps I've wrote enough[89]

Poetic content has appeared throughout this study, illustrating some persuasion or another. Poetic form has seemed worthy of some modest consideration in and of itself. Whatever else the resort to that form meant, it involved a desire to order and to discipline the language; it involved a parallel or yet another extension of the "social" inclination to order and discipline the self. Expression heedless of rules and forms may have come from the humble for lack of knowledge; it seems not to have come from them for lack of concern. Even the physical form of writing had significance, so much so that an Alabama schoolboy could put it in this grandiloquent way: "American Penmanship Commands Mankind."[90] Ordinarily, language command was imposed not upon mankind but upon self. As Richard Rollins has shown, Noah Webster had "social control" purposes in the definitions he worked, and unelevated Americans would not have taken offense at the effort to make them "submit their hearts and minds to an authoritarian God and mold themselves in the image of Quiet Christians."[91]

The popular poetry of that era was full of bathos, but at least structure was imposed upon that sentimentality. Byronic abandon had almost no place in the values of these folk who were only passably literate. While discussing the popular literature of that era, E. Douglas Branch has noted the prolific output of some writers and the seeming haste and carelessness with which they wrote: "Poets blossomed as lushly as the wild flowers they celebrated" in that "age of effervescent, unlabored expression."[92] The poetry written or transcribed by the people of this study would lead to a quite different conclusion, however. "O God she cried in accents wild"—but, whatever the demands of melodrama, she maintained the couplet: "If I must perish save my child!"[93] An upstate New York farmer, Henry W. Dean, pleaded, almost incoherently, with his wife to finish her search for medical relief of some unspecified ill and return to the Lebanon Center farm. "Helen I am nearly distracted," he wrote; a visual suggestion of that state came in the much emphasized, "Oh! *Helen Helen*." In a postscript, the twenty-four-year-old Dean managed a word about form before again lapsing into anguish: "Helen[,] will Helen try for Henry to spell some of her words different?" Even when "nearly insane," the young farmer would not accept "here for hear."[94]

Concern for order and propriety tugged at Henry Dean, and he responded. And a South Carolina woman entered the standard sentiment in metered salute to "Rural Felicity."

> With reason we taste of such heart-stirring pleasure,
> With reason we drink of the full flowing bowl;
> Are jocund and gay, but all within measure,
> For fatal excess will enslave the free soul.[95]

The expansive trappings of the Romantic mood occasionally came into the popular culture, but the ideal yet sought to keep "all within measure." Thus suspicious scrutiny was often directed to fiction and the springs of fantasy which fed it. Thus Francis W. Squires, a farmer of Oswego County, New York, attended a debate in January 1855 on whether "fictitious reading is more deleterious to society than dancing."[96] Here the matter was determined in the affirmative, and, in some form or another, the question seems to have come rather often to formal and informal consideration. The uneasiness about reading fiction came, it seems to me, not from a concern over sin, as Henry James once contended,[97] but rather from a concern over the breakdown of disciplined thinking. Reason and accurate perception of reality were at stake, and therefore society itself was threatened. In restraining the imagination, vestigial Puritanism found an ally in Scottish common sense philosophy. "Upholders of the social structure," one scholar has concluded, accused the imagination of "subversion."[98] And those "upholders of the social structure" had the assistance, by and large, of those in the lesser orders.

In the much discussed Chapter 35 of *Moby-Dick*, Melville warned against the"opium like listlessness of vacant unconscious reverie" indulged in by "romantic, melancholy, and absent-minded young men, disgusted with the carking cares of the earth. . . ." Such young men would sight no whales while assigned to "The Mast-Head." Had simple folk made their way through the Melvillean complexity, they would have recognized the nemesis called "castle-building." Few things so impeded positive accomplishment, spiritual or temporal, and so deluded man into error.

A good illustration of the dangers of the imagination appears in letters written by Ephraim Thompson from the gold reaches to his mother in Daviess County, Indiana. However vexing and disappointing the California venture had proved, he said, it at least put an end to "building Castles in the air." At the outset when imagination had ruled, all had seemed "a golden dream," one "where a feller dont wak up untill he finds himself out of money and digging in mud and watter to make enough to buy Grb."[99] Most viewed the imagination as a pleasure-giving instrument one should avoid. "It is pleasant," Jennie Ake-hurst wrote to her fiance while teaching in Georgia, "to forget *uninteresting* reality and on the wings of fancy to visit a world of ones own creation; yes it is *pleasant* but not profitable. . . ." The man she would marry, Jennie stated, was sufficiently *"strong-minded"* to avoid the indulgence of such a "weakness."[100] "Talulah's Dream," a school composition written by Mary Copp of Savannah, portrayed daydreaming as far worse, indeed as "the most destructive of all habits." Here the dramatic warning came in involuted form. Sitting by a brook, Talulah transformed it by reverie into a silver-hued lake dotted with resplendent vessels and lined by great trees bearing golden fruit. While seated on the shore of that apparitional lake, Talulah saw a female form of "surpassing loveliness" approaching her. " 'You find yourself here in my abode,' " the spectral beauty remarked gently. Your fantasying, she continued, is very pleasant, " 'but alas! so fatal.' "[101] One might wake up digging in mud and water for the day's grub. Or as mariner Melville admonished the "sunken-eyed young Platonist" who hovers over "Descartian vortices" while at the masthead on lookout for whales, "perhaps at mid-day, in the fairest weather, with one half-throttle shriek you drop through that transparent air into the summer sea, no more to rise forever."

A previously cited poem "To My Dear Charlotte" opens with what at first seems a puzzling juxtaposition:

> There may be romance in that gentle feeling
> Which visiteth my heart when at thy side
> I feel a soft hand through mine gently stealing
> Yet there is something real in a bride

In the concluding line which is so pedestrian compared to the preceding three lines, Charlotte's husband simply wished to get at reality. He seemed to suggest that the mind, even in the genuine and moving language of love, must show the discipline necessary to appreciate reality, even unto the "sin sick spirit" on its way to the grave, as Charlotte's husband wrote elsewhere in that poem. That involved a normative consideration, the obligation owed to reality. But it also involved a descriptive consideration, the demands imposed by reality. After a year's stay in her native New England, Elizabeth Smith rejoined her husband in Illinois. Describing their joyous reunion, she noted that some people traveling with her "said they would like to see our meeting, but I assured them there was very little *romance in real life*."[102] Or as Jennie Akehurst wrote, "Fancy and romance cannot linger in such dull light, surrounded with so much common reality. . . ." Such people studiously sought to employ the mind as the "reflector of external objects," not as "a radiant projector which makes a contribution to the objects it perceives." The mind acted as "mirror" not as "lamp."[103]

Humor, Constance Rourke observed, is a "matter of fantasy,"[104] and because of their wariness of fantasy and the imagination, the comon people studied here are not a good source of the humorous. "Levity" aroused concern not only for spiritual but also for mental considerations, as is the case in Isaac Watts' warning in the opening rules for working *The Improvement of the Mind*. F. O. Matthiessen's contention that, in the fun-loving Sut Lovingood, George Washington Harris brought us "closer than any other writer to the idigenous and undiluted resources of the American language, to the tastes of the common man himself" appears earlier in this study. In the same work, Matthiessen cited Whitman's strongly negative reaction to Harris. Whitman's Civil War experience had impressed him with the more sober attributes of the " 'common soldier' "—his " 'decorum,' " " 'good manners,' " and even " 'good, real grammer.' "[105] Whitman came closer to the truth than Matthiessen did with his often-quoted comment on the creator of Sut Lovingood. In order to work his hilarity, Sut foreswore almost all inhibitions, whether of action or of language. He cavorted through the world with spontaneity and, as Edmund Wilson particularly has noted, with downright malevolence.[106] Whether Sut had flesh-and-blood counterparts is beyond the province of this study, but that Sut resembled the spirit, let alone the ideal of common men, as they expressed such in their writings, belongs in the airier realms of the bizarre.

The humorous propensity had little place in humble writings. The general attitude concerning order and restraint helps account for that, as do considerations regarding time and space. " 'Why is a fashionable dressed Lady now a-days like a Flour Barrel?' " Because, San Francisco bartender James Jones wrote to his mother in Baltimore, " 'you are obliged to lift the Hoops before you can put the head in.' "[107] That one had been uttered on the stage of Maguire's Opera House, much to the harm of that establishment and to the harm of Christy's Minstrels. One's fund of the witty gets pitifully little nourishment from scanning the writings of the unelevated—a handful of quips such as this and scattered instances of unwitting drollery.

In *The Comic Tradition in America*, Kenneth S. Lynn avoids unduly stressing "the popular origins" of our humor. "On the contrary," he states, "I would prefer to play down this aspect of our comic tradition" in order to compensate for what he considers the overemphasis others have given. Here he takes exception to the notion that Harris, Mark Twain, and others "were no more self-conscious than the oral tradition on which they drew. . . ."[108] They did more than convey, reflect, and report; they fabricated and created.

This seems a tenable position for the fact that what humor surfaces in the writings studied here has an upward orientation. In part, it came from those above the common people, as in the case of that off-color story told at Maguire's Opera House. Andrew Jackson Sterrett operated within the ranks of the humble, but he had the talent and training that gave him at least a part-time ability to contrive and affect. Sterrett learned the printing trade in the same Erie, Pennsylvania shop where Horace Greeley had once worked. He drifted west into small-time land speculation, but his training with the language probably fitted him to work some identifiable humor. He had an earthy unrestraint that was rare, and by it he could inform a brother of a party where "Polka, Poker, Euchre and Stinkfinger occupied the time I am told." When he returned to the Erie area in the fall of 1859, he found himself in the midst of a protracted meeting. His waggish vexation came in almost literary terms:

I hope the Lord doesn't get as tired of their long-winded pharisaical prayers as I do. They go up garret & into the clothes-presses for *secret* prayers; and then pray so that they might be heard up at John Kreider's; tell the Lord all the news, how kind & good & gracious & merciful He is; instruct Him in regard to His duty toward their ungodly friends & neighbors, & how He ought either to convert them or cut them off! Oh, it's almost intolerable! Bob proposes to put up a sign: 'Small-pox and Horse-distemper here!'[109]

In turn, the rare instances of dialect humor and of tall talk or tall story generally give clear evidence of posturing. At Monticello, Maine, for example, someone wrote a school composition containing contrived dialect. This episode at "Mount-a-cellar" involved the narrator's riding to a party. When nearly there, the fictive party-goer "heerd the tarnalist squeakin that ever was, an I thot they had got me over just to help scrape a hog, but twant."[110] This same collection contains letters replete with sad evidences of subliteracy. But this item, by whosever hand, bore the unmistakable marks of affectation. In their own way, these were efforts to be literary, as was the one use—a contrived use—of "absquatulate" that came to my attention.[111] Having noticed one instance of that word in *Pierre* (Book XXIII, Part 4), it might behoove me to conclude that Melville's characters were as likely to employ it as were ordinary folk.

In the popular writings, gross imagery and abandoned metaphor are largely absent. A South Carolinian wished a Mexican War friend a speedy return to the Forks where he could "mash some of those Girls as flat as a disinterry tird with a saw log roled over them."[112] This example may represent the "indigenous and undiluted resources" of the language, but such illustrations are most rare. The warnings against vulgarity, profanity, and obscenity (and these by men and women who were little given to prudery) may have been more effective than the seekers of the robust and the Rabelaisian have led us to believe. The view of a Tennessean was the generally accepted one: "nothing puts a man down so quick with me" as the use of vulgarities. If those given to such practice knew how others reacted, they would forthwith "lay down this badge of 'Niggerism.' "[113]

People at the South apparently guarded rigorously against the indecorous form of the word Negro; but this young man wrote in exasperation. And he recorded a sentiment that appears elsewhere—the gross and the fantastic in expression stemmed from the influence of the blacks. At Mills Point, Kentucky, in 1848, an unsavory rumor circulated regarding John B. Clark and a certain widow. "The Desisision of the Friends of J. B. Clark on a Report" contained the quasi-official findings of six men, including a village merchant and a blacksmith. They found a particular man responsible for the story, "not that any of us believe that he intended either of them an injury but that he inadvertently used the Language undoughtedly which he learned from Negroes &c &c."[114] With less literacy but with at least a fugitive sense of propriety, D. A. Cary of White Plains, Alabama, wrote apologetically to friends whose welcome he had burdened: "you all got tyrd of me a gone on With mey fre nigar shines."[115] That southern tactic had a northern counterpart. There, responsibility for the boisterous and the abandoned went to the Irish. As a Pennsylvania mechanic remarked of Irish immigrants with whom he rode a Mississippi riverboat, "all is noise and agitation, tumult and disorder; nothing of composure and gravity, but the very reverse."[116]

Composure and gravity have not occurred to many as the essence or even the ideal of pre-Civil War America; many scholars have held almost the opposite. All the same, it might be well to bear in mind that this was not the land of Brobdingnag. Although people probably enjoyed the half-horse-half-alligator talk and antics, they did not mistake them for reality. Such play partook of caricature and grotesquerie which plain people sought to avoid, much as Whitman contended. If the speech of common men in any way resembled those outbursts, they assuredly almost never wrote that way. Perhaps they were too slow and unimaginative to do so; the more likely reason is that they were too self-disciplined and restrained. In general, linguistic abandon and acrobatics came from the borderland between fact and fiction—the Mississippi of Mark Twain, the Rocky Mountains of Joe Meek and Black Harris, the New England of Birdofreedum Sawin or the Tennessee of Davy Crockett and Sut Lovingood. As Whitman's remarks suggested, the common man, except in moments of purposive diversion, would have avoided the verbal excesses coming

from those fugitive locales for their unmannerly, undecorous, and ungram-
matical qualities. Bernard DeVoto's warning about *The Literary Fallacy*
ought to be heeded, even though he did not always do so himself.[117]

Finally, insofar as Americans occasionally enjoyed tall-talk in speaking or
writing, it appealed to them on the basis that it, like poetry, was a discipline.
Certainly, it involved a deceptive virtuosity, and to some later scholars, it
seemed quite instinctive and unrestrained. Actually, however, it, too, was contrived and had a well-defined structure. Are we seriously to imagine that
rough-and-tumble, untutored raftsmen of the Mississippi could launch effort-
lessly into a sustained flow of earth-defying and heavens-stretching rhetoric of
the sort that Mark Twain ascribed to them as they prepared for bare-knuckle
action? The man who identified himself as " 'Sudden Death and General
Desolation' " warned that " 'I'm about to turn myself loose!' "[118] But neither
he nor the "Pet Child of Calamity" turned himself loose; they employed images which, however fantastic, breathe the spirit of the artistic. Even in the
boisterous fiction, there was no stumbling and muttering unintelligibility.
According to Daniel Boorstin, Americans sought and found "A New Uni-
formity" of language. That provided a means of skirting verbal license and
linguistic chaos. And here Boorstin employs James Fenimore Cooper's assessment in *Notions of the Americans*: "... we speak our language, as a nation,
better than any other people speak their language."[119] We were not linguistic
adventurers but linguistic regulators.

In treating "The Spaciousness of Old Rhetoric," Richard Weaver sees
"homogeneity of belief" as the basis for free use of "the uncontested term."
That "chief offender against the modern sensibility" represented the orator's
conviction that he spoke for "corporate mankind," and thus "he always talked
like a big man." But rhetoric has fallen on sorry times, and as Weaver notes at
the beginning of that essay, the kind of discourse our forefathers "would ride
miles in wagons to hear, or would regard as the special treat of some festive
occasion, fills most people today with an acute sense of discomfort." Having
lost "homogeneity of belief," we urge each individual to think—and to mumble
unintelligibly—"for himself." In that essay and others, Weaver does much to
illuminate "a logic, an aesthetic, and an epistemology" of what we now dis-
parage as "spread-eagle" oratory.[120]

What bears even more emphasis than Weaver gave it is the unalloyed fondness that listeners apparently had for simple command of language. There is
scant evidence that humble people countenanced linguistic corruption or
vandalism. Language, like other things, must be brought to refined order.
When their leaders talked their very tallest, they employed unrestrained substance but not unrestrained form. At least from de Tocqueville forward, commentators have paid overmuch attention to the apparent substance. From that
content we have teased rather too many purported dimensions of such things as
a political mythology. What has not been sufficiently remarked is the fact that

people then, if not now, took straightforward satisfaction from hearing an exhibition in language mastery, matters of substance probably being of secondary consideration. Social and educative forms sought to bridle sentiment, argument, and imagination. In turn, unbridled language seemed, if not as bad as unbridled self, then certainly a baneful corollary of it.

Social Control Worked by Circumstance and Experience

Thus far, we have examined some of the positive processes whereby "society" guarded the individual from self. The negative processes, those involving the chastening force of circumstance and experience, deserve at least some mention here. The self would be bridled, whether by blandishment or by woe. This darker theme in American life might require little more than passing mention were it not that so many scholars so emphasize the ebullience and assertiveness of pre-Civil War America. One almost fancies an entire nation (excluding Hawthorne, Melville, and Poe) leaping into the air like flatboatmen, clicking their heels together three times, and shouting defiance in resounding "Whoo-oops." The writings of the plain folk reveal almost none of that spirit.

In a deliriously unguarded moment in "The Transcendentalist," Emerson emitted an abstract Concord version of "Whoo-oop": "You think me the child of my circumstances: I make my circumstance."[121] Perhaps one should resist the puckish urge to put the gentle sage in a tall-talk context. Still, aside from muscular exhibitionism such as clicking his heels together three times in a single leap, even Mark Twain's "Pet Child of Calamity" could not match him. " 'When I'm playful' " the river rowdy averred, " 'I use the meridians of longitude and the parallels of latitude for a seine, and drag the Atlantic Ocean for whales!' " No mean feat, of course, but hardly of the resourceful dimensions outlined coolly by the philosopher Emerson: "I—this thought which is called I—is the mould into which the world is poured like melted wax." Whatever the case with fictive river roughs and real Concord thinkers, America was not singing this refrain. In recent years, some scholars have detected some signs of disquietude in the early republic. Unfortunately, the more common motif for the period centers on the likes of Andrew Jackson, a man who, in John Ward's language, "objectified the belief that man was not the creature of circumstance but the master of his own destiny."[122]

Circumstances, those things surrounding the individual, represented a secular parallel to providence. Providence was, of course, absolute; circumstances, while not absolute, approached that condition. Plain folk left it to the Emersons to tame or circumvent such agencies. During a temporary separation, Mary Conkling sent words of reassurance and counsel to her husband, Enos. "I am philosopher enough," she wrote, "to make the best of that which cannot be otherwise. . . . There is no use in making ourselves miserable—because we cannot have things as we would—but endeavor to be happy under all circumstances."[123] Mary Conkling did not make her circumstances; she managed to accommodate herself to them. As a Baltimore man wrote to a friend in South Carolina, "we are creatures of circumstances. . . ."[124] The mobility and transience of American society during that period probably heightened rather than lessened that sense; it probably involved as much a feeling of being moved as of moving. On July 4, 1850, a few days beyond Fort Laramie, George N. Wheeler meditated on such matters as his twenty-sixth birthday approached: "Ah! how different and what different Sircumstance. . . . Shurely our life is all change[.] [O]ne knows not to day his destination tomorrow[.] Where I shall be a year from to day no one but God alone can tell."[125]

"Where do we find ourselves?" With that question Emerson opened his essay "Experience," and then, in keeping with the Transcendental denial of the formative influence of externals, he dismissed experience as a means of locating oneself. Emerson went to unusual, even callous, lengths to show that the outside had no effect upon him whatever. "There are moods," he wrote, "in which we court suffering, in the hope that here, at least, we shall find reality. . . , for contact with which we would even pay the costly price of sons and lovers." Then, in an unfortunate capitulation to dogma, he adduced the death of his own son two years before. Like all the other "scene-painting and counterfeit," that, too, "does not touch me."

I grieve that grief can teach me nothing, nor carry me one step into real nature. . . . The dearest events are summer-rain, and we the Para coats that shed every drop. Nothing is left us now but death. We look to that with a grim satisfaction, saying, There at least is reality that will not dodge us.[126]

This is partly philosophical and epistemological doctrine; in lesser part, it suggests the Romantic drive to meet life head on. Neither element has much relation to the moods of common men. Most assuredly, they could not summon the sort of Transcendental braggadocio that pronounced experience to be inconsequential; they could not work the monumental dissimulation that Emerson did when he noted that his son died and "it leaves no scar."[127] In the other regard, fronting life boldly and directly had scant charms. Experience, except in the trade sense of practice, had far more to condemn it than commend it. When men learned by experience, they learned sadly. The word itself had almost no warm and attractive connotations; it came with none of the purring vibrations that a later age would draw into association with "experiencing" this or "experiencing" that.

If common men of that era did not quite view experience as Tennyson's "dirty nurse," they often enough employed a morose observation of Benjamin Franklin. A disillusioned teacher in Talladega, Alabama, recalled "the old but true adage, 'Experience keeps a dear School, but fools will learn in no other.' "[128] George Boaz's school had indeed been too dear, too costly, too hard. Now he meant to return to farming. People hoped to learn by precept; if they failed of that, they had, as it were, to learn the hard way, by experience. Experience was not the "best" teacher, as later maxim-mongers would transmogrify the stern contentions of Shakespeare, Franklin, Tennyson, and others. Experience was the dearest, the most hurtful teacher. Unlike the Romantic agonizers, common folk did not lust after the lessons of the school of life; those lessons came inevitably and without invitation.

No literary excursion into the realm of experience was more popular among the common folk than that produced by John Godfrey Saxe in "The Blind Men and the Elephant." Particularly in the 1850s, that "Elephant" became a shorthand designation for encounters with reality.

> It was six men of Indostan
>   To learning much inclined,
> Who went to see the Elephant
>   (Though all of them were blind),
> That each by observation
>   Might satisfy his mind.

Perhaps because it involved a journey, the parable of the six blind men lent itself especially well to that most demanding of experiences, the California trek, a matter to be treated more fully elsewhere.

The homey, subjectivist epistemological "moral" with which the New England poet concluded seems not to have impressed those humble folk who borrowed his imagery. Common men saw in Saxe's fable, not precisely what the author had meant to convey, but rather a metonymous designation for experience. In turn, experience was, for them, no gentle and enhancing thing. Thus, the "Elephant" nearly always took on threatening proportions for them. Often, of course, there was a hyperbolic element, as when James Bell wrote to Augusta Hallock from Illinois telling her that he had seen "the Elephant of Kaneville," that being a western dance.[129] Nearly always, however, a seriousness accompanied the seemingly comic usage. The "Elephant" appeared most frequently and discernibly at such places as Cape Horn, or the isthmus, or the most barren and challenging spots on the overland route, or at the end of the trail. "The Elephant is in California," a carpenter wrote to those who would follow him West, "you'll all get a sight in good time. look out."[130]

Conventional wisdom could hardly have been stated more concisely. In a generic comparative sense, people of pre-Civil War America may have appeared adventurous, self-assertive, and confident, but Douglas T. Miller and others who have offered qualifiers deserve fuller attention. As Miller observes, ". . . the pervasive pessimism of Hawthorne and Melville, and the macabre melancholy of Poe were not out of touch with the age, but were sensitive responses to America's anxieties."[131] Miller presented those anxieties in ways rather more political and cultural than I would use; but general contentions such as his are well borne out by "you'll get a sight in good time. look out."

Conclusion

The most fundamental dimension of getting "a sight in good time" involved reaching adulthood when one left the comforting matrix of "society" in its most direct sense—family and home. When Zuar Jameson took stock of himself on his twenty-first birthday, he expressed the then standard complaint: "I am afraid it is true," he remarked, that the best part of life was now gone. Now self, that least reliable of all things, would have to be relied on more fully. Now the five-foot four-inch Vermonter would have fuller encounters with the "Elephant." He would continue his connection with surrogates such as the local debating society, but, as he gloomily noted of the childhood now behind him, "Those days are past away never to return."[132] A Georgian put it in poetic form:

> O why did sorrow come so soon
> To cloud my youthful brow

Then that characteristically sad refrain got fuller treatment.

> The past is like a cherished dream
> The present Oh how drear
> The futer darker yet doth seem
> Dispare is hovering near[133]

A seventeen-year-old Virginia woman who described herself as "poor, humble and innocent," as "too high souled and proud to equalize myself with the ornery and too course and inexperienced for quality," expressed the refrain of seemingly premature dolorousness in this way: "Wretched indeed would our lot be were we confined to the poor precincts of the present, but, blessed be God! we have rich possessions in the storehouse of memory . . ." Nearly five years later, the man she had married in the interim, the man who had saved her from "the miserable years in solitude" that she feared, made the final entry in her pensive document: "This Journal is done! The author being Elizabeth A. McClure died March 28, 1843. Tho happy in Christ Jesus being the only consolation left me!! She was 22 years 7 months and 12 days old."[134]

The nostalgia of "Ben Bolt," of "The Old Oaken Bucket," and of such Stephen Foster songs as "Gentle Annie" has full consonance with a view of reality holding that the greatest happiness was that of childhood wherein self and circumstances made fewest impingements. After that came maturity and the painful necessity of relying on the self and, in turn, the dissolution of society by the departure of friends, family, and companion. It was a doleful inuring to disillusionment, woe, and death.

Politics and the Nation 6

Of secular matters, society demanded attention and solicitude foremost. Beyond that small and comforting area, the common people somewhat dimly discerned the larger dimensions of politics and nation. The attention they gave to those larger concerns seems to vary in two ways from the conventional accounts. First, their attention to such matters was not as unwavering as is often depicted; and, second, their attention was less rapt and confident than many have contended.

A Comparative Indifference

In 1843, Lucius Salisbury left Vermont for a four-year stay in Missouri. He and Harriet Hutchinson, the girl he left behind, corresponded during the separation that ended with their marriage, and over a century later parts of their letters were published with commentary by Allen F. Davis. Davis made no large claims for that correspondence; indeed, he considered it "more interesting than . . . important." The young couple made no mention whatever of the brewing slave controversy, and only occasionally did they allude to politics at all. "Perhaps their chief usefulness," Davis intimated, "is to illustrate that there were ordinary men and women with ordinary human problems in an age often pictured as dominated by writers and politicians, by economic and intellectual forces."[1] Davis arrived at a standard, if somewhat uneasy, conclusion. In editing a lengthy set of Tennessee letters written by people of the same social standing as Lucius Salisbury and Harriet Hutchinson, Chase Mooney observed the "lack of concern over such events as the War of 1812, the Texas problem, and the War with Mexico."[2]

In 1932, the Connecticut State librarian perhaps felt sensitive about a ten dollar expenditure for the acquisition of the diary kept by Oren Lee, a blacksmith-farmer who served several terms in the state assembly over a hundred years before. Despite his political background, Lee's sporadic entries in the politically exciting year of 1828 fail to mention that it was a general election year. Making his priorities more explicit four years later at age seventy-two, Lee could write that his being chosen delegate to a Universalist meeting was greater honor than his terms in the general assembly. In the same year he made his only mention of Andrew Jackson, recording simply that the president was born in South Carolina in 1767. Oren Lee's diary reveals almost nothing about politics; not surprisingly, the state librarian described it as showing the "narrowness" of places like North Granby a century before.[3]

In the "Divinity School Address" in 1838, Emerson bemoaned what he saw as the erosion of spiritual concerns: "Genius leaves the temple, to haunt the senate, or the market."[4] What for Emerson was a metaphor—genius leaving the temple to haunt the senate—has assumed concrete proportions for some modern observers. "The motives, the processes, the mysteries that made man accept religion and expect God to accomplish what he was unable to do," Jacques Ellul has written of the modern passion he called *The Political Illusion*, "leads him nowadays into politics and makes him expect those things from the state."[5] Whatever the accuracy of Ellul's assessment, Emerson seems to have been somewhat premature. "Genius" may have been hastening from the "temple" to the "senate," but the ordinary people were making that move far more slowly than the sage and others have suggested. Those "ordinary men and women with ordinary human problems" found other things more compelling than politics. As Part One of the present study shows, immediate mundane tasks such as plowing, baking, digging, selling, and sewing did not preclude their thinking in terms of larger categories. Among these larger categories, politics was not as high a priority as has often been supposed. An analysis of common notions about politics may not yield many original insights, but it ought at least to qualify conventional views such as that stated in Carl Russell Fish's *The Rise of the Common Man*: "Aside from the making of a living or the accumulation of a fortune, the main preoccupation of most American men was politics."[6]

Fish used that sentence to open the chapter titled "The Politicians." The next chapter, "The Religious Scene," began this way: "While politics was the predominant preoccupation of the men, religion was that of the women."[7] As a young man wrote from Virginia back to the family in Maine, "I suppose the men folks would like to know something about the recent election. . . ."[8] Items of this nature appear only occasionally in the writings of ordinary folk, however. Fish presents the difference in interests far too starkly. Religion attracted nearly universal attention, and while politics attracted vastly less and did indeed occupy men more then women, it surfaced almost as frequently in the written expressions of women. They, too, showed guarded interest in political developments, and often they simply conveyed political news.

On city election day in early Detroit, a mechanic who had a penchant for arch observations wrote that he "did not vote. I'll none of sin."[9] Such explicit rejections appear only infrequently; most people apparently became somewhat interested in the political scene, at least now and then. With the 1860 election approaching, a man in Princeton, Missouri, put it in uncontestable terms: "Politicks is all the go hear."[10] No doubt it was, but the overall impression from such sources is that of a nation far more lackadaisical than many have contended. The widespread failure to note political developments and the almost grudgingly terse mentions of elections and voting suggest that many Americans did what Rodney Loehr's Minnesota farmers did: " 'Voted today.' "[11]

Beyond disinterest, the people had an almost inconsistent apprehensiveness about politics. "I dont mean anything political," William Jackson hastened to assure an old friend when writing that his Goshen, New York, area was experiencing "hard times and plenty of it."[12] Better mute or avoid, Jackson probably reasoned, what might not readily be restrained. Hurtful self-consciousness for bad writing and gross misspellings became even more intense when, in an Indiana to Illinois family letter, the sensitive subject almost surfaced: "I came very Near to running my letter in to Politicks."[13] People simply wanted to avoid controversial subjects. "I seldom talk politics," a Kentuckian generalized in a letter to his Indiana brother in November 1860. "I refrain," he continued, "because I feel that I can gain nothing by discussing such subjects with my friends, and that I may by differing with my friends become angry myself or make them so."[14]

All of the above suggests that at least some political matters were of consequence; otherwise, there would be no reason for benign avoidance. It also suggests that as political issues became graver the need for silence and avoidance increased. Here we encounter the sort of paradox, or simple reality, of which Santayana wrote in *Character and Opinion in the United States*: "In a hearty and sound democracy all questions at issue must be minor matters; fundamentals must have been agreed upon and taken for granted when the democracy arose."[15] Fundamentals were waxing, as were the perplexities of William Jackson and so many others like him.

The debating societies, in those occasional instances when they considered political matters, also showed caution and hesitance on them. (Near Erie, Pennsylvania, in 1859, a debate was scheduled treating the dangers of territorial expansion. It proved a total failure because the ladies of the area were invited to observe, and their presence, plus the fact that they engaged in "whispering, tittering and hand squeezing" quite befuddled the debaters.)[16] The previously mentioned Mount Hope Debating Society of Orange County, New York, provides a better illustration. In the comparative tranquility of February 1857, the group debated the possible repeal of the Fugitive Slave Law. As late as December 1860, the question of whether a state had the right to secede came under consideration, but after that such subjects were no longer chosen for debates. The issues became abstract—did poverty or wealth do more for the development of "moral & intellectual" character?; or academic—had phrenology attained the rank of science?; or specific and technical—was the application of manure effective in getting better yields?[17] Little wonder that in the writings of the common people one finds much more written reaction to the high-jinx of 1840 than to the debacle of 1860. In 1840, one could bemoan or exult, as persuasions dictated: in 1860, one inclined far more to prayerful quiescence.

A Guarded Enthusiasm

Americans appear to have been more guarded about the benefits of political activity than has generally been supposed. Although their pride in the nation was quite overt, they were not as rambunctious in their patriotic emotions as has often been contended. The word "liberty" did most to inform the celebrational outbursts that did appear.

> Oh! Liberty thou art worth possessing
> Since upon earth there's no greater blessing
> Than all mankind to be free
> Americans then pursue that course
> That will repel aspirants force
> In crushing your Liberty

The young man of Andover, Ohio, who wrote this poem also stated that "The term Liberty carries home to the heart of every true American, such a sensation of pleasure, as, is, impossible for, man's pen to describe, or even, imagination to conceive."[18]

That, of course, is standard, ritual panegyric which appeared fairly frequently in the somewhat programmed form of school essays. Others concentrated on the contrast of America to countries where liberty seemed to suffer.

> There spreads Victoria's realm away
> 'Tis sad yon lonely shore
> Sould tremble 'neath a monarch's sway
> And fear the Lion's roar

Twenty-two-year-old New Jersey printer George Wurts wrote this poem as he stood aboard a boat on the Niagara River between Canada and the United States, between "a monarchy and a republic." To the one side he could hear the lion roaring, but gentler images informed the opposite shore.

> Now turn we where the eagle flies
> The empire of the West

Our country neath yon spreading skies
Lies beautiful and blest[19]

While fretting away six days of quarantine in the harbor at Rio de Janeiro, Maine argonaut Seth Whitehouse noted that it was particularly galling because the men aboard had been accustomed to "so much liberty at home."[20] In *White Jacket*, Melville, who had been in Rio de Janeiro five years before Seth Whitehouse, had a New England "Jonathan" utter defiant words about a similar situation in that port.[21] Seth and his comrades were soon at sea again, where they could reconstitute their temperance society and where they could enjoy the Sunday sermons of Reverend "H," perhaps most notably one that took the much-worn text of Luke 10:42—Mary choosing the one thing needful.[22]

The Andover, Ohio, youth did his partly poetic soliloquy on "Liberty" on the Fourth of July, and the printer on the Niagara River made his comparison when the clamor of the national birthday had hardly died away. Much has been made of the ritual utterances of that day, and it was, of course, the hypostasized moment for celebration. On the 1853 commemoration, Mrs. Ashman Butler, a native of Kentucky and a former resident of Illinois, Missouri, and Iowa, could hear the "minut guns" sounding at Jacksonville, Oregon, near which town she and her family had recently located. Though the rattle of gun fire would again be heard in Indian wars in the area, that sound had a reassuring effect upon this woman. "They have not," she noted, "forgoten the past. . . ."[23] During the pre-Civil War period, the people's awareness of their nation's past was intensified on the Fourth of July, as it was to a lesser degree on February 22 and January 8.

In *History in the United States, 1800-1860*, George H. Callcott states that writers and publishers recognized the selling power of the word "history." America had come to the conclusion, Callcott asserts, that "history was fun."[24] The literary use of the word could be explained in part by Jacques Barzun's contention that for a long time the novel "thrived parasitically upon history."[25] Beyond that possibility, and accounting for other illustrations of what Callcott considered knowing misappropriations, there is a matter of alternate definition. One legitimate use of the word had no necessary connection with the past. Thus, the 1855 Webster's began the fourth definition of history this way: "Description; an account of things that exist. . . ." Given this definition, old Isaac Carr of upstate New York, for example, was not inept in asking his son Caleb to send a "correct history" of the conditions in Wisconsin, specifying such things as quality of soil, distances and availability of land.[26]

Using history as a synonym for description without regard for the time element was fairly common, but the ordinary meaning is of greater concern here. Where history was concerned, foremost attention went to the founding of the nation. "This is the day," John B. Orton of Lockport, New York, wrote on July 4, 1845, "above all others calculated to incite in us, feelings of gratitude to our noble sires. . . . All thanks to the brave heroes of 69 yr ago who were firm and unflinching in the cause of *freedom*."[27] Solemnity abounds here, as this farmer routinely sought renewed faith and inspiration from the feats of those who, in a blend of myth and history, annually performed their heroics. But there was more than solemnity.

"How different the American people celebrate this day," a New Hampshire diarist wrote on July 4, 1839, "some for dinners, some tem[perance] meetings, Abolition, colonization, peace &c.[,] some fishing gunning swimming, riding and many other things . . . whilst many work all day."[28] This fellow chose a temperance meeting and found it poorly attended. In another July, a man from Maine who was surveying in Minnesota "went to church" on Sunday, July 3. The terse entry from the next day indicated that he "got drunk." The two-word entry for July 5 is illegible, but in juxtaposition to its fairly firm predecessor, it suggests clearly that the writer again "got drunk." A ready inference can be drawn from the lack of entries for the remainder of the week, but it is reassuring to find that the surveyor went to church on Sunday, July 10, and that on July 11 he returned to the work which had been interrupted to commemorate the founding of the nation.[29] For the surveyor, that Minneapolis Fourth was a sizable diversion.

The young printer mentioned earlier who wrote a poem on the glaring disparity between "a monarchy and a republic" while on a boat between Canada and the United States on July 8 had not shown such a solemn spirit in Utica four days earlier. To be sure, he had been "fortunate enough" to gain admission to the State Lunatic Asylum where he witnessed, apparently with unraised eyebrow, inmates engaged in patriotic exercises. But sportiveness surfaced unmistakably earlier in the entry when the writer announced the "glorious 4th" and the intention of having a good time by, among other things, parodying a grand oration.[30] Countless people played, fought, drank, and otherwise seized an occasion for breaking drab routine. And it would be quite idle to mention the fact, were it not for the latter-day penchant for depicting a nation soberly and literally accepting the orators' herculean metaphors and fervent visions.

In the preceding chapter the contention appeared that Americans of that era had a prodigious appetite for forensic display, and no day so put speakers and listeners to the test as did the 4th of July. On that day supremely serious matters surfaced; indeed the proceedings involved, as a student of nineteenth-century oratory put it, "a ceremonial incantation." However, other elements, even of the oratory itself, were not in keeping with that gravity. As the same student of oratory pointed out, there was a matter of form or style as well as a matter of substance. Aristotle had named and described that style long before, and Hugh Blair, in particular, commended it to early nineteenth-century

America. Bluntly stated, it involved a "preference for ornamentation and elegance over simplicity." To those who knew their Aristotle, that was the "epedeictic" style;[31] to a good many others it was tall-talk. For a people with a seemingly insatiable hunger for displays of language mastery, the ornate form must often have taken precedence over the solemn substance. Writing from the "Editor's Easy Chair" in 1870, George William Curtis noted that the orator of the day felt challenged by the "painful consciousness that he is to compete with ginger-pop, gunpowder, and the circus, and that he must somehow produce the impression of remarkable 'somersets,' or the clown over the way will bear the bell."[32] As Barnet Baskerville and others have observed, play and parody (conscious and otherwise) had intruded upon the Fourth of July speech even before the Civil War.[33] Some such recognition probably moved John Kouwenhoven to the following observation:

nobody but an ass could have taken us very seriously in our moods of slapping ourselves on the back, and—as a matter of fact—few people did take it seriously. . . . Not even the writers who "made the eagle scream," as the saying was in the nineteenth century, took themselves seriously; often they were being intentionally funny and fooled nobody except humorless English travelers and some uncommonly stuffy politicians.[34]

Progress and Young America

The plain folk appreciated the comparative blessings they enjoyed, and they awaited future blessings with a spirit of quiet prayer rather than of thunderous assertion. They seem to have left it almost entirely to intellectuals to expand on the theme of progress. A search of popular sources for intimations of that "most popular philosophy"[35] is to little avail. The idea of progress as gradual and inevitable betterment had not reached the 1855 Webster's dictionary, let alone the sources used in this study.

The popular sources seem to convey about as much about degradation as of progress, though there are few comments on either. One of the well-known slogans of muscular assertiveness—Young America— did appear in three sources, but its spiritual kin, manifest destiny did not appear at all. The term Young America has been employed in various ways: in retrospect, as a designation for part of the early national period; as the label for an aggressive element within the Democratic party centering upon Stephen A. Douglas; and as a watchword of a New York City literary clique that espoused a form of cultural nationalism.[36] "Unhappily," Perry Miller wrote, "Young America were not numerous."[37] He meant that assertion to apply to the constricted world of creative literature; but it is an assertion that might readily be extended without loss of accuracy.

At the end of a diary, a twenty-one-year-old Indiana farmer appended some miscellaneous names and observations. There, with no supporting context, appears "Young America." What the term might have meant to him is not known, but the mood ordinarily connected with that term does not comport with a sentiment written nearby: "Remember thy Creator in the days of thy youth."[38] "Young America has got the upper hand," a resident of Beverly, Massachusetts, happily exclaimed as he told of the discomfiture experienced by the "Old Fogies" at revelations of scandal at the local workhouse. Along with the standard vis-à-vis, Young America and the Old Fogies, this writer well conveyed the brash irreverence often connected with the insurgency known as Young America. Thus, in telling of a man who had risen to local prominence in marine insurance he described a "nervous" way of greeting, "as if he had poisoned your dog, or seduced your sister."[39]

To some, Young America meant the youth of America, and specifically the wastrel youth of America. Early in 1858, a Greenbush, New York, man—himself only twenty-one—wrote in his diary that while out for an evening stroll he had encountered some specimens of "Young America" reeling home after a binge. A diary entry of a few weeks earlier mentioned a good snowfall and the fact that "Young America is improving the same." This simple observation assumed a pejorative tone when a moment later the writer asked rhetorically: "Why was not I born to a fortune that I could drive fast Bays [?] to death and get drunk" without concern?[40] This young man used the expression Young America several times, but not always clearly. Where it is clear, it is censorious, even though the writer, by his own telling, was no paragon of sobriety.

Emerson uttered some stern words when he addressed himself to "The Young American" in Boston in February 1844, but he also showed large confidence. "America," he wrote, "is beginning to assert herself to the senses and to the imagination of her children. . . ."[41] All may have had to agree, but not all had to approve. National self-assertion may have had little more to commend it than did personal self-assertion. Herman Melville had once been connected with the literary phase of the Young America movement, but in the section entitled "Young America in Literature" in *Pierre* he derided that spirit as a compound of immaturity and ostentation. In artistic simile, Melville contrasted the age of the portrait with the age of the daguerreotype: "How natural then the inference, that instead of, as in old times, immortalizing a genius, a portrait now only *dayalized* a dunce."[42] Whether in the real setting of Beverly, Massachusetts, and Greenbush, New York, or in fictitious realms, sarcasm often informed the depictions of something known as Young America.

In Joseph G. Baldwin's Alabama, Simon Suggs, Jr., took the measure of his father in a game of "*seven up*" played for a race mare, and, here as elsewhere, "it was the old fogy against young America." With the game tied, Young America, after executing a "brilliant" shuffle, laid his snuff box on the table. Father Suggs took a pinch, not knowing that it was laced with cayenne pepper. As the "old gentleman" recovered from a sneeze, the first thing to meet his eye was a jack turning in the hand of Young America. Fatherly pride struggled against a sense of individual loss, and then the Old Fogy congratulated Young America, "and swore that he was wasting his genius in a retail business of 'shy-keenry' when nature had designed him for the bar."[43]

Mortimer Thomson, writing as Q. K. Philander Doesticks, compounded the parody in his 1856 *Pluri-bus-tah*. The meter of this saga of the leader of the Yengah nation derives from Hiawatha; its theme centers on the wastrel course of Pluri-bus-tah's son Yunga-Merrakah. Pluri-bus-tah, the founder, had been avaricious, but his wife restrained him somewhat. Yunga-Merrakah defied all restraints, devoting himself totally to the pursuit of money and of pleasure, a totally downward course.

> One by one, he lost the virtues,
> Lost the few and scanty virtues

Then, injecting apocalyptic prophecy into sardonic social commentary, Doesticks brought his epic to an end. Yunga-Merrakah had "fizzled."

> And the mighty Yengah nation
> Now was perished and forgotten,
> While its only trace or token,
> Was the last, Almighty dollar.[44]

However representative the views of Thomson, Baldwin, and Melville may have been, the assertion that "Young America's grand ideal really expressed the feelings of many Americans"[45] is doubtful.

Elections and Disruptions

As all know, excitement and intensity prevailed on the Fourth of July, though the mood of the day, as I sought to show, was informed by feelings that may have been neglected in our historical reconstructions. Much of the same can be said for election day. Periodically at least, strenuous attention went to the political sphere, so much so that scholars such as Roy F. Nichols and David Donald have seen the political hurly-burly, not just as an effect, but as part of the cause of the disruption leading to armed conflict. Nichols wrote of a "deep-seated enjoyment of political activity by Americans which proved dangerous. . . . A great disruptive fact was the baneful influence of elections almost continuously in progress, of campaigns never over, and of political uproar endlessly arousing emotions."[46] There may well have been, to use David Donald's expression, an "excess of democracy,"[47] but a qualification or two may be in order. Generally, politics provided the occasion more than the cause of the turbulence to which Nichols and Donald have called our attention.

For an example, let us return for a moment to the Fourth of July celebration.

An 1859 gathering on that occasion in northwest Georgia proved even more exciting than one young lady had anticipated. Unpleasantness arose. A challenge to a "fist and skull fite" from one received a derisive dismissal by another. Then, as the hand of one raised an axe and the hand of another responded with a fence rail, "you aut," as the distressed witness wrote a few days later, "of heard me hollow."[48] Conviviality and celebration can, of course, take untoward directions. "As is always the case," a shipboard argonaut mused on a July 6, some of the celebrants did not feel "independent enough until they were drunk and laid away in their Berths."[49] On another founding day—what appears to have been the formal incorporation of Lodi, Illinois—the townsfolk felt the need to "rejoice." "So," as one of the less ecstatic among them wrote later, "they got out the old anvill and blased away and the third time they fired her she burst[,] killed one man and broke one other man's leg."[50] A "fist and skull fite," an ocean-borne commemoration observed not wisely but too well, and a sixteen-pound piece of blast-propelled metal cutting a man nearly in two did not inhere in the spirit of the occasions that begot them. When one Jim who had been involved in the tumultuousness at that Georgia barbecue stalked away saying that "he never enten to pray un tell he whirps" someone, it seems powerfully unlikely that niceties regarding the Declaration of Independence were at issue. And, in turn, when politics itself was "all the go," the attendant boisterousness probably had far more to do with setting and form than with doctrine and substance.

One does not get an impression of political beliefs held so firmly as to invite rancor. Diaries indicate that many people attended political meetings with almost blasé indiscriminateness—Whig one day, Democrat another, Native American or Republican another—apparently availing themselves of whatever talent, show, and excitement they could find. To be sure, they occasionally expressed and explained their party affiliations, sometimes vehemently, but from those expressions it is supremely difficult to discern attitudinal patterns. Once past such unarguable and generally undefined categories as liberty, little appears but occasional mutterings about aristocracy, the monster bank, Federalism revived, mobs, demagogues, or whatever. One could readily succumb to the conclusion that there was indeed a consensus of political belief and that the apparent differences represented little more than a choosing of sides for display and mock conflict. On a day in the fall campaign of 1852, thirty-five-year-old Michael Luark, at the time a carpenter in the Anderson, Indiana, area left some bedsteads unfinished in order "to hear the candidates expose one another," but, he added with apparent disappointment, "they was quite friendly for candidates."[51] Politics provided diversion. Evidently, the sound and the fury often signified very little.

The diversion was usually innocent enough. In the fall of 1844, Seaborn Jones of northcentral Mississippi wrote playfully that the Whigs and Democrats thereabouts were competing so fiercely for the sponsorship and consumption of free dinners that he feared that the campaign might "bring on hard times again." Even more interesting than that possibility, Jones continued, was a development at nearby Grenada at a Whig gathering which included a procession of twenty-six ladies on white horses, each signifying a state. The emblematic South Carolina was wearing a fur hat to mark the great victory of four years before, but alas, as Seaborn Jones noted with one degree of embroidery or another, her horse gave a start "and down came South Carolina and she showed her Coon Skin."[52]

While Seaborn Jones was delighting in such spectacles, a young clerk in New York City concerned himself especially with "Julia," but he also made frequent mention of sporting events, shows, and politics. Indeed, for him there was little difference among these three categories. A horse race on "Beacon Course" in which the American winner did "10 5/8 miles within 60 min." against two English entries which had been brought expressly for the race was given as must space in his writings as the general election that would issue in the presidency of James K. Polk. He enjoyed the "fireworks and displays" sponsored by the Native Americans; he watched the Democrats in torch parade; he noted regretfully that the Native Americans had to cancel theirs because of inclement weather; and he remarked the good fortune of the Whig young men who had a fine day for one of their parades and who basked in the festive accompaniment of "the smiles of the ladies, the cheers of their friends and the groans of their political enemies."[53] As one of a group of visitors in a rural area of northern New Jersey expressed it on another election day, they had a good time "carrying on ourselves, & looking at others" doing likewise.[54]

Straight political fare does not seem to have been sufficiently enticing— hence, the prodigious number of free dinners made available for political occasions. Moving between his Ohio birthplace and an Iowa farm in 1840, young Cyrus Sanders had the opportunity while in Saint Louis to attend a Whig rally and hear a speech by "a gentleman from Illinois, introduced by name Ned Baker." That effort by Abraham Lincoln's close friend was, Sanders allowed, "the best speech I ever heard of the kind." Later in that spring, the young farmer encountered two men who were even more note-worthy than Ned Baker. While aboard a steamboat on the Ohio, he had the happy chance to see "the Kentucky Giant," seven-foot four-inch Jim Porter who caught the attention of many. He impressed Sanders as "one of the greatest curiosities I ever beheld." So impressed was he that he was led to an invidious comparison to William Henry Harrison. Recently, while in Cincinnati, Sanders had received an introduction to Harrison. The twenty-year-old farmer considered that an honor, "but I would rather have seen Porter, than had half a dozen such Introductions."[55]

Those wishing more than a speech by Ned Baker, a free dinner, or a look at the "Kentucky Giant" did not have far to go, at least not around election time. These less restrained activities reveal very little about political beliefs and ideas, but they do have intrinsic interest. Henry Miller, a young Pennsylvania carpenter working in Saint Louis in 1838, described the period of city elections as the times that tried not men's souls but their bodies. The patriotism of the local citizenry consisted in "Cursing, drinking, sometimes fighting, getting Black eys, bloody noses." Visitor Miller did not participate in these patriotic endeavors, but he did become involved in the state elections later in the year. In contrast with the "midling quiet" of the city elections in April, "the Politics ran high" in August when the young carpenter set about casting the first ballot of his life. When voting traffic became too heavy at the courthouse on the Saint Louis waterfront, both Whigs and Democrats rented steamers to carry the faithful to a polling place at Carondolet a few miles downriver.

Arriving at Carondolet with the Democratic cohort, Miller found that the Whigs had stolen a march and already had "possession" of the polls: " 'Whigs, Stick to the Polls, don't let the damned Democrats vote.' " That Whiggish resolve did not go unchallenged, and, with some in the ranks imitating the "Barking of Dogs, some the roaring of Bulls," the following discourse ensued:

Hurra for the Whigs, Pull down the Banner, Lick them, drive them away, Keep the Polls, Hurra for Darby, Hurra for Sublette, Hurra for Benton and Democracy, Hurra for Clay, down with the damned Democrats, Hurra for Jackson, Hurra for Hell, see who'll get there first.

Fundamentals such as liberty and freedom did not escape attention, the excitement notwithstanding. When, for example, the outnumbered Democrats were temporarily driven back from the voting place, our chronicler observed that the Whigs, "seeming to think that they were in a Free country," had therefore "a right to let vote who they pleased." Democrats, too, stood on principle, perhaps because they stood only precariously anywhere else. Feeling like a "whipped dog" after having been thrown down a flight of stairs, Miller offered his antagonists at the top "some remark on the Liberty of suffrage, &c., &c." Finally, he managed to cast his ballot for Thomas Hart Benton, but he did so in a setting that featured more fighting than he had witnessed in his entire life. And, regrettably, our carpenter's discourse on "the Liberty of suffrage" probably availed him less than did the compelling logic which he observed in the form of bloody "derks, Bowie Knives, clubs, handkerchiefs with stones" in them and other such aids to political reflection.[56]

"It is well known," Winthrop Jordan has written, "that liberty trees and poles served as rallying points for both the destructive and ritualistic activities of Revolutionary crowds. Precisely *why* is less certain."[57] A half century and more later, some people were still erecting poles, others were yet cutting them down, and the *why* remained elusive. On the afternoon of March 8, 1845, the Democrats of Ellington, Connecticut, spliced and re-erected a "Hickory tree" which had been chopped down the night before. Once the pole was again in place, the Hickoryites gave vent to their defiance of the malefactors; they gave those "Coons [the Whigs] a national salute of 28 guns from a 4 pounder and 3 for Texas and 3 for Oregon." Minions of the "Coon" element had cut the pole, and an angry hatter who was a staunch Democrat entered this indictment in his diary:

Fuller Ransom [,] White Ransom and one Fitts known as the Old Indian Chief from the similarity of his looks & his bad temper and disposition with malice aforethought not having the fear of God before their eyes but being moved and instigated by the Devil did with force and arms, viz axes cut slash hew and fall the aforesaid Hickory tree.[58]

The hatter had once served a politically appointed term as clerk of court, and the expression of his wrath shows it. However, that helps almost not at all in gaining, as Jordan put it, "some insight into the meaning, the psychic content, of these symbols." But in light of the fact that poles were erected, cut down, and replaced to the accompaniment of a "4 pounder," it does seem safe to venture that a good deal of just plain sport entered in, along with a rowdyism which paraded as acceptable political ceremony.

The outrage worked by the "Coons" probably involved the same "Hickory tree" that had been raised during the preceding fall campaign, from which emerged the presidency of "Young Hickory," James K. Polk. The angry hatter's account suggests the trials of that campaign and indicates that political participation could be as hazardous in Ellington, Connecticut, as in Saint Louis, Missouri. In those frenzied fall days, "Coons" systematically undid the "Hickory" monuments, but the Ellington Democrats persevered. Finally, they undertook to raise a particularly impressive pole measuring, according to hatter Edwin Olmstead, 131 feet in length. Unfortunately, something went amiss in the engineering; "John Tobey of Vernon" was struck on the neck and killed. According to the Democratic hatter, the fifty-two-year-old man was "some deaf and withal stupid with Liquor or he would have got out of the way." Nonetheless, his fellow Democrats "acted like men" after the mishap, putting him in a coffin, carrying him home, and starting a fund-raising for the widow.[59]

Writing to his Covington, Indiana, parents from Weaverville, California, in 1852, John Tice indicated that one feature of life in a mining town had a familiar quality. A recent election had been "an old-fashioned one like they used to have in Covington, drinking and quarreling and gambling."[60] Time and again, such comments appear in our sources, more often than not expressing worry and vexation about rowdies and loafers, about noise and meaningless excitement grown to turbulence, and about the degradation of political practice into inflammatory factionalism. Carpenter Henry Miller and a great many others—including Mrs. John Tobey, if not her pole-raising husband—would have seen merit in David Donald's analysis of pre-Civil War society. Donald states that that society exhibited the divisive marks of an "excess of democracy" and, in turn, the erosion of necessary restraints: "Simply because Americans by the middle of the 19th century suffered from an excess of liberty, they were increasingly unable to arrive at reasoned, independent judgments upon the problems which faced their society."[61]

For all that humble people were bombarded with celebrations of some vague quality called liberty, their own use of the term had important limitations. They associated liberty so completely with the Revolutionary era that the word meant hardly more than national independence, and that was just the constriction placed by the 1855 Webster's dictionary on "Political liberty." John B. Orton of Lockport, New York, presented "our noble sires" as having been "unflinching in the cause of *freedom*," but that was freedom from the British Empire. Those "noble sires" struck for "Independence and Universal Liberty," but for Orton "Universal Liberty" had no denotative quality whatever. In fact, our forefathers "stood like a rock for the Separation & Dec. [laration of Independence] come life or death & only with our invincible leader, & patriot, Washington [,] maintained their rights against fearful odds," that is, they maintained the independence which they had declared.[62] Liberty also meant the perpetuation of the inspired thoughts and systems of the Founding Fathers, and little elaboration or improvement could or need be done. In keeping with the spirit of the day—January 1, 1838—the operator of an Ohio tin shop turned his attention to large themes, including the legacy of the Founding Fathers who—in expression almost unmatched in currency—"swore to die or be free." Before castigating the "aristocracy" for, among other things, ill-concealed debauchery on New Year's Day, Oren Wiley elaborated his prayerful invocation of the founding spirit:

May our happy government roll on to the latest posterity in the annals of time, and may its rulers ever be governed by the same patriotic principles that our venerable forefathers were when they rebelled against the tyrents yoke. May their ashes be at rest, and everlasting peace be their happy lot.[63]

The liberty engendered by the Founding Fathers did not mean the din and riotousness of campaign tactics. With the 1840 campaign coming to its end, Matthias Zahm, a brushmaker, beekeeper, fireman, sometime tipstaff and crier of the Lancaster, Pennsylvania, court, mused about the now dying year: "1840—Things as they now are." Such things included coon skins, hickory poles, log cabins, cider kegs, "stratagem and foolery," "blaguardism and newspaper slander," "trash and nonsense disgracefull to the morals of a civilized society," and various other devices causing both parties to "waste more money in keeping up the excitement than would buy the winter wood and clothing, for all the needful poor in the whole U. States. . . ." Social upheaval and similar considerations concerned the fifty-one-year-old Zahm much more than material utility. For months now, "marching with drum and fife through the streets at night by both parties is every night except sundays, speeches are made in the open air at night, and shouts and huzzas rent the air, rowdies can get drunk every night free gratis on both sides of the question. . . ." God grant, came Zahm's resigned hope, "that the most honest of the two Candidates may be elected, so that the people may again be restored to their sober senses, and the country be settled down to the proper order and decorum. . . ."[64]

"Proper Order and Decorum"

In wishing a return to "proper order and decorum," Zahm showed a concern that was in no way idiosyncratic, and it involved him and others like him in philosophical matters. In his perceptive study of pre-Civil War thought, Rush Welter refers to some "relatively philosophical statements about self-government" that he encountered. Then, parenthetically, he adds that "Unphilosophical Americans simply ignored the philosophical issues and clamored for their 'rights.' "[65] Perhaps no one would argue with the first part of that formulation, but the present study suggests a qualification of the second. The world never lacks those who "clamor for their 'rights,' " but, though there was evidently much of that clamor in the 1830s, 1840s, and 1850s, it is out of keeping with the restraints and inhibitions which simple people seem to have revered, and probably often evinced.

"Proper order and decorum" involved government in its institutional, overt form, and it involved government qualified as self-government. The term self-government seems almost never to have entered the vocabulary of the sorts of people upon whose writings this study is based; but again, by implication, these lesser sorts revealed their values. To revert to earlier discussions by way of reminder, it is well to bear in mind that, in general terms, the enhancement of the self seems to have aroused apprehension rather than approbation. Except insofar as it denoted no more than national independence, self-government would have involved very little more than self-control or self-restraint. The 1855 Webster's rendered it with almost disarming succinctness: "The government of one's self."

But two fundamentally different constructions may be placed upon that seemingly unarguable terseness; and those constructions derive from differing views of human nature. To those taking a fond view of human nature, self-government would mean letting the self do as it pleases. To those who take a contrary view of human nature, self-government would mean controlling or governing the self. The former has generally been seen as having by far the greater pertinence to pre-Civil War America; John W. Ward, for example, readily distilled statements by Andrew Jackson and John L. O'Sullivan into the political premise that "the people are virtuous and capable."[66] However, Jackson and O'Sullivan notwithstanding, the people may have taken a somewhat different view of the matter.

Put another way, common ideas bear more resemblance to the informing principles of "The Politics of Whiggery" than to those of "The Politics of Democracy," as those are depicted in Rush Welter's intricate analysis. In the views of the Democracy, according to Welter, "the ultimate tendency" was "to turn to self-government as a way of avoiding government." He reminds us, of course, that people of democratic persuasion were "not literal anarchists," and that George Camp, of whom John W. Ward made much in an essay referred to earlier, incorporated "limitations on the self" in his theory of democracy. But the emphasis falls definitely upon undoing restraints— "throwing off external authority" and "throw[ing] off every trace of subordination to political institutions."[67] At least in theory, all things were allowed to the self. The people who are the subjects of this book may have often voted the Democratic ticket, but they were at best indifferent Democrats.

Conversely, the Whig spokesmen portrayed by Welter tended to think in terms "which equated self-government with deference to an objective moral order." Though Welter gives it little attention, that involves an individual, religious consideration, but at least here the emphasis has come around to self-restraint or to popular government generalized as political self-restraint. In one context, Welter refers to it as "a sort of involuntary self-government," which translated precisely as self-restraint. In the "conservative doctrine" of the Whigs, "men of a suitable disposition were entitled to govern themselves politically because they were already able to govern themselves as individuals; ... self-government tended to follow from the claims of character."[68] This much resembles the mood of the lower classes, but again a refinement is in order.

Self-government or self-control did not so much "follow from the claims of character"; in the most basic sense, it *was* character. It had its own satisfactions in virtuous conduct. In practical terms, the Burkean formula—if restraint comes not from within, then surely it will come from without—would have impressed these humble folk as the common sense of the matter. The Ohio tin shop operator mentioned earlier was a staunch Democrat, but his comments on the Harrison campaign of 1840 are redolent of Whiggish doctrine, if not of Whiggish practice. All of the "unmeaning" hoopla, the "drinking of hard cider," and "imitating the cries of birds and the howl of wild beasts" was not only "disgraceful to the country." It unmistakably said "to the people, you are too ignorant for self government. ..."[69] His views are echoed in those of an upstate New York farmer who wrote in 1844 that "if there was half as much excitement about religion as there is about Politicks we should not be so stupid, vital piety is very low."[70] The similarity of mood between common people and some Whig theoreticians probably does little to explain why many of these people voted for William Henry Harrison but looked askance at other Whigs. The similarity was there, but it was little more than what Rush Welter calls the "broadly Calvinist view of human nature"[71] that yet pervaded the land. That view of human nature was very fundamental, and it could cause some to regard formal political divisions as inconsequential, as many later scholars have contended. According to a traveling Tennessee daguerreotypist, after noting his own preference for the Whig ticket in 1852, "the distinction between whig and democrat is almost nominal."[72]

In 1856, another young man who traveled in his trade was in Leavenworth, Kansas Territory, at the conclusion of the national election. Paying particular attention to his home state of Pennsylvania, he observed that she went Democrat, "and be d———d to her; and Old Buck's elected, and be d———d to him too." Now at least he could dismiss politics for four more years.[73] Thus another qualification of the supposed hold that political enthusiasm had upon the land involves the simple fact that, however frequent the elections for this or that, there was more of an ebb and flow to America's political life than a political reading of our history might suggest. Matthias Zahm, that jack-of-all-trades in Lancaster, Pennsylvania, remarked during the 1840 election that the "poor drudges"—the riffraff who maintained the constant uproar and who could therefore get drunk every night "on both sides of the question"—would forthwith be ignored by their "late leaders and treaders" until it came time again for the "political drums and fifes" to call them into disruptive action.[74] Compelling as Roy Nichols' argument in this regard may be, those "political drums and fifes" did not always impose their will. In August 1843, Thomas Jefferson Ingersoll, a native of Massachusetts then residing in Cheneyville, Louisiana, wrote that, as of the moment, "there is little said upon politics. . . ." In August of the next year, however, in another letter to the same brother back in the hometown of New Salem, he had a far different report: "Politics are very exciting here already and getting more so."[75]

According to David Donald, people of that era had an ultimately insupportable "excess of liberty." They sought to "escape their freedom" and consequently, "Fads, fashions, and crazes swept the country."[76] In this aside, he indicates that the fervor that often centered upon the political arena frequently took surrogate form elsewhere. There is general truth in that idea, of course, and one might cite, for example, the case of Matthias Zahm. In 1840, he fumed about campaign excesses in a way that would almost suggest rational detachment, but he developed some causes of his own. After having derided the temperance movement as a mercenary creation of New Englanders, he became a staunch temperance man; in 1842 and 1843, he became absorbed in the animal magnetism (hypnotism) craze; in 1844, he mixed support of Whig candidate Clay with an intense nativism, describing the Democratic victory as one of "Foreigners over American born Citizens" and predicting the Pope's dominion over America. The man who had reviled both parties in 1840 had become a Whig to the core, even to the fiendish degree of concocting (or at least transcribing) doggerel in the cause:

> The Friends of Taylor met in Mass
> And laugh'd at poor old Lewis Cass

Though exulting in the victory of Old Taylor here in November 1848, a more contemplative Zahm recognized his own enthusiasms as well as the propensity of his age. Upon learning that the Division of the Sons of Temperance in the Conestoga community a few miles to the south had "blow'd out," Zahm mused resignedly: "Too much of a good thing will give one surfeit, as well as too much evil, (time will tell)."[77]

But orthodox religion did far more to mute singleminded concern with politics than did all the "fads, fashions, and crazes" of the era. Politics waxed as vital piety waned. Though far away in Cheneyville, Louisiana, Thomas Jefferson Ingersoll considered it his first duty to his brother at home, not to convey the warming and cooling of political affairs, but to remind him of ultimate spiritual considerations, most importantly, "our eternal destany."[78] On October 5, 1840, a roving Tennessee carpenter wrote to inform his father that he could not oblige him with the news of a recent camp meeting at Dover because he had attended a Whig rally at Nashville. "We dont do much else," he explained, "but talk polliticks now a days," but in a month things would change and discussion would return to basics.[79] Horatio Chandler of Chesterfield, New Hampshire, had enough political interest to condemn "the foul & contaminating influence of British Whigery." But in the fall of 1840 when he worked in a store in Montrose, Pennsylvania, his attention shifted to other things, notably the forthcoming fall and winter revival. When he returned to New Hampshire in late February 1841, Chandler did what he could to further the good work there. On February 27, he attended a meeting and had, in the spiritual terminology of that era, "a very happy time." That same evening he talked "very seriously" with his wife, that is to say, he "begd her to seek the Lord." Such sublime doings occupied Democrat Chandler so thoroughly that his only comment on the inauguration was that William Henry Harrison was "crowned President."[80]

A more dramatic illustration of religion's higher priority came at the January 7, 1847, meeting of a debating society in New Hartford, Connecticut. Young Democrat Walter Merrell went to that gathering abundantly prepared to oppose the proposition that the administration ought to be censured for the Mexican War. When the matter came up before the open house, however, only one vote was cast for censure. Then, to Merrell's irritation someone proposed that the lyceum or debating society itself be dissolved and transformed into a prayer meeting. Merrell was so annoyed that he walked out when it was moved, seconded, and voted that the lyceum close " '*sine die*' and that a prayer meeting be substituted in its stead." After overcoming his anger, he returned a month later to a meeting that proved, as religious meetings so often did, to be "quite an interesting" session. Now that vexing matter of military conflict was referred to a higher tribunal than a debating society; a prayer was offered "to have the Mexican War come 'to a speedy and perpetual End.' "[81]

It is very small wonder that George Camp should emphasize the similarity between religion and democratic politics: "I cannot refrain from noticing some strong points of similarity between the history of religion and of democratic liberty. . . ."[82] Writing in 1841, Camp must have known that politics of whatever stripe had first to make peace with religion. The religious bias was preeminent, and politics could fall out of accord with it only at its own peril. As a temporal force, religion provided the fundamental basis of self-control, and the extension of that could hardly be other than social control. Social control seems to have assumed negative connotations in the late twentieth century. It would not have frightened our ancestors, as long as that control involved Protestant Christian values and not the exactions of the Pope, monarchy, or other alien force.

One scholar, attempting to remove the stigma attached to the " 'social control' " inclinations of pre-Civil War America, has urged us to think of it more as "social improvement" than as " 'social control.' "[83] In part that is a commendable effort, but, in terms of unelevated perceptions, two problems arise. First, for the common people social control would have seemed far more necessary than sinister. However labeled, it would have been seen as a means of preventing necks broken by falling liberty poles or bodies sorely tried by dirks and Bowie knives. Second, the label "social improvement" suggests reform activities far too much to be in keeping with the notions of common folk.

Reform

In an undated school composition entitled "Pride," a Maine youth identified a challenge which he and others like him faced: "and it has been left for us to crush and destroy those evils which to the disgrace of our country are now alowed to range abroad unreproved and unrestrained."[84] He never identified those evils that ranged abroad. Alexander Pope's line indicating that the poor man contents himself with "the care of heaven"[85] rather than the reform of those around him may overstate the passive quality of common people in pre-Civil War America. That era has a reputation for activism, and Carl Degler, for example, espied a great many in that period who set out "On the Road to Damascus."[86] But attempts to determine the common man's feelings about and involvement in reform causes is to little avail. "Huza for Jackson & reform," a young Maryland store clerk expostulated in 1834, but here reform referred only to banking policy.[87] What a later age might construe as a reform thought probably rarely, if ever, occurred to him.

Mary Paul of Barnard, Vermont, was one who, after finding other roads painful and wearisome, tried, in the figurative sense, that road to Damascus. In the fall of 1845 the fifteen-year-old girl who was then working in Woodstock, Vermont, asked her father for permission to go to the Lowell mills where "I could earn much more to begin with than I can anywhere about here." Having prevailed upon her father, she was by late November at work in the spinning room of the Lawrence Corporation's Mill 2, and she liked it "very well." A month later, she could "doff as fast as any girl in our room," and her optimism continued: "I think that the factory is the best place for me and if any girl wants employment I advise her to come to Lowell." In time her opinion changed. A letter written after an unexplained two and a half year break in the correspondence suggests that her health had failed, but now she was back in Lowell where she had "never worked so hard" in her life, and another reduction in wages was imminent. Evidently, Mary found that she could not bear the physical pace, and she drifted into existence by work of the needle.

"I have," Mary informed her father in November 1853, "a plan for myself," one that would take her to the North American Phalanx in New Jersey. Her reasons for joining the Fourierist experiment were practical, not abstract. She explained that she could get "better pay without working as hard. . . . The price for work there being 9 cts an hour, and the number of hours for a days work, *ten*. . . ." She happily envisioned doing various kinds of work "without degrading myself, which is more than I could do anywhere else," particularly at house-work which drove women, Mary contended, to exist on twenty-five cents a week rather than submitting to the way "servants are *treated*." "At the 'Phalanx' it is different, *all* work there, and all are paid alike both men and women have the *same pay* for the *same* work—There is no such word as *Aristocracy* there unless there is *real* (not pretended) superiority. . . ."

With high hopes and her father's approval, Mary joined the phalanx, but the "strange ways" there disturbed her. Then in the fall of 1854 the mill burned, and Mary Paul recognized that this elusive dream of Horace Greeley and others was doomed. The world, she concluded, was not "ready" for Fourier's idea. She now saw the "confinement of the needle" ahead of her, but some two years after her last letter from the New Jersey commune, Mary, now twenty-seven years of age, became the wife of Isaac Guild of Lowell. It would appear that he brought her that comparative ease and comfort that the mills, the phalanx, and the "confinement of the needle" had not provided. Once she married, the enthusiasm of a girl starting at Lowell and the hope of a young woman bound for the phalanx apparently vanished. Five months after becoming Mrs. Guild, Mary wrote in a tone of philosophical resignation: "The world jogs on, and we jog with it. . . ."[88]

Mary Paul's letters contain some women's rights sentiments, but the fundamental dimension of her quest involved simply a decent and comfortably rewarding job. By and large, people of Mary's station in life rarely wrote about reform movements, and when they did so their comments generally fell somewhere between banter and hostility. For example, aside from being a debatable abstraction for lyceum meetings, the women's rights movement seems often to have been little more than a ready source of drollery. A Pennsylvania farmer who, like so many others, had an indiscriminate penchant for lecture-going, entered this reaction in his diary to one champion of the movement:

"She spoke very well, but her speech like all others on Womans Rights was of very little practical use, being at least 5000 years ahead of the time. . . ."[89] Often, simply hearing the word "bloomer" was enough to provoke hostility. In July 1856, traveler Andrew Jackson Sterrett put up for a night with an Iowa family of which the wife was "an Oberlin Bloomer." The next morning he left in a foul mood, indeed "with a mental curse upon all strong-minded, long pan-talleted women. . . . They may show off well enough somewhere, but they fail in the Kitchen."[90]

When Mary Paul Guild wrote to her father preparatory to his coming to live with her and her husband, she noted that she owed it to her husband Isaac to broach a sensitive matter. Mary felt compelled to ask that, when her father Bela joined them, he "refrain from that *one* habit which always brings naught but trouble & an ill name. . . ."[91] Whatever the reason, Bela Paul did not stay long with his daughter and her husband, and one can only infer what that "*one* habit" was that worried Mary. But the inference seems safe and ready; Mary's concern centered upon what was by far the most compelling reform urge in humble America. Fifteen years earlier, as the nation readied itself for the election of 1844, Bela Paul received a letter from his brother-in-law, Ira Coolidge. Assuming a jocular tone, Ira chided Bela for his support of Henry Clay; "from my very Soul," Ira remarked, "I believe he cant come it." Having chided his brother-in-law's political persuasions, Ira Coolidge then became earnest. How, Ira asked, was Bela doing "without old king Alcahol." Apparently, both men had attempted to overthrow that ruler, and Ira expressed the hope that Bela kept him as subdued as he was "about my diggins . . . *total Absti-nance.*!"[92] "King Alcahol" very likely had again assumed dominion over Bela Paul when his daughter remonstrated with him in 1859.

Probably in May 1853, Hannah Coffin and Adaline Wright addressed the weekly session of the "Economy Union of the Daughters of Temperance" of Economy, Indiana. Early in their brief prepared message, Hannah and Ada-line told of the organization's "precious privilege" which was "to lend our feeble aid, & to throw out our influence to the world in prohibiting the great reformation of mankind." The storekeeper's daughter and the shoemaker's daughter had bungled the phrasing, but the "Dear Sisters," ranging in age from fifteen to fifty, could not have missed the meaning. These "leagued sisters" had gone into combined action primarily because of intemperance—"the ring leader of all the vices," "this earth-blighting and soul-destroying demon."[93]

On an early November day in 1856, twenty-three-year-old Jane Conine of Perry, New York, wrote to a married sister mentioning the possibility of a visit. Whimsically, she remarked about chances of finding a man in her sister's western neighborhood, and she indulged the fancy by giving some specifications of what her sister should have ready for her. Much playfulness and a bit of earn-estness came into blend in the imaginative description; but one part rang totally of seriousness: ". . . he must be PERFECTLY TEMPERATE!"[94] That ideal, far more sought than realized, involved, as much as anything, a restraint upon the self. On a steamboat on the way to Saint Louis and the overland trail for California, a Mississippi farmer worried the possible defiance of principle when he drank some brandy as an aid against the ravages of the cholera. He had meant to keep his temperance pledge, and he resolved "not to drink only in the case of immergency."[95] In pre-Civil War America, "immergencies" abounded, especially on the Fourth of July, muster day, and the like. But at least an effort was made. "This night is the last of A.D. 1839," a man from New Hampshire wrote, "& what has been done for the temperance cause by me?" Perhaps remembering that he had had free drinks on the militia captain at George's tavern after drill, he had to admit that he had done little. He ended the entry and the diary with the somber observation that "much is to be done before we can say we are a temperance people."[96] The unblinkable reality of "King Alcahol," far more than some chimerical "King Andrew" or another, "this earth-blighting and soul-destroying demon" of the bottle more even than a slave-power conspiracy of the South brought forth what energies humble Americans had for working "the great reformation of mankind."

"Burning Kansas" and Other Controversies

The editor of the Conine family letters, in one of which Jane called for a "PERFECTLY TEMPERATE" spouse, admitted that "Politics and politicians are completely absent from the correspondence. . . , nor is there any mention of the burning issues of slavery and sectionalism." With the Conines perhaps rather more than most, the "unwavering focus on the writers' day to day lives and concerns"[97] did not extend to such matters. Diary after diary and collection after collection of letters make no mention of war in Mexico or violence in Kansas. In regard to the Mexican War, the reaction of two New England brothers—one in the home state and one in Louisiana—may have accurately reflected the country's mood. Apparently in reaction to the word that little was said of the war in the home locale, the brother in Louisiana wrote as follows: "The war with Mexico excites us here as little perhaps as it does with you."[98] In the summer after the settlement of the conflict, a young clerk in Albany noted that the city had made arrangements to have the body of a local hero disinterred from its Mexican grave and brought home for reburial. Without hesitation that soldier had gone to "defend & protect his precious land & countrymen." In terms of zeal, this entry does not approach one of some three months earlier when the diarist told of the endeavors of John B. Gough, a man who waged war against the bottle rather than against Mexicans. Though himself not inclined to abstinence, this clerk rhapsodized on this "brilliant star," this "great intellectual" who was "breathing forth to the world the pure & unoffending breath of the Temperance cause," who was smashing the "Alcoholic Bowl in atoms."[99]

The upheaval in Kansas in the 1850s should have elicited a loud reaction, but our sources are relatively quiet on the subject, thereby reflecting ignorance, indifference, or, perhaps, apprehension. There are few guides to the meaning of silence. Perhaps the common people knew little or cared little about Kansas; or perhaps they knew and cared but thought it better to attempt the sort of benign avoidance suggested earlier in the chapter. On a spring night in 1858 a young man who was employed in Greenbush across from Albany took the trouble to explain his lack of attention to what we deem important. Hearing cannon fire across the river and not knowing the occasion for it, James A. Brown archly conjectured that the artillerists were "shooting slavery out [of] Kansas," or perhaps celebrating some stroke of the "Presidents deviltry." It was of no moment "as I am not interested in politics or the Administration." With that peremptory dismissal this twenty-two-year-old man who so enjoyed temporal pleasures composed some after-midnight thoughts on "the terrors of death." He dwelled on "men wrestling for happiness & finding a grave"; he nightmarishly conjured the deck of a storm-stricken vessel where "human nature was then striped of all self-deceit before the presence of death"; and at 3:00 A.M., having filled the last page of his notebook but not his capacity for mordant revery, and having sent politics packing hours before, young Brown sought repose.[100]

Others, of course, were most concerned about the trouble in Kansas. When the man whom she hoped to marry wandered as far west as Iowa and thought of going farther, Augusta Hallock of New York warned him against Kansas: "I dont want you to go there and get killed. no no!"[101] Generally, however, even those in Kansas itself were often silent on political matters. A young man from Canal Dover, Ohio, who was a childhood schoolmate and acquaintance of William Clark Quantrill, revealed in his diary exceedingly little of the political tensions existing in the territory when he was there for six months in 1857.[102] Another youthful diarist, this one from New Castle, Pennsylvania, kept a Kansas diary from April 1855 to November 1860, the early parts of which were written on a claim near Dutch Henry's crossing on the Pottawatomie, a locale immortalized by John Brown. James R. Stewart's account reveals his love of daydreaming, drinking, reading, and other diversions. In the summer of 1856, he did a brief stint in James H. Lane's free-state army. As the martial spirit spread, Stewart set out to give "the damed ruffians hell," but that endeavor had its drawbacks and a weary and frustrated young man concluded that "war," even that on the Wakarusa, was "a hell of a thing."[103] Considering the writer's at least momentary involvement in the Kansas controversy, his diary is strikingly devoid of intimations or evidence of political or ideological issues and tensions. Aside from the entries treating his two weeks of ignominious campaigning, Stewart gave his readers almost no reason at all to picture Kansas bathed in gore. And even those few entries breathe more the spirit of trial and vexation than of anger and intensity. If God's wrath were to be meted out in Kansas, it would have to be done through people of far different spirit.

Evidently, most people concentrated on things more prosaic than political imperatives. In remarking about the "danger of collisions" in Kansas Territory, Joseph Trego, who was engaged in the mill business at Sugar Mound, stated simply that he and others like him were "so absorbed in business that we do not have time to think about the matter."[104] To be sure, Trego probably wrote this statement to comfort a wife back in Illinois, but his wish that people would stay "absorbed in business" may not have been an idle one. Next to religion, business afforded the surest anodyne for political ideology. A man who should have had great political interest but who at the moment was "very economical of opinions on political questions" wrote to a brother from Leavenworth in November 1856, "a man's politics can only be obnoxious here."[105]

Writing from the gold reaches in 1850, young John Paul Dart mentioned statehood for California. He remarked that if one believed the San Francisco newspapers and the speeches in Congress, one would imagine that Californians were very "anxious and indignant" about the matter. "Humbug!" the young Mississippian snorted, "There is not one man in a hundred that cares a dam about it one way or another."[106] And Joseph Trego told of the "hearty laugh" that he and others had enjoyed when reading yet another of the "Kansas yarns" concocted by the press.[107]

In general, the sources used for the present study discuss politics pretty much in proportion to their respective station in life, particularly if that station related to journalism or law. In the fluid society of that era, moves into such realms might occur without much scrutiny of credentials, especially in the western reaches. When he learned that his brother John was practicing law in California, James Kinkade wrote to inquire how attorneys were "manufactured" in that state. John's answer should not be taken literally, but in parodying the questions put to him in the bar examination, he intimated the ease with which some could move into functions where political instincts had fuller sway: "Are you a good judge of Cogniac and Bourbon? . . . Have you got money enough to treat the Court and Committee with Shampaigne and Cigars?"[108]

Occasionally, some common men took a real interest in political activity. Charles E. De Long left his Duchess County, New York, farm and went to California where, among other things, he was a miner, saloonkeeper, hotel clerk, and deputy sheriff. On March 8, 1854, the young man went to the state capitol where he "heard the Senators and Assemblymen Spout out some of their superfluous Gas."[109] Despite his derision of politicians, he soon achieved some political prominence as "California's bantam cock." Francis W. Squires made the move away from the New York farm more slowly, but in the fall of 1860, after having been a passive observer, he became active in Republican organizational efforts. On August 4, farmer Squires took a long step toward

modernity when he "traded a testament for a Political Text Book."[110] Within
several months that trade brought him the appointment as village postmaster.

The Necrology of Politics

Many people who seemed to have an almost scandalous lack of concern for
the effect their political leaders had upon the world at least bothered to note
when those leaders left the world. Rather like Hawthorne's gravestone carver,
they were careful "to label the dead bodies."[111] Two weeks after the death of
President Harrison, a woman in Erie, Pennsylvania, wrote to another woman
in Franklin telling her of the "solemn and imposing" observances by which the
people "of both parties" in Erie had paid their last "sad Honours to their dearest President." Whatever else that death signified, "Still it is but one of the
tokens of the frailtie of all human power."[112] In that same spring, another
Pennsylvania woman wrote to a cousin telling her that the prayer meetings
continued their nightly supplications "for a revival of religion in this Church."
To this letter she appended some "Lines on the Death of William Henry Harrison," a transcription of the efforts of some versifier who had blended Pope and
Gray for the occasion. Part of the poem advised against despair, for "the power
which raised" a Washington and a Harrison

> To save their country in a dangerous day
> Can raise another great and good as they.

But the central point of this poetic message reiterated the prosaic one from
Erie, "the frailtie of all human power" and man's ultimate insufficiency:

> With all his power his life he cannot save:
> The path of glory lead but to the grave.[113]

The age's prodigious appetite for necrology required that deceased leaders
be given so many ceremonial funerals and "burials" that an unsuspecting
modern reader might imagine that there were repeated interments. In this
regard, a combination of entries by a Maryland diarist might arouse some
wonderment: on August 5, 1834, he recorded that the "burial of Gen¹
Lafayett" took place at a village just across the Potomac, and on October 16 he
wrote that "the Burrial of Gen¹ Lafayett took place today in Hagerstown."[114]
Funerals were routinely delayed for weeks or even months after burial in order
to allow a gathering of the family and friends. Hence, there was nothing
untoward about solemnities conducted at far remove in time and place from
actual interment. The "funeral procession for our much beloved Jackson"
required three hours and twenty minutes to pass Chatham Square in

Manhattan over two weeks after the remains of the old general had been committed to its Tennessee grave.[115]

When a housewife in Wheeling, Virginia, wrote to an old friend in her home area of upstate New York, she included some description of the house in which she lived. "Over the mantle," she noted, "hangs General Harrison's tomb in a black frame."[116] This woman's letters often had an arch, sometimes even earthy quality; but politics and politicians made their entry only by way of the tomb of William Henry Harrison. An observation from Richard II might well have aptness: "More are men's ends mark'd than their lives before."[117] Not only did people observe the death of public figures more than their achievements, but they also often specified the very moment of departure. Thus, one frequently encounters such diary information as that Daniel Webster died *"24 inst at 2.38 AM."*[118]

There were, of course, noteworthy deaths in realms other than politics, and one of them may help to elucidate moods. When Hawthorne beheld the Genesee Falls on a visit to Rochester, he confessed that his

chief interest arose from a legend, connected with these falls, which will become poetical in the lapse of years, and was already so to me as I pictured the catastrophe out of dusk and solitude. It was from a platform raised over the naked island of the cliff, in the middle of the cataract, that Sam Patch took his last leap, and alighted in the other world.[119]

When Patch stepped off into eternity in the fall of 1829 he assured that, for the next two or three decades, those passing through Rochester would be as disinclined to miss the scene of that death leap as a visitor to Boston would be to miss Mount Auburn Cemetery. "Led by curiosity," wrote a young New Englander while in Rochester, "to look upon the scene of Sam Patch's immortality." Then, unfortunately, he undertook to rhapsodize:

> The gaping multitudes might stare,
> Patch took his stand aloft in air[120]

Sam Patch may have had, as Richard M. Dorson contended, "attributes for American apotheosis." His "fondness for brag, antics, drink, and danger . . . reflected the ebullient Jacksonian United States."[121] In what is known of that fellow who made a series of extraordinary plunges leading to Genesee Falls, the modern eye discerns a strong resemblance to James Thurber's "The Greatest Man in the World." But, as Hawthorne realized, Patch's fame came by "immortality," by death. If for a time he was an "American apotheosis" that may have derived more from his death than from his life. That inconsequential braggart and rounder elevated himself by an act of deathly showmanship, taking his "last leap" into "the other world" in a peculiarly public and spectacular way. Even more than vital heroics, death was on exhibition at the Falls of the Genesee.

In the wake of the election of 1852, a man in Buffalo briefly mentioned politics in a letter to his son. Webster and Clay, he said, "have both departed," and their equals will be long in arriving. Webster in particular had towering capacities, and, "his failings" notwithstanding, he had been "a great man."[122] Here, as in the infrequent similar references to Webster and his peers, the specific nature of the greatness is not described. "It was Daniel Webster's destiny," Irving Bartlett has written, "to become 'godlike' while he lived."[123] The man in Buffalo had a far different final concern about Webster: "On his death bed did he pray for pardon and for acceptance with God." Though the particular implications of it may have changed with time, the Shakespearean dictum retained its general force: "Nothing in his life became him like the leaving it."[124]

Impending Crisis

Late in December 1860, Iowa farmer Michael Luark, a self-styled "Green Hoosier" with a poetic inclination, versified about the weather and brooded about the future of the nation. Born in Virginia, this forty-two-year-old man was the quintessentially mobile American. After four years in Virginia, he grew to manhood in Indiana. In subsequent years, he lived in Illinois and Iowa; he followed mining booms to Colorado and California; and he spent the mid-1850s in Washington Territory to which he would later return for the remainder of his long life. Now it was the rigors of "Winter in Iowa" that inspired the poetic farmer: "Ever changing blow, Blow, *BLOW*." In the meditative last entry of the year, Luark, returning to prose form, translated the challenges posed by nature into those encountered by the ship of state. Foreboding colored his expectations of the coming year, in which there might well occur some "startling developments in our Political History," possibly even the "Dissolution of the Union and Civil War with all its train of horrors." On the next day, in the initial entry of the fateful year, he somberly commented on the grim portents. If President-elect Lincoln allowed free rein to those "most ultra sectional and Abolition" men who had secured his victory and who would wish now to trouble the "vexed Slavery question" even further, "then farewell to our beloved Union of States."[125]

One would assume that literate people of whatever class would have recorded their reactions to this moment of crisis. Such is not the case, however. The "Green Hoosier" went somewhat beyond his fellows. On the basis of such sources, however, there is little to prepare us for the inexorable tragedy of Civil War. In these writings, sectional sentiments appeared far less frequently and intensely than approaching war suggests. The sparse data in the writings of the unsophisticated in those pre-war years suggest that, insofar as North and South bore antipathy one toward another, the antipathy sprang from sources other than the one perceived by many leaders of the time and, of course, by countless others of whatever attainment after the fact of the disaster.

"Wildness," Ralph Waldo Emerson contended, was the cardinal attribute of the southern character. Folk from the South were "more civilized than the Seminole," the seer conceded, "a little more." William R. Taylor has noted a paradoxical quality in Emerson's scorn for southern "wildness," for it is contradictory to Emerson's almost inordinate fondness for the "unhandselled savage nature" of "terrible Druids and Berserkers" which he expressed in the same year that southern "wildness" gave offense.[126] Unsophisticated Northerners had a much less intense view of the South, but a much more consistent one. Insofar as the South aroused their apprehension, it did so for much the same reason that Emerson's outburst suggests. The fundamental basis for suspicion of the South derived from a perception of a land suffering a comparative lack of restraint and discipline; a land with a comparative propensity for the natural and the spontaneous. The quiverings and murmurings, however great or small, generated by the South in the American moral imagination moved along almost the same lines of force as those generated by the West.

It was a "melancholy tale" indeed that a Steubenville, Ohio, man reported in July 1837. He had learned that his brother who had been working in a Shreveport, Louisiana, store had been "litteraly butchered" by two "incarnate devils" in what began as a trivial altercation. "God of heaven cool my burning brain," he prayed; heeding the pleas of his wife and children, he decided against a trip to that community where the slayers of his brother not only enjoyed freedom but also boasted of their deed.[127] This Ohioan did not pronounce a general indictment of the South. In cases where such an indictment was made, it reflected the general belief that such nasty incidents were characteristic of the South, a land where self-restraint was rare.

"The way they kill men here," a young jewelry salesman wrote from Mobile, Alabama, "is a caution to others." His parents both threatened and pleaded with him to forsake his business venture and return home to New York City.[128] "Stay no longer among them Southerners," an Ohio father admonished a son in Canton, Mississippi. Realizing that his son might have a mind of his own in the matter, the father assumed a more positive tone. If he stayed, the son should choose the least "vitious" company available.[129] A young upstate New York woman of simple background, working as a teacher and governess on a Georgia plantation, complained that the planter's wife was "not capable of giving one word of advice or making one wise suggestion in regard to the taming of her own children." Because the South lacked "taming," it suffered what Jennie Akehurst called "this half civilized mode of living."[130] Even more than the enslavement of blacks, the license and self-indulgence of whites aroused the Northerners' misgivings about the South.

"Pardon me when I say to you *do not go*[;] indeed I cannot bear the thoughts of it." In that way, Fanny Barber beseeched Lawrence Parker, the man she would marry, as he prepared to leave on a clock-selling expedition in the South. Lawrence went, however, and Fanny made the best of it in the Sheldon, New York, area. Fanny's imagination created more compelling scenes of "traversing the wilds of the South with you," of traversing what she styled the " 'far west' "—Tennessee and Alabama. Lawrence went to improve his health and his finances.[131] As a young New Englander confided in his diary upon his arrival in New Orleans, "I am going regardless of consequences, into an unhealthy climate amongst lawless and vicious men, with but one object—money getting—and this with the hope that I may be enabled to return to my native state and enjoy life free from the vexation attendant upon a short purse."[132] Any fears the South aroused were apparently overcome by possibility of material betterment.

In his treatment of the impact which the South had upon the imagination of the abolitionists, Ronald G. Walters narrows his focus to "their [the abolitionists'] drive to control man's animal nature, particularly his sexuality."[133] He reminds us that reformers of that era, even radical ones, sought man's betterment more by imposing controls than by lifting them. Without narrowing the matter to sex and slavery, the unabashed conviction that "man's animal self had to be conquered"[134] serves well as the central normative precept of the "mute inglorious Milton." Restraint assumed the proportions of an admonitory byword. Whereas the abolitionists saw the South as "a society in which man's sexual nature had no checks put upon it,"[135] the common men simply saw the South as a society in which human nature generally had insufficient checks.

Mr. and Mrs. Abner Goddard had left their native Pennsylvania to settle in Missouri. Now in early 1847 they intended to get out of the "land of Ague & Slavery," as Abner called it. His wife, Catherine, explained that she was reluctant to raise their children where "they might hear guns and hounds all day Sunday."[136] Here she meant the sounds, not of the fugitive chase, but of leisure, diversion, and, because Sunday was in the equation, abandon. "Oh! How different from the Sabbath at home . . . ," was the plaintive word of a Yankee schoolma'am in that "strange land" of Louisiana.[137]

These sources contain very few overt negative reactions to slavery. Fanny Barber for one expressed her opposition to that institution. Her clock-selling fiancé, Lawrence Parker, had more complicated feelings, perhaps because he had been in the South. With regard to religion, he considered himself "a child of nature," and possibly that natural condition, which so many Northerners ascribed generally to the South, caused him to equivocate about what Fanny considered this "very cruel mater" of slavery.[138]

In the writings of people who had lived in the South, unqualified antislavery sentiments almost never appear. A Vermont woman who was a teacher or governess in the Greenville, North Carolina, area was very ambivalent. She felt certain that she was seeing slavery in its "most desirable garb," but she insisted that that only made her the more opposed to it. "And yet—I cannot see for my life what can be done. The case is desperate." She had seen no brutality; indeed, in her experience, slaves received good food and appeared contented. Still, they had no "liberty." This distraught and well-meaning woman found no happy way out of her quandary. "Poor *creatures*—how I pity them— yet what can be done! 'Mas's'r' 'Mas'r' I fear ever will be the watchword of Afric's poor sons."[139] Even Jennie Akehurst who was so self-consciously northern in attitude and so diligent in guarding against lapses into the less restrained and less spiritual southern ways, dismissed the South as " 'Darkiedom.' " Its residents of one color aroused her sympathy no more than did those of another.[140]

Young carpenter Henry B. Miller, whom we saw embattled for Benton at the polls in Carondolet, Missouri, went down the river to the Natchez area in December 1838. There he described the observation of Christmas week "which in slave states is always a great time." He told of the southern custom of giving the slaves the week off from Christmas to New Year—this in an era when Christmas Day itself often went unobserved in the North. (Protestant misgivings about Christmas had not yet disappeared, and for the North the intense and extended celebration of it in slave areas might have been taken as disquieting evidence of prodigality on the one hand and susceptibility to popish ceremonialism on the other.) Miller described the jubilation from one plantation of an area to the next, with the consummate event being "a Grand Niggah Ball." In seriocomic tone, he complained that in such a setting we do not have "the niggah in his originality," but rather we have "the White man nigahafied." That last irregular verb form apparently meant that, at the "Grand Niggah Ball," the black man aped the white man's ways: "When into de saloon he lead de blushing damsels, Dare eyes outshine de moon. . . ."[141]

In his efforts at humor, the carpenter illustrates the tendency of Northerners to employ adventurous descriptives and to resort to potentially offensive parody. Apparently, Southerners were downright finicky by comparison. For a northern example in 1854, an Iowa farm woman wrote home to the western New York area to report that her husband had drifted toward the Whig and anti-Kansas-Nebraska persuasion, and thus had become "a nigger man."[142] That corruption of the word "Negro" appears very rarely in sourthern sources. A passage from a letter written by a small-time Georgia slave trader suggests the comparative fastidiousness that seems to have been practiced. "Tell all the Negros," he urged his wife while he was away on a trading and selling venture, "if they dont mind and Doe right and wait on yew it will be hard times with them when I get home."[143] Perhaps such usages mean very little, but from the scant remarks one finds regarding race and slavery, one gathers that the average Northerner felt no great moral outrage over the "peculiar institution" or any intense solicitude for those fettered by it.

In 1857, a young Pennsylvanian recounted one of those episodes in slavery which was "so often the subject of description by Northerners": the separation of a slave man from his wife and child. When the owner of a slave named John decided to move west from Macon County, Missouri, another man who owned John's wife and their child pleaded, as did others, with the migrant to sell John rather than break up the family. An offer of $1300 did not overcome the adamance of John's owner, so John and Eliza were separated. Indignation surfaces in this man's description, but what borders on callous mockery appears as well. "John's wife," he wrote of the final meeting and the final separation, "was bawling so that I heard her before they got within 20 rods. John kept a pretty stiff upper lip until Eliza went out & met them & set up her bawl; then he began to whimper & finally he roared too."[144]

Earlier in the same letter, the Pennsylvanian undertook a light parody of the Sunday afternoon watermelon socials held by the blacks outside the Macon County home where he was staying temporarily. The writer was apparently familiar with the black-face shows of the era, and what he penned here smacks much of the spirit of minstrelsy. Robert C. Toll's assertion in *Blacking Up*, that "For a decade, Northern audiences could view slavery as little more than part of the minstrel show,"[145] may be unguarded, but the ease with which the Pennsylvanian slipped into descriptions evocative of the black-face show— "such unprovoked & boisterous yah, yah, yahing & such gallantry & coquettishness you never saw"—suggests that the profound and tragic condition of those in slavery was more easily borne when kept in comic euphemism. They were, as he styled them himself, "niggers."[146]

Always, a cautionary word of some kind came forth to defuse the potential for positive action against slavery, or almost anything else. A Maine housewife who was never near slavery listened to a Wendell Phillips lecture with general sympathy but with reservations. "Very many good things," she noted, "but very sarcastic & many hard thrusts at ministers in particular & religion generally. *Everything* must bend & give place to the *one great thing*—the *Abolition of slavery*—man's laws & God's ordinances if need be." A week later, this inveterate lecture-goer heard Theodore Parker, and she was pleasantly surprised: "Contrary to my expectations, he had nothing exceptionable in sentiment—rather humorous, & on the whole a very good lecture."[147] In one of the infrequent mentions of *Uncle Tom's Cabin*, an Alleghany, Pennsylvania, man who had gone to the California mining reaches urged his wife to read the novel. Miner John Eagle did not specify why she should read it, but he did suggest that if she were too busy she might have her sister Net read it to her while she worked. Two months later, Net's brother who was with Eagle in the mines wrote a word to Net that may have been meant to forestall untoward inferences being derived from a reading of Harriet Beecher Stowe: "Net I dont want you to be gowing to Niger Church."[148] Young Pennsylvania farmer John Cummins finished Stowe's *Dred* at the end of 1856 and considered it "a well written book" in which "the evils of slavery are graphically displayed." "But practically, Slavery is very far from its abolishment though much to be desired."[149]

Conclusion

In *The Liberal Tradition in America*, Louis Hartz mentions the "sad resignation of America,"[150] a quality that permeates the writings of common people. Their almost instinctive reaction to troubles was resignation. Thus, the young man closed his account of slave John's removal from his wife and child with sardonic use of the words of "pious justification" uttered by his host: "he 'reckons that's what John was made for!' " Whether a Macon County, Missouri, innkeeper, a Pennsylvania farmer, a Maine housewife, a Forty-niner, or even this first-hand witness to heartbreak, the common man in pre-Civil War America would show little more than wariness and suspicion when a Wendell Phillips threatened "man's laws and God's ordinances." "I do not believe in slavery," a young store clerk wrote from Detroit after an untidy incident there involving some runaways, "but I believe in protecting the laws which are made for us."[151]

Such people would have been mildly surprised to be informed that slavery and race were sundering the beloved union. And to conceive of such people fighting a long and bloody war over slavery poses a staggering challenge to the imagination. Whatever it was that rent the union and paved the way to devastation, the response to the concrete fact was predictably prayerful. On November 2, 1860, Sarah Johnson, the wife of a small businessman in Oswego, New York, felt "very gloomy about the election. God help this distracted country." Four days later, Mrs. Johnson repeated the invocation: "again I say God help the country."[152]

Pauline Stratton, a native of Pennsylvania who had moved from Virginia to Missouri in 1855 with her husband, children, and half-dozen slaves, regularly sought God's aid for a variety of sore burdens. Now in November 1860, she sought surcease for a troubled country wherein talk of secession was open and earnest: "I pray that God would avert such a thing from our beloved country." Almost twenty years before, when seventeen-year-old Pauline wrote to accept Thomas Stratton's proposal of marriage, she said that she was embarking upon her new life with the hope of God's assistance and with the prayer that, so assisted, the days of their union would "glide sweetly." Those nineteen years had not glided very sweetly at all. Pauline Stratton knew that God's solicitude, though infinite, was unfathomable. At the end of December 1860, she concluded that only His intervention could spare the country war.[153] She did not need to add that it might not serve His cosmic purpose to intervene.

Nature and Art 7

Nature was whatever bore no marks of man, whatever was unshaped, unculti-
vated, or undomesticated. Art was what man had done. These very basic
definitions serve as a point of departure for consideration of a sizable wonderment experienced by the common people of pre-Civil War America.

The General Religious Framework

An old farmer in Delaware County, New York, had some sad news to convey at the beginning of February 1841. An aged relative had died; "the light of
the candle gradually sunck down into the socket and was extinct, and she
seeast to exist." The old man sent glad tiding as well: "I hasten to tell you not
withstanding God afflicts he also sends joy and gives song in the night, even
songs of great deliverance. . . ." In the standard winter setting, protracted
evening meetings had been under way for "some time past," and "the spirt of
the Lord had ben hovering around some lost siners and found them in a waste
wilderness where there was no way." "Songs of great deliverance" came from
those who had emerged from "natures darkness" into God's "marvellus
light."[1]

It would not do to force Niagara Falls, the Natural Bridge, or the Rocky
Mountains into this conventional Christian dichotomy of nature and grace as
rendered by a farmer on the western slopes of the Catskills, for he spoke in
similitudes. Still, one must bear in mind that, for an intensely Christian people,
any discussion of nature must have involved, at least vaguely, the imagery of
hostile chaos and downright threats to the soul in pilgrimage. "Nature's darkness" on the one hand and the "marvellus light" on the other hand involved
absolute and mutually exclusive categories. Religious deviation such as
Transcendentalism might alter the perception, and changing aesthetic canons,
which at least in hackneyed expressions made their way into popular language,
might accelerate the drift to a positive view. But the transformation from the

gloom of "waste wilderness" to the glory of nature ennobled and idolized probably moved along rather more slowly than a reading of Emerson might suggest.

Though concerned mostly with literary and aesthetic considerations,
Marjorie Hope Nicholson does give some attention to "The Theological
Dilemma" in *Mountain Gloom and Mountain Glory*:

'Cursèd is the earth'—perhaps in this old idea, so old that we had forgotten it, lies one
explanation of the superstitious awe with which Nature was surrounded, from the Dark
Ages to Rip Van Winkle, in the minds of men to whom the "haunted air and gноmèd
mine" were filled with malign and awful presences and powers.[2]

To put the matter another way, the overwhelming consideration in our ancestors' minds was the subduing of nature. Earthly paradise was unattainable,
least of all in nature. The much-remarked garden of the world, for example,
was simply that and no more. However much temporal comfort might derive
from it, it was of the world, while the ultimate goal was the garden of the other
world.

The polarity of nature and grace paralleled the duality of things temporal
and things spiritual. In both cases, the imperative was to move from the former
to the latter—from nature and things temporal to grace and things spiritual.
Nature and things temporal stood unmodified and unregenerate. Grace and
things spiritual stood modified and regenerated. As the old farmer in Delaware
County put it in regard to those who had recently been led from "natures darkness,": "they say that they hardly know themselves." Different categories and
considerations were emerging, however. With the help of such theorists as
Edmund Burke, Hugh Blair, and William Gilpin, Western man had moved
toward a positive aesthetic appreciation of the untamed and the illimitable.
Here in the aesthetic realm, the tension involved nature and art. Trouble arose
in reconciling the religious perception and the aesthetic perception.

Somewhat oddly, when common folk turned to the matter of the tension between nature and art, they took their stand, at the village debating societies and
elsewhere, for nature. Though viewed as refractory and sinister in religious
terms, nature came, in this small step toward modernity, into some favor. It did
so because of a combination of inadvertence, transcendence, and humility.
With heedless inadvertence common folk appropriated some cliches of an
aesthetic language, the implications of which they seem not to have understood. The ethic of that insinuating rhetoric augured ill for the old convictions.
In turn, with almost inspired pedestrianism they relied upon Alexander Pope
to work a feat of transcendence whereby nature could be argued past the credentials committee. In this formulation, nature, however frightening and
chaotic it might appear to be, had cosmic design and was, of course, God's art.
In the immediate view, nature bedeviled and destroyed, but, in a variant of
cosmic optimism, its ultimates were purposeful and beneficent.

All Nature is but Art, unknown to thee;
All Chance, Direction, which thou canst not see;
All Discord, Harmony not understood;
All partial Evil, universal Good:[3]

God orchestrated nature, and, though one might not perceive the harmony, one could at least look with Pope "thro' Nature up to Nature's God."[4] And here, born of God-fearing humility came the ritual warnings against prideful celebration of art, the works of man.

Observing Nature and Enchaining Fancy

When Hattie Kendall wrote from Maine to a relative in Minnesota Territory, she spoke her wish to be in the West when the prairies were in "the height of their bounty," that being, she imagined, "well worthy, the pen of a poet, or the pencil of the painter."[5] Had they had a chance, the Hattie Kendalls of the world would not have been able to "muse on Nature with a poet's eye," as Thomas Campbell expressed it in "The Pleasures of Hope."[6] The people could not often indulge in the luxury of musing. As a Texan who had been captured after the Mier battle in 1842 and who now was a prisoner marching hungry, thirsty, and weary in the Monterrey area noted morosely, "[I] had no taste for the beauties of nature."[7] A few days out of Fort Laramie, a California-bound Hoosier admitted that the scenery might have been judged "sublime" by others, "but what charm had barren praries to us who wanted grass and water."[8] Lack of opportunity was one thing, but lack of ability loomed even larger. With some moments for sunset reverie in the waste country beyond South Pass, another migrant sensed the magnificence of the setting; "what a field I have before me but my untutored mind must let it pass. . . ."[9]

In fact, his untutored mind did not let it pass entirely. Both before and after his disclaimer, he attempted the rhapsodic, as, for example, this flourish while viewing California's mountains: "whose proud summits, were decked with white shining snow, purest of earthly things, and fittest to rest against the blue heaven."[10] Something impelled these unlettered people to make such verbal efforts and to do so with surprising frequency.

Much of that attention came from the hope of improving the mind. Not long before going to work in an Albany store, young William Hoffman lolled about the farm and sought to keep himself out of difficulty. He undertook to improve his time by reading Isaac Watts' *Improvement of the Mind*, that religious popularization of Locke's *Essay Concerning Human Understanding*. Just what "rare; yes superexcellent ideas" this young man got from Watts is unclear. (He did learn one of Watts' hymns, thus indicating that he was using an edition incorporating both facets of that cleric's talents.) Possibly Watts impressed him with his remarks on the first of those "eminent means or methods whereby the mind is improved," that being "Observation"—"all that Mr. Locke means by sensation and reflection."[11] By inference we might move from Watts on observation to Hoffman on nature six days later: ". . . as the gorgeous Sun gradually raised its disk above the horizon & reflected its luminous rays against the Hills. . . . Extending & expanding throughout & over the great Face of Nature."[12] In other cases, one needs no inference. "You must keep a journal of your trip," a young man wrote a cousin bound for California, ". . . nothing is so improving as the exercise of *description of places*."[13] The discipline leading to improvement of the mind could be intensified by resort to verse form, often with lamentable results such as those worked by a New Yorker writing atop one of the heights in Panama City:

> here the winds are soft the air is mild
> the forests a perpetual green
> the winterry winds are never felt
> the whitening snows are never seen[14]

Of course, one need not ascribe all portrayals of nature to Lockean calculation alone. Perhaps as Gray put it in the "Elegy," some of the common folk did indeed have hearts "pregnant with celestial fire" (line 46).

> See the patriarchal forest
> Clothed in hues that never fade[15]

A self-styled "Green Hoosier" and irrepressible poet penned those and other "Fugitive Thoughts" while on his way to the Pike's Peak gold area in 1860. Michael Luark had at least some "fire," and he seems never to have lost it as he lifted himself from farming, carpentering, and gold-chasing into the main chance of the "patriarchal forest," a small sawmill in the Puget Sound area. Writing from nearby Sauvie Island in the lower Columbia, Charlotte Whipple told of having given birth to a daughter in the latter stages of the overland trip. Here, Charlotte revealed a straightforward spirit that seems in keeping with her apparently indomitable nature. She wrote of the childbirth that "the fuss was all over in an hour" after an evening encampment just short of the Boise River. In the morning she walked from the tent to the wagon, the train "not lying by one hour on my account"—"wasn't I right smart as the Hoosier says." Perhaps that whimsy belies her imaginative side, the side that gets expression elsewhere in the same letter home. In terms of her present condition, she told of being snugly ensconced in a cabin on the banks of the "great & beautiful Columbia," a river "truly far surpassing all the rivers in the states being from one to four miles wide along here[,] clear as crystal & moving along with a calm grandeur which insensibly enchains the fancy."[16]

As has been contended through much of this study, people such as Charlotte Whipple had views that were fundamentally pre-Romantic. They generally sought to enchain the fancy in a way which was quite different from that suggested by Charlotte's rapt comments on the Columbia. The conventional wisdom almost invariably held that building castles not only wasted the immediate moment, but also posed a threat to the very capacity to employ right reason. Charlotte's genuine regard for nature probably did not overcome those unanswerable precepts instilled in her years before as she grew to womanhood in the Catskill region. She had internalized that penchant for keeping intrepid scrutiny upon a "mind to[o] prone to wander," even "the necessity of more vigilant watchfulness over a heart too prone to cling to earth." A heavy rain that prevented Sunday church attendance seems to have elicited from her the sort of enchaining indictment she might otherwise have received from someone else: "Oh what a wicked heart I have[,] continually prone to wander[.] How far short I come of performing my duties or keeping the commands." We seem to get beyond this spiritual censoriousness when Monday dawned gorgeously. "Oh what a delightful morn," came the word from this twenty-five-year-old woman. But the mood of the previous day quickly reasserted itself. The ecstasy came into check and was channeled into prayer for attunement with God, "if only I prove an obedient child."[17] For the sake of the soul itself, all must be brought into discipline, even the splendor of a Catskill sunrise.

Discipline, order, and subjection were the bywords; nature as well as human nature needed tailoring. The disarray of nature suggested or meant abandon, and, at least in principle, these people eschewed abandon. To make the point with an extreme illustration, we can go to a Mexican War volunteer who luxuriated in being a private soldier and in being subjected to army regimen. In one instance, a Byronic sentiment flowed from his perfervid pen:

"To me high mountains are a feeling
But the hum of human cities torture"

But he contrived this usage as rhetorical counterpoint: "Such *used* to be my feelings. . . ." Having left Byron in his wake, he could now urge a policy whereby, through some paramilitary arrangement, 100,000 men would be sent to subdue nature in the West, even to extirpating its animal population: *"No living thing save men."*[18]

Flourishes of outright fanaticism came rarely; most people expressed the drive to bring nature into ordered subjection in a more moderate form. In a negative instance, a young New Yorker, as he made his way by steamer up the Alabama River in the fall of 1840, showed a variant of the apprehension about southern wildness. "As yet," he grumbled, "we have not come to the place that wears the least appearance of civilization or the rudest improvement."[19] In like vein, a man from Maine wrote to his wife, who was home on the farm near

Milo, that it would be nice to live in Bangor. The scant thirty-five miles from Bangor to the village in Piscataquis County measured the chasm separating "the advantages of *civilized society*" from "a kind of half civilized and heathenish" condition.[20] A schoolgirl's composition entitled "Flowers" kept the focus mostly upon the positive side of the equation. She did not dwell upon the wild profusion that this form of nature's bounty might show but rather upon the idea that, insofar as flowers gave "medecine to the mind," they did so in "well-cultivated" gardens. To see such exercises in orderliness by the mansion of the great or the cottage of the lowly was to know that therein resided a person of "correct habits."[21]

The neatness that reflected correct habits in dominion over nature made its way, with ever lessening force, even into the plains and the mountains. Graves, those most arresting places, gave ironic testimony to man's presence, and satisfaction of sorts could be drawn from the care taken with them. In the early stretches of the California trail in the spring of 1850, Elias Daggy of Indiana made the characteristic references to graves passed, adding such comments as "head board inscription neat," graves "all neat." Farther along on June 10, "an Allwise Providence" through the agency of cholera claimed a member of Daggy's party, and the deceased was left under "a neat little mound" some 140 miles east of Fort Laramie.[22] Back along the trail in that same spring, another argonaut envisioned greater triumphs over nature than neat mounds and headboards. As he gazed out upon the "vast expanse of prearie" in western Iowa, he foretold the day when it would "all be subdued, fenced with wire and hedges."[23] This prophet lived an even hundred years, long past the time needed to show the accuracy of his forecast.

At the outset of his study *Wilderness and the American Mind,* Roderick Nash calls attention to a compelling etymological matter regarding the word "wilderness." "In the early Teutonic and Norse languages, from which the English word in large part developed, the root seems to have been 'will' with a descriptive meaning of self-willed, willful, or uncontrollable."[24] Here, to the humble eye, was something of frightful mien indeed. No more was needed to arouse fearful apprehensions than the spectre of human nature freed of restraint. And nature as a physical dimension, for threatening just that release, assumed the proportions of "dark and sinister symbol," as Nash puts it in regard to wilderness per se. "A more subtle terror than Indians or animals," he remarks elsewhere, "was the opportunity the freedom of wilderness presented for men to behave in a savage or bestial manner."[25] Here we have a truth which, however conventional, deserves underscoring and bearing in mind because some quite different views of more sophisticated people are sometimes ascribed to far too many.

An arresting illustration can be found in a work which Nash mentions as taking a view of the matter different from his own. In *The Golden Day,* Lewis Mumford impressionistically located some Rousseauvian origins for the western spirit and movement of the pioneers themselves. According to Mumford, such people were undertaking "an experimental investigation of Nature, Solitude, The Primitive Life."[26] In fact, however, in the purview of the plain folk, "Nature, Solitude, The Primitive Life" posed threats to human felicity and the human soul matched perhaps only by those of the devil himself, who, by the way, was generally seen to have free play, if not sovereignty in precisely those domains.

When Herman Melville's confidence-man assumed the guise of herb doctor—" 'one who has confidence in nature, and confidence in man, with some little modest confidence in himself' "—he met his match, perhaps for the only time in his series of chameleon appearances, in a "hard case" from Missouri. Before encountering the herb doctor himself, that stubble-chinned "hard case" with the double-barreled gun and the "Spartan manners and sentiments" carried on the following exchange with a tubercular miser who had risen to the confidence-man's lure and had purchased some of the medicine—" 'nat'ral yarbs, pure yarbs' ":

'Because a thing is nat'ral, as you call it, you think it must be good. But who gave you that cough? Was it, or was it not nature?'

'Sure, you don't think that natur, Dame Natur, will hurt a body, do you?'

'Natur is good Queen Bess; but who's responsible for the cholera?'

'But yarbs; yarbs are good?'

'What's deadly-nightshade? Yarb, ain't it'[27]

Confidence-men abounded, perhaps a good many of them in the role of herb doctor, but where nature in the generic and philosophical sense entered the consideration, Melville's ursine "hard case" had a great many counterparts. And, of course, even Ralph Waldo Emerson saw other susceptibilities for man vis-à-vis nature than becoming a transparent eyeball. Emerson, too, could be a hard case. "Our Western prairie," he noted as illustration of a general contention, "shakes with fever and ague." That and many other things like it gave "hints of ferocity in the interiors of nature." "Let us not deny it up and down," he urged; "Nature is no sentimentalist,—does not cosset or pamper us."[28]

The Agrarian Myth

As would be expected, our sources express an admiring attitude toward agriculture and pastoralism. The common man's pleasure in the pastoral, however, derived not from his comparative proximity to nature but from his recognition that, in agricultural and pastoral settings, nature had been subdued and rendered orderly.

My reading of the sources leads me to perhaps a significantly different emphasis from that which John Ward gives to this matter. "They celebrated nature," Ward wrote of Jacksonian Americans, "but not wild nature."[29] Waiving for the moment questions as to whether it is possible to celebrate "nature" but not "wild nature" and recognizing that Ward's perception of the ideal American scene of that era as being a "corn field surrounded by a split rail fence" has much to commend it, one yet ought to remember the most rudimentary fact that nature had little positive attraction to those bereft of the luxury of contemplating it in comfortable abstraction. Many people of that generation perceived, as Ward contends, a spectrum running from pure nature to full civilization, and they accepted an obligation to maintain a middle position. But the obligation antecedent to all other considerations was to move away from nature. At sufficiently long remove from nature, contrary feelings might be allowed.

When, in Leo Marx's depiction, the train whistle breaks the author's meditation in Sleepy Hollow, we are left with a sense of harsh intrusion and defilement. The machine had gotten loose in the garden.[30] From his home near Irasburgh, a scant few miles from the Canadian line in northernmost Vermont, Zuar Jameson made a trip to Montpelier and Northfield just before harvest in 1855. The young man made the standard vists to the state capitol and to burying grounds, but nothing captured his attention more than the railroad yards and equipment at Northfield. "I love to hear the whistle of the engine, ringing of the bell and rattling of the cars on the iron track," he wrote fondly. "It appears," he continued, "as though there was business going on, it is like civilized life." How long, he wondered after returning to the Orleans County home to test his small, slight frame against the demands of the rye harvest and to look with foreboding to the long winter months with their equally trying necessity of taking a school, would it be before the people in his locale will be able to hear "the steam whistle sound through these vallies."[31]

The paeans to country life came far more from those who did not reside in the country than from those who did. "Of all situations in life," a Pennsylvanian wrote to a relative in Ohio, "I do think the Farmers the most to be envied."[32] This writer kept a store, and, as was frequently the case in such exchanges, the recipient was a farmer. "I suppose you are passing the winter in happy farmer fashion," a traveling clock peddler wrote to his brother in Connecticut. "Your evenings pass with your good wife and little what do you call him. A cheerful fire cider and apples with other good things to sweeten and happy your life are yours—and may you long enjoy them." Whether such expression of admiration for bucolic pleasures and virtues was sheer flummery cannot readily be determined, of course. What is explicit in this letter is what was probably tacit in many others like it: "My business I doubt not is more lucrative than yours."[33] Then came the turn, genuine or affected, to those more than compensating categories.

The key to such celebrations of rural felicity came not from nature but from

contentment. The farmer, it was commonly thought, knew not pride nor ambition; come what might, he did not fret nor murmur. According to this notion,
the farmer was happy for being contented. Happiness involved what happened
to a person, and contentment meant full spiritual acquiescence in whatever
happened. Thus, writing to his brother Nahum back on the farm and talking the
somewhat circular language of happiness and contentment, clock-peddling
Milo Holcomb confessed his full acquaintance with "the feelings of an
ambitious youth."[34] Nahum, one is allowed to infer, suffered no such familiarity. Perhaps his name was his spirit, God's comfort; but it might be hazardous to envision him laying the curse of his namesake, the prophet, upon
Ninevah—"Woe to the bloody city!"[35] The merits of country existence seem
to have involved a variant of willing and voluntary subjection more than
nature's ennoblement, or even more than some real or fancied economic independence. It was no accident that Savannah schoolgirl Mary Copp devoted
most of a composition dealing with "City and Country Contrasted" to the advantages "we of the city" possess. That fact notwithstanding, she moved
undaunted to the conclusion that such things as the "nut gathering, the
Whortleberrying and the sociable visits of the country people" overshadowed
those advantages. If the likes of "nut gathering" did not establish fully enough
the credentials of those people whose choice of an agrarian life seemed, in
popular perception, to translate into vows of abstinence, there was ready recourse to the unanswerable imagery of a "low white church of a country
village, situated in a graveyard and surrounded by trees."[36] Few could ask for
more than a church surrounded by a graveyard.

Mary Copp of Savannah had a counterpart in Fanny Fryatt of New Jersey,
school-notebook author of a "Country Life composition," among other things.
"How much more pleasant," came the opening flourish, "is a country than a
city life." The reasons did not emerge readily, but a "neat cottage by the wayside" was featured prominently. Here one wonders how Fanny would have
reacted had she found the cottage not to be neat. Her other writings provide
almost tailor-made illustrations of the philosophical disinclination to revere
naturalness. The farm could not be exalted on that ground. To be sure, in her
"Country Life composition" she did not neglect the flowers, the birds, and the
"clear sparkling river." But those birds and flowers had to behave themselves
in order to pass muster, for when untamed nature intruded upon Fanny's
imagination, her reaction was a blend of horror and loathing.

Reflections on slavery, for example, gave the opportunity to dwell on the
"animal disposition" of blacks, and that soon gave way to the metaphor of the
jungle and to an attenuated version of the great chain of being—from "the
worm up to the *white* man" with the "Ourang Outang" doing conventional
service in illuminating racial connections. More melodramatically, in "A
Dream" Fanny watched savages dancing wildly around a "young white girl"
whose father had preceded her in satisfying the cannibalism of their desolate

island captors. When the fiends returned to their ghastly repast, Fanny became dream-life actor rather than observer. She crept to the now unattended girl, but as she started to undo the ropes the savages espied her and set up a "horrid" yell, to which Fanny responded by shrieking herself awake. Because it appears in variorum, "The Winds!" evidently came from Fanny's own febrile imagination. Precisely what it meant to convey remains unclear, but the nightmarish connotations surrounding nature are unmistakable. The "mystic chaunts" of the "choir of winds" enwrap the "bleak hills and cliffs" and drive to "froth the maddened waves." This is no matter of an aeolian harp at open window giving hushed tones of gentle melancholy. "Conflict reigns" in this natural realm where all is "tumultuous," "fierce," "dread," "dusk-winged," and "solemn."[37]

Progress and the City

On a day in the course of an unusually easy turning of the cape on the California voyage, some argonauts from Maine caught three albatrosses, probably with baited fishhooks. A diarist in the group observed that some of the sailors aboard had "great veneration" for that bird, "but," he continued, "we had no scruples believing that man has dominion over the fowl of the air as well as the fish of the sea."[38]

> He prayeth well, who loveth well
> Both man and bird and beast.[39]

Not even the fabled fate of the "Ancient Mariner" nor these parting words of injunction to the wedding guest could secure albatrosses from the thirst for sport and diversion among bored and idle men on their way to golden destinies. The aforementioned "dominion" was absolute, and, as a result, almost everything was fair game. Diary entries of grown men in which appear casual mentions of the toll taken in woodpeckers, jays, robins, or whatever strike the modern reader as anomalous at best.

On an outing in the White Mountains, another New Englander gave a somewhat frolicsome account of a day's hunting, in this case not at all connected with concern for provender. He fired at a squirrel and, he noted wryly, "*frightened* him *tremendously*"; then he unsuccessfully stalked a jay; and then he chased another squirrel, flailing at it with his ramrod. Though thus far unharmed, the squirrel may have been so awestruck as to delay while the nimrod employed his ramrod in more conventional fashion, after which interlude he fired and killed his quarry. Evidently, the charge far exceeded the challenge; after the blast, the squirrel-slayer found only a bit of head and tail, thus bringing to mind the tale about "Jim Crow's" hitting a man so hard that nothing remained but a grease spot. Having imperiled wildlife in this fashion, our chroniclcr cnded his entry with brief mention of the "great railroad fever" in the area.[40]

With railroad fever prevailing, we again approach that supposedly pervasive notion of progress. Given the dominant contentions about pre-Civil War views, one might construe things in such way that albatrosses, squirrels, or jays had to give way before some inexorable working that begot temporal, human betterment. As has been observed briefly in another context, however, one finds almost embarrassingly little in the sources to sustain such a construction.

"This idea," in J. B. Bury's rather constricted definition of the notion of progress, "means that civilization has moved, is moving, and will move in a desirable direction." This beneficent process, he states, "must not be at the mercy of any external will; otherwise there would be no guarantee of its continuance and its issue, and the idea of Progress would lapse into the idea of Providence."[41] Defining things this way would allow us to end abruptly any discussion of the idea of progress in popular thought. As W. Warren Wagar has recently written, "Christian thinkers for their part subjected everything to the will of divine providence and took no real interest in the prospect of terrestrial improvement." Although here he is referring to post-classical Christianity, to the world view that prevailed until the sixteenth or seventeenth century, much of his assertion could also pertain to the common man's thought in mid-nineteenth century America. As Wagar remarks in what I take to be a chiding tone in the same essay, recent scholarship often has as its motto, " 'It happened later than you think. . . .' "[42]

To expand somewhat upon the quite limited subject of progress, it would be well to note the very sparing use of the word itself in our sources. In some small part at least, the word "improvement" served in its place. Whether the word was progress or improvement, however, the sentiments expressed nearly always had a concrete and retrospective focus that keep them almost entirely out of the realm of progress seen philosophically as the dynamic of society or as law of history. For one thing, sources of the sort used for this study had, as befit their lack of sophistication, a good deal of matter-of-factness. When Isaac Metcalf of Maine wrote from Minnesota Territory home to "Dear Ettie," he told her of the Falls of Saint Anthony where the "presumptious Yankees have stuck in a Saw Mill." Isaac, himself one of those "presumptious Yankees," then turned his eager attention to Lake Minnetonka, and he did not at all need prescience or faith in progress to perceive that it would one day be "a great place of resort, with fine Steamboats and Hotels."[43] Purblindness of an almost inspired sort would have been required not to have seen what Isaac saw. Writing to his wife from Cleveland, Charles Rich, a native of the same part of Maine as Isaac Metcalf, told of the delights of railroad travel: "this flying along at the rate of from 30 to 50 miles an hour is a lively business to what a wagon with a lazy horse is."[44] Again, this distinction resulted in no philosophical construct; no comtemplation of human destiny came into play to make the separation between this "lively business" and "a wagon with a lazy horse."

When Emily Lewis of New York composed "Thanksgiving," she had abundant opportunity to specify the nation's blessings, but here, as was generally the case, the writer maintained a prayerful tone and a focus on the past. Having reviewed past developments and accomplishments, she could arrive at the assertion that "we are astonished at the wonderful progress."[45] The word "progress" here has no teleological burden; it meant nothing more than the generally happy change from what previously obtained to what now obtained. It was descriptive and denotative, not connotative and projective; it was de facto, not de jure. This fairly rare use of the word "progress" does not put it in the role of god-term, with its first letter susceptible to capitalization. About the only remove from the realm of retrospect to that of normative anticipation came in prosaic recognitions that hard work applied to bountiful resources generally resulted in desirable effects.

That is almost precisely what the "Green Hoosier" meant to convey in his "Fugitive Thoughts" which were written as feuding erupted in his party as it neared the end of the Pike's Peak trek. This long poem gives exciting but commonsensical intimations of what could be realized where human diligence and cooperation combine with nature's remarkable stores.

> Peace [!] be still ye jarring discords
>   Nor disturb our camp again
> We are seeking precious treasures
>   Where theres thousands seek in vain

Success gave no guarantee, even in realms of plenty. But,

> If we seek with single purpose
>   Like a band of brothers true
> Rich rewards shall be our portion
>   Happier days for me and you

Then, from the microcosm of his own party, the Hoosier enlarged the scope of his didactic poem, even to civilization's most arresting clarion.

> See the towns and cities springing
>   As if built by magic skill
> Soon you'll hear the railroad whistle
>   Wake the echoes keen and shrill[46]

All of this was a matter of enterprise, not lawful formulation. It involved "Yankee enterprize," as a Californian put it, "the untiring industry and perseverance of the Yankee Nation."[47] Writing from the North Fork of the American River, another new arrival mentioned the belief that it had never been known to thunder in that region "until the yankeys came." He went on to an unintentionally droll embroidery of that theory: "I do not dout but the yankeys will metimorfis the country Over so that it will be showery the year Round instead of a Rainey and dry season[.] The yankeys do wonderful things some times."[48]

As those Yankees who sometimes did wonderful things so well knew, however, God made the final determinations. The "idea of Progress," to employ J. B. Bury's terms, did not exactly "lapse into the idea of Providence." Providence had simply preempted the ground, and there was no place for Progress considered as a grand law of history, though there was some small place for progress considered as the undramatic result of plain hard work. And progress or improvement generally took the form of taming wilderness, whether in human nature or in nature. As Emily Lewis put it in her "Thanksgiving," Americans could look about "and behold this thickly settled country, towns, villages and even cities, where but a few years ago, were spread forests, and where the Aborigines wandered unmolested with here and there a wigwam to tell that human beings inhabited the wilds of America."[49] The spiritual dangers posed by the "wilds" probably informed the thinking of people such as Emily vastly more than did some inevitable process which spontaneously and necessarily enhanced the human condition.

"And even cities" had arisen. The concern about that dimension of human affairs, though apparent in the sources, does not have the intensity that one might expect. The misgivings that do appear have little that smacks of the mythical or even the biblical; rather, they partake of the specific, and, very likely, they possess a good deal of prosaic accuracy. Fears for physical well-being in the city, particularly in summer, derived from perceived reality. When a mother sadly reported that she and her husband would be unable to lend their son money, she urged him to return with his family to the Winamac, Indiana, home. Her greatest anxiety was for her grandson, little Willie. "I fear," she noted in this July letter, "if you keep him in the Citty you may lose him."[50] During the heat of another July, a Boston engraver, who was without the resources to get the medical attention he needed, commiserated with his wife who had had to go to an even hotter New York City. Writing on Sunday and stating that Reverend Stearns had done well in the morning sermon despite the temperature, Oliver Pelton went on to a fanciful depiction of places that would be "paradise in comparison to a city of brick walls & stone pavement." Beset by heat and ill health, the straitened engraver took wishful refuge in "the country in a farm house anywhere that I could look out on the beautiful landscape and be free from care & toil."[51]

As focuses of worry about the city's hazards, bodily health and comfort ranked well behind spiritual well-being. "And for the Christian," Roderick

Nash has written, "wilderness had long been a potent symbol applied either to the moral chaos of the unregenerate or to the godly man's conception of life on earth."[52] When the young man whom we encountered previously in the chapter as he read Isaac Watts went on to become a clerk in New York City, he longed to get away from that city "with all its Mammon."[53] This is conventional metaphor, ready for service when needed, but again it seems not to have slipped from the pen with quite as much ease and frequency as one might expect. The city was, of course, as Bunyan's Pilgrim and many others knew, the wilderness of the world, and it had evils and dangers paralleling those of the forests and the mountains. In both realms unrestraint prevailed. While in New York City awaiting California passage, John French, a native of New York who had long resided in Michigan, wrote in his diary as follows: "Went alover the citty. To church twise while in York. A most misrabel set of cut throats I ever saw."[54] One supposes that French encountered that "misrabel set of cut throats" in the "citty" at large rather than at church, as the sequence might suggest.

In 1854, Elam Slagle of rural North Carolina spent some time in Baltimore enlarging his talents in the tanning trade. Elam went only at the strong urging of his employer who wanted him to absorb some northern knowhow. His shock at hearing a Universalist sermon and some other of his reactions appear earlier in this book, but here his judgment of the city bears mention. He arrived at his fullest indictment on a Sunday. Even on a holy day, temptation beckoned in Baltimore. After strolling to the waterworks, some of his acquaintances at the tannery asked thirty-year-old Elam to join them for a drink. "This was a trial for me," he admitted, particularly because of their reassurance that he could order "pop water." But it was a parting of the ways. "When I got to the door the thought struck me where am I[,] what am I gowing to do." Though he liked some things about the city, he realized that there was "a great deal of meanness," and he saw clearly "the danger young people is in." "No some of money" could keep Elam Slagle in a city.[55] "We are quite astonished," an Ohio mother wrote to a wandering son upon learning that he was in New Orleans. This was not only a city but a southern city, and thus doubly unrestrained. After making that point, Mrs. Johnson urged self-restraints because society would impose few: "it will require you to put a strong guard upon your *thoughts* & actions." Only by so doing could he make his way safely through a wilderness fitted out with "the gaming table, the wine cup, and last though not *least*, the Syrens voice."[56]

All in all, the much-remarked tensions regarding progress, nature, and civilization took rather different shape in popular thought than one might suppose on the basis of studies deriving from other sources. Progress, for example, might be vaguely entertained by the common mind insofar as it involved matters of fact, but as a matter of faith, it simply could not contravene providential doctrine. In turn, both the attraction of nature and the worry about

civilization were less pronounced than inference from the intellectual formulators would lead us to believe. "The reader may object that I am talking
nonsense"—thus writes Perry Miller in an essay treating the almost obsessed
dismay that America, "Nature's Nation," felt because "the defiling axe of
civilization" was slashing into "our sublime wilderness."[57] It is not nonsense
at all, as long as the notions of Thomas Cole, Asher Durand, Emerson, and
Thoreau are not imposed upon Fanny Fryatt, Isaac Metcalf, Elam Slagle, and
Emily Lewis.

In Miller's views, a "virtually universal American hostility to the ethic of
utilitarian calculation" was "mobilized into a *cri du coeur* against Gradgrind." Whether the "nameless magazine writers" or the sages of Concord,
these people "identified the health, the very personality, of America with
Nature, and therefore set it in opposition to the concepts of the city, the railroad, the steamboat. . . . If here and there some still hard-bitten Calvinist
reminded his people of ancient distinctions between nature and grace, his
people still bought and swooned over pseudo-Byronic invocations to Nature."[58] Again, this is not nonsense, far from it, but the prevalence of the new
views is indeed overstated.

Prosaic people had little fear of the spirit of Gradgrind. Steamboats on Lake
Minnetonka aroused no dread, nor did they on the Ouachita River. Giving a
"View from my window" as it opened out upon that Louisiana waterway,
Yankee schoolma'am Caroline Poole may have verged upon a pseudo-Byronic
invocation to nature, but in the right of her scene "lies the steamboat (Dan O'
Connell) 'the symbol of life & power.' " Caroline Poole could take satisfaction
from that steamboat, as it reflected glassily in the still surface of the Ouachita.
She labored in an area where grown men yet crawled under wagons to obtain
refuge from wild animals, where nature's sway was evidenced by women
nursing children during Sunday service, where the preacher might unleash
himself all the more by quaffing "water made strong" during the sermon, where
Indians yet wandered by selling game, and where the "blackness" and violence
of the storm evidenced nature's recalcitrant fury.[59] The likes of Caroline Poole
needed fewer reminders of the ancient distinctions between nature and grace
than Miller's assertions would lead us to believe.

"Surely this society," Miller writes in expressing his hypothetical reader's
objections, "was not wracked by a secret, hidden horror that its gigantic exertion would end only in some nightmare debauchery called 'civilization.' "[60]
Common men harbored no great illusions about civilization, but that was not
because they were idolators of nature. They took a chary view of man's
potential, and civilization—the works and orderings of man—was, in the
Christian world view, faulty and vain. But in this real world where the web of
restraints worked upon nature was all too tenuous, only madmen or anchorites
abandoned civilization. Indeed, the *cri du coeur* of common men was probably
a good deal less *against* Gradgrind than it was *for* civilization.

Allowing the imagination to play for a moment on the "future city" that would arise as Breckinridge, Minnesota, encouraged young Daniel Hunt as he laid out a claim nearby in the summer of 1857. True exhilaration came that fall when his party prepared for the return to the towns on the Mississippi: "It really seemed like life to be bound towards civilization again & my spirits were boyant . . . [with] the hope of again seeing people in the persuits of happiness as well as gain."[61] A literal *cri du coeur* burst from Fancher Stimson's party about noon of July 16, 1850, as it plodded hot, dirty, and tired toward Placerville. A sound came "which caught all ears" and arrested "every step." "It was the crowing of a cock near by. Instantly, every hat in the party was swinging in the air, and more than two dozen throats were shouting hurrah, hurrah!" The chanticleer, so much employed as a literary symbol in the era, gave "a most certain indication that we had passed from a wilderness into some sort of civilization."[62] It was only a miner's shack with "Hang Town" not far beyond, but that was enough. To those who would insinuate the mass of pre-Civil War society into accord with the fashionably Romantic post-Christianity, parading its aversion to Gradgrind and its intoxication with nature, must go to the reminder, "It happened later than you think."

Nature Challenges the "Gospel of Civilization"

Aside from overstatement, Miller was on the right track. Near the end of the same essay he generalizes as follows: ". . . the American, or at least the American artist, cherished in his innermost being the impulse to reject completely the gospel of civilization, in order to guard with resolution the savagery of his heart."[63] Miller's mis-focus, if such it be, came from his failure to keep that qualifier—"or at least the American artist"—more firmly in our attention. The "American," of course, moved with vastly more hesitance and trepidation than did the "American artist." Still, the "disturbing challenge" to American religion deriving from "the course on which it so blithely embarked a century ago, when it dallied with the sublime"[64] involved in a direct and active way the prosaic as well as the inspired. The "American" as well as the "American artist" dallied with the sublime, but for plainer folk that dalliance came in a particular misadventure, the misappropriation of aesthetic terms and categories. As stated at the beginning of this chapter, when the focus became aesthetic, people who should have known too little to have been gulled were indeed gulled. They chose nature over art.

In the debating societies, the matter of art versus nature was debated as frequently as Columbus and Washington were compared. However oddly, the results seemed more predictable when nature contested art than when the discoverer of the country confronted its defender. "Unlucky for me," as a bright, pert young woman of upstate New York put it after having been bested, "I was on the side of Art."[65] How was it that art should have been looked upon as a handicap? In an earlier reference, it appeared as a blend of inadvertence, transcendence, and humility. The first involved a matter of semantic fashion pointing to the future along the "course" which Miller describes. The latter two, along with easing doubts about the heedless use of fashionable cliches, show the indisposition of plain folk to break away from the categories of the past, in this case, theonomous categories.

Once again, basic definitions must be considered. In the usage of that era, the word "art" applied to vastly more than is commonly the case now. In part, the difference may derive from a semantic intensification or channeling, rendering a word applicable to only some part of what it had previously encompassed. Words such as love and intercourse have undergone noteworthy constriction, and the ascription of a modern sense to past uses of such words sometimes produces droll results.[66] In addition, the change in usage regarding art probably involves unthinking attenuation; we use the word "art" where our ancestors used the expression fine arts. For example, Hawthorne employed the word in the conventional sense of his era in the opening sentences of "The New Adam and Eve":

We who are born into the world's artificial system can never adequately know how little in our present state and circumstances is natural, and how much is merely the interpolation of the perverted mind and heart of man. Art has become a second and stronger nature; she is a stepmother, whose crafty tenderness has taught us to despise the bountiful and wholesome ministrations of our true parent.[67]

Whatever was manmade—"the world's artificial system"—was art. Art nearly translated into civilization. The eighteenth-century separation for aesthetic purposes of the useful and the fine arts had not yet become so fully ingrained as to go without saying. It had to be specified. Thus, Hawthorne gave a seemingly redundant title, "The Artist of the Beautiful," to a tale that has aroused much pondering among modern critics. Farther down the intellectual scale from Hawthorne, a young man from a comfortable Connecticut background could pronounce the Mount Pleasant waterworks outside Philadelphia to be "a great work of art."[68] A Southerner of similar situation offered the following exclamation at what was probably his first railroad ride: "What a triumph of art is this mode of travelling."[69] Both directly and by implication, the comprehensive definition appears in even less sophisticated sources. It is suggested in the endless visits common people made to waterworks such as Croton and Mount Pleasant and to other physical developments, and, too, it is suggested in the visits, where allowed, to the penitentiaries, asylums, and academies. There were, of course, moral and didactic implications in these visits, but matters of art were involved as well. Art was manifest in the bricks and stones and iron bars on the one hand. It also took form in the much applauded routine and discipline characterizing the human dimension within the institutional confines. Nature had been reduced to order.

In many cases, there is no need to resort to inference. Early in his work on American thought, Ralph Henry Gabriel makes symbolic use of "the most daring engineering enterprise yet undertaken within the United States,"[70] that being the damming of the Connecticut River a few miles above Springfield, Massachusetts. In the summer of 1850, young A. F. Niles took a job as cook on a raft making the trip from Haverhill, New Hampshire, to Springfield, thus affording himself the opportunity to see the recently completed project. In humble perception, the community growing up by the dam had not yet taken on the dignified identity of Holyoke, "New Ireland" seeming to have greater aptness. Whatever the name of the place, our riverborne cook, as was his wont, took in the sights, particularly the dam itself. It was, he wrote, "the most splendid piece of artificial workmanship" he had seen.[71] No derogation attached to the word "artificial"; here it had descriptive rather than normative application. It meant work of art, work of man, mark of civilization. So when they threshed out the matter of art versus nature at the village debating societies, they were doing far more than, say, comparing the sunset's glow to a Thomas Cole painting.

Romance and the Sublime

When a New Englander mentioned New York City's enjoying "natural and artificial advantages,"[72] there was no suggestion in the latter adjective of meretriciousness. Intimations of that sort were coming, however, as likely they did at a previously mentioned session of the "Alder Creek Paulemic" when the "fowling query" was posed: "which is the most butiful to the eye[:] Art for the one part or nature for the other."[73]

Here in DuBois County, Indiana, as elsewhere, some altered definitions of beauty very likely came into play, however unwittingly. The aesthetic categories derived from Burke, Blair, and Gilpin were in the process of redeeming the American landscape, but, as Perry Miller recognizes, the effect of that change upon American religion was less happy. As nature rose in esteem, grace sank. Now the untamed and awesome limitlessness of the American continent could be viewed, given the help of the notion of the sublime, in psychesthetically positive terms. In treating "The Picturesque Versus the Sublime," Roland Van Zandt has written that "the main battle of the nineteenth century" took place "between the scenic qualities that make up the 'beautiful' and/or the 'picturesque' and those that form the 'sublime.' "[74] For taking on the aura of the imponderable and the unutterable, the sublime poses almost endless difficulties. In general terms, however, that doctrine of the sublime "dispelled," as Roderick Nash has put it, "the notion that beauty in nature was seen only in the comfortable, fruitful, and well-ordered."[75]

The picturesque and the beautiful possessed something called association, another category about which aesthetic battles were waged. Association meant the marks of man upon the landscape. "Productions of art,"[76] to use Hugh Blair's terms, or some intimations of art enhanced the natural setting and could be the key to rendering it beautiful or picturesque, or, simply, pleasing to behold. Thus, in the 1790s George Vancouver expressed delight at the islands of Puget Sound and the lower mountain reaches surrounding it because he saw " 'extensive spaces that wore the appearance of having been cleared by art.' " Farther north along the coast where there was no suggestion of "art," no association, Vancouver, yet unversed in sublime appreciation of chaotic vastness, recoiled in distaste.[77] A half century later, Francis Parkman took with him on the Oregon Trail a wider range of sensitivities. In a qualified way, as Roland Van Zandt has shown, the sublime entered his depictions of western nature, particularly in that stock catalyst of the sublime, the thunder and lightning of the storm at night. But, again and again for Harvard-trained Parkman as well, "a scene in nature," as Van Zandt put it, "is saved from a total lack of aesthetic appeal"[78] by some association—an Indian village, a Mexican herder, or the false but pleasing impression of artful tailoring given by the small groves dotting the prairie. Two years earlier in his commencement address, Parkman became involved in the epidemic of concern about the superiority of European nature: "Its streams and mountains are hallowed by associations that ours have not, and may never have; and the hand of art has polished the rough features of Nature."[79]

"The prairie and the timber are so blended," a new Minnesota farmer wrote of the Glencoe area, "that it looks like an old settled country."[80] That high approbation came from John R. Cummins because the scene possessed the comforting intimation of art, of the hand of man, of association. On the Oregon Trail, where the neat mounds and headboards gave poignant and ironic signs of human presence, a man from Indiana conveyed nicely the conventional sense of the picturesque or the beautiful as he surveyed the country a day beyond Fort Laramie. In one direction loomed the mountains with their disquieting awesomeness, but turning elsewhere his eyes swept over hills which reminded him of "gentle rolling waves—and all so neatly set with pine trees that we are reminded of the well cultivated and thrifty Orchard of some enterprising farmer...."[81] Bound for the same destination by the sea route, another diarist underscored the psychological dimension of association as an element of aesthetic appreciation. For an hour or so, he had watched another ship on the horizon, but then it was gone, and

we again were alone, the sole tenants of the ocean—it is indeed a cheerful sight to look and watch a distant sail even tho there is but a spec that breaks the well defined outline of the horizon—It is refreshing to the mind, and interesting to the feeling.[82]

Insofar as unsophisticated people preferred what might be called the beautiful or the picturesque, they did so because it contained association. That crucial factor removed or at least muted the sense of solitude, a condition which they took great pains to avoid. As has been stated previously, abundant scholarly depiction of such things as individualism has obscured that fact. In turn, association in its general sense is sometimes skewed by those who would limit it to political, legal, financial, or some other explicit organizational form. For example, in a recent work on attitudes toward the Indians, one scholar hit upon a statement in an 1849 *Baptist Missionary Magazine* urging that there be instilled among the red men " 'those associations . . . by which men express their interest in one another, and aid one another.' " Drawing upon a passage that appeared later in that same essay, this author interpolated in this way directly after " 'those associations' ": "[such as 'chambers of commerce, insurance companies, banks, joint stock associations']."[83] That has an arresting effect, but to get to "associations" such as banks it was necessary to bypass and ignore what the *Baptist Missionary Magazine* used for its first illustration: "homes for orphan children, asylums for the insane. . . , [and] provision for the sick and suffering." In the general sense, what most aroused the disdain and pity expressed by this Baptist for those bereft of "associations" was the fact that they "live almost, as it were, alone."[84]

What Roland Van Zandt calls "The Romantic Debate" issued in "The Romantic Apotheosis," an aesthetic and philosophical underwriting of the sublime which, among other things, redeemed the American landscape by obviating the need for association.[85] At least to some degree, the common people of that period gravitated in that modern direction, and they did so in part by inadvertence. They came, unthinkingly it seems, to incorporate an abundant amount of expression and mood which were not in keeping with their own considered beliefs. These stodgy pre-Romantics let down their guard. They reminded themselves again and again that there was precious little romance in real life; they gave warning after warning about the likely course from introspection to melancholy; and they fumed about the idle reverie which they styled castle-building. A seductive rhetoric had been unleashed, however, and the unsophisticated took some of the rhetoric, if not yet the social and ethical consequences of it.

The word "romantic" itself came into heavy use, with seeming aptness for the cemetery, the waterworks, the view from the capitol at Albany, or the scenery on the Oregon Trail. A lumber company employee at Minnesota's Mille Lacs Lake—"a beautiful sheat of water"—enumerated a variety of elements before him, including the lake that stretched farther than the eye could reach, canoes, waterfowl, dogs, and Indians. The scene beggared his powers. One "ought to be like Harriet Beecher Stow the author of uncle toms cabin," he remarked, "a little given to romance." The diarist continued in the conjectural vein for a moment longer, adding that "I am romantic enough myself but lack the head[;] cant get it in my wool right."[86] A good many others like him were not deterred by the fact that, where aesthetic categories were concerned, they could not get it in their "wool right." And for the sake of their values, they would have done better to temper even more the emergent Romanticism with the sort of prosaic worldliness that a Pennsylvanian used as he viewed a stretch of Schuylkill River country from a cemetery: "romantic, and beautiful *but worth considerable money.*"[87]

" 'Why to yon mountains turns the musing eye whose sun bright summits mingle with the sky—

> Why do these cliffs of shadowy
> tint appear more sweet than
> all the landscape smiling near
> tis distance lends ench
> antment'

This rendition of a "thought of the poet" Thomas Campbell came from a young man from Centerville, Tennessee, while he served as a clerk for a trading venture to Bent's Fort in the summer of 1855. Those white-capped peaks in the distance lent enchantment indeed when one had to suffer at short range the "vileness" of "mean bloodthirsty" Indians.[88] The distance and the murkiness of the "shadowy tint" bespoke the Romantic and intimated the sublime. "All writers on sublime subjects," according to William Gilpin, "deal in shadows and obscurity."[89] Thus, a form of the often-eschewed castle-building could be practiced at such evocative Oregon Trail landmarks as Chimney Rock and Court House Rock. Not yet that far on the route, an Irishman pelting a skunk with buffalo chips and receiving for his efforts an arresting but "unexpected salute" represented the real life of the trail to a twenty-one-year-old farmer's son from Annapolis, Indiana. But a week later at Court House Rock, the fancy was served in a way that was more romantic than comic. Our traveler had not accepted a report of a snake with a head at each end, but he would try harder where the "ancient bluff ruins" were concerned. "They bear some resemblance to ruins," he conceded, "and with a little imagination it is easily pictured out."[90] In the plains section of the route, another argonaut exclaimed that the "eye could wonder [wander] and be lost in seming nothingness." In the Scott's Bluff area, the eye could mold its own enchanted reality. "Here can be seen," this Alabaman remarked as part of the chorus of answer to the envied "Romantic association"[91] of Europe's ruins, "churches forts castles and everything the mind can imagine. . . ."[92]

The imagination had more sway, and it was beginning to take on a discernible tinge of melancholy. Robert Burton's anatomy of that mood, of course, suggests the illimitable sources of melancholy and perhaps its agelessness as well. And George Boas has reminded us that the so-called Age of Reason was rife with "melancholy tombstone poetry, weeping willows, the sublime and the awful."[93] Still, the psychesthetic conjunction of pleasure and melancholy seems particularly identifiable with the Romantic mood, most notably in its sublime dimension.

> O lead me, queen sublime, to solemn glooms
> Congenial with my soul; to cheerless shades,
> To ruin'd seats, to twilight cells and bow'rs,
> Where thoughtful Melancholy loves to muse[94]

Thomas Wharton the Younger certainly did not stampede our plain folk with that 1747 apotheosis of "The Pleasures of Melancholy," but he and others like him did move some of those inglorious folk at least an appreciable way toward the modern world.

"There is pleasure in dreamy melancholy," a young Ohioan mimicked the message for the benefit of the woman from whom he was separated.[95] Lovers are not renowned for restraint or neat logic, and one can hardly expect anything more than melancholy from those who reflect at the grave of a loved one. Given the charm rather than the dread of melancholy, however, yet other dimensions and settings could be brought into acceptance. Solitude, for which the common people had mostly aversion, bred melancholy, and at least occasionally there came a willingness to dress the lonely dolefulness in positive garb. The grave served well for this purpose if properly placed. "There is a mournful pleasure far away from home and in a savage land," a New Yorker wrote in viewing the final resting place of a predecessor on the southern trail east of El Paso, "to contemplate his death under a lonely tree. . . ."[96] From here, only a step was needed to embrace the manforsaken setting itself, not just the grave. In that same spring of 1849, looking out over "dreary wilderness" on the Oregon Trail, a Hoosier took just that step in pronouncing the "wild and melancholy beauty of the scene."[97]

"I have not given you a touch of the sublime this time, (as you will see,)," Alcina Baldwin playfully wrote to a male acquaintance in Buffalo, "but I trust you will excuse me, knowing I am but a rough country girl."[98] Whatever meaning or lack of meaning attached to it, the word "sublime" was sweeping the country. Roland Van Zandt refers to that "endlessly repetitious, nineteenth century obsession,"[99] and the obsessed included at least some who should have been sufficiently ignorant to have had immunity, rough country girls, for example. Sadly, Perry Miller did not live to write the prologue to his grand, projected study of the intellect of that era, a prologue titled "The Sublime in America." Certainly, we could have used his spirited guidance through "queen sublime's" growing dominion.

Much of the usage of a term that had grown to such proportions that rough country girls could gently parody it involved nothing more than voguish adoption. As all know, there are fashions in words, as well as in clothes and ideas. For example, let us return to our Connecticut River raftsman and admirer of the dam at "New Ireland." Continuing downriver to the Hartford area, he visited his sister who was a mill girl in a brush manufactory, and he accompanied her to a showing of a panorama of Bible scenes. He considered the paintings "very beautiful and sublime," most likely intending the latter descriptive, not to counter the former but rather to serve as a handy and fashionable reinforcing of it.[100] And Elias Daggy, the argonaut who turned away from a sublime mountain prospect because it was "buoisterous" in order to praise that which was in fact beautiful or picturesque—the rolling hills west of Fort Laramie dotted by trees in such way as to suggest a "well cultivated and thrifty Orchard"—nonetheless called the latter scene sublime. That was no isolated personal judgment; "without a dissenting voice we pronounce it the most sublime our eyes ever beheld."[101] Subtle points of aesthetic categorizing most likely did not enter the deliberations of weary men stopping for a moment in their arduous trek, but it is noteworthy that, where something was accorded very high favor, none had misgivings about calling it sublime.

Such people did not always mistakenly appropriate the notion of the sublime. In one sense, no one had greater claim to the term than the uninformed. Insofar as the term connoted "what was commonly called the 'indescribable,' "[102] it was peculiarly suited to those with an insufficiency of descriptive powers. And, of course, all irony aside, these less sophisticated mortals did apply the term—at Niagara Falls, say, or in a storm at sea—with ineffable aptness. Another aptness, which is more crucial and one might say more worrisome, involved the occasional congruence of humble usage of the sublime with that intended by the theoreticians.

Whatever is fitted in any sort to excite the ideas of pain and danger, that is to say, whatever is in any sort terrible, or is conversant about terrible objects, or operates in a manner analogous to terror, is a source of the *sublime*; that is, it is productive of the strongest emotion which the mind is capable of feeling.[103]

As Edmund Burke stated it, so did others sometimes employ it. The category of the sublime not only did much to render the wildness, vastness, and chaos of the American landscape acceptable, but it also did somewhat in rendering other, hitherto objectionable things less objectionable. In contrasting the old and the new literary conventions, an admiring reviewer of Mrs. Hemans' gently archaic poetry expressed it this way in 1827: ". . . if heaven, earth, and ocean had formerly been plundered of their *sweets*, the universe was now ransacked in quest of *images of terror*."[104] The surprising thing about the common people is that they flirted as much as they did with the terror-laden sublime, that they did not heed even more rigidly Pope's warning about the course from pitying to enduring to embracing.

The fascination with the horrific has been, one assumes, a constant part of human affairs, but the category of the sublime did much to legitimize that fascination. The common people sometimes defied instinct and training by accepting the legitimacy. "It looks very black & angry—thunder loud and

flashes of forked lightning playing with great rapidity . . . tis on us[,] tis ter-
rrible—we have no such storms in Penna . . . the scene [is] terrible & sublime . . ."[105] Writing from a hotel in Fort Madison, this newcomer to Iowa hit
upon the most compelling natural instance of the sublime—a thunder and lightning storm. He lacked the artistry that Francis Parkman brought to a similar
setting, but the result is the same. A city ablaze had similar evocative power,
and here, too, the less sophisticated sometimes obliged. When a large section
of Broadway burned in July 1845, a New York City onlooker brought his description into keeping with emergent usages; it was "a scene awfuly grand and
sublime."[106] Three thousand miles away, when Sacramento went up in flames
in 1852, a like protrayal emerged: "The sight filled spectators with sublimity
and terror. . . ."[107] The language of the sublime gave a positive gloss to the terrible, the vast, and the chaotic, and at least in some small degree it worked an
incursion upon the humble loyalty to order, neatness, and restraint.

Most folk, however, probably avoided the pitfalls in this rather inadvertent
drift toward the sublime, and they did so by a previously mentioned act of
transcendence in which a phrase from Alexander Pope did yeoman service.
The awe and terror bred of chaos and limitlessness gave way to other sentiments when one looked "thro' Nature up to Nature's God." Thus, when an
aurora borealis particularly impressed a Brookfield, Connecticut, farmer in
January 1837, he described it as "a sublime sight—one calculated to fill the
mind with astonishment and reverence."[108] In proclaiming about sunsets and
other "works of God," a farmer in Minnesota Territory concluded that "thay
are incomprehensible and sublime."[109] In such cases, the sublime—whether
properly or not—lost its frightening associations, to be veiled in providential
reverence. Indeed, one writer who made the routine effort to describe the indescribable at Niagara Falls appropriated a line from somewhere indicating
the ineptness of sublimity. As he, too, looked " 'through nature to natures
God,' " he perceived, not " 'awful Sublimity,' " but " 'Soul filling beauty.' "[110]
Imperfect mortals could not fathom the aurora nor comprehend Niagara's
thundering vastness, but God could, for such things fell within His design.
Spectres of meaninglessness and visions of accidental collocations of atoms
had not yet beggared humble mankind's hopes and efforts to see purpose in the
universe. "This is the most wonderful production of Nature I ever beheld," a
Connecticut clock peddler wrote home after viewing Virginia's Natural
Bridge, "It cannot be looked on without wonder[.] It leads the mind up from
nature to natures God[.] Surely such a production is not the work of
chance."[111]

Conclusion

Surely, too, God-fearing humility demanded that greater homage go to the
immediate works of His hand than to those works (whether they be paintings,
steamboats, or barns) which were His at second-hand, works done by the sub-

contracted agency of man. Art (the barns and all the rest) was, in this fundamental sense, inherently inferior, as those village debaters doubtlessly reminded one another. Here again, nature, whether death, disease, hardship,
sunsets, or the aurora borealis, fell into place in the providential schema. The
first duty was to overcome nature, as it was to avoid death and disease which
were among its components. Those village debaters, for example, were busily
engaged in overcoming nature by disciplining themselves and their talents as
they made their predictable way to the conclusion that, in the cosmic sense,
nature excelled art. When confronted by God's nature in its occasional smiling
aspects—a rainbow, a grove-dotted plain, a sunset, or the Natural Bridge—
such folk remembered full well whence such blessings came. When confronted
by God's nature wearing other aspects—a storm at sea, a conflagration in a
city, death, and disease—they attempted unmurmuring accommodation,
bearing always in mind that God's ultimate purposes were being served.

> And now he bids adiew to all
>   Resigns his mortal breath
> Obeys the voice of natures call
>   And sleeps the sleep of death[112]

The West 8

Four days short of Fort Kearny, a "hard-working, God-fearing farmer" from the Athens, Ohio, area remarked on the size of the movement along the trail to California and to the gold that lured him and the others. "The multitude that is going is wonderful," he wrote on May 24 of the *annus mirabilis*. "It seems as if the whole world was going to market."[1] Though John Edwin Banks had rather more expressiveness than most of his peers, he probably did not attach any particular significance here to "going to market." Still, that phrase does suggest Emerson's discernment of a drift in American society from the "temple" to the "senate" and the "market."[2] Much of this study has meant to show that that drift, where common values and perceptions were concerned, was less dramatic and rapid than the seer concluded in his 1838 address. Insofar as the common man's writings registered the matter, however, the catalyst, if not the central cause, of that drift resided here in the West, whether in the gold reaches or elsewhere. The previously discussed flirtation with nature and the sublime would, as Perry Miller notes, bear problematical fruit in time, but among ordinary people it was too occasional and unthinking to do more than foreshadow. The West did more than foreshadow. It came directly to bear upon the individual and the general consciousness, and in so doing it proved profoundly unsettling.

All sensed the magnitude of the gravitation toward the West. The "whole world," a Kentuckian who went as far as western Missouri in the spring of 1852 wrote, "seems to be in motion for Oregon and California."[3] "Nothing but the Pacific," came the word of wonder from a new Minnesotan, "will stop this mania for the west."[4] All sensed the consequences of this unprecedented movement, generally without the gleeful recklessness which has so frequently been ascribed to them. Rowland Berthoff has described the Americans of that era as a people "who made economic progress their preeminent value" and who therefore "could discern only dimly the fundamental but far less salutary upheaval that was undermining the primary institutions of their social order." They appeared heedless of the dangers "for the individual to get along without the non-economic values of life that had been embedded in the old social order." Indeed, to them "the consequent slackening of the strands that had bound the old institutions of society together seemed quite acceptable, even desirable."[5] What Berthoff calls the "society of individuals" was indeed in the making, but, if it did not come "later than you think," it came, in humble perception, more with awe and resignation than with verve and celebration. Perhaps not quite as dimly as we imagine, such folk discerned the unrestraint and worldliness attendant upon the western movement. "I suppose you know," Peter and Eliza Nevius wrote to a brother, "that our relatives is not only moveing towards the grave, but to the west." Expressing it in that way may have been meant to do little more than convey the sense of inexorability, but that same letter probably hit upon a worrisome contrast in telling of the writers' visit to some Pennsylvania or Ohio relatives who apparently had not joined the western migration. They were of the sort, the letter fondly told, who followed "the old fashioned way not careing much about the good things of this world."[6]

The good things of this world worked their greatest enticement and effect in the West. Indeed, the West stood as a veritable synecdoche for the much-remarked and much-resisted drift from things spiritual to things temporal. Here, perceived more sharply than Berthoff's excellent study might lead one to suppose, was the worrisome spectre of an agency causing the move, to use William A. Clebsch's terms, from sacred to profane America; from the temple, in Emersonian terms, to the senate and the market; from the garden of the church to the garden of the world, or, even better, to the wilderness of the world. Such lines of tension aroused a pronounced disquietude. The allurement was irresistible, but the course from east to west seems almost reducible to the course from past to future—the small, tailored, cramped, but comforting past making way for the open, expansive, independent, but abandoned future. The West and what it meant played a major part in filling the vial with the acids of modernity. Those less sophisticated sorts who witnessed the corrosion reacted to it in mumbling parallel of a latter-day Jeremiah who viewed the plight of twentieth-century people liberated from social, institutional, and religious bonds: "They stagger out into trackless space under a blinding sun. They find it nerve-wracking."[7]

A Word About Motivation

A word about the motivation of those who went west seems as unavoidable as it does, I fear, futile. In making some remarks about the "broader aspects" of that "climactic manifestation of an American pioneer impulse," the California Gold Rush, David M. Potter reminded us in 1945 of the dangers of simplistically explaining what moved our ancestors:

The discovery of gold was the superficial cause of their restlessness, but whatever may explain it fundamentally, the money value of the gold certainly cannot. Economic determinism is as inadequate to explain the Forty-niners as it is to account for the Crusades. Regardless of its cause, however, an overpowering compulsion enlisted men in this hazardous journey, drove them to the limits of human capacity in its prosecution, and enabled them to achieve the symbolical mastery of the American West.[8]

Potter helped to redress a balance, but he may also have worked a greater effect than he had intended. Those Forty-niners and their counterparts elsewhere may have failed to achieve symbolical mastery, but twentieth-century students of American culture, particularly after Henry Nash Smith's *Virgin Land*, have bid fair to do just that. Those reaches where the deer and the antelope played seem now almost overpopulated with romping symbols and gamboling myths.

Much of that has been salutary, revealing, as it often does, the conscious and semiconscious persuasions of intellectual formulators who generally operated at a very comfortable remove from the realm about which they conjectured. But it was a far different matter with the less intellectual. With all respect for and partial agreement with David Potter, there is precious little evidence to show that a drive for "symbolical mastery" had much at all to do with the efforts of those who made the western move. However compelling the "idea of the West" may have been, it comes only very uneasily into accord with the moods of the common people. Here again, even in the case of Loren Baritz's thoughtful treatment of the theme, more caution may be in order.

Appropriately enough, it was Henry David Thoreau who personified the American mythology of the west. The west meant freedom: "Eastward I go only by force; but westward I go free." It was the way of the race: "I must walk toward Oregon, and not toward Europe. And that way the nation is moving, and I may say that mankind progresses from east to west." To the east lay history, while westward was the apocalypse, the future, and "adventure."[9]

One is constrained to remark that that crotchety, small-town recluse probably had scant company in the rapture bred by the advent of "the apocalypse, the future, and 'adventure.' " "In his own person, Thoreau, as American, combined the west of happiness and eternity, the west of millennium, and that of empire, the west of direction, and the west of place. He could do no more."[10] Where quintessential Americanness is concerned, a candidate unlikelier than Thoreau would be hard to find. And that isolate backyard traveler could have done one more thing; he might have tried the real West.

Whatever was in the person of Thoreau (and granting readily the significance of that), what was in the written expressions of his more ordinary counterparts had a disarmingly straightforward quality where their steps toward Oregon or elsewhere were concerned. They minced few words about the nature of their quest or their move; they sought lucre. On April 16, 1849, David Jackson Staples left Boston as member of an argonaut company which departed with the "purpose of bettering our condition on monetary matters and seeing the country."[11] This young man who had been employed in millwork, farm work, and shoemaking possessed the spiritual values of his time. The tandem threat expressed by Pope as "the lust of lucre, and the dread of death"[12] weighed heavily upon him, as it did upon so many others. With Boston far behind and with the ocean-like limitlessness of the plains broken only by the dolorous associational counterpoint of "new made graves," Staples mused at the demise of one of his own group. We must, he noted, "content ourselves with the thought that God's ways are best." Perhaps with "money matters" at the back of his mind, he concluded that "our ways are not his ways and our thoughts not his thoughts."[13] In the afterglow of reminiscence, things other than lucre and its derivatives pushed readily to the forefront of the pioneer mind. But in anticipation and at the moment, explanations of the western migration—however myriad may have been the variants and however wild may have been the idiosyncrasies—centered upon the realm of worldly substantives.

It might be flattering to some of us to accept the construction whereby Henry Seidel Canby brought Henry David Thoreau and the average American into a community of belief and impulse. After reminding us that Johannes George Zimmermann's "much read book on 'Solitude' was suggesting a retreat for solitary reflection as a cure of souls," Canby rendered much of the path to the West almost immaculate in the following way:

Nor should it be forgotten that no Transcendentalism was needed to draw the young, nature-loving American of the early nineteenth century toward the life of the Indian in the woods. Thousands with no spark of philosophy in them had yielded to the attraction of waste spaces and the independence of a self-sustaining life. Even in the forties they were still drifting off Westward, not to be pioneers or land speculators, but to escape from the money system or the pressure of stale morality or the idea of progress by getting rich.[14]

The unprepossessing people whose jottings appear in the present study would have had great difficulty recognizing themselves in Canby's assimilative portrait. Indeed, many of them would have taken umbrage.

In September 1850, twenty-six-year-old George N. Wheeler, a native of Cortland County, New York, who had farmed and taught in Ohio, began a "new Era" in his life as he came down out of the Sierra Nevada toward Marysville: "I am finely in Callifornia and from this time my success or failure to make a fortune must commence."[15] It is unlikely that young Wheeler or the others who wrote in similar terms were money-mad, but the things of the world did need tending. A Mississippi farmer who left for the land of gold in the previous year showed the characteristic, troubled reflection and the characteristic effort to explain the move, more to satisfy his wife and his own conscience than to indulge "the busy gossips of our little village." Jackson Thomason well knew the ready surmise regarding those who left a wife to go to California, and so he took pains to clarify. "Avarice," he noted candidly at the outset, "has to bear its *position*" in the equation. That amounted to no concession, but rather to statement of fact, once by which the farmer suggested derivatives such as the possibility of more ease for his wife and himself. That could mean enhancement of their "society," which probably stood for no more than enjoyment of one another.[16]

Perhaps nothing was more freighted with temporal connotations than was gold, the West's most powerful allurement. As the people who sought it knew, however, gold and the other material riches of the West had the seeming potential of smoothing the way to spiritual ease. Those temporal categories which asserted themselves in such dramatic and unprecedented ways in the West had the capacity of shading into and overlapping spiritual categories. As is perhaps ever the case, no neat line separated the serving of mundane interests from the serving of otherworldly ultimates. In the West, the problem of discriminating between the two intensified, a fact that augured ill for those otherworldly ultimates. After outlining the hazards of the trip and the short-comings of existence at the end of it, a new Oregonian nonetheless urged a Missouri cousin to join him. In his blunt injunction, he blended the major components of the humble world-view, the major sequential elements of the present study, and the drift which that sequence is meant to represent: "I close by saying become trewly religious get you a kind wife and come to oregon [;] the donation [land law] is extended two years."[17]

Whether gold or the Donation Land Law, the promise of the West was material, but, of course, that material promise could betoken much more. In 1852, Tom Charles of Vicksburg contrived a reason for visiting New Orleans, and then he kept going. "You know," his wife Ellen who suddenly found herself alone dutifully explained to a sister-in-law, "how unfortunate Mr Charles has been the last few years." The Vicksburg lack of fortune, as Tom wrote without gloss or euphemism, had centered upon liquor and cards and the encumbering of others in his debts. Now, a job in a San Francisco grocery and then one in the customshouse began to pay, but in ways other than the monetary. Ellen, having surmounted her amazement and having joined her husband, could report that Tom had not been out of an evening, except on two occasions when she had declined going with him to see Lola Montez. "I would have been willing," wrote this woman who had refused the move to the Far West until her husband rendered it a *fait accompli*, "to come to Cal to see this change in him if nothing more." In spite of the enticements—"piles of gold" on the tables and "beautiful women" dealing—Tom had not "played a card or bet a cent" since arriving. But he knew very well that it was all or nothing at all: "when you hear of Tom gambling or getting drunk just say that he has given up all hopes . . . and intends to devote himself to cards in the future." Strange that a Tom Charles, afflicted with a love for the cards and the bottle, should have retained his "hopes" and should have survived at all in the abandon of San Francisco. Yet, after two years there, despite the temptations, exorbitant costs, and burdens on Ellen who scrimped to the point of downright illness, Tom Charles could conclude that "there is nothing like a new country for poor folks."[18]

In a community far different from Vicksburg, young Richard Ela rankled at still being at the farm home a full year after he had meant to leave. Ironic deprecation "(I almost forgot to tell you about Richard)" entered a letter to his brother when the disaffected youth turned to his own affairs: "he is almost eighteen years old: he does nothing (feeding the pig and getting in a little wood excepted) but build castles in the air which are continually falling to the ground. Poor dog!" Four years later, still at home in the Lebanon, New Hampshire, area and still having the nominal liberty to leave, Richard Ela verged on despair. "I envied my mother her grave," this "most desolate and unhappy of beings" confided; "if I could die fairly I should die gladly." As was the case with Tom Charles of Vicksburg, however, there was a way out: "The West is our object; there is no other hope left for us." In the next summer, Richard wrote from Buffalo where he worked in a joiner's shop in order to finance the further venture toward his destiny: ". . . and if Providence spares to me my health and faculties I will yet be in possession of my hearts desire[,] an honest *independence*."[19] Providence did so spare Richard Ela, and in Wisconsin he more than achieved that "honest independence," the term here referring not to independence of spirit or mind, but to the "ability to support one's self."[20]

This young man had wearied of the "poverty" of home. He had concluded that "there was not a single peg for me to hang a hope upon," and he had at last managed to overcome his querulous and unbecoming irresolution. In 1836, writing from Will County, Illinois, where he stayed for a time before moving on to Wisconsin prosperity, Ela admitted that New England yet held first place in his "admiration and affections." Yet, his future was here in the West: "If I cannot live here I cannot live anywhere. . . ." To be sure, the country seemed a bit "drear and desolate" to the New England eye, and the "speculation mania" let loose upon the region troubled him. "But," came the conclusion, "it will one day be a great country—a fine country—*the garden of the world.*"[21]

Here we have a convention of which much has been made, and perhaps properly so. However, one must guard against overly generous translation of the occasional appearances of this metaphor in our sources. It had, of course, a compelling quality and a large currency, and the common people could employ it, when they saw fit, for persuasive or playful reasons. In November 1844, John Kinkade and his family, having left Ohio, resettled in Washington County, Iowa, "to enjoy the pleasures of the garden of the world within two miles of Skunk river a stream as well adapted for navigation as any in Ohio and it will be known abroad over the hole world. . . ."[22] This letter, which seems genuinely to have had the purpose of causing some relatives to "flee from the land of Ohio to the land that flows with milk and honey," is uncharacteristically inflated; it is possible that simple irony, sensed and shared by brothers but lost to later readers, entered in. Certainly, cautionary marks were almost always more in evidence than is the case here, and those cautionary marks bear more attention than they often receive.

First, the much-remarked garden condition lay, where the West was concerned, in the future. Thus, a Forty-niner, looking out over the Platte Valley, judged that it "one day will be the garden of the world."[23] Richard Ela, who was able to make distinctions and keep things straight, explicitly made the garden a matter of projection—"it will one day be. . . . " Of course, the future tense often went unstated, largely, I suspect, because of stylistic attenuation. In addition, in some places the garden seemed very imminent. "All seems," an Aztalan, Wisconsin, settler wrote in 1846, "to have been expressly fitted by the Divine Being for easy settlement."[24] In large portions of Illinois, Wisconsin, Iowa, and Minnesota, the landscape bore an almost tailored appearance, as if the work, or much of it, had already been done. "You have but a faind eyedeea of the prrary heere," the wife of a new Illinoisan learned in 1836; "thay are a purfect flour bead of the choisest seclections that I ever saw in the most purfect gardins in our state."[25] Whatever the condition of the orthography, the imagery was sound, as was the general description of the countryside around Galesburg. In comparison to what had gone before, it all seemed so commodious, inviting, and malleable. Hearkening to the grimmer images of the wilderness of the past, Ambrose Bierce gave an impressionistic sketch of the ease enjoyed by more recent pioneers, as contrasted with the trials of those who had in earlier times "reclaim[ed] from Nature and her savage children here and there an isolated acreage for the plow. . . . " "The woodman pioneer is no more; the pioneer of the plains—he whose easy task it was to subdue for occupany two-thirds of the country in a single generation—is another and inferior creation."[26] Compared to real nature, much of the Middle West was indeed a garden.

To be even more blunt, the association in popular thought between garden and nature was at most tenuous and often nearly nonexistent. When plain folk resorted to imagery regarding the garden of the world, they referred not to the natural, but to the unnatural, to the tamed, the domesticated, and the social. Those conditions required effort, and where happy valleys were concerned, immaculate conceptions entered the formulation not at all. In 1852, when aged Asher Freeman recalled his experience in the Lakes Cayuga and Seneca country in 1796, he made explicit the working of the process. That area, the old man wrote, had had the finest land he had ever seen in the "state of nature," and he surmised that it must now be "the garden of the west."[27] For an Asher Freeman, the hard work lying between a "state of nature" and "the garden of the west" did not need to be specified; it stood as a given. Many did, of course, specify. Silas Seymour, that settler who wrote of God's having tailored

Wisconsin for "easy settlement," knew that the ease was only comparative. Even there, if people were to make a go of it, they had to be "self-denying"; they had to have "gumption and some foresight."[28]

Self-denial, gumption, and foresight were ingredients of art, not of nature. Those were the qualities that got the garden tilled, and, indeed, there was no such thing as an untilled garden. The 1855 Webster's reinforced the sense of cultivation, discipline, and structuring by drawing the etymological connection between the word "garden" and city names such as Stuttgart and Novgorod which were variant derivatives of it. Viewing with awe and admiration the fountains, temples, and civic buildings of the conquered City of Mexico, a Pennsylvania sergeant made the sort of association suggested by the dictionary: "Governed by good men and inhabited by an educated people, it would be the garden of the earth. . . . "[29]

"Do not think I looked for Eldorado," Silas Seymour told his sisters back in New York State.[30] Of course, he did not, nor did others. It might well be protested that such could go without saying, as surely it could were it not for the fact that our scholarship has promoted mythical inflations whereby it would seem that a westering nation, like Poe's "gallant knight," seriously sought Eldorado, or paradise, or Eden, or the big rock candy mountain, or some such. Insofar as our ancestors had a compelling destination, it was heaven, and nearly all of them had the good sense to consign that to the afterlife. Having arrived in Wisconsin, Richard Ela informed his brother in standard common-sensical terms that the "chances to get wealth certainly are better than in the old States." But, " 'tis not Eden," came the unnecessary reminder; "a man has something to do besides to *plunk* and *eat*, he has got to *sow* and *reap, plan* and accomplish. . . ."[31] In some generic, subconscious (and therefore unfathomable) sense, "the Edenic myth" may have been, as Charles Sanford states, "the most powerful and comprehensive organizing force in American culture."[32] However, one ought to prepare for a long quest in finding intimations of paradise in the writings of the common man. Not sober citizens but soothsayers trafficked in that sort of thing.

In treating the "romantic vision of the nineteenth century" whereby "the North American wilderness" came to be "fondly called Nature," George H. Williams undertook to correct or extend Henry Nash Smith's treatment of the American West as "symbol and myth." It seems that Smith had neglected some of the more rapturous visions. According to Williams, "Smith seems to have been unaware of the millennial elaboration of the biblical garden-desert theme, which will have been as much in the minds of the nineteenth-century denizens and interpreters of the wild West as, according to his thesis, the French Physiocratic agrarian theory!"[33] Getting yet more mileage out of the millennium, Klaus J. Hansen seconds Williams:

Clearly, George H. Williams is correct when he argues that Henry Nash Smith's brilliant study of the symbolic significance of the virgin land is in need of revision. Nineteenth-century Americans, in their westering, were as much impelled by apocalyptic visions as by physiocratic theories. . . . I do not deny that the average settler was, of course, first of all interested in land. . . . Still, the average settler could not help but have encountered millenial ideas in one form or another, while the ideas adumbrated by Smith would be found primarily among the intellectual elite.[34]

One ought not to succumb to the impish urge to use for ironic illustration of biblical, garden-desert imagery the Forty-niner setting off with his sack to "gather Buffaloe chips as the Israelites did the manna."[35] But Smith's contentions—loaded with quite as many symbols and myths as they will bear—seem the more defensible. If there were primal cultural compulsions moving those "average settlers" and those "denizens" of the "wild West," as contrasted with the "interpreters" thereof, those compulsions lay not in paradisiac or millennial ecstatics but in the prosaic notion that hard work applied to pregnant resources could yield a garden, a place of comfort, and modest competence in and for this world. If an "intellectual elite" worked a monopoly, it lay far more in the realm of millennial dithyrambics than in the realm of the comparatively pedestrian agrarian didactics. Of course, there was no Eden in Wisconsin, but Richard Ela settled, as did almost all of his fellows, for the comparatively better, or at least the promise of it: ". . . if sowing brings a better crop, or planning is attended with richer results, than elsewhere, it is enough."[36]

Vitality, Opportunity, and Worldliness

Vitality characterized the West, but that vitality derived from a material base, not a spiritual one. "It appears to me," a Minnesota farmer wrote in 1856, "that there is greater energy in the very air of the West." In this and in other diary entries, he specified what he took to be the generally happy consequences of that greater energy, including such things as more potatoes sacked, more corn planted, and twenty-mile walks that would have been considered a "great act" at the East routinely undertaken at the West.[37] As this young Pennsylvanian himself intimated, however, the impressive feats derived mostly from the comfortable circumstances, from the comparative lack of physical hindrances. The air, though purer than in eastern cities, was not charmed, but here the soil was better soil and there were fewer roots and rocks. "My boys," a Maine man who was starting anew in Illinois informed the folks at home, "like working on the prairies where they have no stones nor roots to trouble them."[38] This was not the food for ecstasy, but it did generate a lot of enthusiasm. Thus, a Hoosier who had relocated in the Chariton, Iowa, area allowed his prose to degenerate into regrettable poetry in telling that, thereabouts, it was "an easery matter to make a farm and easery to get the stuff to make it of an healther and pleasanter bouth winter and summer and soil that will last till gabrel blows his horn and produce well every year

If I oned property in Indiana
I'd sell the land first of any
And start that self same day
and toddle along towards Iowa[39]

Here we have the unadorned lure and vitality of material opportunity. "I tell you Mas. Boby . . . it's enough to make one walk tiptoe to see his labours prospering so abudantly." That good word from the new home near Natchez back to South Carolina told that the writer had seen several men, as "poor as myself" on arrival, now owning three or four hands. Another man involved in the same move urged the friend at home to remain there if he was doing well, but, if not, "take *Scotch Courage*, and come to this land of plenty."[40] Catherine Woods of northern Maine meant to take courage of some kind or another. She did common housework, and that for a pittance. The West appealed mightily, and when a family for which she had toiled made the move to Minnesota, poor subliterate Catherine sought to join them. Among other devices, she attempted to play on the sympathies of one of the younger members of that family, but to little avail—"Old saing is true out of Sit out of mind." And so she faced the prospect of doing housework for a dollar and a quarter per week, with the galling awareness that a Minnesota acquaintance had made a dollar a day waiting tables. She felt impelled to leave her current location. She considered returning to the "rust tick" [Aroostook County] but sensed that that would be little better. She could not get the money to go west, and so, for Catherine Woods, Boston became the safety-valve. There she obtained better work, and she came to like it "furste rate."[41]

In an 1832 letter to relatives and friends at the old home in Pennsylvania, a couple newly arrived in Indiana made this general observation on their changed location and their changed condition: "You may think that we are out of the world but we seem to have just got into it."[42] That way of expressing it betokened distance and separation, but the explicit meaning of Martha and Solomon Fussell's assertion illustrates very nicely a key part of the common man's perception of the West. Vitality and opportunity there abounded. But for people philosophically predisposed to resignation and acquiescence, and for people constitutionally ill-prepared, as William Dean Howells painstakingly showed, for the visit of easy fortune, the surge of vitality and the intrusion of opportunity posed large challenges. Vitality and opportunity were indeed forces of the world, forces that readily gave rise to things far more unsettling than calm, agrarian accomplishment. "Unrestraint," Frederick Jackson Turner pronounced in the last paragraph of his 1893 address on the frontier condition, "is triumphant."[43] Here again one might readily envision our forefathers rejoicing in that fact, but given the spirit of Martha and Solomon Fussell and their kind, more may have been lost than gained by the westward movement. They now lived in a "wonderful place for trade and business of all kinds." They had not left the world at all, but rather had "just got into it." Now more than before they had to accommodate to worldly forces.

Simple movement itself militated against the observance of cherished ways, as the perplexity and haggling about the Sabbath on the overland trails so well attest. A few years before those dislocations, a New Yorker reconnoitering the land in Illinois in 1836 probably took pains to mention to his wife that he had attended a Methodist quarterly meeting. However, he could not deny that it was hard to keep the "mind on religion when a purson is a travling and in such a variety of company. . . ."[44] As frontier historians have so frequently called to our attention, the search for a particular piece of land, in which endeavor the above writer was engaged, often had no settling finality. Sending word to relatives in Weewokaville, Alabama, a Union County, Arkansas, couple told of the standard practice, vintage 1849. One could, "as a great many others about here" do, get land at government prices, "make a little improvement and then sell it for from 100 to $200" profit,[45] then repeating the process further on. As a New Englander in Minnesota Territory noted in general observation, the spirit of "go-ahead" and "drive on" prevailed, "mingled with a great degree of restlessness" which caused farmers to settle and improve a location, only "to sell out & *go west*." "Onward & onward," he wrote of his fellow Westerners of the 1850s, "always settling & never settled. . . ."[46] Such people were not settling the country; they were unsettling it. And it was indeed hard to keep one's mind on religion.

Vitality translated into movement, and it translated as well into business. When Hawthorne remarked on the push and hubbub of Rochester, which for him was a western city,[47] he matched the reaction of plainer folk who time and again hit upon the business aura as a salient feature of the new areas. Of course, in some form or another business was, after all, the fundamental reason for being there. "Verily," an argonaut wrote, "California is a go-ahead country," one in which he meant to remain for about two years. That amount of time would allow him and his partners to square their accounts in the world, an achievement "which we could not have done at home in ten or fifteen years."[48] "The *West* I do admire," a newly arrived shoemaker wrote of Cincinnati. In time, Augustus Roundy left the Ohio city for his native Massachusetts, but here in 1839 he relished Cincinnati's "continual hum of business from Monday morning 3 oclock when the mail boats arrive until dark. I do very much like to be where there is plenty of business. . . ."[49] Hardly off the boat in San Francisco in 1850, a man bound for the mines pronounced it "a bisness place. Bisness of all cinds." To be sure, "all cinds" included gambling and even worse, but they did not prevent this sojourner's predicting that it was "going to bee the gratist place in the world."[50] Here we have the seeds of the western perception and the western spirit which James Bryce analyzed so compellingly some three decades later. If business had not yet become, as Bryce would suggest in his chapter "The Temper of the West," a "kind of religion,"[51] it certainly was already doing much in western locales to undermine the preeminence that traditional religion had enjoyed.

In this western realm, "Booster Talk"—what Daniel Boorstin calls "The Language of Anticipation," worldly anticipation—was emerging as the accustomed mode. When people gave in to the temptation of "describing things which had not quite yet 'gone through the formality of taking place,' "[52] speculation, flummery, and fraud came without delay or welcome. It could hardly have been otherwise. The West was not the arena of personal isolation, natural communion, or even intentional adventure. It was the arena of business and the main chance, and the opportunistically mobile farmer or homesteader participated almost as fully as did the architect of grandiose railroad or town-building schemes. But, participate though they did, these Americans felt strong qualms and expressed them.

"The western world is all alive," a Vermont tinsmith observed as he relocated in Ohio. "The lakes, the streams, the prairies and forests are teeming with life and exhibit all the noise and bustle of human industry and enterprise."[53] Much of what Oren Wiley discerned in 1836 had not quite yet " 'gone through the formality of taking place,' " but it was the aura described and suggested by a great many. Some, of course, reveled in the main-chance frenzy. A day's work in Kansas in 1856 merited this entry by a small-time land speculator with a penchant for the wry: "I managed by dint of hard blustering & swearing to bring in my 'bogus claim.' " Eight days later, he sold it. When noting that a railroad land-grant rumor had "set a good many folks crazy" and that they were frantically bidding up land that was mostly under water, he ended his account with an arch "Let em rip!" In Minnesota Territory on one occasion, he bought eighty acres one day for $480 and sold it the next for $585. Andrew Jackson Sterrett well knew that by "watching the chances, & picking up bargains, & turning them in the spring" a "man with a pile of money, could *clear* a pile of money."[54] That working aroused the unabashed relish and envy of this comparatively worldly young man. But here, as in such other ways as his chiding of religion nearly unto irreverence, Sterrett did more to foreshadow the coming age than to bespeak his own.

However much these rococo prospects intoxicated Sterrett and his ilk, they sobered and worried many more. Aboard a steamer on the way to Saint Paul in the summer of 1855, New Englander Isaac Metcalf sidled into conversational range of Willis Gorman, "friend and pet of Frank Pierce" and now territorial governor of Minnesota. Perhaps assuming a chidingly confidential tone, Gorman admitted that he had not known where Minnesota was when his comrade of Mexican War days made him governor of it. Now, however, having become acquainted with the area, he enjoyed it, profited by it, and showed no hesitance in sharing the secrets by which people rose in it: "Men have made foirtunes by hiring money at 5 per cent per month to speculate upon! I told him I could not understand that. 'Oh! Corner lots — Corner lots' said he."[55]

Eyeing the world sardonically and his fellow bartenders suspiciously, James T. Jones, manager and bartender in a San Francisco establishment, understood such things far more fully than did Isaac Metcalf, but he had scant patience for "Corner lots" whatever form they took. "Anybody that knows anything of the west," he informed his mother, "knows there is no more money there, than in an eastern village, and that no man possesses *anything* that is not *mortgaged*. . . . I cant help but laugh and wonder what the *next spec* will be." Bartending in a building owned by Sam Brannan had its attractions; indeed, Jones had never had "such a chance for *filthy lucre*." But soon he drifted on to his "*next spec*," marketing an ointment for piles. People of his own dour persuasion may have looked upon that product as "all gammon," to use an expression that he applied to other things, but surely, again to employ his terms, it was not "the biggest humbug of the day," else he would not have sent his mother a supply for her own use. Whatever the case in these regards, the acerbic sailor turned bartender endured California "to make money," and, he added in characteristic resolve, "when I get it, I am off."[56]

Telling of her trip west to Michigan by road, rail, canal, and lake boat, Lucia Sparhawk ascribed whatever scant satisfaction there had been in the venture to "Kind Providence." Providence had not seen fit to ease every step, however. Aboard a canal boat "everybody looked sad and felt dirty," and the only refuge was the "refuge from torturing thought." However galling other aspects of the West proved to be in 1836, "the most discouraging feature is the immense land speculation now going on, to the injury of the country and the permanent settlers."[57] The "speculating tricks of 1835 & 36,"[58] as a young Pennsylvanian in Missouri styled them, passed quickly into lore, and a great many of the cities projected in them gave their challenge to ancient Athens and Rome for only a moment before translating into triviality or oblivion. The "big cities of '36"—nothing but a few crumbling foundations kindly veiled by weeds in one, and only the enduring mockery of a shabby tavern in another—could indeed give rise to "discouraging" thoughts. Ridicule such developments as he might, this young man from Connecticut who had ventured west to work for a merchant in Michigan City, Indiana, and who now told of still-born metropolises, could not elude the spirit which had informed those very places. Now, twelve years after the "big cities of '36" had been conceived, in the same letter that described their demise he stated that there was "right smart of an excitement" regarding a railroad. If it came through Michigan City, the future of that place was assured; if not, Michigan City "will only be on the records of citys past and gone."[59]

Perhaps it was that tenuousness and transience that moved Gertrude Stein to be "always explaining to French people that Europeans do not know anything about disillusion, Americans have to have so much optimism because they do know what it is to have disillusion. . . ."[60] As a New Yorker explained while visiting Madison, Wisconsin, in 1840, "the people are very avaricious, are professed enemies & take every possible advantage of strangers, & to me the whole fabric seemed founded on selfishness, reared at the expense of the credulous & duped people & tottering now to its very base with the ague of speculation."[61] The western dimension with its "ague of speculation" did much to breed fear and distrust and disquietude.

The Hazards of New Fortunes

Lo, a vision! . . . gaunt dogs howling over grassy thresholds at stark corpses of old age and infancy, . . . fields, with turned furrows, choked with briers; . . . a thousand paths marked with footprints, all inland leading, . . . Oh; over forest, hill, and dale. And lo! The golden region!. . . thousands delve in quicksands and sudden sink in graves of their own making, . . . other thousands slave and pile their earth so high they gasp for air and die, . . . Here, one haggard hunter murders another in his pit; and, murdering, himself is murdered by a third. Shrieks and groans! Cries and Curses! It seems a golden hell! . . . "Ah! Home! Thou only happiness! Better thy silver earnings than all these golden findings. Oh, bitter end to all our hopes; we die in golden graves."[62]

Thus did Yoomy, Melville's minstrel in the circumnavigation of *Mardi*, tell his lugubrious phantasm of California and its consequences. Of course, poetic license has here been intensified almost beyond calculation: a writer of fiction inventing an intricate allegory at one point in which a mythic bard offers a trance-like perception. Elsewhere, perhaps most notably in the same book, Melville draped the West, particularly when images of raw greed did not intrude, in far more positive garb. Nonetheless, this nightmarish vignette, derived as it was from the West's apotheosis, should be remembered as a counterweight to the happily assertive sounds with which the era is so frequently connected. In sentiment, "Oh! Susannah" avoided being substantially fraudulent only by being thoroughly nonsensical.

Yoomy's vision had far more power and clarity than what could come from the modes of expression at the command of the common people, but they made do. Time and again for purposes of gently ironic euphemism, they relied upon the trope made famous by John Godfrey Saxe's poem about the blind men and the elephant. As shown in an earlier chapter, the elephant usage appeared as a general synonym for experience, and, given some point of reference, it could serve as designation for almost any part thereof. In concluding an analysis of an episode in a Ned Buntline story in which two "wicked" sisters fought for the "honor of seducing" a young man brought ill into their household, a modern scholar had this to say: "When the young man recovered, they made a compromise and both 'showed him the elephant,' as it was euphemistically termed in 1850."[63] Textual analysis of *The G'hals of New York* might prove unavailing even for the well-equipped, let alone for this reader, but in the section under consideration, Ned Buntline did not employ the elephant metaphor, thus allowing one to infer that our modern scholar made the seduction-elephant equation. The drollery of that constriction of use would not have escaped our generally somber ancestors. In an age not renowned for openness of expression regarding the physical aspects of sex, the popularity of a song titled "Seein' the Elephant"[64] suggests that other things ordinarily came to mind at such mention.

That song came, it is almost needless to say, in 1849. In rhetoric and imagination the elephant might roam anywhere, but his special habitat was the American West. The piquancy of the Saxe poem and the studied nonchalance of letters home to loved ones could not veil the fact that that creature was neither gentle nor friendly. Fools would not settle, lore had it, for a purely vicarious acquaintance with him because, though he kept a "dear" school, they could learn in no other. But, where the elephant as West was concerned, a quick introduction, or perhaps just intimations, or "tracks" often sufficed. Remarking on some Pike's Peakers who changed their minds and their direction at Iowa City, one migrant described them as "satisfied with this view of the *Elephant*."[65] With time on his hands on the isthmus, a New Yorker bound for California looked about for an amusement to replace his shipboard delight in the torments of a seasick Jew. The Jew—apparently indisposed every day afloat from New York Harbor to San Francisco Bay, and exposed to the baiting of our diarist—persevered, but other people, as the devilish John P. Bannan wrote in Aspinwall, turned back after seeing only "part of the Eliphant." (In that community Bannan, who liked to "take a smile" (drink) almost as much as he liked to badger a seasick Jew, passed a shop kept by another Jew, and "when I called him a Chatham St he said I was a tam New York lofer.")[66] Whatever the values of John P. Bannan, the values of the era would have retained their integrity longer had more people been satisfied with seeing only "part of the Eliphant."

The elephant sign always became more prominent the farther west one went. On May 27, 1850, after a miserably cold and windy night near Fort Laramie, one sojourner had "no doubt the 'Elephant' gave us a slight brush of his tail."[67] Four days later in the same year and near the same place, another man, whose gathering of buffalo chips "as the Israelites did the manna" appeared in another context, "imagined" that he had seen "the tracks of the Elephant," though he could not be certain for the dust in his eyes. As the dreary trail stretched toward South Pass and beyond, all doubt disappeared: "Elephant tracks have been growin more plenty for the last 300 miles." Because he was soliloquizing in a diary rather than conversing by letter, this writer could specify the nature of some of those "tracks." "Graves were quite thick and ded cattle everywhere," he noted. In the course of the day, he did something in comparison with which gathering buffalo chips was an exercise in delicacy— making "soop from the washings of a number of putrid carcasses."[68] Less literately but yet softly evocative of hardship came the word from the Fort Laramie area back to the Indiana wife of a harness maker-farmer turned argonaut: "tel becky i seen the elephants tale." The writer left it at that, probably deeming it better not to burden Mrs. Sponsler and "becky" with disquieting details.[69]

The elephant often made the most dramatic impression upon those who continued and completed their temporo-spatial projection into modernity. The previously mentioned Charlotte Whipple gave birth to a child near the Boise River, and she wrote home in good spirits when located in the gentle bosom of the lower Columbia. But "one thing is certain," she averred; back there along the trail, "the elephant hoof & horns is to be seen."[70] For James Jones, whether he was selling whiskey in Sam Brannan's building or concocting ointment for piles, "the California Elephant is a dreadful sight."[71] Obadiah Ethelbert Baker did not have Jones's glum outlook, but he never forgot the burdens of the western trek.

> We saw the Elephant sure enough
> O never mind, but you bet 'twas rough

From the shakiness of the hand and from the similarity it bears to dated items, one can infer that Baker composed his lengthy poem in the 1890s, some forty years after the events chronicled. In the next to last of the twenty-five stanzas of "Seeing the Elephant," the impact of Baker's glimpse becomes most clear and concise:

> God has been good, the world has been rough
> Seeing the Elephant has been tough
> Think we've seen the Big fellow enough[72]

The hardships of the West also came to bear upon those in the East who suffered because fathers, sons, or husbands had ventured afar. Yoomy's troubled vision included that dimension, and nearly all commentators—poetic, scholarly, or whatever—would recognize it, though the happy and assertive aura that surrounds the depiction of the westward movement probably mutes it unduly. There is no measuring the "last look of anguish" on a mother's face as a son turned westward, never again to be beheld, and there is no reason to doubt that the memory of that look stayed with the prodigal "unfaded to the grave."[73] The intangible toll upon that mother, and in turn upon the son whose quoted words came at learning of her death, defies calculation, but one can locate some tangible and partly calculable dimensions of the burden shouldered by those who stayed behind. "If you ever want to see me again alive in this world," an ill and despairing Forty-niner wrote from Sacramento, "do you get 150 dollars and remit to me."[74] Whether Mrs. William Goodridge managed to borrow that sum is not known, but her husband died in California shortly after informing her of the cost of his return. The California urge that drew Goodridge away from Beverly, Massachusetts, had an especially strong effect upon John Eagle of Alleghany, Pennsylvania, because of the hurt he had so often experienced at seeing his children and his wife "dressed so poorly" that it was an embarrassment for them to go out, while "other men's wives could dress up and run out when they pleased." Now, with her husband gone to be replaced by the abstract, ironic comfort of a thousand dollar life insurance policy, Margaret Eagle drifted even closer to poverty while trying to keep the little store going.[75]

If Mrs. Eagle scrimped more than she had before, at least she seems not to have been called on to send her husband money. The size of individual and private money flow to the West probably cannot be estimated, but that flow was a recurring fact of life, or of death as in the case of William Goodridge. For James Jones, the San Francisco bartender, "*steamer day*" evidently meant better business, that being the day when, given the arrival of a ship bearing letters from the East, "all are after money."[76] Here the impact remains in the realm of the impersonal. In other instances, it became far more dramatic. Though they had "nothing to Doe and Nothing to Doe it with," Isaac and Lucy Carr sought to show good cheer in writing to a son and his wife who had made the move west to Wisconsin. Isaac knew that times were always difficult in a "new country," but, as he encouragingly pointed out, "you will Son Be worth more than Either of your fathers." Isaac meant nothing ironic when he wrote that in June, but soon that comparison would be more hurtful than inspiring. As money gave out at the upstate New York home, a pathetic tone surfaced in the correspondence. After noting that he had again borrowed in order to send them help, father Carr remarked simply that he and his wife "must have something to live on." His wife Lucy's message to the Wisconsin children bordered on despair and hysteria:

Dear Children[:] [I]t is with awful felings that I attempt to say a few words to you. [I] cannot endure my feealings much longer[.] [Y]our father thought he should go to see you this fall but if he has to send you his money he cannot go[.] [W]e do not allow our selves any luxerys[.] [T]he tim has come that we cannot work and we do not want to go to the poor hous[.] [W]e cant go to meting for the want of cloaths nor any whear for the want of a wagaon[,] so you see we cannot take any comefort in this world . . . this world is not mutch to us[.] [T]he anguish of my hart this morning . . . I wil stop[.] I hope yore takeing more comfert than I am   Lucy Carr[77]

How often this sort of thing attended the settling of the West is well beyond determination, but the dread instilled by such prospects appears frequently. At least for old Isaac Carr, only a few more months of that comfortless condition intensified by the spectre of the poorhouse lay between him and his eternal destiny.

Another minor elaboration of the perception of hardship entailed in the westward movement involves the Indian. The westward impulse and reality

generated an amplitude of dismal prospects, but the writings of the unsophisticated reveal very little of those extremes of tropistic hate, revulsion, and fear
toward the Indian that one might anticipate. To be sure, these sources do not
express a gentle or solicitous attitude towards them, though the debating
societies occasionally deliberated as to whether the Indian or the slave had
greater claim to America's compassion, and diary entries sometimes registered outrage at abuses worked upon the natives. But it would require great
talent to wheedle from humble sources even an intimation of the gore-bathed
phantasmagoria that supposedly characterized more sophisticated sources.
In one analysis of the sanguinary "mythopoeic perception" appearing in
"printed literature" we encounter a "savaged landscape" begotten of a
"tortured mind," and in both the "archetypal enemy" is the red Indian.[78] The
instructed vision of plainer folk, both unimaginative and anti-imaginative,
seemed not to have entertained those dark fancies.

Even when the West itself was under discussion, the common people found
so many things other than the native inhabitants to occupy their writing attention. They said very little about the Indian, and so little of what they did say
has any compelling interest to the modern mind. Ideas of natural goodness in
some way reflective or suggestive of primitivism hardly occurred to them. Nor
did they apparently have any acquaintance with the doctrine or notion of progress against which the Indian might have been judged. Nor did visions of the
Indian's dark diabolism seem to have seized or tortured their imaginations. To
be sure, solicitous urgings to beware routinely came from mothers, wives, and
other loved ones. "I dont much expect to ever see you again," Prudence Kelley
of Danby, Vermont, wrote sadly to a nephew and his wife who were considering the California move. To young Joseph she urged the recognition that
"an interest in Christ is worth more than all the gold in California," but,
looking at what she had written and perhaps reflecting on changing times, she
surmised that "this looks verry simple to you." However wedded to doctrines
of old, Prudence lived in this world as well as the other, and so she reminded
her willful relative to "take good care of number one" and to go by sea rather
than by land in order to avoid being "cruilized by the Indians."[79] Prudence
Kelley could hardly have done other than offer that advice. Those in the West,
however, even those in the exposure of the overland crossing, seem rarely to
have perceived the Indian as threat or as enemy. Theirs was, of course, the
language of reality, not that of literary drama. Hence, perhaps for that reason,
their imagery has almost no place for the "American hero" and in turn for his
obligatory "archetypal enemy."

Writing at Cannon Falls, Minnesota Territory, in 1855, a New Englander
mused on the difficulties that his generation ("degenerate children of the
Puritans," he seriocomically styled them) would have had, had they faced the
bleak prospects of seventeenth-century New England shores rather than the
comfortable tailoring of the area upon which his eye rested. "Ridiculous 'Pil-

grim fathers' " we " 'westerners' " would have made, he concluded, "but
fortunately this soil & these Indians are just about wild enough to make the
labor on one & the sight of the other interesting without being tedious or
dangerous." As did others, this writer came prepared with a line from Thomas
Campbell to help indicate that the Indian too was best viewed from afar: " 'distance lends enchantment to the view.' "[80] With the Minnesota massacre yet
seven years in the future, this sentiment came not from fear but from mild pity
and disgust.

These unsophisticated people employed a conventional designation for the
Indian. The Indian very frequently appeared in their writings as the "red man
[or son or child] of the forest," and he appeared so whether he was encountered in verdant Minnesota, the sere plains of western Nebraska, or the
desert wastes beyond South Pass. For them, the Indian's character remained
constant regardless of circumstances or setting: a vexing and somewhat
pitiable blend of gluttony, improvidence, beggarliness, cowardice, and fil-
thiness. The red sons of the forest—these "quer Chaps," as one argonaut
called them[81]—were regarded with condescension but with indulgence as well.
An encounter with an encampment of Sioux in the Platte River country moved
a man from Indiana to remark that "a Hoosier could be very much amused by
observing the savage customs. . . ." Then he provided some physical description—"The color of the Sioux is that of a dark mulatto—wellformed—keen
eyes—& black hair"—before getting on to his most concerted effort to maintain a charitable posture: "fond of presents and very much inclined to friendship."[82]

Needless to say, those "quer Chaps" could arouse much less charitable
feelings, but what a westering Michigander called "the hard side of the Golden
Picture"[83] had more fearsome prospects than the red man of the forest. For
those going west, cholera alone pushed the Indian into comparative triviality.
Perhaps because the hazards to physical well-being were so abundant
wherever one was, the West posed its most worrisome threats in realms other
than the corporeal.

The Land of "Unrestraint"

What historian Turner called the "unrestraint" of the frontier process
appeared to contemporaries as the decay of morals and the rending of the
fabric of association. Numerous physical hardships and hazards awaited the
pioneers, but they were of far less consequence to those who went west or to
those who stayed home than the subtler and less palpable assaults of the westward trek upon the soul and society. Worried descriptions of the realm one
entered when one left the "land of steady habbits"[84] to venture beyond "the
bounds of civilization" are legion in their writings: a realm "where no church
bell is heard[,] no Sabbath known[,] and no divine law regarded";[85] where, for

example, "gaming and drnkn are Virtues"[86] and "the truth cannot be uttered";[87] and "where every one 'doeth that which is right in his own eyes.' "[88] The twentieth century, with its appetite for antinomianism and primitivism, sometimes has scant patience with the crabbedly restrained ways of its immediate ancestors. And the memory of Frederick Jackson Turner can now be subjected to stern lecture for having perpetuated and extended the "myth of civilization."[89]

Of course, our present fondness for "unrestraint" works no obligation upon our predecessors; they can be rejected, but they cannot be changed. To the modern taste, John P. Bannan may seem somewhat amusing, but, here too, distance may lend the enchantment. After reaching California in the late 1850s, he drifted to mining flurries farther north. Trudging along in the Walla Walla country after a particularly disappointing venture, he and his party came upon a Methodist minister. The man of the gospel traveled with them for a day, and he set about to enhance their spiritual life, but alas, he soon despaired. In his summary judgment of their character, he estimated that, were Bannan and his fellows only a hundred strong, they could drive the devil from his stronghold in hell.[90] When argonaut Bannan was not discommoding Methodists, he was diverting himself in such ways as getting drunk, provoking brawls aboard ship, or baiting a seasick Jew.

"I want you to tell Bayless," the word went from the Iowa District of Wisconsin Territory to a brother in Ohio in 1838, "that I disregard him as there is neither law nor gospel here and I am at his defiance."[91] At least for the time being, Bayless would not receive any judgment that might be awarded him by a court against frontiersman John McCleary, and all recall lore regarding zones where the Ten Commandments and other niggling constraints are rendered void. People of archness or the more affluent might welcome the liberation, but common folk did not. "Great Kountry this," a Mississippian sardonically wrote of the Sonora, California, mining area after having witnessed a man stab another to death for "impropriety with his wife." "The devil gets in the women here," he observed, but then he commented on human nature and on the way the West affected it. Perhaps the devil did not so much get into women in places such as Sonora; perhaps the devil "merely comes out of them."[92] On the second Sunday out of Boston Harbor bound for California, a comparatively sophisticated young man unhappily detected faces still sufficiently long to symbolize "the *strictest* phases of Puritanism."[93] It comforted him, however, to see that change was occurring, and already the effort on one man's part to read a sermon met with disinterest and disdain. The avoidance of a "dry" sermon ten days out of comfortable Boston seems innocent enough, but in the minds of the common people it could betoken much more and much worse. At the end of July in that same magic year, other Bostonians camped on the Green River, and among them there occurred a "brutal affair." In the course of an argument, a man named White pushed and kicked a man named Ayer. The latter grabbed a hatchet and hurled it at his opponent, thus inflicting a ghastly wound in White's thigh. This sorry business, according to a diarist who witnessed it, resulted from "having all restraint thrown off."[94]

That, of couse, was the indictment made against the South—too little discipline, too little restraint. In the cartography of the mind, the West bore a close relation to the South. South and West enticed and menaced in similar ways; and it could indeed be that the man of the South was a more skilled frontiersman than his northern counterpart because he was more at home in the unrestrained setting. That some would later consider such things as the shootout on the dusty cowtown street as little more than a variant of the peculiar ways of the South would have come as little surprise to those of the pre-Civil War generation.[95]

Mayhem and impropriety were only the outward signs of a dislocation that was quite as much spiritual as it was spatial. "There are too many," pronounced the "reforming synod" in the throes of cultural self-scrutiny in the wake of King Philip's War, "that with profane Esau slight spiritual privileges."[96] To many, the expanse of time separating the era of Philip's War from the era of the Gold Rush may appear as having rendered worry about "profane Esau" and solicitude for "spiritual privileges" unutterably archaic, perhaps void. But they were yet alive, and not only in the mind of Ralph Waldo Emerson. Indeed, he and other, later commentators, as has been previously suggested, may well have exaggerated the degree to which American society had drifted from its religious moorings, but, of course, the drift was undeniable. In the common view, the most evident harbinger and the most effectual catalyst of the "new profane epoch," to use William A. Clebsch's expression, was the West. Therein, as they well knew, resided an overabundance of those who roamed with "profane Esau." These people would very likely have understood the idea of "a nation profaned," what in Clebsch's close and nonpejorative definition was "a society standing *pro-fanum*, outside of religion's temple," a society bereft or neglectful of its "privileges."[97]

Having gone west for lucre, the migrants rarely troubled to assure others that the Indians were, say, friendly, or docile, or impotent. Nor did they spend much time expatiating about the egalitarian or democratic implications of the unsettled arena. In an uncommon expression of the theme a new Minnesotan wrote that "the rich are brought down nearer to a leavel with the poor than in almost any other place for they all have to live in small houses[,] ride to meatings on double sleads & so on."[98] As others of his letters reveal, this man quickly became enamored of the comfortable Minnesota setting, especially because his settlement had an abundance of "Ministers Professors Deacons and class leaders & most of them are first rait neighbours."[99] Horatio Houlton and the vast majority of the others went west to better their material condition; their incumbent argumentative obligation consisted in muting their own fears and the fears of others regarding their spiritual well-being. Insofar as humble contentions about the West were positive in other than the material depiction, they were so in their occasional, overly protested assertions that the Westerner did not have to sacrifice his "privileges," ones that were far removed from what one young man dismissed as "this insignificant privilege"[100] of voting.

"Contrary to your fears," a Connecticut Yankee in Grundy County, Missouri, advised the folks at home, "I *know* the voice of supplication to Heaven sometimes breaks upon the stillness of the western wilds and we may confidently trust it will become more and more frequent."[101] Sometimes, by way of invidious comparison, the West took the offensive, as it did when a native of Granby, Connecticut, wrote the following home from Warren County, Illinois, in 1835: "In point of Morality and Sobriety, the citizens of Warren County taken as a body are far above the citizens of Granby." With the "eye or ear of the Christian" rarely being offended, and with plenty of preaching available, Warren County seemed on its way to becoming "the garden of the United States."[102] Writing to the family back in Saline County, Missouri, Thomas Hayter told of good times in his part of Oregon Territory. Religious excitement, particulary among the Baptists and most particularly as evidenced by his own condition, moved him to claim much. His way of formulating the glad tidings, however, admitted even more than it claimed. "That," he remarked of his having joined the Baptists, "Surprised you i Should guess[,] for to leave an Old settled Country and Come to a new among All Classes of People for to Better Prepare for a future Existance is somewhat Singular." As plain folk saw the matter, it was somewhat singular indeed.[103]

The unnerving admissions, the regrets, and the forlorn hopes expressed by those going west came far more commonly, forming something of an unanswerable countercurrent to the heady visions and the specious mouthings. For the American Pilgrim, the West provided even less of a home than that which he had left; he found no Delectable Mountains and overmuch of Vanity Fair. To review some of his categories, when he spoke of privileges, he meant, unless otherwise specified, religious privileges; when he spoke of meetings, he meant, unless otherwise specified, religious meetings; and when he spoke of society, he meant, unless otherwise specified, a religiously wreathed joining of family and intimates. The West threatened all of these overlapping dimensions of the spiritual realm. Writing home to Connecticut from Ohio in 1831, Lydia and Erastus Bingham wearily noted that they no longer lived where they could enjoy "every religious privilege."[104] A year later, a new Illinoisan sent word to her native area that what was needed was "orchards and privileges."[105] That refrain about privileges echoed around the western reaches, as it did from Missouri even as late as 1857: "That want of Church privileges is our greatest cross."[106] To narrow the focus and indicate a specific area of those privileges denied them, they referred to meetings: the "worst difficulty is meeting";[107] "My greatest complaint is the want of meetings."[108] Society construed as spiritual microcosm rather than as profane macrocosm, showed the same deficiencies. Do not catch the California fever, an Ohio gold-seeker wrote to a friend at home, for he could derive more pleasure and comfort from one hour "in the society of his wife" than any man in California could in a year.[109] In a discouraging word describing the Platte Purchase country of northwest Missouri in 1840, a Virginian who had been employed in the survey told that "society is very bad, the Sabbath is hardly known, and religion almost discountenanced."[110] Envying the people at home in Deerfield, Massachusetts, a woman who had relocated in the Richfield, Illinois, area made the following assessment of those whom she now encountered: "They want no society [,] nether are they fit for any. . . ."[111] One wonders what the surveyor from Virginia and the housewife from Massachusetts would have thought had they been informed that, by "Emerson's generation," the wilderness had come to be viewed as "the redemptive West."[112]

Not all lamented their new society. The young man who had gleefully watched "the *strictest* phases of Puritanism" slipping from aboard the *Rudolph* only ten days out of Boston Harbor again marked the liberating progression two Sundays later. Now with Boston almost a month behind, George F. Kent felt free to spend the Sabbath cleaning his gun and doing other such "worldly" business.[113] Kent was a man of some attainment and, if not worldly, at least somewhat so inclined. Earthy and sardonic Andrew Jackson Sterrett luxuriated in the West, in the realm of " '100 per cent.' " For him, Leavenworth, Kansas Territory, in the fall of 1856 did not wreak of political or ethical or religious imperatives. Indeed, such considerations had no place among the melange of fraud, chicanery, and promotional bluster that this small-time speculator described in terms that Bryce would have relished: "Religion—there is but one here and that is '100 per cent.' Business—there is but one here and that is '100 per cent.' Generally speaking there is nothing here but '100 per cent.' "[114] The West was for people of the world, people who had position or unwonted independence. Melville brought the type to mythic apotheosis in his fictionalized Ethan Allen, a man who remarked of himself that " 'in my younger days I studied divinity, but at present I am a conjurer by profession' ":

Allen seems to have been a curious combination of a Hercules, a Joe Miller, a Bayard, and a Tom Hyer; had a person like the Belgian giants; mountain music in him like a Swiss; a heart plump as Coeur de Lion's. Though born in New England, he exhibited no trace of her character. He was frank, bluff, companionable as a Pagan, convivial, a Roman, hearty as a harvest. His spirit was essentially Western; and herein is his peculiar Americanism; for the Western spirit is, or will yet be (for no other is, or can be), the true American one.[115]

The common people would have been reluctant to celebrate those who drifted from divinity to conjuring, those who were jokesters or fighters or gallants. The West, the future, and the world *pro-fanum* were nearly interchangeable dimensions, but plain folk did not rush to embrace them. They were drawn to those dimensions inexorably, as to a lodestone, but they went moodily, apprehensively, and resignedly. The "Green Hoosier" on the Oregon Trail mused that Sunday and the things it represented were now "failing," "as such things inevitably must fail when men who act from improper motives are freed from the restraints of society." The "Green Hoosier" had flexibility, however, and could accommodate himself to the world: "So took up the line of march with the moving tide."[116] "O!" a young married couple who had made the move west from upstate New York to Wisconsin repined; there was such danger of "constantly sining" against a "forbearing Redeemer." In fact, on one of the rare occasions when they heard a minister of the gospel, the minister pronounced Wisconsin the "Hardest place to live Religion" that he had ever seen—"so much worldly business[,] so many changes buying & selling farms that Christians are almost buried up in the rubbish of the world."[117] Hawthorne's dour imagination contrived a celestial railroad which would allow the Pilgrim to circumvent the hazards and obstacles which Bunyan had made him overcome. In Wisconsin, that "hardest place to live Religion," a New York family mortgaged their newly acquired farm in order to invest in a terrestrial railroad, the Milwaukee and La Crosse. They lost the money but managed to keep the farm. From the family home came the parental and generally sound doctrine of the era, that being the hope that the migrants were "seaking to lay up A large t[re]asure not all in rail rode stock but in that world ware we shall need nothing of this world."[118]

Elizabeth Cooley McClure and her new husband, James, left Virginia in 1846, and they, too, encountered what their Wisconsin counterparts called the "rubbish of the world." Not wanting to "live like a dog," the young McClures left their unprepossessing situation for something better; as James wrote aboard a steamer between Memphis and New Orleans, "I think to do well after while and make money plenty." Those happy thoughts were not readily realized, and for a few months the peregrinations of Elizabeth and James amounted to a study in suffering and frustration. "O[,] I am tired of the world," the distressed young wife wrote when the fruitless western wandering reached the Independence, Missouri, area, "I want religion!!" The world-weary woman did not have long to endure. Eight months later, an illness brought her the routine doses of laudanum and calomel as well as the prayers of the man who had loved his poor, proud, and aspiring wife, perhaps not always wisely— "God of heaven have mercy on her." Then, with her own diary hand shaking into illegibility with disjointed phrases such as "feel doubtful of whether" and "through the valley of death," the "world" ended.[119]

Twenty-three months earlier, having just crossed the line from Virginia into Tennessee, Elizabeth had lain awake late at night musing and listening while beside her James accepted the fitful sleep allowed by the first of a series of illnesses. Her mind went to the agony of parting, something she had experienced only a week before; her mind went as well to that realm known as heaven, where parting is no more. Her ear brought soulful accompaniment to her reverie by suffusing it with Isaac Watts's "Hark from the Tomb" as it was being rendered "slow and melancholy" by the slave segment of the wayfaring party. A few nights before, the newly married and pioneering couple had gone to rest by the "Glorious Light of Zion."[120]

Conclusion

How jarringly inappropriate that human dislocation yielding intense physical and spiritual suffering for nearly all concerned should have ridden forward in historical recollection to the jaunty strain of "Oh Susanna." As at the Virginia-Tennessee line when the young McClures paused in their trek, America sang hymns near Fort Kearny on the evening of June 17, 1849.[121] The nation, as Bernard De Voto so dramatically showed in his study of the forces concentrated in *The Year of Decision*, was being catapulted into an alien future, particularly by "some people who went west."[122] In the lower echelons, however, many refused their destiny and poignantly clung to the past; there with darkness gathering near Fort Kearny "it seemed like home to hear old hundred."[123] Polk County, Oregon, was one of the places where the westering ended, and there, as the year 1851 expired, Sarah C. Buckingham, a native of Missouri, received a call from her newly arrived cousin Tom Hayter. Twenty-one-year-old Tom had not yet found religion on the frontier. When he "sung his two favorite songs" for Sarah, however, he intoned sentiments powerfully informed by the spirit in which Americans anticipated and confronted the West: one was "the White Pilgrim[,] the other O let me go to my home that is far distant east."[124]

APPENDIX:
Some Thoughts Regarding Procedure, Related Scholarship, and Sources

Many historians contend that it is important to delve into the shadowy recesses of the popular mind. For example, in 1954, John Higham complained that intellectual history deprived itself of "much of its complexity and significance" by neglecting or eschewing "the study of the moods and beliefs of the man in the street."[1] Today, Higham can take satisfaction from the rechanneling of effort in American intellectual history that came from examining "the less refined level of consciousness the French have taught us to call collective mentalities."[2] H. Stuart Hughes admits that "every declaration of mankind more explicit than a bestial cry may in some sense be considered the subject matter of intellectual history."[3] What comes from intellectual historians as injunction and justification comes from others as something bordering upon exhortation. Armed with a righteous "sympathy for the powerless," the historian should, Jesse Lemisch urges, approach "past societies from the bottom rather than the top." That would involve "nothing less than an attempt to make the inarticulate speak."[4]

But alas, sober second thoughts arise and problems intrude. "Sympathy for the lot of the common man is commendable," Merrill Jensen allows, before going on to remind a new wave of seekers of lowly truths that "it can lead to distortion...."[5] Perceiving that the infatuated scholarly and artistic hearkening to *Vox Populi* represents yet another form of primitivism, George Boas labels it an "easy way." In precisely the same context, he quotes Spinoza: "'The will of God is the refuge of the ignorant.'"[6] Thereby, Boas intimates another pitfall, one upon which some may reflect more if they have persevered in the reading of the present tome. Simply put, readers may find that the voice of those people adduced in this study bears painfully small resemblance to the voice of gods they themselves heed. And as historians will recall, some spirited discussion has emerged from the concern as to whose gods were being echoed by the messages wheedled from inarticulate people such as Jack Tars and White Oaks.[7]

Aside from the possibility that the common man—whether Jack Tar, White Oak, or whatever—may not have been thinking what he should, there is the burdensome fact that he left so little record of what he thought. "Bestial cries" will not suffice, and almost nothing "more explicit," according to the nearly universal, humbling admission or supposition, yet remains. Thus, the mood of the common man, so frequently deemed consequential, is probed almost solely by indirection, and we are left with inferences, sometimes of awesome breadth. We have studied what the common man thought, not by what he said, but by what he did or by what others said. Given the seeming fact that the common man left precious little, if any, record of what he believed, then it almost necessarily follows that studies of popular thought would derive from popular actions or from thoughts generated elsewhere.

On the one hand, Jesse Lemisch, who would have us "make the inarticulate speak," himself speaks only metaphorically. He seeks to illumine "conduct and ideology," and he quickly admits that written expressions of "the people on the bottom" entered the consideration very little: "Mostly they were inarticulate, and we must read their purpose in their actions. . . ."[8] Of people literally at "the bottom," that goes almost without saying, and Lemisch, aside from openly espousing the cause of the lowly, does what many others have done: he infers "purpose" from "actions."

In cultural and intellectual history, however, it has been more common to infer popular thought (or "purpose," or mood, or attitude, or belief) from intellectual thought. Time and again, implicitly and explicitly, we are bade to envision the radiation of ideas through a society, from adventurous theoreticians at the top of the cognitive pyramid down, with varying degrees of cultural lag, to the ignorant, the lackadaisical, and the recalcitrant. In instructing the intellectual historians, Crane Brinton evidently had something of this order in mind as he called upon them "to follow ideas in their often torturous path from study or laboratory to the market, the club, the home, the legislative chamber, the law court, the conference table, and the battlefield."[9]

In one variant of this approach, some figure acts as ideational representative or surrogate; he acts as one whose thought reflects and articulates what remained as unexpressed hope, mood, or urge in the common man. Even for cultural and intellectual historians, often this procedure strongly resembles the way in which social historian Jesse Lemisch sought to reveal the common man's thought by his action. (Indeed, in his much-remarked call for history "from the bottom up," Lemisch spent a good deal of time treating uncommon people such as John Woolman and Thomas Paine, apparently on the ground that they spoke for those who themselves could not speak.) It seems that certain proclivities are discerned in mankind, and then some thinker whose pronouncements appear congruent is adduced as spokesman of his age. As an example, we can look at a book which literary historian Henry Seidel Canby wrote about Thoreau. "And it was Thoreau," Canby asserts, "who spoke direct to the condition of everyday men caught in the quiet desperation of difficult careers—men who were not speculative, not even religious, yet unable to do what they wanted, even to know what they wanted."[10] Very little is asked of those "everyday men," other than to oblige someone with an opportunity to speak for them.

Likewise, in anatomizing American popular culture of the antebellum period, Carl Bode evidently felt constrained to do something with Emerson and Transcendentalism. Having admitted that "no literary historian would assert that Transcendentalism had a marked influence on mass attitudes," Bode faced a situation that was challenging to him and instructive to us. The admission notwithstanding, we find Emerson, at the end of the same paragraph, preaching "the gospel of sincerity and ideality to more and more people." A page later, we learn that Emerson received at least "a limited response in American culture" in spite of the fact that "no one but a mystic—or a professional philosopher—could grasp" some of what he said, and that other things he espoused "were, literally, un-American ideas and emphatically not those of a large majority of Americans." While his less intellectual counterparts could not understand some parts of what he said and could not accept others, Emerson emerges in Bode's account as herald of his age for "Self-Reliance," if for no other reason. Therein, Emerson wrote "sentence after sentence in a way to fix them in the American mind."[11] And, for illustrative purposes, to contemplate even more dizzying heights in another area of history, we can watch as one scholar who, after decrying the historians' inclination to "look at their material from the top down" and to treat the common man as "an apparently static object of speculation," undertook to explicate "the mental world of the common man" by "the application of humanistic psychoanalysis to an historical evaluation of the life and work of A.J.P. Taylor."[12] Perhaps this prepares us more for the Emersonian assertion in *Representative Men*: "We need not fear excessive influence."[13]

Bode's *Anatomy of American Popular Culture* illustrates yet another variant of the general approach to the study of common thought: the views or moods of the common man are derived from things they supposedly read, heard, or saw. Bode states that he sought, among other things, "to suggest how the American character may have revealed itself through its cultural preferences." Thus, he could find no place for *Walden* because, he noted, "popularity has been my touchstone. . . . This is a book on the people's choice."[14] This tactic has been employed countless times, ordinarily without Bode's use of Jungian archetypes. Indeed, on a spectrum of likelihood this method oscillates somewhere between highly attractive and inevitable. Surely, the world is as one in concluding that we learn something about the 1850s from the fact that *Ten Nights in a Bar-room* sold tremendously while Thoreau's classic which appeared in the same year sold almost not at all. That conveys a message, but it comes through with far greater volume than clarity. Great as were other problems he faced in his anatomizing, they were, Bode remarked, "nothing compared to the problem of inferring American character from cultural preferences."[15]

Despite the barriers encountered, the efforts at "inferring" have been many. When, for example, Roderick Nash reconstructed American thought of the years 1917 to 1930, he devoted a chapter to "The Mood of the People," that being an amalgam of "Heroes" such as Babe Ruth, "Books" such as those written by Gene Stratton-Porter, "Crusades" such as the Ku Klux Klan, and a "Faith" dramatized by Aimee Semple McPherson.[16] Other works have more pertinence to my area of consideration.

"The heritage of ideas which may be reckoned as distinctly American may be sought among the soiled pages of old textbooks which have captured the modes of thought appropriate to their own age."[17] In that way, Richard Mosier begins a methodological explanation of the devices whereby he analyzed the McGuffey Readers of the nineteenth century in order to reconstruct the process involved in *Making the American Mind*. In a similar undertaking, Ruth Miller Elson opens with the statement that finding what the ordinary man thought poses "one of the persistent problems of intellectual history." She, too, went to the schoolbooks, explaining her course this way: "What the averbal man of the past thought about anything is probably lost forever to historical research, but one can at least discover those ideas to which most Americans were exposed by examining the books they read." It seems reasonable enough to assume that, by this method, one could arrive at what Elson calls "the lowest common denominator of American intellectual history."[18]

Those who draw inferences from cultural consumption do not, of course, limit themselves to schoolbooks. Popular songs, poems, paintings, and novels provide rich veins for historians and others, and the yield from them has been high and lively, if not always precise. For a particular example, the popular stage has given us some of the more dramatic indications of what energized the hearts, if not always the minds, of our less sophisticated ancestors. The melodrama, "that most banal of dramatic forms," became for David Grimsted, as it has to a lesser extent for others, a means whereby "to glimpse that most devious of historical objects, the popular mind of an age."[19] With even more venturesomeness, Robert C. Toll went to the minstrel show of the nineteenth century in an effort to shed light, not just upon the antics of "Brudda Tambo" and "Brudda Bones," but upon the way that "minstrelsy helped shape the way Americans conceived of and thought about each other and their country."[20] In "A Note on Method," Toll asserts that "many scholars are searching for ways to uncover the history of 'common people.' " By "using computers to process vast stores of statistics," such scholars have at least a start in constructing their "lives," but, he adds, "they have yet to find ways to recapture common people's thoughts, concerns, desires, fears, and hopes." For Toll as for others, the answer was to infer popular thought from popular culture. "The problem, of course, is sources," Toll explains. "Average people rarely kept diaries, wrote letters, or authored books." Given that view, the "materials" of "popular culture" provide "virtually the only sources for the popular thoughts and feelings of the past." From those "materials" Toll chose the minstrel show as one means of gaining "at least partial access" to the moods of "average Americans."[21]

According to Crane Brinton, some social historians have "in a sense" become intellectual historians by "focusing on what went on in the heart and head of the man in the street."[22] It is only fair to note that there are more invidious ways of stating the relationship about which Brinton remarked. John Higham (for whom the embrace of intellectual history had sufficient reach and warmth to encompass "Little Orphan Annie as well as Adam Smith") admits nonetheless that "perhaps a preponderant part of the academic world relegates to social history the study of the moods and beliefs of the man in the street, reserving for intellectual history the study of high-level ideas."[23] And with the "*via regia* of intellectual history" stretching before him, H. Stuart Hughes betrays a decided fastidiousness when turning to "the level of popular acceptance" of ideas. That involves "a constituent part of general social history," or even of " 'retrospective cultural anthropology.' "[24] While trying to keep at least a toehold on the *via regia* for the study of popular and common notions, R. Richard Wohl concedes that such endeavors fall within the "plebeian" dimension of intellectual history as contrasted with the "aristocratic."[25]

I earnestly hope that this present study deserves to be called history, and I readily leave to readers, if not necessarily to posterity, to supply whatever qualifiers might seem appropriate. But the in-house discussion of definitions bears at least momentary attention. There is a sobering aspect to the placement—by relegation, descent, or ascent—in the realm of social history, particularly for one who does not think of himself as a social historian. Where the study of the common man is concerned, a certain tension or even testiness obtains, and that atmosphere is not confined to general essayists and nonhistorians. So the historian, even if he deems himself an unwilling and unlikely participant in the action, ought at least to determine the lines of fire.

"History will be better written in the ages to come," Edward Eggleston, president of the American Historical Association, announced in the last year of the nineteenth century. The peroration of his address gave the general sense of this grand envisagement as Eggleston addressed the twentieth century: ". . . when the American Historical Association shall assemble in the closing week a hundred years hence, there will be, do not doubt it, gifted writers of the history of the people. . . . We shall have the history of culture, the real history of men and women."[26] In those remarks about "The New History," Eggleston assumed something of a prophetic role, but it is well to remember that, even in 1900, he could cite various precedents and precursors in the attempt to portray "the real history of men and women." Thus, it seems both inevitable and supererogatory that a Merrill Jensen, for example, should in 1970 remind a Jesse Lemisch, for example, that efforts to view history "from the bottom up" were at that late date not at all unprecedented.[27]

What some heard as glad tidings sounded far differently to others. "With the emergence of social history," Ralph Henry Gabriel fondly asserted in 1936, "the guild has returned to its ancient claim that the domain of history is bounded only by the circumference of human life."[28] Twenty years later, Philip Jordan animadverted to the very session at which Gabriel enthused by noting that "a caravan of wise men journeyed by day and by night to Providence, Rhode Island, to stargaze."[29] Jesse Lemisch unburdened himself of the conclusion that there was an elitist bias in those unredeemed by the sounds of inarticulate silence.[30] H. Stuart Hughes, striding unperturbedly on the *via regia*, dismissed efforts to obtain meaning from " 'lower' " levels of thought as futile and as likely to degenerate into "a mechanical and boring catalogue of curious notions."[31] "We insist," Solon Buck pronounced in the halcyon days of the new dispensations, "on knowing something about the lives and thoughts and ideals of the people as distinguished from those of rulers and leaders."[32] A moment later, Louis Pelzer seconded the motion: "A study and appreciation of the contributions made by Plain Men is a distinct phase of the newer history."[33] To those who thought otherwise, that insistence only accelerated the growth of "the nefarious 'cult of the common man,' " with its appetite for "social trivia" and its bent for replacing "politics" with "pioneer pancakes."[34] In the "virgin" fields of history, one seeress espied "such interesting facts as the date on which canned fruit was first handled in the local grocery, when the first oysters were sold, and what was apparently the first appearance of commercial candy in the village."[35] But sad to say, Henrietta Memler's time spent in the "priceless source of information" yielding those "interesting facts" had already been diagnosed by Wilbur Cortez Abbott as "merely a symptom of lowering human values."[36] We can expect more exchanges of this nature. The tempo may change and the deployments may become obscured in the frenzy of strife, but the war itself will likely endure while there remain "aristocrats" and "plebeians" to fight it.

The present study does not seek involvement in that troubled arena, though some may well draw it there. It seeks rather to help bridge a gap in historical understanding, a gap that is as frequently admitted as bemoaned and for which there has been little more than the kind of inferential leaps noted earlier. For their glimmerings of popular attitudes, scholars have gone mostly to items of popular cultural consumption because, they contend, there is no other recourse. The "problem," David Grimsted remarks, is "essentially one of sources, or rather the nonexistence of sources." Where direct "sources" yield nothing, the melodrama, in this case, gives at least some intimations. The solution is far from perfect, however: "One cannot be sure how well the melodrama echoed the notions of the historically voiceless, or that we can today accurately catch the cultural reverberations. It is always hard to identify whose voice one hears when listening to echoes, or to be perfectly sure what is being said."[37] The qualifiers always place severe limits upon certainty. "The scholar cannot simply assume," Robert C. Toll notes, "that popular culture accurately reflects popular thought. If it is a mirror at all, it is like a funhouse mirror that presents distorted or partial images of the subject."[38]

Mine has been a more direct approach, and there is little that is unprecedented in it, though some people would pronounce it novel and others fruitless, if not impossible. Most of the earlier endeavors along this line have been limited, or incidental, or illustrative. For example, when William A. Clebsch investigated the broad sweep of American religious moods, he sought at least some intimations of what the common people were thinking, and to that purpose he used at the Huntington Library sources similar to and in some cases the same as I used at that location.[39] Far removed from Clebsch and at a more popular level is Stewart Holbrook's account of the *Yankee Exodus* from New England; Holbrook occasionally employed family correspondence and diaries in a way bearing some resemblance to my own.[40] *The Life of Johny Reb* and *The Life of Billy Yank*, as recreated by Bell Irvin Wiley, consisted at least in part of the life of the mind. And various scholars—Wilson Clough, Rodney Loehr, Blake McKelvey, David Potter, Charles Sanford, Alice Felt Tyler, and Charlotte Erickson[41], to name only some—have edited or studied the popular writings of this period. To one degree or another, they have all advanced suggestions as to how the jottings of this family, or of that storekeeper, or of that Forty-niner might reflect pervasive notions and values. Perhaps the most arresting item among those attempting to convey and delineate popular writings is an essay by Jesse Lemisch. In this essay, Lemisch did more than infer humble thought from humble action; he actually listened more closely to the inarticulate. Although Lemisch may have been overbold in his conclusions and have shown undue impatience with the fellow historians whom he sought to bestir, he did offer the salutary, if inflated, reminder that "the most fragile and evanescent sort of historical evidence can be retrieved."[42] That assertion is much too unguarded, but there indeed exists a large store of source material which is roughly of a kind with that 1781 dream of a seaman named William Widger.

To forestall at least some of the displeasure of those who suspect their fellow historians of concealing and ignoring method, or of relegating it to "prefaces and footnotes and an occasional methodology article,"[43] something better will have to be found than Jacques Barzun's "history has no method or methods."[44] Readers of this book may quickly conclude that that is true of at least one historian. Those readers will very likely conclude that that one does indeed believe that "a historian's modus operandi should be carried by how he does it and not by what he says about doing it."[45] So, a few words about how this study developed may be in order, but, insofar as these words suggest method, they do so by way of the metaphor that Barzun allowed, that being as indication of an effort to be "rational and resourceful, imaginative and conscientious."[46] Others will decide how frequently, if ever, the effort was successful.

As a period of study, the pre-Civil War generation had some bases of attraction beyond my own interest in it. First of all, probably no amount of discouraging words and sober second thoughts will efface the notion that that period somehow involved, to use Carl Russell Fish's title, *The Rise of the Common Man*. Because of that, or coincidental with it, an especially large number of scholarly works regarding that era address themselves in some way or another to the moods of the common man. Nearly all become enmeshed in categories deriving from some hypostasized being called the common man. For example, F. O. Matthiessen's exquisite analysis of the major literary figures of that period did not maintain a loftiness of subject matter totally in keeping with the loftiness of presentation. A glance at the index column above and below Poe reveals the likes of Pietro Perugino, Petrarch, Phidias, Pindar, Pliny, Plotinus, Plutarch, Alexander Pope, Ezra Pound, Praxiteles, Proclus, Propertius, Proudhon, and Proust. But Pecos Bill is there too, and that is perhaps an indication that the author intended to bring his writers of genius into relation "through their varied responses to the myth of the common man."[47] Most readers would adjudge Matthiessen's way to be the *via regia*, but it nonetheless led to generous amounts of Sut Lovingood in the final chapter. The pre-Civil War period also commends itself to us for seeming to be a manageable package, an integral unit of some thirty years. At its outset, the new nation had just buried its eighteenth-century exemplars, John Adams and Thomas Jefferson. It then turned, supposedly with relish, to the less restrained ways typified by Andrew Jackson, that consummate man of the people whom it had chosen for leader. At the end, Harpers Ferry, *Origin of Species*, the election of Lincoln, and Fort Sumter adumbrated much that was different. The break may appear vague, but it is certainly perceptible, and one may indeed say with Henry James that "the Civil War marks an era in the history of the American mind."[48]

The antebellum period is inviting for a combination of other factors: high literacy and mobility; cheap paper and postage—which would suggest that many people must have occasionally put pen to paper. But locating a sufficient supply of the remains would seem to many an insuperable challenge. Jesse Lemisch's dictum notwithstanding, perhaps those remains had been too "fragile and evanescent." In 1936, Samuel Rezneck urged historians to reconstruct that level of thought "whose chief and only distinction is that it is common," and he opined that there might well be a good deal of the "casual writings" of our ancestors lying "neglected and dusty in the attic of many an old house."[49] Not all of it has stayed in those attics. "Enclosed find two old letters which I found among the papers of an estate I represent." Thus wrote J. H. Bankhead, Jr., who would in time follow his father to the United States Senate. Perhaps the New History and social history had not yet been fully assimilated in Jasper, Alabama, in 1904 because Attorney Bankhead continued in this fashion: "They were written by a soldier in the Mexican War and may be of some interest as curios. I do not see anything in them of historical value."[50]

If those letters which Talulah's uncle sent along to his friend at the Alabama Department of Archives and History had been of "historical value," they may have been published. A good many like them have been, as the notes and bibliography of the present study may demonstrate. But here, too, there is a selectivity, some generally tacit but incumbent basis upon which popular writings have been deemed worthy of publication. When I finished my stay at the Manuscripts Division of the New York Public Library, the top call slip of things which I had not covered was for a diary kept by one

John Q. Roods. Along with many others, that item would not, I thought, enhance or enliven my appreciation of pre-Civil War attitudes. That was a mistaken surmise, however. In the course of later research in published sources, it came before me between the covers of the *Wisconsin Magazine of History*. Therein, Earl Pomeroy, who edited the diary, explained that "in somewhat sub-literate and hurried fashion" it provided "some of the flavor of the boom" that Roods encountered during his visit to Wisconsin in 1847.[51] An even more compelling source of modern interest in popular writings can be seen in the case of three letters which were published in the *New England Quarterly* a century after they were written by two people whose names have long since been forgotten. One of them, a New Hampshire farmer's son, had gone to Kentucky as a schoolmaster, and he had an exchange of letters with the clergyman who had taught him. It seems safe to assume that that clergyman's fear that his former pupil might grow "indifferent to the infamy of slavery" did nothing to prevent those letters from being dignified by modern print.[52]

Civil War letters and diaries have, of course, done remarkably well, but, by and large, they do not fall within the purview of this study. The most important antebellum counterparts are those deriving from the Gold Rush and from related or similar movements such as the Oregon Trail. However fatiguing those treks may have been in reality, they seem never to overburden reader interest, of whatever generation. "So many of these journals have been published," John Walton Caughey remarked somewhat wearily as he introduced yet another to print in 1941, "that it is incumbent today to give good reason for presenting another."[53] The Gold Rush was, far and away, the great occasion of the era, so great that it assured both that people would write about it and that their writings would later be available in readily researchable form, thanks to John Walton Caughey and so many others. Less dramatic occasions have also brought the writings of "plain men" to publication—a new home in the West, volunteer service in the Mexican War, a visit to Niagara, election high-jinx, a steamboat trip, and so on.

"A correlation ought to exist," Caughey noted with just an intimation of normative loftiness, "between the importance of events and their recording."[54] That seems reasonable enough, but where the common man and his writings are concerned, the credentials committee sometimes takes a generous and latitudinarian view. At times sheer curiosity can suffice, as it did on one occasion when the *Missouri Historical Society Bulletin* published some correspondence of "people who were so nearly unlettered that they spelled their words as they pronounced them."[55] But the embrace of social history has more warmth and breadth than this indulgence of the quaint, and that fact is illustrated especially well by certain historical publications in certain years.

Arthur Wallace Peach's twenty-year connection with the *Proceedings of the Vermont Historical Society* (later *Vermont Quarterly: A Magazine of History*, and then *Vermont History*) provides an excellent case in point. Interestingly enough, Peach taught "the fine art of English expression,"[56] not history. He wrote poetry and fiction, and he edited plays as well as the writings of Thomas Paine. Whatever muse guided him most directly, he discerned and registered the new emphases in Clio's realm. In 1936, he expounded upon the enlarged sphere of historical interest by noting that historians "in recent years have been turning more and more from the older, more limited conceptions of historical study."[57] Two years later, in introducing for his readers an autobiography written by an obscure Vermonter in the nineteenth century, Peach underscored the significance inhering in the nation's little-known John Whittemores, men who had performed "the little tasks of everyday life 'in the light of great principles.' " Here in 1938, "in the face of corroding changes of a softer, more cynical, perhaps less courageous, more faithless day," it behooved people to recollect and to appreciate: "If Vermont would keep faith with the past, it must remember its Whittemores."[58] In 1941, the same year in which John Walton Caughey betrayed a doubt or two, Peach, perhaps for the very fact that he was in part a poet, spoke the most direct assertion of faith as a preface to an account of village life in "Lympus and Lilliesville in 1855":

We confess that we believe in the history of the common man, in the faithful following of his footsteps, no matter how transitory they may have been. Earlier issues of the *Proceedings* have reflected this faith of ours in that we have printed pioneer records and journals, of no value in their relation to major movements of men and events, but significant in their revelation of the common man at work, building with his hands the greater destiny of a state and its future.[59]

Peach could not have subscribed to the verdict later pronounced by Norman K. Risjord that the " 'common man' "—"mute, colorless, and timid"—"can never be rescued from anonymity, but he can be analyzed, at least in numerical terms, and traced through the course of time."[60] To Peach and those like him, it would have seemed an affront to the common human circumstance for the John Whittemores to be consigned to an oblivion from which emerges, as another scholar put it, "only bare and colorless entries in public records to testify to their ever having lived."[61] John Whittemores had flesh and blood, personality and identity. Some historians have sought to raise them above the slough of statistical ciphers. Their destiny was heaven, not a computer.

In 1941, the year of Peach's confession of faith, Yale University Press with sponsorship of Vassar College published a full volume containing the diary of a young New Yorker who, if his self-assessments are to be believed, was the quintessentially common American. By such publications we were, it would seem, keeping faith with our past almost with a vengeance. In a review of that published diary, Arthur Bestor drew a compelling contrast between its author and his aristocratic, diary-keeping contemporary Philip Hone: "In almost every particular,—social position, politics, religion, literary taste and reforming zeal,—the two diarists were at opposite poles."[62] Perhaps the quest for representative common men—John Whittemore, Michael Floy of Bowery Village, and whomever—involved a contradiction in terms on the one hand and a redundancy on the other. Anyway, Philip Hone remains vastly better known than Michael Floy. The aristocrat yet outdoes the plebeian. Even so, Floy and his kind have at least had a respectful hearing, and those seeking to broach the murkiness of popular beliefs are thereby benefited.

Beyond the items which, for one reason or another, have appeared in print, one goes to manuscript sources. At this point, whatever precise or denotative or scientific meaning might inhere in the word "method" goes by the boards. This is a matter of hit-and-miss, educated guess, meandering, uneducated guess, instinct, catch-as-catch-can, stark obstinacy, and serendipity. My letters of inquiry to manuscript repositories generally proved unavailing, not because of professional inadequacy on the part of those who received the letters but rather because I was asking about things which, if they were there at all, had little or no claim upon the professional time and attention of those I addressed. Such letters of mine begot puzzled, bemused, courteous, and uninformative responses. John Whittemore and Michael Floy notwithstanding, people at manuscript institutions know their prestige material, not the ephemeral, trivial, anonymous tidbits which I seemed to be seeking.

Of course, repositories differ vastly in their yield of the kind of sources which go into a book such as this one. As all manuscript librarians know:

An important phase of preservation is selection of material. There can be no hard and fast rule, and just because a letter was written two hundred years ago does not necessarily make it of historical importance. The writer must record something of value which may have been news, but is now history. Opinions are important too, but a recital of aches and pains, and inquiry into Aunt Suzy's health and general complaints of hot or dry weather are not worthy of storage space and the expense of cataloguing. When light, heat, cleaning, burglar and fire protection are added together, shelf space is surprisingly costly.[63]

Some institutions have more patience with reports of Aunt Suzy's health and with that hot or dry weather, about which, some vehemently suspected, I meant to write a book. Places with an especially large amount of material pertinent to my uses and with research control of it included the Collection of Regional History at Cornell University, the Southern Historical Collection at the University of North Carolina, the University of Georgia Libraries, the Minnesota Historical Society, the Henry E. Huntington Library and Art Gallery, and the Indiana Historical Society (which last is in the same building with the also fruitful Indiana Division of the Indiana State Library). But this tack of discussion could lead to the anecdotal, and, though the philosopher John Passmore pronounced that to be the "natural mode" for historians and even excused it in them,[64] it perhaps ought not to be over-indulged.

People who have discussed this study with me have almost invariably directed their questions along sectional lines, most notably, of course, North-South sectional lines. As may already be apparent, the research was not confined to a geographical area, and such questions have a perfectly understandable quality. Indeed, my own preconceptions and projections for the study gravitated far more toward some North-South duality or antinomy than does the finished product. Whatever the anticipations, however, it became apparent to me that the integrity of the sources did not sufficiently accord with dualistic architectonics. To be sure, Northerners occasionally recorded their perceptions of and fancies about the South, and Southerners reciprocated. They both espied disparities of conduct, mood, and persuasion, and those disparities occasionally and roughly fit patterns that are suggested by such titles as *Yankees and God, The Militant South,* or *The Lazy South.*[65] Now and again, the present study explicates some of those variations and tensions. But, however appropriate it may be to focus upon the *Cavalier and Yankee*[66] in the literary imagination or however uneasy I may be about repeating what Chard Powers Smith called the "common mistake" of treating "our two ancient cultures together,"[67] it seemed a greater error to attempt some organizational separation than to employ a reflection of what was there in reality—an occasionally dissonant syncretism. Perhaps an analogue involving the East-West, rural-urban dimension will illustrate, if not substantiate, my point. In his previously mentioned review of the Michael Floy volume, Arthur Bestor gave us the salutary reminder that "historians have sometimes underestimated the extent to which ideas usually associated with the rural democracy were held as firmly by the urban middle classes."

Matters of North vis-à-vis South and East vis-à-vis West enter this study, and the latter provides something of a basis of organization at the conclusion. Attempts to describe double or multiple regional mentalities or of somehow speaking to the onset of war fall outside the purview of this volume, not so much by prior design as by matter of fact. The juxtaposition of a "Puritan Ethic"[68] and a "Southern Ethic,"[69] to use the formulations of Edmund S. Morgan and C. Vann Woodward respectively, surfaces now and again because both were there in antebellum America. The major emphases in this book, however, derive not so much from an antagonism or a tension or a dialectic as they do from pervasive moods, which pervasive moods appeared in sometimes variant form in the South.

One danger I encountered was the greater volume of writings from the North. Whatever else the Puritan might have done, he and his descendants waged inveterate educational war against the old deluder Satan. The literacy rate was higher in the North, and so more writings from those in the lower echelons of the northern society are available than are those of their southern counterparts. As a reviewer of Frank L. Owsley's *Plain Folk of the Old South* put it, "The plain folk of the South seldom left diaries and letters behind them. . . ."[70] Therefore, one inevitably runs the risk of giving disproportionate weight to the views of that more literate Northerner. If one reconstructs on the basis of written remains, one necessarily heeds those who wrote. In some sense then, here we may have a problem of inference. The risk must be taken, however. For one thing, this study does not profess to be a recreation of the moods of the truly inarticulate or averbal. It has sought and found written expressions of those who seem to typify the common man. Hence, it has seemed wiser to undertake a reconstruction of common attitudes in full recognition that there may well be some imbalance in sources. And, of course, common men and women in the South did leave written remains. They are fewer and more fugitive, but they are there.

Also, a certain aptness inheres in the very fact of that possible imbalance, and not only because of disparity of population. There was a matter of assertiveness, almost aggressiveness and conquest involved here. It does not burden the fancy unduly to perceive the enduring Puritan spirit striving mightily and with some success to tame, discipline, and educate the two wild sectors on its flanks—the West and South. The new New Hampshire farmer's son illustrates the larger reality. If a further moment of allegory does not boggle, we might say that, only after having deemed his educational errand into the southern wilderness to have been insufficiently fruitful, did the Puritan go there bearing firearms rather than primers. Domingo Sarmiento, an Argentine statesman and educator, used imagery of that sort when he visited the United States in 1847. He disliked the South, largely because it reminded him of South America. More importantly, he openly admired the "Puritan" and "Pilgrim" capacity for taming, ordering, and improving. "I am becoming a Yankee to such an extent," he remarked in playful fondness, "that I speak with a nasal twang while reviewing these ideas." Sarmiento perceived civilization and amelioration radiating outward from Boston and its surroundings, going forth embodied in "the descendants of the Puritans and Pilgrims," and curbing the "barbarism" of the Westerner, the immigrant and, perhaps to a lesser degree, the Southerner. The Puritans were the Brahmin race of the United States. Like the Brahmins coming down from the Himalayas, the inhabitants of these old states have spread out toward the Western reaches of the Union and have educated by their example and methods the people who, without skill or science, are prospering on the newly cleared land. . . . They carry to the rest of the Union the manual aptitude which makes an American a walking workshop, the iron energy for struggling with and conquering difficulties, and the moral and intellectual aptitude which makes him equal if not superior to the best the human species has produced to date.[71]

To speak of Brahmins and barbarians leaves the matter in the metaphorical realm, and, of course, one undertaking a study such as this must do something to assure that his sources indeed derive from people who were, in some general sense, "plain folk"— whether they be found in the North, South, East, or West. First, the people included in this study were literate; they had at least the rudiments of education. Other than this qualifier, I make no attempt to define neatly or rigidly the social classes included or excluded. First, those included were not themselves intellectual formulators.[72]

Intellectual formulators are not the only ones who have been excluded. The evidently wealthy have no place herein, and, insofar as my imprecise measures and criteria allowed, neither do those who might be styled well-to-do or even comfortable. Needless to say, one can enjoy no great certainty in such matters unless one limited severely the number of individuals whose writings were to be studied. In order to obtain volume of material and representative coverage, this study embraced far too many individuals to allow rigorous and meticulous scrutiny in each case, however. In many cases it would have been almost impossible anyway. One difficulty of research in such sources is that it is not possible to ascertain exactly how many people wrote them. A single letter may bear two or more signatures and show the characteristics of yet a different number of hands; unsigned letters may or may not be ascribed to a person whose penmanship bears a resemblance; people wrote letters for others; diaries assigned by manuscript repository to some one person suggest more than single authorship; and so on.

Another problem stems from the fact that family fortunes ebbed and flowed. Would it be admissible, for example, to employ pre-Civil War letters or diaries—supposing there to be such for conjectural purposes—of one "Wm Rockefellow," his wife Eliza, and family? The 1850 census—town of Owego, Tioga County, New York, dwelling visitation number 1192—lists no real property for them, but it does credit them with five children, including an eleven-year-old son named John. Here, the quandary is hypothetical and the case extreme. What is one to do with an individual who was not a Rockefeller but who was born and raised in unimpeachably certifiable commonness or even poverty and then rose far above it? Does the ascent render him uncommon and inappropriate? Or is he common until some point in his rise? At what point? Since I found no absolute criteria or formulae, I must repose in the trust that common sense and the rule of reason served me well most of the time.

Because they were intellectual or attitudinal conveyors, if not formulators, journalists, ministers, and educators only rarely gain admission to these pages. To be sure, no great fastidiousness can be exercised because, particularly in the case of teachers, the inhabitants of that less specialized age wandered back and forth across occupational boundaries. As a man born in England told a native of this country in 1858, " 'you Americans can turn your hand at anything but it is quite difficult in the Old Country.

There a man has but one business.' "[73] Thus, for example, to exclude all who might have taken a common school for a few weeks in the slack wintertime would leave few in the available literate ranks. But people who were consistently or permanently engaged as journalists, ministers, or educators have been excluded.

That exclusion has applied to certain other categories, and in these cases it may arouse some misgiving. I have neither sought nor incorporated sources that derived from subcultural or alien elements. My focus was on the common, not the uncommon. However toweringly important it may be to discern and delineate the moods of recent immigrants or racial minorities or self-consciously sectarian religious groups, that is not the purpose of this study. I humbly and respectfully leave those endeavors to others. The challenges and vexations entailed in locating and analyzing the written remains of a couple thousand unelevated, mainstream Americans—Americans whose views might be supposed to have been conventional, characteristic and concentric rather than dissident, exotic or eccentric—have been fully sufficient unto all of these many days.

Generally, where published materials are concerned, determinations as to who should be included or excluded can be made from the editors' remarks. Occasionally, I deviated from their qualitative assessments—as, for example, when I suspected that a certain inconsequential Forty-niner had far less of the poet in him than his modern editor discerned.[74] In general, of course, editorial introductions and notes have been invaluable.

Their counterparts—the descriptions of manuscript holdings prepared by their holding institutions—can save prodigious amounts of time. Such descriptions vary vastly from institution to institution and from collection to collection within a given institution, and unfortunately, such descriptions are the thinnest where my kind of sources are concerned. If little or nothing was known of a collection, it became my practice to take a look at it. Apparently out of some cataloguing error at the Vermont Historical Society, the Henry Stevens Letters came to have an unnatural adjunct. The catalogue description points out that, with the letters of that prominent man, there have been filed some "which have absolutely no connection with Henry Stevens, and are if [*sic*] fact an entirely different family...." In this case there fell to my lot, not even poor relatives, but the Lilly family of Woodstock, Connecticut, and the Jacob Stevens family of South Strafford, Vermont, from which "quite illiterate" folk I gleaned some very usable material.[75] Material which I used in a collection was often of an ancillary nature, the writings of poor relatives rather than the writings of those whose written remains were deemed worthy of preservation.

Without such aids as those just discussed, it would have been difficult and time-consuming to determine the social class of the writers. Rarely does the opening letter of a nondescript collection or the January 1 entry of an obscure diary vouchsafe the information that the writer was impeccably common. Lacking that, one resorts to other means, among which internal evidence comes foremost. Inappropriate professions generally reveal themselves, sometimes quite abruptly. In 1846, Arthur P. Thompson of Hickman, Kentucky, felt that he could not visit an old friend in Madisonville for the financial fact of "Beaing por." For "common popel," he added, "times is hard."[76] "Here I am," Cyrus Sanders wrote moodily five years after having arrived in Iowa with little but high hopes, "in poverty and obscurity a solitary old Bachelor." Because Sanders' journal has been edited, one does not need his attestation of the "*sad reality*,"[77] but, time and again, writers directly or indirectly revealed their stations in life.

In some cases, internal evidence was the sole evidence because the writer's identity was unknown. Where anonymous writings met all of the specifications, they were included. Such people have been styled "Anonymous Americans" and some are that in fact. The diary kept by an unidentified Bostonian indicates more than one problem encountered in the use of common sources. This twenty-four-year-old man did menial work, cleaning, weighing, and packaging in "the dust and gloom" of what probably was a publisher's warehouse. Whoever he was, however, his taste in reading and lecture attendance and his powerful fear of "*living* as the herd of ordinary people"[78] rendered his credentials too suspect. He was therefore excluded.

If we had the name of the writer of such a source, we might be able to use some external means to determine his calling and station. Depending upon the time and place from which the source derived, tax lists, city directories, probate court records, and county histories might be helpful, but these are at best occasional and unwieldy aids. The present research does not involve compact blocks of people—towns, townships, counties, city units, or whatever. Because of the purpose and nature of this study, the people whose sentiments appear in its pages come together only in these pages. They constitute a random scattering from hither and yon. For example, when I was researching in the ample holdings of the Minnesota Historical Society, most of my time was spent in material which had been written by people elsewhere, people in New England, and New York, and Pennsylvania, and so on. Letters have a spatial dimension, and a society that generates a large amount of personal correspondence is a society on the move. In part, the same holds true of day-by-day accounts, as the relation between journey and journal (not to mention the inclusion of diary by connection with Latin ancestry) would well indicate. Time and again, the researcher deals with his subjects at far long range—reading in North Carolina what a man had written in Mississippi, reading in California what had been written in Vermont. This all but precludes comprehensive employment of such things as probate records and tax lists.

Even when the writer's identity was known, a source often proved imprecise as to a location whereby he might be traced. The rationalization of American society, even unto social security and zipcode numbers, was hardly underway, and in the South, almost not at all. A diarist can emerge in the mind's eye of the researcher with full flesh and blood, and yet at the same time remain beguilingly enigmatic. Place names came and went; they were duplicated, triplicated, confused, and abused mightily. A diarist might write year in and year out without ever bothering to state directly his location. He, of course, had no doubts as to who and where he was. His was a realm wherein evanescence now obtains. As the poet knew, people such as he did indeed keep "the noiseless tenor of their way."[79]

Tracking down these plain folk can be rewarding because occasionally one can unveil part of their obscure destiny or stumble upon some enticing items in their own right. There is some satisfaction in determining that the Henry Putnam Diary and Account Book at the New-York Historical Society was written by someone other than Henry Putnam, probably his brother Hiram;[80] that to Vernon Louis Parrington's father, while at Waterville College, it may have fallen the debater's lot to speak to the affirmative of this question—"Ought the particular religious sentiments of candidates for public office to influence our votes?";[81] that the two segments of the Orville Nixon Journal at the Huntington Library probably came from different men;[82] that the anonymous Diary Record of Farm Labor at the Connecticut State Library was written by

William Bassett of Watertown;[83] or that the Monroe Sullivan Letter at the Kentucky Historical Society was written in Mexico City by James Sullivan whose destiny became even more obscure for the fact that he angrily scrawled at the end of his letter that he meant to write home "nomore," and for the fact that a tear in the paper effaced the James of his signature, leaving it "nomore" Sullivan, or, reasonably enough, Monroe Sullivan.[84]

On September 11, 1850, an upstate New York farmer talked with the census taker, and that functionary managed to mis-do the farmer's middle initial and last name.[85] On a similar occasion, an Alabama woman found herself "hindered" one evening by a census taker, and to his requests for information she "gave in ours, partially."[86] A mistaken middle initial, a letter dropped from a surname, and the Alabama woman's telling qualifier underscore the need for caution, as Stephen Thernstrom advises, for those using the manuscript schedules of the United States censuses.[87] While those schedules provide the most readily available means of getting an idea of worth and occupation of an individual, they have, for my purposes, shortcomings other than erroneous or partial information. For one thing, the census provided, when it provided anything, mostly corroboration of my own perceptions or suspicions. Rarely did census information about an individual in whose correspondence or diary I had been reading surprise me.

Beyond the fact that it generally yielded what I had already discerned, a far larger gainsaying of the census for a study of this nature is that it frequently could yield nothing at all. Given the mobility of the American people and the random nature of this research, it was in some cases probably impossible and in many others unfeasible to do a census check. The census schedules have a lack of adaptability to this research similar to that of such devices as probate records. Even where the schedules have been indexed, one suffers frustration after frustration. Individuals who can be identified and located in the mid-1850s, say, seemed not at all enslaved to an obligation to get registered on the census of that area in 1850 or 1860. Often the researcher will know who and where people were for substantial periods of time; but unless he knows who and where they were in the summer or fall of 1850 or 1860, the federal census schedules are totally unavailing.[88] And where an index is not available, going to the census schedules for discrete, often vaguely identified items can be distressingly time-consuming.

If I had confidence in the usability of a source, I often did not attempt a census check, unless I had solid and sustaining information on which to operate. Of course, I did many census checks, by and large, insofar as time, patience and ingenuity allowed. But, where a fairly large number of scattered people of vague description and location are concerned, thoroughness and certainty were either unattainable, or unattainable within reasonable procedural limits. Ranging across a thirty-year period, I sought to analyze a large and representative body of writing done by Americans of no special attainment. This involved the exclusions previously indicated. I trust that my efforts in that regard have been generally successful; but I well know the likelihood that an occasional source of mine will be revealed, possibly by the astute local or regional historian, as having been less common than it should have been. Credentials came under scrutiny; but the light was nearly always dim. When almost no light could be shed, common sense, as it is meant to do, prevented impasse if not, in each and every case, error.

In sum, the research for this study represents an effort to follow the "good rule" that C. V. Wedgwood appropriated from G. M. Young: one should " 'go on reading until he hears them talking.' " "We do not know an age," Wedgwood herself continued, "until we are at home with its way of thought and manner of expression, until we can recognize its central idiom, the commonplaces of its daily vocabulary, its special tone of voice."[89] That is a very tall order; it will be left to others to determine if it was ever approached in this book.

NOTES

Introduction

1. Joseph Wood Krutch, *The Modern Temper: A Study and a Confession* (New York, 1929), pp. 130-33.

2. "Is The Common Man Too Common?," in Joseph Wood Krutch (ed.), *Is The Common Man Too Common? An Informal Survey of Our Cultural Resources and What We Are Doing About Them* (Norman, Okla., 1954).

3. Ibid., "The Taste of the Common Man," p. 146.

4. Albert Jay Nock, *On Doing the Right Thing: And Other Essays* (New York, 1928).

5. *The Adventures of Tom Sawyer*, Chapter 21.

6. Philip Wylie, *Generation of Vipers* (New York, 1942), Chapter 8.

7. "On Observing Some Names of Little Note Recorded in the *Biographia Brittanica*," lines 1-2.

8. Diary of Rapin Andrews (Indiana Division of the Indiana State Library).

9. George F. Kent Journal, February 8, 1849, HM 524 (Huntington Library).

10. *The Huntington Library Bulletin* 11 (April 1937).

11. Isaac Watts, *The Improvement of the Mind: Or, A Supplement to the Art of Logic* . . . (New York, 1822), p. 30.

12. G. B. King to Uncle, January 12, 1861, William S. Powell Papers (Southern Historical Collection, University of North Carolina).

13. Mary David Butler to Lyman Hodge, January 29, 1850, Benjamin Hodge Papers (Huntington Library).

14. Susan Kuhlmann, *Knave, Fool, and Genius: The Confidence Man as He Appears in Nineteenth-Century Fiction* (Chapel Hill, N.C., 1973), p. 123.

15. "The Journal of Jane Voorhees," *Proceedings of the New Jersey Historical Society*, 65 (April 1947), 91.

16. James Jones to Mother, October 4, 1858, JTJ63, James T. Jones Papers (Huntington Library).

17. J. H. Bankhead, Jr., to Thomas M. Owen, December 30, 1904, J. W. Triplet Letters (Manuscripts Division, Alabama Department of Archives and History).

18. J. W. Triplet to J.A.F. Kirkpatrick, February 20, 1847, J. W. Triplet Letters

(Manuscripts Division, Alabama Department of Archives and History).

19. Richard Albert Edwards Brooks (ed.), *The Diary of Michael Floy Jr. Bowery Village 1833-1837* (New Haven, Conn., 1941), p. 1.

20. Amelia J. Akehurst Diary, August 17 and 23, 1859, Akehurst-Lines Collection (Division of Special Collections, University of Georgia Libraries).

21. *Annals of Iowa*, Third Series, 23 (January 1942), 254-57.

22. Floyd and Marion Rinhart, *America's Affluent Age* (New York, 1971), p. 322. The Rinharts are students of photography, but this book is quite creditable social history. The concluding chapter, which has reproductions of death photographs, aptly bears the title, "Obituary."

23. James A. Bell Collection (Huntington Library).

24. "'A New Home—Who'll Follow?' Letters of a New England Emigrant Family in Ohio, 1831-1842," *Ohio History Quarterly* 65 (April 1956), 153.

25. Mrs. Lucy Furber Diary, March 7, 1855 and August 26, 1856, Pierce F. Furber and Family Papers (Minnesota Historical Society).

26. Charles W. Dudley Journal, 1856-1857, HM28295 (Huntington Library). This undated notation appears to have been written as the diarist began his 1856 entries.

27. John Eagle to Wife, February 10, 1853, John H. Eagle Correspondence, EGL 16 (Huntington Library).

28. John B. Orton Diaries, 1845-1907, November 1, 1848 (Manuscripts Division, New York Public Library).

29. F. L. Lucas, *The Decline and Fall of the Romantic Ideal*, Cambridge University Press Paperback (Cambridge, 1963), p. 235.

30. As quoted in Robert E. Kelley and O. M. Brack, Jr., *Samuel Johnson's Early Biographies* (Iowa City, Iowa, 1971), p. 119.

31. M. van Beek, *An Enquiry into Puritan Vocabulary* (Groningen, 1969), p. 28.

32. Diary kept by an unidentified student while living in Massachusetts in 1833 and 1834 (Manuscripts Division, New York Public Library). This entry was probably written sometime in 1834.

33. Levi Countryman Diary, July 11, 1858, Levi M. Countryman Papers (Minnesota Historical Society).

34. James T. King (ed.), "'I Take This Opportunity to Inform You . . .': The Gold Rush Papers of Andrew Cairns," *California Historical Society Quarterly* 46 (September 1967), 214.

35. Ibid., pp. 214, 221.

36. Elizabeth Adams to Sister, July 23 (probably 1840), John Thompson Kinkade Collection (Huntington Library).

37. G.O.A. (ed.), "A Gold Rush Diary," *Historical Society of Southern California Quarterly* 36 (December 1954), 287.

38. Andrew Jackson Sterrett to Brother, September 29, 1857, Andrew Jackson Sterrett Papers (Minnesota Historical Society).

39. George Lewis Diary, November 9, 1846 (Connecticut State Library).

40. Elijah Smith Memoir, Elijah Smith Papers (Collection of Regional History, Cornell University). Smith seems to have been seventy-eight years old when he wrote this in 1858, and he seems to have been writing about an occurrence of the spring of 1839. The 1840 census shows that he had a wife and two children, but the children do not correspond in age with those who were the children of the lady doing the packing. Did the

lady of the packing stay? Did Smith so soon replace her and her children? Sometimes only a fine line separates curiosity from perversity, and perhaps it would be well to ponder the matter no further.

41. (Charles Henry Smith), *Bill Arp's Scrap Book; Humor and Philosophy. Letters 'Pendente Lite,' Letters Historic, Domestic and Pastoral, with Some true Stories Added* (Atlanta, 1884), pp. 242-43.

42. Ibid., p. 243.

43. Sophia Mackres to Uncle, July 2 (approximately 1850), Lucien Parker Correspondence (Huntington Library).

44. Rosanna McCullough Copy Book (South Caroliniana Library, Columbia, S.C.).

45. William Gladden to John and Drusilla Cassil, April 10, 1831, John Thompson Kinkade Collection, KI 18 (Huntington Library).

46. Donald E. Baker (ed.), "The Conine Family Letters, 1852-1863: 'Just Think How We Are Scattered,'" *Indiana Magazine of History* 70 (June 1974), 138.

47. "Elegy Written in a Country Church Yard," lines 83-84.

48. "John Clark's Journal (1824-1842)," *Proceedings of the Vermont Historical Society*, New Series, 10 (December 1942), 187, 191.

49. Quoted in Robert Allen Skotheim, *American Intellectual History and Historians* (Princeton, N.J., 1966), p. 3.

50. Richard M. Dorson, *Folklore: Selected Essays* (Bloomington, Ind., 1972), p. 257.

51. George Boas, *Vox Populi: Essays in the History of an Idea*, The Johns Hopkins Press Paperback (Baltimore, 1969), p. 247.

52. Daniel Boorstin, "The Myth of an American Enlightenment," in *America and the Image of Europe: Reflections on American Thought*, Meridian Book Paperback (New York, 1960), p. 66.

53. David Hackett Fischer, *Historians' Fallacies: Toward a Logic of Historical Thought* (New York, 1970), pp. 195-200.

54. Ibid.

55. Ernest Leisy, "Fatalism in Moby-Dick," in *Moby-Dick Centennial Essays* (Dallas, 1953), p. 88.

56. *His Fifty Years of Exile*, Chapters 24-25.

57. *The Complete Works of Ralph Waldo Emerson*, Autograph Centenary Edition (Cambridge, Mass., 1904), xi, 330, 331, 335.

58. Cyclone Covey, *The American Pilgrimage: The Roots of American History, Religion and Culture*, Collier Books Paperback (New York, 1961), p. 109.

59. "Cock-A-Doodle-Do! Or, The Crowing of the Noble Cock Beneventano," *Harper's New Monthly Magazine* 8 (December 1853), 83-85.

60. *Mosses From an Old Manse*, in *Complete Works of Nathaniel Hawthorne*, Riverside Edition (Boston, 1882), II, 496.

61. Andrew Hacker, *The End of the American Era* (New York, 1970), pp. 10, 26.

62. Henry Atwater Note Book, Plymouth, Connecticut, 1836-1846 (Connecticut State Library); and Jesse W. Owen to John B. Clark, May 30, 1846, John B. Clark Papers (Kentucky Historical Society).

63. Paul Elmer More, "The Solitude of Nathaniel Hawthorne," *Atlantic Monthly*, 88 (November 1901), 590.

64. Fred Landon, "Extracts from the Diary of William C. King, A Detroit Carpenter, in 1832," *Michigan History Magazine* 19 (Winter 1935), 65.

Chapter 1

1. Unidentified Daily Journal kept on a voyage from New York to San Francisco in 1848, April 26 to 30, 1848 (New-York Historical Society).

2. Jackson Thomason Diary, April 10, May 6, May 9, 1849 (State of Mississippi, Department of Archives and History).

3. Robert Beeching Journal, September 11 to 27, 1849, HM17430 (Huntington Library).

4. Richard Albert Edward Brooks (ed.), *The Diary of Michael Floy Jr. Bowery Village 1833-1837* (New Haven, Conn., 1941), p. 1.

5. Susan Fox Diary, January 2, 1844, Bibbens Family Papers (Collection of Regional History, Cornell University).

6. Sally Waters to Smith Lipscomb, November 21, 1849, Lipscomb Family Papers (Southern Historical Collection, University of North Carolina).

7. Julia Adams to James A. Matters, January 9, 1843, Phinehas Adams Papers, 1759-1892 (Huntington Library).

8. *The Complete Works of Ralph Waldo Emerson* (Cambridge, Mass., 1904), vi, 41.

9. William Hoffman Diary, 1847-1850, March 3, 1848 (New-York Historical Society).

10. Josiah Campbell to Caroline Ward, March 29, 1847, and June 9, 1847, Carrie Ward Campbell Letters (Indiana Historical Society).

11. Kenneth B. Murdock, "William Hubbard and the Providential Interpretation of History," *Proceedings of the American Antiquarian Society* 52, Part 1 (April 1942), 17.

12. Robert P. Hay, "Providence and the American Past," *Indiana Magazine of History* 65 (June 1969), 79, 100.

13. Paul Nagel, *This Sacred Trust: American Nationality 1798-1898* (New York, 1971), p. 53.

14. John W. Ward, *Andrew Jackson: Symbol for an Age* (New York, 1955), p. 110.

15. Fred Somkin, *Unquiet Eagle: Memory and Desire in the Idea of American Freedom, 1815-1860* (Ithaca, N.Y., 1967), p. 205.

16. Arthur Ekirch, *The Idea of Progress in America, 1815-1860* (New York, 1944), pp. 166, 267.

17. Martin Marty, *Righteous Empire: The Protestant Experience in America* (New York, 1970, pp. 188-89.

18. Quoted in Robert W. McLaughlin, *The Spiritual Element in History* (New York, 1926), p. 226.

19. Ward, *Andrew Jackson: Symbol for an Age*, p. 148. Ward's index entry for "Manifest Destiny" ended this way: "*see also* Providence."

20. Alfred K. Weinberg, *Manifest Destiny: A Study of Nationalist Expansionism in American History* (Baltimore, 1935), p. 482.

21. Perry Miller, *The Raven and the Whale: The War of Words and Wits in the Era of Poe and Melville* (New York, 1956), p. 109.

22. John W. Ward, *Red, White, and Blue: Men, Books, and Ideas in American Culture* (New York, 1969), pp. 52-53.

23. Andrew Lester Diary, 1836-1888, April 11 and 12, 1843 (New-York Historical Society).

24. William Williams to Brother, February 27, 1834, in Chase C. Mooney (ed.), "Some Letters from Dover, Tennessee, 1814-1855," *Tennessee Historical Quarterly* 8 (September 1949), 263-64.

25. "The Law of Progress of the Race," *United States Magazine and Democratic Review* 15 (August 1844), 197.

26. Diary of William W. Hoppin, May 13, 1842, Hoppin Family Diaries (Manuscripts Division, New York Public Library).

27. Edwin Olmstead Diary, November 4, 1844 (Connecticut State Library).

28. Jackson Thomason Diary, August 19, 1849 (State of Mississippi, Department of Archives and History).

29. E.A.B. Phelps to Samuel W. Phelps, March 25, 1848, Edward Ashley Bowen Phelps Letters and Diary, 1847-1848 (Manuscripts Division, New York Public Library).

30. "How Ought American Mind to Be Cultivated?" *Harper's New Monthly Magazine* 15 (June 1857), 121-25.

31. "The American Mind," ibid. (October 1857), 692-98.

32. Ibid.

33. Frederick Merk, *Manifest Destiny and Mission in American History: A Reinterpretation* (Baltimore, 1963), p. 261.

34. David W. Humphrey to ?, June 23, 1855, David W. Humphrey Papers (Minnesota Historical Society).

35. "How Ought American Mind to Be Cultivated?," p. 122.

36. Wiley Vester to Benjamin Vester, September 1, 1838, Elijah Vester Papers (Southern Historical Collection, University of North Carolina).

37. M. L. Hodge and others to Lyman Hodge, October 2, 1849, Benjamin Hodge Papers (Huntington Library).

38. Lois Lillie to Jacob B. Stevens, February 19, 1842, Henry Stevens Letters, 1851-1853 (Vermont Historical Society).

39. Augustine Holcomb to Nahum Holcomb Jr., May 25, 1830, Holcomb Family Letters (Connecticut State Library).

40. Edward F. Travis Diary, 1843-1847, March 1, 1845 (Manuscripts Division, New York Public Library).

41. Tom Turner to Mother, September 8, 1836, in John H. Jenkins (ed.), "Texas Letters and Documents," *Texana* 2 (Fall 1964), 217-18.

42. Pauline H. Stratton Diary, 1841-1870, January 9 to 20, 1850, and January 20, 1852 (Western Historical Manuscripts Collection, University of Missouri, Columbia).

43. Ira McCall to John M. and P. Hanford, July 25, 1840, Hanford Family Letters (Collection of Regional History, Cornell University).

44. Seth C. Whitehouse Journal, December 11, 1849 (Maine Historical Society).

45. "Journal of a Trip from Brooklyn to Niagara Falls in June 1841 John Read Barrows," *New York History* 23 (April 1942), 193.

46. Mary Hodge to Lyman Hodge, April 8, 1850, Benjamin Hodge Papers (Huntington Library).

47. E. M. Olcott Diaries, 1856-1858, February 21, 1857 (New-York Historical Society).

48. John Drake Diary, December 30, 1832 (Collection of Regional History, Cornell University).

49. Levi Countryman Diary, November 2, 1858, Levi N. Countryman Papers (Minnesota Historical Society).

50. *The Complete Works of Ralph Waldo Emerson* (Cambridge, Mass., 1904), VI, 14.

51. John Brophy to Mary Rebecca Brophy, December 2, 1849, Brophy-Beeson Papers, BB97 (Huntington Library).

52. Abraham and Keziah Taylor to Nicholas Spinney, April 28, 1833, and October 16, 1836, Spinney-Hunt-Wildes Papers (Maine Historical Society).

53. Lovina Smith to Joseph H. Smith, December 19, 1841, Lovina Smith Letters (Collection of Regional History, Cornell University).

54. John Brewster to Brother, December 29, 1852, John Brewster Letter (Connecticut State Library).

55. Ernest Lee Tuveson, *Redeemer Nation: The Idea of America's Millennial Role* (Chicago, 1968), Chapter 4.

56. "Bartleby, the Scrivener. A Tale of Wall-Street," *Putnam's Monthly Magazine of American Literature, Science, and Art* 2 (December 1853), 601.

57. John Wm. Bugg to Bela Paull, April 22, 1834, Mary Paul Letters (Vermont Historical Society).

58. Horatio N. Chandler Account Book, April 15, 1841 (New Hampshire Historical Society).

59. William F. Heard to Sister, October 20, 1856, George H. Tunnell Collection (Six Vault, Georgia Department of Archives and History).

60. Crane Brinton, *Ideas and Men: The Story of Western Thought* (Englewood Cliffs, N.J., 1963), p. 147.

61. Joseph Willard Diary, January 26, 1853 (Massachusetts Historical Society).

62. Andrew Jackson Sterrett to Brother, July 8, 1855, and August 27, 1855, Andrew Jackson Sterrett Papers (Minnesota Historical Society).

63. Ward, *Andrew Jackson: Symbol for an Age*, p. 213.

64. Stephen Goddard to Abner L. Goddard, August 4, 1842, Orrin F. Smith and Family Papers (Minnesota Historical Society).

65. Samuel Nichols to Wife, March 26, 1850, Samuel Nichols Collection (Huntington Library).

66. Louise Fogle (ed.), "Journal of Ebenezer Mattoon Chamberlain," *Indiana Magazine of History* 15 (September 1919), 238.

67. James Amsted Brown Diary, 1858-1860, March 8, 1860 (Vermont Historical Society).

68. Josiah M. Hickman Diary, September 19, 1848 (Indiana Division of the Indiana State Library).

69. Thomas S. Bennett to Thomas S. Espy, April 23, 1836, Espy Family Papers, 1800-1900 (Western Historical Manuscripts Collection, University of Missouri, Columbia).

70. Webster Abbott to Mother, Brother, and Sister, January 12, 1851, Peck Family Papers (Collection of Regional History, Cornell University).

71. James M'Cosh, *The Method of Divine Government, Physical and Moral* (New York, 1852), p. 44.

72. *Complete Works of Ralph Waldo Emerson*, VI, 31.

73. Ibid., pp. 6-8.

74. Rose G. Spinney to Nicholas Spinney, May 10, 1846, and Rose G. Spinney to Niece, January 1, 1860, Spinney-Hunt-Wildes Papers (Maine Historical Society).

75. Lizzie Robbins to Julia Pelton, September 8, 1858, Oliver Pelton Correspondence (Connecticut State Library).

76. Augustine Holcomb to Milo Holcomb, December, 1830, Holcomb Family Letters (Connecticut State Library).

77. Abigail Day Williams to Mrs. A. Willard, July 5, 1835, Fred Rider, Jr., *Collector*. Family Papers, 1784-1856 (Collection of Regional History, Cornell University).

78. *Tupper's Poetical Works: Containing "Proverbial Philosophy," "A Thousand Lines," Etc. With a Portrait of the Author* (Auburn and Buffalo, n.d.), p. 111.

79. Cordelia Randall to Miss E. E. Lewis, January 30, 1839, Papers of Abiathar Hubbard Watkins and Emily Lewis Watkins, 1836-1894 (Manuscripts Division, New York Public Library).

80. Augustine Holcomb to Nahum Holcomb, n.d., Holcomb Family Letters (Connecticut State Library).

81. Mary Bunting to David James Bunting, February 18, 1845, Mary Bunting Letter (South Caroliniana Library, Columbia, South Carolina).

82. William Hoffman Diary, 1847-1850, August 17 and 19, 1848 (New-York Historical Society).

83. Jesse W. Owen to John B. Clark, September 22, 1846, John B. Clark Papers (Kentucky Historical Society).

84. Charles Peterson to Elam Slagle, April 9, 1847, Elam Slagle Papers (Southern Historical Collection, University of North Carolina).

85. N. Chapin to Asa Chapin, June 27, 1847, Lyman Stuart *Collector*. Stampless Covers (Collection of Regional History, Cornell University).

86. *Religious Interpretations of American Destiny* (Englewood Cliffs, N.J., 1971).

87. H. Richard Niebuhr, *The Kingdom of God in America*, Harper Torchback Edition (New York, 1959), p. 179.

88. *White Jacket or The World in a Man-of-War*, Chapter 36.

89. Edward McNall Burns, *The American Idea of Mission: Concepts of National Destiny and Purpose* (New Brunswick, N.J., 1957), p. 28.

90. Russel B. Nye, *This Almost Chosen People: Essays in the History of American Ideas* (East Lansing, Mich., 1966), pp. 164, 206. A part of the renowned quote is employed similarly in Arthur Schlesinger, Jr., "America: Experiment or Destiny?," *American Historical Review* 82 (June 1977), 516.

91. "The American Mind," p. 695.

92. Weinberg, *Manifest Destiny*, p. 128.

93. Mary Orme, "Providence," *Democratic Review* 18 (February 1846), 141.

94. J. G. Tasker, "Providence," in James Hastings (ed.), *Dictionary of the Bible* (New York, 1951), p. 769.

95. Lawrence Parker to Fanny Barber, November 8, 1834, Fanny Barber to Lawrence Parker, November 5, 1836, Lawrence Parker to Fanny Barber, November 19, 1836, and October 15, 1838, Barbour-Parker Family Letters (Collection of Regional History, Cornell University).

96. Lawrence Parker to Goodrich Barbour, September 15, 1848, Barbour-Parker Family Letters.

97. Mother to Children, July 16, 1850 (or 1851 or 1857), George Harbold Letters (Kentucky Historical Society).

98. Hannah Newcomb to Mrs. Patty Garrett, July 12, 1836, Newcomb-Johnson Col-

lection (Huntington Library).

99. Sophia Mackres to Uncle, July 2 (?), (perhaps 1850), Lucien Parker Correspondence (Huntington Library).

100. Lois Lillie to Jacob Stevens, December 30, n.d., Henry Stevens Letters, 1851-1853 (Vermont Historical Society).

101. George Henry Dickenson to Aunt, September 11, 1859, and A. Dickenson to Sister, November 14, 1859, Joel Crane and Eunice Fitch Family Correspondence (Indiana Historical Society).

102. Andrew Jackson Sterrett to Brother, May 9, 1860, Andrew Jackson Sterrett Papers (Minnesota Historical Society).

103. Unidentified Daily Journal kept on a voyage from New York to San Francisco in 1848, August 26, 1848 (New-York Historical Society).

104. Thomas J. Hayter to Elizabeth Coleman, October 21, 1855, Coleman-Hayter Letters, 1840-1900 (Western Historical Manuscripts Collection, University of Missouri, Columbia).

105. James Duffe Diary, 1844, March 30, 1844 (New-York Historical Society).

106. *Complete Works of Ralph Waldo Emerson*, II, 93.

107. Robert Spinney to Nicholas Spinney, March 31, 1834, Spinney-Hunt-Wildes Papers (Maine Historical Society).

108. M.A.H. and L. T. to Polly Tarble, n.d. (1830s), Haile Family Papers (Vermont Historical Society).

109. Pauline H. Stratton Diary, 1841-1870, January 7, 1858 (Western Historical Manuscripts Collection, University of Missouri, Columbia).

110. Perry Miller, *The New England Mind: The Seventeenth Century* (Cambridge, Mass., 1963), p. 208.

111. Sarah Grimes to Mary, May 20, 1855, Grimes Family Correspondence (New Hampshire Historical Society).

112. Mary E. Copp Composition Book, December 13, 1848, Daniel Dennison Copp Letters (Manuscript Department, William R. Perkins Library, Duke University).

113. *Complete Works of Ralph Waldo Emerson*, VI, 5.

114. Ibid., pp. 5, 23.

115. Chapter 31.

116. Andrew Lester Diary, 1836-1888, April 12, 1843 (New-York Historical Society).

117. Abraham and Keziah Taylor to Nicholas Spinney, April 28, 1833, Nancy Taylor to Seth Burgess, April 7, 1842, and Abraham and Keziah Taylor to Nancy Taylor, (probably May) 12, 1842, Spinney-Hunt-Wildes Papers (Maine Historical Society).

118. Emsley Burgess Diary, April 4, 1847, Emsley Burgess Papers (Southern Historical Collection, University of North Carolina).

119. James Malin, *The Contriving Brain and the Skillful Hand in the United States: Something About History and the Philosophy of History* (Lawrence, Kans., 1955), p. 14.

120. M'Cosh, *Method of Divine Government*, p. 44.

121. John Bunyan, *The Pilgrim's Progress*, Part II.

122. Ward, *Andrew Jackson: Symbol for an Age*, p. 213.

123. Henry Hewes to William H. Garland, September 6, 1844, William Harris Garland Papers (Southern Historical Collection, University of North Carolina).

124. *The House of the Seven Gables, and The Snow Image and Other Twice-Told Tales*, in *Complete Works of Nathaniel Hawthorne*, Riverside Edition (Boston, 1883), III, 72.

125. *Pierre or, The Ambiguities*, Book V, Section v.

126. Russel B. Nye, "The Search for the Individual: 1750-1850," *Centennial Review* 5 (Winter 1961), 19.

Chapter 2

1. *The Complete Works of Ralph Waldo Emerson*, Concord Edition (Boston, 1903), I, 119, 123, 131-32, 144-45.

2. Robert Elliot Fitch, *Odyssey of the Self-Centered Self, or Rake's Progress in Religion* (New York, 1960), p. 20.

3. "Divinity School Address," p. 144.

4. *The Complete Works of Ralph Waldo Emerson*, Autograph Centenary Edition (Cambridge, Mass., 1904), IX, 251.

5. Lyman Benson to Nathan Hale, August 9, 1837, Haile Family Papers (Vermont Historical Society).

6. Peter Oliver to William Oliver, April 5, 1836, W. K. Oliver Correspondence (Alabama Department of Archives and History).

7. "Divinity School Address," pp. 140, 143.

8. William A. Clebsch, *From Sacred to Profane America: The Role of Religion in American History* (New York, 1968), p. 64.

9. Ibid.

10. Memoir, Elijah Smith Papers (Collection of Regional History, Cornell University).

11. J. W. Canfield Diary, March 10, 1852, Leander Crawford and Louisa (Canfield) Purdy, *Collectors*. Family Papers (Collection of Regional History, Cornell University).

12. Andrew Jackson Sterrett to Dear Charley, March 15, 1854, Andrew Jackson Sterrett Papers (Minnesota Historical Society).

13. Abel and S. Holton to Nathan and Maryann, October 31, 1858, Haile Family Papers (Vermont Historical Society).

14. Jonathan Parker to Eunice Parker, January 16, 1843, Lucien Parker Correspondence (Huntington Library).

15. J. Lindsay to John Shuff, August 22, 1840, J. Lindsay Letter (Kentucky Historical Society).

16. Lucy Ann to Cousin Charlotte, June 29, 1851, Sherman-Safford Papers (Vermont Historical Society).

17. *The Complete Works of Nathaniel Hawthorne*, Riverside Edition, (Boston, 1882), II, 445, 451, 455.

18. J. Lindsay to John Shuff, August 22, 1840, J. Lindsay Letter (Kentucky Historical Society).

19. Abraham and Keziah Taylor to James Douglas, March 4, 1832, Spinney-Hunt-Wildes Papers (Maine Historical Society).

20. Joseph McCool to Aaron C. Nevius, September 5, 1840, Orrin F. Smith and Family Papers, 1829-1932 (Minnesota Historical Society).

21. Amarilly Lines to Dear Children, January 22, 1860, Akehurst-Lines Collection (Division of Special Collections, University of Georgia Libraries).

22. J. R. Green to Dear Josh, October 10, 1858, Lipscomb Family Papers (Southern Historical Collection, University of North Carolina).

23. Ephraim S. Wilson to Mary Ann Covington, May 6, 1854, Mary Ann Covington Wilson Papers (Southern Historical Collection, University of North Carolina). Contrary to inferences that might be drawn from this citation, Mary Ann did not marry Ephraim; she married his brother.

24. J. W. Owen to John B. Clark, October 25, 1846, and ——— Owen to John B. Clark, n.d., John B. Clark Papers (Kentucky Historical Society).

25. Lawrence Parker to Fanny Barber, October 15, 1838, Barbour-Parker Family Letters (Collection of Regional History, Cornell University).

26. LeRoy P. Graf (ed.), "The Journal of a Vermont Man in Ohio, 1836-1842," *Ohio State Archaeological and Historical Quarterly* 60 (April 1951), 198.

27. "Selections from the Plymouth Diary of Abigail Baldwin, 1853-4," *Vermont History* 40 (Summer 1972), 218.

28. Joseph Haroutunian, *Piety Versus Moralism: The Passing of the New England Theology*, Harper Torchback Edition (New York, 1970), p. xxii.

29. Archibald B. Knode Diary, May 19, 1833, Archibald B. Knode Papers, Diaries and Account Books (Indiana Historical Society).

30. Nathan E. Parkhill Diary, December 1859, Nathan E. Parkhill Diaries, 1852-1901 (Vermont Historical Society).

31. Moses Coit Tyler, *A History of American Literature During the Colonial Period 1607-1765*, Agawam Edition (New York, 1898), I, 192.

32. Francis W. Squires Diaries, December 14, 1851 (Collection of Regional History, Cornell University); Perry Miller, *The New England Mind: The Seventeenth Century* (Cambridge, Mass., 1963), p. 68.

33. Mary A. Nearing Diary, February 12, 1857, Berry Collection (Collection of Regional History, Cornell University).

34. William Hoffman Diary, 1847-1850, March 13, 1847 (New-York Historical Society).

35. Charles W. Dudley Journal, 1856-1857, July 3-12, 1856, HM28925 (Huntington Library).

36. Manuscript Journal of a young man of Burlington (Vt.) who in 1839 journeyed to Va. and other places, July 4, 1839 (Vermont Historical Society).

37. William Hoffman Diary, 1847-1850, September 8, 1850 (New-York Historical Society).

38. Clebsch, *From Sacred to Profane America*, pp. 7, 161.

39. Josiah B. Chaney Diary, April 2, 1848, Josiah B. Chaney Papers, 1792-1917 (Minnesota Historical Society).

40. John Drake Diary, August 1, 1830 (Collection of Regional History, Cornell University).

41. *Moby Dick or the White Whale*, Chapter 8.

42. F. O. Matthiessen, *American Renaissance: Art and Expression in the Age of Emerson and Whitman* (New York, 1941), p. 126.

43. Daniel H. Hunt Diary, 1854-1859, November 26 and 30, 1854 (Minnesota Historical Society).

44. Daniel H. Hunt Diary, 1854-1859, November 22 and December 3, 1854, September 6, 1855, May 23-26 and June 1, 1856 (Minnesota Historical Society).

45. William ——— to Dear Sister, January 29, 1860, Spinney-Hunt-Wildes Papers (Maine Historical Society).

46. Victor L. Dowdell and Helen C. Everett (eds.), "California Diary of John French 1850-51," *Michigan History* 38 (March 1954), 34-35.

47. "Journal of Cyrus Sanders," *Iowa Journal of History and Politics* 37 (January 1939), 84.

48. *New York Times*, July 4, 1856.

49. July 3, 1839.

50. Clebsch, *From Sacred to Profane America*, p. ix.

51. Carl Bode, *The Anatomy of American Popular Culture 1840-1861* (Berkeley, Calif., 1959), Chapter 10.

52. *The Complete Works of Ralph Waldo Emerson*, Autograph Centenary Edition (Boston, 1903), II, 132.

53. Henry Peck Diary, November 28, 1830 (New-York Historical Society). This diary was catalogued as that of Henry Peck, but the diary reveals that it was kept by Henry's brother, Hiram.

54. Joseph Willard Diary, January 10 (or 9), 1853 (Massachusetts Historical Society).

55. Horatio N. Chandler Account Book, April 2, 1841 (New Hampshire Historical Society).

56. Richard Albert Edward Brooks (ed.), *The Diary of Michael Floy Jr. Bowery Village 1833-1837* (New Haven, Conn., 1941), p. 146.

57. Josiah M. Hickman Diary, January 6, 1849 (Indiana Division of the Indiana State Library).

58. Seth H. Willard Diary, June 7, July 10, and October 12, 1859 (Maine Historical Society).

59. Eben Weld to Martin Weld, February 10, 1846, in "A New Englander in the West: Letters of Eben Weld, 1845-50," *Minnesota History* 15 (September 1934), 306.

60. Vincent Hoover Diary, 1849-1850, August 19, 1849, HM27628 (Huntington Library).

61. Nancy Aiton to John Felix Aiton, n.d. (catalogued in folder for 1835-1839), John Felix Aiton Papers, 1835-1888 (Minnesota Historical Society).

62. James A. Padgett (ed.), "A Yankee School Teacher in Louisiana, 1835-1837: The Diary of Caroline B. Poole," *Louisiana Historical Quarterly* 20 (July 1937), 662.

63. Carl Russell Fish, *The Rise of the Common Man* (New York, 1927), p. 183.

64. Ray Allen Billington, *Protestant Crusade: A Study of the Origins of American Nativism* (New York, 1938), pp. 68-69.

65. Brooks (ed.), *The Diary of Michael Floy Jr.*, p. 216.

66. J. W. Canfield Diary, September 22, 1853, Leander Crawford and Louisa (Canfield) Purdy, *Collectors*. Family Papers (Collection of Regional History, Cornell University).

67. Kate White (ed.), "The Diary of a '49-er—Jacob Stuart," *Tennessee Historical Magazine* 1 (Series II) (July 1931), 282.

68. Sidney Ahlstrom, *A Religious History of the American People* (New Haven, Conn., 1972), p. 559.

69. Jules Zanger (ed.), *Captain Frederick Marryat: Diary in America* (Bloomington, Ind., 1960), p. 78.

70. Padgett (ed.), "A Yankee School Teacher in Louisiana," pp. 662-68.

71. David Brion Davis, "Some Themes of Countersubversion: An Analysis of Anti-

Masonic, Anti-Catholic, and Anti-Mormon Literature," *Mississippi Valley Historical Review* 47 (September 1960), 217-21.

72. Billington, *Protestant Crusade*, p. 108.

73. John Higham, "Another Look at Nativism," *Catholic Historical Review* 44 (July 1958), 149, 151.

74. Oscar Handlin, *Boston's Immigrants: A Study in Acculturation*, Atheneum paper edition (New York, 1968), p. 185.

75. John R. Bodo, *The Protestant Clergy and Public Issues 1812-1848* (Princeton, N.J., 1954), pp. 82-83.

76. "Religions of the Christian Perimeter," in James Ward Smith and A. Leland Jamison (eds.), *The Shaping of American Religion*, I, *Religion in American Life* (Princeton, N.J., 1961), 178.

77. Albert Post, *Popular Freethought in America, 1825-1850* (New York, 1943), p. 195.

78. Stephen and Phebe Humphrey to Marcus Humphrey, January 13, 1834, Noah Marcus Humphrey and Family Papers (Minnesota Historical Society).

79. Lois Lillie to Jacob B. Stevens, February 19, 1842, Henry Stevens Letters, 1851-1853 (Vermont Historical Society).

80. Thomas Maitland Marshall (ed.), "The Journal of Henry B. Miller," *Missouri Historical Society Collections* 6 (1931), 257-60.

81. T. S. Eliot, *American Literature and the American Language: An Address Delivered at Washington University on June 9, 1953* (Saint Louis, 1953), p. 4.

82. Marshall (ed.), "Journal of Henry B. Miller," p. 223.

83. "Religions of the Christian Perimeter," p. 177.

84. Second Presbyterian Church of Bath to Sister Eveleine Ostrander, April 3, 1835; and Same to Same, n.d., John Ostrander Family Papers (Collection of Regional History, Cornell University).

85. Elam Slagle to Wife, April 22, 1854, and April 28, 1854, Elam Slagle Papers (Southern Historical Collection, University of North Carolina).

86. Mary (Covey) to Lucetta Abbott, n.d., Peck Family Letters (Collection of Regional History, Cornell University).

87. J. E. Clayton Diary, February 10, 1850 (Manuscripts Division, Alabama Department of Archives and History).

88. Post, *Popular Freethought in America*, p. 195.

89. Thomas J. Hayter to Sarah Hayter, October 10, 1854, Coleman-Hayter Letters, 1840-1900 (Western Historical Manuscripts Collection, University of Missouri, Columbia).

90. Post, *Popular Freethought in America*, p. 214.

91. Thomas J. Hayter to Sarah Hayter, October 10, 1854, Coleman-Hayter Letters, 1840-1900 (Western Historical Manuscripts Collection, University of Missouri, Columbia).

92. Oren Lee Diary and Journal, July 9 and 18, 1829, February ?, 1831, December ?, 1831, March 3, 1833, October 15, 1835 (Connecticut State Library).

93. John Brown to Mrs. Lucy Nims, February 26, 1833, Brigham Nims Family Papers (New Hampshire Historical Society).

94. Quoted in Raymond M. Weaver, *Herman Melville: Mariner and Mystic* (New York, 1921), p. 316.

95. Francis W. Squires Diaries, August 8, 1851 (Collection of Regional History, Cornell University).

96. A. Dickenson to Dear Sister, March 18, 1860, Joel Crane and Eunice Fitch Family Correspondence (Indiana Historical Society).

97. L. Mattison and Sister Polly to Dear Brother, March 28, 1852, Sherman-Safford Papers (Vermont Historical Society).

98. Grace Adams and Edward Hutter, *The Mad Forties* (New York, 1942), p. 215.

99. William to Dear Sister, May 21, 1855, Spinney-Hunt-Wildes Papers (Maine Historical Society).

100. Lewis Macy to William W. Wood, February 6, 1852, and Same to Same, March 24, 1852, Thomas Marshall Family Correspondence (Indiana Historical Society).

101. Lewis Campbell Diaries, June 19, 1857, April 11 and July 25, 1858 (Manuscripts Division, Iowa Historical Library, Iowa State Department of History and Archives).

102. Lewis Campbell Diaries, September 12 and 26, 1858 (Manuscripts Division, Iowa Historical Library, Iowa State Department of Archives and History).

103. Lewis Campbell Diaries, September 19 and October 17, 1858 (Manuscripts Division, Iowa Historical Library, Iowa State Department of History and Archives).

104. "The Diary of James R. Stewart, Pioneer of Osage County, April, 1855-April, 1857; May, 1858-November, 1860," Part One, *Kansas Historical Quarterly* 17 (February 1949), 2-36.

105. James Jones to Mother, July 19, 1858, James T. Jones Papers, JTJ61 (Huntington Library).

106. Ahlstrom, *A Religious History of the American People*, p. 489.

107. Lewis Campbell Diaries, July 15, 1858 (Manuscripts Division, Iowa Historical Library, Iowa State Department of History and Archives).

108. Clara Day to Sister, December 12 and 19, 1858; Clara Day to Brother and Sister, September 11, 1857 (or 1859); Alfred A. Day to Brothers and Sisters, July 17, 1858; Lydia Day to Children, February 1, (probably 1859), Schuyler Hendryx Papers (Minnesota Historical Society).

109. R. Laurence Moore, "Spiritualism and Science: Reflections on the First Decade of the Spirit Rappings," *American Quarterly* 24 (October 1972), 486.

110. Alfred A. Day to Brothers and Sisters, July 17, 1858, Schuyler Hendryx Papers (Minnesota Historical Society).

111. Nancy Williams to Dear Uncle and Aunt, April 20, 1859, Boody and Mowers Papers (Collection of Regional History, Cornell University).

112. Lydia Day to Children, February 1 (probably 1859), Schuyler Hendryx Papers (Minnesota Historical Society).

113. See J. Stillson Judah, *The History and Philosophy of the Metaphysical Movements in America* (Philadelphia, 1967), p. 70.

114. Lewis Campbell Diaries, August 16, 1858 (Manuscripts Division, Iowa Historical Library, Iowa State Department of History and Archives).

115. "Diary of James R. Stewart," pp. 12, 22.

116. Robert W. Delp, "Andrew Jackson Davis: Prophet of American Spiritualism," *Journal of American History* 54 (June 1967), 47.

117. James Jones to Mother, June 5, 1858, James T. Jones Papers, JTJ59 (Huntington Library).

118. Ibid.

119. Lewis Campbell Diaries, August 15, 1858 (Manuscripts Division, Iowa Historical Library, Iowa State Department of History and Archives).

120. Alice Felt Tyler, *Freedom's Ferment: Phases of American Social History to 1860* (Minneapolis, 1944), pp. 79, 84-85.

121. Ibid., p. 79.

122. Raymond M. Weaver, *Herman Melville: Mariner and Mystic* (New York, 1921), p. 318.

123. *The House of the Seven Gables, and The Snow-Image and Other Twice-Told Tales*, Riverside Edition (Boston, 1883), pp. 290-91.

124. Russel B. Nye, "The Search for the Individual: 1750-1850," *Centennial Review* 5 (Winter 1961), 13.

125. Book XX, Section 2.

126. Signet Classic paper (New York, 1963), p. 116.

127. Andrew Hacker, *The End of the American Era* (New York, 1970), Chapter 11, p. 212.

Chapter 3

1. James Tuthill to Mrs. Robert Case, August 8, 1842, Freegift Tuthill Papers (Collection of Regional History, Cornell University).

2. ———— to Sally Stebbins, February 1, 1832, Stebbins Letter (Collection of Regional History, Cornell University).

3. Robert Baird, *Religion in America; or, An Account of the Origin, Progress, Relation to the State, And Present Condition of the Evangelical Denominations* (New York, 1844), p. 206.

4. Philip Greven, *The Protestant Temperament: Patterns of Child-Rearing, Religious Experience, and the Self in Early America* (New York, 1977). See, for examples, pp. 13, 103.

5. Zach H. Burnett to Atlas A. Burnett, June 30, 1845, Burnett Family Papers (Southern Historical Collection, University of North Carolina).

6. Mary Harris (Lester) Diary #1, November 25, 1847, Andrew Lester Diary, 1836-1888 (New-York Historical Society).

7. Donald H. Welsh (ed.), "Martha J. Woods Visits Missouri in 1857," *Missouri Historical Review* 55 (January 1961), 111.

8. Mary J. Nutt to Miss Mortimer, March 13, 1838, Mrs. William Adams Papers (State of Mississippi, Department of Archives and History).

9. Matilda Drew to Sarah Drew B————, n.d., James M. Drew and Family Papers (Minnesota Historical Society).

10. Norman Woods to Jane Woods, July 21, 1843, in L. U. Spellman (ed.), "Letters of the 'Dawson Men' from Perote Prison, Mexico, 1842-1843," *Southwestern Historical Quarterly* 38 (April 1935), 263.

11. H. G. Woods to Norman Woods, November 24, 1843, in Spellman (ed.), "Letters of the 'Dawson Men'," p. 269.

12. R. Owen to Mrs. Sarah Owen, March 5, 1834, Julia Bryce Lovelace Letters (Manuscripts Division, Alabama Department of Archives and History).

13. E.A.B. Phelps to Samuel W. Phelps, February 13, 14, and 20, 1848, Edward Ashley Bowen Phelps Letters and Diary, 1847-1848 (Manuscripts Division, New York Public Library).

14. John G. Cawelti, *Apostles of the Self-Made Man* (Chicago, 1965), p. 90.

15. D. H. Lawrence, "Model Americans," *Dial* 74 (May 1923), 507.

16. Russel B. Nye, "The Search for the Individual: 1750-1850," *Centennial Review* 5 (Winter 1961), 2.

17. Sarah B. Russell to William Houlton, November 1, 1852, William H. Houlton and Family Papers (Minnesota Historical Society).

18. "Selections from the Plymouth Diary of Abigail Baldwin, 1853-4," *Vermont History* 40 (Summer 1972), 218. The quote comes from introductory remarks.

19. Sarah Smith to William Alger, April 4, 1844 (or 1845), Elijah Smith Papers (Collection of Regional History, Cornell University). Alger's wife was Sarah's sister Lydia.

20. Susan Seymour to Silas Seymour, April 17, 1854, in Ruth Seymour Burmester (ed.), "Silas J. Seymour Letters," *Wisconsin Magazine of History* 32 (June 1949), 469-71. Part of the letter speaks directly to Silas's wife, Mary.

21. Paul Carter, *The Spiritual Crisis of the Gilded Age* (DeKalb, Ill., 1971), p. 130.

22. Philip Schaff, *America: A Sketch of Its Political, Social, and Religious Character*, edited by Perry Miller (Cambridge, Mass., 1961), p. 117.

23. Milo Holcomb to Nahum Holcomb, January 29, 1831, Holcomb Family Letters (Connecticut State Library).

24. Jennie Akehurst to Maria (sister), October 16, 1851, Akehurst-Lines Collection (Division of Special Collections, University of Georgia Libraries).

25. Max Eastman, *The Sense of Humor* (New York, 1936), p. 24.

26. Schaff, *America*, pp. 116-17.

27. Daniel Boorstin, *The Americans: The Democratic Experience* (New York, 1973), p. 162.

28. William A. Clebsch, *From Sacred to Profane America: The Role of Religion in American History* (New York, 1968), p. 66.

29. Martha B. Caldwell (ed.), "The Diary of George H. Hildt, June to December, 1857: Pioneer of Johnson County," *Kansas Historical Quarterly* 10 (August 1941), 269.

30. The renderings of Harris's language vary widely. This version comes from Kenneth S. Lynn (ed.), *The Comic Tradition in America* (Garden City, N.Y., 1958), p. 221.

31. F. O. Matthiessen, *American Renaissance: Art and Expression in the Age of Emerson and Whitman* (New York, 1941), p. 637.

32. Fanny and Lawrence Parker to Goodrich Barbour, October 2, 1847, Barbour-Parker Family Letters (Collection of Regional History, Cornell University).

33. Sarah Ames to Eliza and Nancy Kendall, September 12, 1841, William H. Houlton and Family Papers (Minnesota Historical Society).

34. Julia Pelton to Mrs. Maria Walcott, January 8, 1843, Oliver Pelton Correspondence (Connecticut State Library).

35. Mrs. Andrew W. Adams Diary, March 8, 1856, Andrew W. Adams and Family Papers (Minnesota Historical Society).

36. Albina Rich to Charles Rich, April 1, 1854, Rich Family Papers (Maine Historical Society).

37. Arthur Wallace Peach (ed.), "John Clark's Journal (1824-1842)," *Proceedings of the Vermont Historical Society*, New Series, 10 (December 1942), 191.

38. Albina Rich to Charles Rich, December 7, 1853, Rich Family Papers (Maine Historical Society).

39. Mercy Spinney to Ephraim Spinney, March 17, 1830, Spinney-Hunt-Wildes Papers (Maine Historical Society).

40. Sidney Smith to ———, February 6, 1856, William H. Houlton and Family Papers (Minnesota Historical Society).

41. Arozina Perkins to Barnabas Perkins, January 2, 1850, in "Letters of a Pioneer Teacher," *Annals of Iowa*, Third Series, 35 (Spring 1961), 617.

42. G. Perkins to Alvah Avery, August 12, 1848, Ebenezer Brown Papers (New Hampshire Historical Society).

43. Andrew J. Roberts to Matilda Roberts, August 8, 1852, in "Letters from the Past," *Vermont Quarterly: A Magazine of History*, New Series, 20 (April, 1952), 129-30; and Mathilda Roberts to Andrew J. Roberts, September 4, 1852, in "Letters from the Past," *Vermont Quarterly: A Magazine of History*, New Series, 20 (July 1952), 208-10.

44. Nancy Haile to Nathan Haile, January 25, 1851, Haile Family Papers (Vermont Historical Society).

45. ——— to Sally Stebbins, February 1, 1832, Stebbins Letter (Collection of Regional History, Cornell University).

46. James Bell to Augusta Hallock, January 25, 1857, James Alvin Bell Collection (Huntington Library).

47. Brigham Nims Diary, October 5, 16, and 23, 1842, Brigham Nims Family Papers (New Hampshire Historical Society).

48. Horatio Houlton to William Houlton, June 1, 1855, William H. Houlton and Family Papers (Minnesota Historical Society).

49. Whitney Cross, *The Burned-over District: The Social and Intellectual History of Enthusiastic Religion in Western New York, 1800-1850* (Ithaca, N.Y., 1950), p. 41.

50. [Augustus Baldwin Longstreet], *Georgia: Scenes, Characters, Incidents, &c. In the First Half Century of the Republic* (Augusta, Ga., 1835), pp. 212-13.

51. F. Hatch to Mrs. Marlin Johnson, October 22, 1830, Newcomb-Johnson Collection (Huntington Library).

52. Mason Cleveland to Phinehas Adams, September 22, 1834, Phinehas Adams Papers, 1759-1892 (Huntington Library).

53. Charlotte E. Burkhart to Mary Baltzell, May 4, 1845, Charlotte Burkhart Letters (Kentucky Historical Society).

54. Nell W. Kull, "'I Can Never Be Happy There in Among So Many Mountains'—The Letters of Sally Rice," *Vermont History* 38 (Winter 1970), 52.

55. Susan Bibbens Fox Diary, March 18 and 22, 1839, Bibbens Family Papers (Collection of Regional History, Cornell University). An unidentified obituary mentions Fox's capacity for "merriment" and his "excentricity."

56. C. P. Pettit to Joshua Lipscomb, March 2, 1860, Lipscomb Family Papers (Southern Historical Collection, University of North Carolina).

57. Levi Countryman Diary, August 10, 18, and 22, November 21, 23, 25, and 28, and December 2, 7, 8, 11, and 12, 1858, Levi N. Countryman Papers (Minnesota Historical Society).

58. James and Sarah Ireland to David and Mary Ann Ireland, August 7, 1851, James Ireland Family Correspondence (Indiana Historical Society).

59. Andrew Lester Diary #2, April 5, 1843, Andrew Lester Diary, 1836-1888 (New-York Historical Society).

60. Susan Bibbens Fox Diary, March 7, 1840, Bibbens Family Papers (Collection of Regional History, Cornell University).

61. Perry Miller, *The Life of the Mind in America from the Revolution to the Civil War* (New York, 1965), p. 7.

62. Julia Adams to James A. Matters, January 9, 1843, Phinehas Adams Papers, 1759-1892 (Huntington Library).

63. Mathilda Roberts to Andrew J. Roberts, July 3, 1852, in "Letters from the Past," *Vermont Quarterly: A Magazine of History*, New Series, 20 (January 1952), 48-50.

64. Diary kept by an unidentified student while living in Massachusetts in 1833 and 1834 (Manuscripts Division, New York Public Library). The cited material is in a reflection that precedes the dated entries.

65. F. Hatch to Mrs. Marlin Johnson, October 22, 1834, Phinehas Adams Papers, 1759-1892 (Huntington Library); Cross, *The Burned-over District*, pp. 182-84.

66. "From the Covenant to the Revival," in James Ward Smith and A. Leland Jamison (eds.), *The Shaping of American Religion*, Volume I of *Religion in American Life* (Princeton, N.J., 1961), 362.

67. Timothy Smith, *Revivalism and Social Reform in Mid-Nineteenth Century America* (New York, 1957), p. 8.

68. *The Complete Works of Ralph Waldo Emerson*, Autograph Centenary Edition (Cambridge, Mass., 1903), II, 281-82.

69. Smith, *Revivalism and Social Reform*, p. 8.

70. Ralph Henry Gabriel, "Evangelical Religion and Popular Romanticism in Early Nineteenth-Century America," *Church History* 19 (March 1950), 36-39.

71. Miller, *The Life of the Mind in America*, p. 60.

72. Brooks (ed.), *Diary of Michael Floy Jr.*, p. 16.

73. "Evangelical Religion and Popular Romanticism," p. 39.

74. Brooks (ed.), *Diary of Michael Floy Jr.*, pp. 14-17.

75. Lois Lillie to Jacob B. Stevens, February 19, 1842, Henry Stevens Letters, 1851-1853 (Vermont Historical Society).

76. ——— to My Dear Children, April 20, 1851, Haile Family Papers (Vermont Historical Society).

77. Putnam Catlin to Mrs. Clara Catlin, April 23, 1840, in Marjorie Catlin Roehm, *The Letters of George Catlin and His Family: A Chronicle of the American West* (Berkeley, Calif., 1966), p. 160.

78. Horatio N. Chandler Account Book, December 20, 22, and 23, 1840 (New Hampshire Historical Society).

79. J. W. Canfield Diary, February 3 and 4, 1852, Leander Crawford and Louise (Canfield) Purdy, *Collectors*. Family Papers (Collection of Regional History, Cornell University).

80. Zachariah Burnett to Atlas A. Burnett, October 11, 1849, Burnett Family Papers (Southern Historical Collection, University of North Carolina).

81. Frances Lea McCurdy, *Stump, Bar, and Pulpit: Speechmaking on the Missouri Frontier* (Columbia, Mo., 1969), p. 164.

82. Kull, "The Letters of Sally Rice," p. 51.

83. Joanna ——— to Atlas Burnett, May 15, 1843, Burnett Family Papers (Southern Historical Collection, University of North Carolina). Joanna evidently was born a

Burnett, but it is not clear whether she had a married name at the time of this letter.

84. Charles A. Johnson, *The Frontier Camp Meeting: Religion's Harvest Time* (Dallas, Tex., 1955), p. 214.

85. William Hoffman Diary, August 29 to September 2, 1847 (New-York Historical Society).

86. Andrew Jackson Sterrett to Innis (Sterrett), August 16, 1858, and Same to Same, September 4, 1858, Andrew Jackson Sterrett Papers (Minnesota Historical Society).

87. Bryant Redding to "Dear Cosin," July 26, 1855, George H. Tunnell Collection (Six Vault, Georgia Department of Archives and History).

88. Baird, *Religion in America*, p. 217. Philip Schaff saw the protracted meetings as being "designed to compensate for the regularly returning church festivals rejected by the Methodists, as by the Puritans. . . ." *America*, p. 142.

89. Cross, *The Burned-over District*, p. 183.

90. Johnson, *The Frontier Camp Meeting*, p. 247.

91. Perry Miller, *Consciousness in Concord: The Text of Thoreau's Hitherto 'Lost Journal' (1840-1841) Together with Notes and a Commentary* (Boston, 1958), pp. 104-07.

92. Hattie M. C. to Friend Jesse, August 19, 1847, George H. Tunnell Collection (Six Vault, Georgia Department of Archives and History).

93. Miller, *Consciousness in Concord*, pp. 106-07.

94. J. W. Canfield Diary, March 17 and April 5, 1852 (aside from dates specified in my text), Leander Crawford and Louisa (Canfield) Purdy, *Collectors*. Family Papers (Collection of Regional History, Cornell University); Miller, *Consciousness in Concord*, p. 105.

95. Jesse Beaver to A. C. Nevius, January 27, 1846, Orrin F. Smith and Family Papers, 1829-1932 (Minnesota Historical Society).

96. Smith, *Revivalism and Social Reform*, p. 72.

97. David E. Smith, "Millenarian Scholarship in America," *American Quarterly* 17 (Fall 1965), 536.

98. H. Richard Niebuhr, *The Kingdom of God in America*, Harper Torchback Edition (New York, 1959). See, especially, pp. xii, 164-65.

99. Ernest Sandeen, *The Roots of Fundamentalism: British and American Millenarianism 1800-1930* (Chicago, 1970), pp. 42-43.

100. Sidney Ahlstrom, *A Religious History of the American People* (New Haven, Conn., 1972), p. 845.

101. Ernest Tuveson, *Redeemer Nation: The Idea of America's Millennial Role* (Chicago, 1968), pp. 88-89.

102. Ibid., p. 89.

103. Fred Landon (ed.), "Extracts from the Diary of William C. King, A Detroit Carpenter, in 1832," *Michigan History Magazine* 19 (Winter 1935), 67.

104. Blake McKelvey (ed.), "The Autobiography of Asher Freeman," *New York History* 25 (April 1944), 214.

105. Linus E. Sherman and C. H. Sherman to Dear Brother, February 13, 1852, Sherman-Safford Papers (Vermont Historical Society).

106. J. F. Maclear, "The Republic and The Millenium," in Elwyn A. Smith (ed.), *The Religion of the Republic* (Philadelphia, 1971), p. 189.

107. Oren Lee Diary and Journal, January 13 and February 11, 1831 (Connecticut State Library).

108. ———— to Ellen, January 16, 1855, Haile Family Papers (Vermont Historical Society).

109. Jabez Whiting to Wellborn Beeson, July 28, 1855, Brophy-Beeson Papers, BB63 (Huntington Library).

110. Charles Rich to Albina Rich, February 5, 1854, and Same to Same, April 30, 1854, Rich Family Papers (Maine Historical Society).

111. Levi Countryman Diary, November 30, 1858, Levi N. Countryman Papers (Minnesota Historical Society).

112. Jesse W. Owen to John B. Clark, May 18, 1851, John B. Clark Papers (Kentucky Historical Society).

113. John L. Clayton to Wellborn Beeson, May 24, 1857, Brophy-Beeson Papers, BB27 (Huntington Library).

Chapter 4

1. *The Complete Works of Ralph Waldo Emerson*, Concord Edition (Boston, 1903), I, 143.

2. Michael Aaron Rockland (ed.), *America in the Fifties and Sixties: Julián Marías on the United States*, trans. Blanche De Puy and Harold C. Raley (University Park, Pa., 1972), p. 41.

3. Carl Bode, *The Anatomy of American Popular Culture, 1840-1861* (Berkeley, Calif., 1960), pp. 122, 193-94.

4. "Editor's Introduction," *Uncle Tom's Cabin or, Life Among the Lowly* (Cambridge, Mass., 1962), p. xi.

5. Geoffrey Gorer, "The Pornography of Death," *Encounter* 5 (October 1955), 50-51.

6. William Y. Sprague Diary, after the entry of September 17, 1859 (Connecticut State Library).

7. Hiram Peck Diary, undated miscellany at beginning (New-York Historical Society). (This item is catalogued as the Henry Peck Diary, but it was kept by Henry's brother Hiram.)

8. Isaac S. Barr Penmanship Book, Mrs. I. S. Barr Manuscripts (Manuscripts Division, Alabama Department of Archives and History).

9. Charles W. Dudley Journal, undated item, HM28925 (Huntington Library).

10. John R. Cummins Diary, December 31, 1856, John R. Cummins Papers, 1850-1916 (Minnesota Historical Society).

11. *Mardi: and a Voyage Thither*, Chapter 181.

12. Seth H. Willard Diary, April 4, 1859 (Maine Historical Society).

13. Bode, *Anatomy of American Popular Culture*, p. 192.

14. Perry Miller, *Consciousness in Concord: The Text of Thoreau's Hitherto "Lost Journal", 1840-1841, Together with Notes and a Commentary by Perry Miller* (Boston, 1958), p. 75.

15. Robert W. Lovett, "Augustus Roundy's Cincinnati Sojourn," *Historical and Philosophical Society of Ohio Bulletin* 19 (October 1961), 260-61.

16. Sophronia C. Beebe to Jennie Akehurst, February 4, 1858, Akehurst-Lines Collection (Division of Special Collections, University of Georgia Libraries).

17. LeRoy and Jas. R. Upshaw to James Upshaw, August 30 and October 20, 1841, Upshaw Collection (Division of Special Collections, University of Georgia Libraries).

18. Annis Pierce to Caleb and Emily Carr, November 5, 1856, Caleb M. Carr Letters (Collection of Regional History, Cornell University).

19. "On the Death of my 2 brothers & sister," February 1851, Harris Family Papers (Indiana Historical Society).

20. Brigham Nims Diary, February 11 and 12, 1846, Brigham Nims Family Papers (New Hampshire Historical Society).

21. Archibald B. Knode Diary, September 30, November 15, and December 31, 1834, Archibald B. Knode Papers, Diaries and Account Books (Indiana Historical Society).

22. Dily Richards to William Richards, November 2, 1855, George H. Tunnell Collection (Six Vault, Georgia Department of Archives and History).

23. (Mrs. Oswald) to William Garland, September 30, 1839, William Harris Garland Papers (Southern Historical Collection, University of North Carolina).

24. I. P. Blair to W. D. Boaz, January 9, 1853, William Davis Boaz Papers (Manuscripts Division, Alabama Department of Archives and History).

25. Julia Adams to Hannah Watrous, May 2, 1848, Phinehas Adams Papers (Huntington Library).

26. Charles Rich to Albina Rich, December 5, 1853, Rich Family Papers (Maine Historical Society).

27. Albina Rich to Charles Rich, December 7, 1853, Rich Family Papers (Maine Historical Society).

28. Fred Somkin, *Unquiet Eagle: Memory and Desire in the Idea of American Freedom, 1815-1860* (Ithaca, N.Y., 1967), pp. 40-41.

29. *The Gilded Age: A Tale of To-Day* (New York, 1915), I, 44-54.

30. Daniel H. Hunt Diary, June 10, 1857 (Minnesota Historical Society).

31. Andrew Jackson Sterrett to Brother, July 3, 1859, Andrew Jackson Sterrett Papers (Minnesota Historical Society).

32. Thomas Coleman to Father, April 14, 1852, Coleman-Hayter Letters, 1840-1900 (Western Historical Manuscripts Collection, University of Missouri, Columbia).

33. Mary Stuart Bailey Journal, April 14 and 17, 1852, HM2018 (Huntington Library).

34. Walter B. Foster Journal, July 24, 1842 (Missouri Historical Society).

35. John Drake Diary, May 6, 1832 (Collection of Regional History, Cornell University); William Silliman Journal, January 18, 1840 (Connecticut State Library); Thomas Reber Diaries, January 29, 1855 (Collection of Regional History, Cornell University).

36. David Lindsey (ed.), "The Journal of an 1859 Pike's Peak Gold Seeker," *Kansas Historical Quarterly* 22 (Winter 1956), 326-27.

37. Josiah B. Chaney Diary, September 3, 1845, Josiah B. Chaney Papers (Minnesota Historical Society).

38. *Twice-Told Tales* (Boston, 1900), II, 132-33.

39. A. P. Moss to Dear Emily, September 18, 1853, Smith Collection (Six Vault, Georgia Department of Archives and History).

40. Anna and Edward O. Smith to Brother and Sister, December 24, 1839, in Helen

Everett (ed.), "Early Michigan Letters," *Michigan History* 42 (December 1958), 415-17.

41. Josiah B. Chaney Diary, September 17, 1845.

42. Walter B. Foster Journal, January 16, 1842.

43. *White Jacket or the World in a Man-of-War*, Chapter 31.

44. *Pierre or, The Ambiguities*, Book 20, Part 1.

45. *The Complete Works of Ralph Waldo Emerson*, Autograph Centenary Edition (Boston, 1904), VI, 5.

46. Mathilda Theresa Roberts to Andrew J. Roberts, January 30, 1853, in "Letters from the Past," *Vermont Quarterly: A Magazine of History* 20 (October 1952), 300-301.

47. Albina Rich to Charles Rich, March 5, 1854, Rich Family Papers (Maine Historical Society).

48. Augustine Holcomb to Nahum Holcomb, Jr., May 25, 1830, Holcomb Family Letters (Connecticut State Library).

49. Francis W. Squires Diaries, March, 1853 (Collection of Regional History, Cornell University).

50. Simeon Ives to Josiah Crosby, September 8, 1847, Lyman Stuart *Collector*. Stampless Covers (Collection of Regional History, Cornell University).

51. George and Fidelia Baldwin to Lawrence Parker, October 2, 1847, Barbour-Parker Family Letters (Collection of Regional History, Cornell University).

52. R. Owen to Brother and Sister, April 22, 1836, Julia Bryce Lovelace Letters (Manuscripts Division, Alabama Department of Archives and History).

53. *Pierre or, The Ambiguities*, Book 22, Parts 3 and 4.

54. Cyclone Covey, *The American Pilgrimage: The Roots of American History, Religion and Culture* (New York, 1961), p. 105.

55. Francis W. Squires Diaries, March 9, 1860.

56. Lucy Holcomb to Nahum Holcomb, May 10, 1837, Holcomb Family Letters (Connecticut State Library).

57. Fidelia and George Baldwin to Lawrence Parker, November 2, 1845, Barbour-Parker Family Letters (Collection of Regional History, Cornell University).

58. John Barber to Lawrence Parker, November 2, 1845, Barbour-Parker Family Letters (Collection of Regional History, Cornell University).

59. Jabez Whiting to Wellborn Beeson, July 28, 1855, Brophy-Beeson Papers, BB63 (Huntington Library).

60. David D. Anderson (ed.), *The Literary Works of Abraham Lincoln* (Columbus, Ohio, 1970), p. 66.

61. American Century Series Paperback (New York, 1965), pp. 107, 153-54.

62. 46 (October 1850), 352.

63. 3 (April 1843), 509.

64. William Montgomery Journal, June 10, 1850, HM19474 (Huntington Library).

65. Mary E. Copp Composition Book, January 30, 1849, Daniel Dennison Copp Letters (Manuscript Department, William R. Perkins Library, Duke University).

66. "Journal of a Trip from Brooklyn to Niagara Falls in June 1841 John Read Barrows," *New York History* 23 (April 1942), 195.

67. James Bell to Augusta Hallock, June 7, 1855, James Alvin Bell Collection (Huntington Library). Sweet Alice, of course, had "hair so brown." A lock of Augusta's reveals hers to have been dark reddish-brown.

68. Sarah Ames to Eliza and Nancy Kendall, September 12, 1841, William H.

Houlton and Family Papers (Minnesota Historical Society).

69. Barbara Rotundo, "The Rural Cemetery Movement," *Essex Institute Historical Collections* 109 (July 1973), 234.

70. For details and illustrations in this regard, see Mrs. Stewart McCormick, "Death and Adornment," *Missouri Historical Society Bulletin* 25 (April 1969), 201-206.

71. Josiah B. Chaney Diary, September 10, 1845.

72. Mary Ann to Mrs. Cole, undated, Haile Family Papers (Vermont Historical Society).

73. Samuel Nichols to Father, May 21, 1849, Samuel Nichols Collection (Huntington Library).

74. *White Jacket or The World in a Man-of-War*, Chapter 81.

75. David Brion Davis, *Homicide in American Fiction, 1790-1860: A Study in Social Values* (Ithaca, N.Y., 1957), p. 293.

76. Bower Aly, "The Gallows Speech: A Lost Genre," *The Southern Speech Journal* 34 (Spring 1969), 208.

77. Ibid., p. 213.

78. William Hoffman Diary, August 29-30, 1850 (New-York Historical Society).

79. Obadiah Ethelbert Baker Journal, March 12, 1859, Obadiah Ethelbert Baker Collection (Huntington Library).

80. *White Jacket or the World in a Man-of-War*, Chapter 89.

81. Elisha D. Perkins Diary, January 8, 1850, HM1547 (Huntington Library).

82. Mabell Eppard Martin (ed.), "From Texas to California in 1849: Diary of C. C. Cox," *Southwestern Historical Quarterly* 29 (October 1925), 128, 136. This diary was published in three parts in *Southwestern Historical Quarterly*.

83. *Mosses From an Old Manse* (Boston, 1882), pp. 384-85, 388.

84. *Frontier: American Literature and the American West* (Princeton, N.J., 1965), p. 76.

85. Ibid., p. 75.

86. III, 1, 79-80.

87. *Mosses From an Old Manse*, p. 389.

88. Edward D. Jervey and James E. Moss (eds.), "From Virginia to Missouri in 1846: The Journal of Elizabeth Ann Cooley," *Missouri Historical Review* 60 (January 1966), 185-87.

89. Sarah Smith to Sister, July 11, 1843, and Sarah Smith to William Alger, April 4, 1844, Elijah Smith Papers (Collection of Regional History, Cornell University).

90. Mary and James Cole to Brother (John Jones), September 1, 1852, Morgan D. Jones Letters (Manuscripts Division, Alabama Department of Archives and History).

91. Minerva Bacon to Lydia Barnhart, June 27, 1841, Lyman Stuart *Collector*. Stampless Covers (Collection of Regional History, Cornell University).

92. L. Clark to Mrs. Ann Bromley, June 18, 1850, Lyman Stuart *Collector*. Stampless Covers (Collection of Regional History, Cornell University).

93. Julia Adams to Hannah Watrous, May 2, 1848, Phinehas Adams Papers, 1759-1892 (Huntington Library).

94. Augusta Hallock to James Bell, July 4, 1856, James Alvin Bell Collection (Huntington Library).

95. John L. Palmer to John M. Scott, November 12, 1855, John M. Scott Letters (Division of Special Collections, University of Georgia Library).

96. Mario Praz, *The Romantic Agony*, translated by Angus Davidson (London, 1951), p. 27.

97. Amelia J. Akehurst Diary, 1851, Akehurst-Lines Collection (Division of Special Collections, University of Georgia Libraries). Dating within the diary is very difficult. Italics mine.

98. Curtis Dahl, "The American School of Catastrophe," *American Quarterly* 11 (Fall 1959), 388-89.

99. "A Memoir of Lucretia Maria Davidson," in *Lives of Sir William Phips, Israel Putnam, Lucretia Maria Davidson, and David Rittenhouse*, The Library of American Biography Conducted by Jared Sparks, Vol. 7 (New York, 1870), 288. Italics mine.

100. Ibid., p. 290.

101. Anderson (ed.), *The Literary Works of Abraham Lincoln*, pp. 56, 68.

102. George W. ——— to James Armstrong, December 24, 1842, John Milton Armstrong and Family Papers (Minnesota Historical Society). George W. does not seem to have been the brother of James Armstrong.

103. *Mardi: and a Voyage Thither*, Chapter 9.

104. Mrs. Andrew W. Adams Diary, April 12, 1856, Andrew W. Adams and Family Papers (Minnesota Historical Society).

105. A. J. Hayter to Sa. A. G. Hayter, June 14, 1855, Coleman-Hayter Letters, 1840-1900 (Western Historical Manuscripts Collection, University of Missouri, Columbia).

106. Minerva Bacon to Lydia Barnhart, June 27, 1841, Lyman Stuart *Collector*. Stampless Covers (Collection of Regional History, Cornell University).

107. Archibald B. Knode Diary, September 28-29 and November 15, 1834, Archibald B. Knode Papers, Diaries and Account Books (Indiana Historical Society).

108. Joanna to Atlas Burnett, May 15, 1843, Burnett Family Papers (Southern Historical Collection, University of North Carolina).

109. John Barber to Goodrich N. Barbour, March 24, 1848, Barbour-Parker Family Letters (Collection of Regional History, Cornell University).

110. *Uncle Tom's Cabin or, Life Among the Lowly*, Chapter 26.

111. Lawrence Parker to Goodrich Barbour, September 15, 1848, Barbour-Parker Family Letters (Collection of Regional History, Cornell University).

112. *The Guilded Age*, I, 109-11.

113. *Richard the Second*, II, 1, 14-15; *Macbeth*, I, 4, 7.

114. Elizabeth and James Olin to Alfonso R. Peck, July 28, 1850, Peck Family Papers (Collection of Regional History, Cornell University).

115. Pauline H. Stratton Diary, January 12, 1855 (Western Historical Manuscripts Collection, University of Missouri, Columbia).

116. Lizzie Robbins to Julia Pelton, September 8, 1858, Oliver Pelton Correspondence (Connecticut State Library).

117. Horatio N. Chandler Account Book, January 15, 1841 (New Hampshire Historical Society). This item is both diary and account book.

118. Fidelia Baldwin to Goodrich Barbour, April 23, 1848, Barbour-Parker Family Letters (Collection of Regional History, Cornell University).

119. Hiram Peck Diary, June 18, 1831 (New-York Historical Society).

120. C. S. Boardman to Homer Boardman, October 9, 1839, Lyman Stuart Papers (Collection of Regional History, Cornell University).

121. John and Rachel Ricketts to Brother, December 23, 1838 (Kentucky Historical Society).

122. Peter and Catherine Beaver to Mrs. Sarah Beaver, March 11, 1847, Orrin F. Smith and Family Papers, 1829-1932 (Minnesota Historical Society). The quoted part of the letter was written by Catherine.

123. E. A. Slagle to J. F. Slagle, August 31, 1853, Elam Slagle Papers (Southern Historical Collection, University of North Carolina).

124. *Mardi: and a Voyage Thither*, Chapter 9.

125. Sarah Hayter and Elizabeth Coleman to C. J. Hayter, October 9, 1844, Coleman-Hayter Letters, 1840-1900 (Western Historical Manuscripts Collection, University of Missouri, Columbia).

126. Aaron and Eliza Stryker to David Ireland, September 7, 1859, James Ireland Family Correspondence (Indiana Historical Society).

127. Ann Douglas, "Heaven Our Home: Consolation Literature in the Northern United States, 1830-1880," *American Quarterly* 26 (December 1974), 497.

128. Elizabeth Baskin to Miss N. J. Baskin, May 21, 1848, William Davis Boaz Papers (Manuscripts Division, Alabama Department of Archives and History).

129. Clark Sanderson to Nephew, July 22, 1854, James Ireland Family Correspondence (Indiana Historical Society).

130. R. E. Riddick to Charles C. Riddick, March 18, 1852, Charles C. Riddick Papers (Southern Historical Collection, University of North Carolina).

131. Annis Pierce to Caleb and Emily Carr, November 6, 1856, Caleb M. Carr Letters (Collection of Regional History, Cornell University).

132. Ann Woods to Aaron Nevius, October 30, 1843, Orrin F. Smith and Family Papers 1829-1932 (Minnesota Historical Society).

133. Keziah Herrick to Mary J. Bass, February 10, 1854, Joel Crane and Eunice Fitch Family Correspondence (Indiana Historical Society).

134. Morgan Eastman to Lydia Barnhart, July 25, 1841, Lyman Stuart *Collector*. Stampless Covers (Collection of Regional History, Cornell University).

Chapter 5

1. H. N. Rhodes Diary, September 24 and 27, 1850 (Vermont Historical Society).

2. Ibid., October 2, 7, and 11, 1850.

3. Herman Melville, *The Confidence-Man: His Masquerade*, Chapter 5.

4. Richard D. Mosier, *The American Temper: Patterns of Our Intellectual Heritage* (Berkeley, Calif., 1952), pp. 201-203.

5. *The Complete Works of Ralph Waldo Emerson*, Autograph Centenary Edition (Cambridge, Mass., 1903), II, 204; III, 77; III, 255.

6. Quoted in F. O. Matthiessen, *American Renaissance: Art and Expression in the Age of Emerson and Whitman* (New York, 1941), p. 5.

7. Stephen Whicher, *Freedom and Fate: An Inner Life of Ralph Waldo Emerson* (Philadelphia, 1953), pp. 139-40.

8. Perry Miller, *Consciousness in Concord: The Text of Thoreau's Hitherto "Lost Journal," 1840-1841, Together with Notes and a Commentary by Perry Miller* (Boston, 1958), p. 35.

9. John O. Lyons, *The Invention of the Self: The Hinge of Consciousness in the Eighteenth Century* (Carbondale, Ill., 1978).

10. *Complete Works of Ralph Waldo Emerson*, II, 74.

11. Philip Greven, *The Protestant Temperament: Patterns of Child-Rearing, Religious Experience, and the Self in Early America* (New York, 1977), Part II, p. 74.

12. Andrew Hacker, *The End of the American Era* (New York, 1970), pp. 159, 168-69.

13. Tom Wolfe, *Mauve Gloves & Madmen, Clutter & Vine and Other Stories, Sketches, and Essays* (New York, 1976), p. 167.

14. "Solitude and Society," *Atlantic Monthly: A Magazine of Literature, Art, and Politics* 1 (December 1857), 229.

15. Mother to My Dear Emily, December 18, 1859, B. B. Griggs Letters (South Caroliniana Library, Columbia, South Carolina).

16. Abner S. Goddard Diary, February 16, 20, and 21, 1850, Orrin F. Smith and Family Papers, 1829-1932 (Minnesota Historical Society).

17. Alfred Kazin and Daniel Aaron (eds.), *Emerson: A Modern Anthology*, Dell Paperback Edition (New York, 1958), p. 161.

18. Augusta Hallock to James Bell, May 23, 1854; Same to Same, June 1, 1854; Same to Same, October 15, 1854; James Bell to Augusta Hallock, April 8, 1855; Augusta Hallock to James Bell, May 20 and 23, 1855; Same to Same, December 19, 1855; Same to Same, March 16, 1856; Same to Same, April 3, 1856; James Bell to Augusta Hallock, April 6, 1856; Augusta Hallock to James Bell, February 1, 1857; James Bell to Augusta Hallock, March 22, 1857; Augusta Hallock to Dear Brother Eddie, November 11, 1863, James Alvin Bell Collection (Huntington Library).

19. Jesse M. Huckabee to Maria Louisa Smith, October 15, 1846; R. A. Moss to Maria Louisa Smith, March 15, 1847; Thomas Curtis to Maria Louisa Smith, January 19, 1855; Eliza A. Patton to Maria Louisa Smith, May 25, 1856, Smith Collection (Six Vault, Georgia Department of Archives and History).

20. Rinaldo Parker to Mrs. Eunice Parker, March 31, 1834; September 24 and October 22, 1837; and February 10, 1841, Lucien Parker Correspondence (Huntington Library).

21. See, for example, T. Mallory to N. E. Mallory, October 2, 1840, Lyman Stuart *Collector*. Stampless Covers (Collection of Regional History, Cornell University).

22. Brigham Nims to Selina Gould, March 5 and June 28, 1853; Selina Gould to Brigham Nims, July 15, 1853; Brigham Nims Diary, July 23, August 8, 17, 27, September 15, 1853, Brigham Nims Family Papers (New Hampshire Historical Society).

23. Morton Hunt, *The Natural History of Love*, (New York, 1959), p. 309.

24. Amelia Akehurst to Sylvanus Lines, August 1854, Akehurst-Lines Collection (Division of Special Collections, University of Georgia Libraries).

25. James Armstrong to Mary Nelson, July 23, 1841, John Milton Armstrong and Family Papers (Minnesota Historical Society).

26. Amelia J. Akehurst Diary, August 23, 1859, Akehurst-Lines Collection (Division of Special Collections, University of Georgia Libraries).

27. Bryant Redding to Dear Cousin Ann, October 18, 1855, George H. Tunnell Collection (Six Vault, Georgia Department of Archives and History).

28. Mrs. A. Badgley to Niece, December 6, 1850, Joel Crane and Eunice Fitch Family Correspondence (Indiana Historical Society).

29. Minutes of the Mount Hope Debating Society, March 2 and March 9, 1857, Leander Crawford and Louisa (Canfield) Purdy, *Collectors*. Family Papers (Collection of Regional History, Cornell University).

30. Levina Lilly to Jacob Stevens, August 7, 1836, Henry Stevens Letters, 1851-1853 (Vermont Historical Society).

31. Charlotte Whipple to Samuel, September 15, 1849, Charlotte L. Whipple Diaries (Manuscripts Division, New York Public Library).

32. Lawrence Parker to Fanny Barber, September 5, 1834; Same to Same, November 8, 1834, Barbour-Parker Family Letters (Collection of Regional History, Cornell University).

33. Miller, *Consciousness in Concord*, p. 88.

34. Ibid., p. 89.

35. Albina Rich to Charles Rich, June 25, 1854, Rich Family Papers (Maine Historical Society).

36. Brigham Nims to Selina Gould, August 13, 1853, Brigham Nims Family Papers (New Hampshire Historical Society).

37. Brigham Nims to Selina Gould, August 1, 1853, and August 13, 1853, Brigham Nims Family Papers (New Hampshire Historical Society).

38. Abner S. Goddard Diary, March 6, 1850, Orrin F. Smith and Family Papers, 1829-1932 (Minnesota Historical Society).

39. Albina Rich to Charles Rich, December 25, 1853, Rich Family Papers (Maine Historical Society).

40. Mother Matilder to Edward B. Drew, June 1855, James M. Drew and Family Papers (Minnesota Historical Society).

41. Amelia J. Akehurst Diary, 1851, Akehurst-Lines Collection (Division of Special Collections, University of Georgia Libraries). This is not a true diary but rather a thematic account or narrative.

42. James T. Johnson, "English Puritan Thought on the Ends of Marriage," *Church History* 38 (December 1969).

43. Mrs. Lucy Furber Diary, Pierce F. Furber and Family Papers (Minnesota Historical Society).

44. Johnson, "English Puritan Thought on the Ends of Marriage," pp. 3, 5, 7-8. For more of Johnson's ideas and findings in this regard, see "The Covenant Idea and the Puritan View of Marriage," *Journal of the History of Ideas* 32 (January-March 1971) and *A Society Ordained by God: English Puritan Marriage Doctrine in the First Half of the Seventeenth Century* (Nashville, 1970).

45. *The Writings of Henry David Thoreau*, II (Boston, 1906), 150. This expression came, of course, in the "Solitude" chapter of *Walden*.

46. Mrs. Lucy Furber Diary, November 24, 1855, Pierce F. Furber and Family Papers (Minnesota Historical Society).

47. Lawrence A. Cremin, *The American Common School: An Historic Conception* (New York, 1951), pp. 16-17.

48. Lewis Campbell Diaries, February 24, 1858 (Manuscripts Division, Iowa Historical Library, Iowa Department of History and Archives).

49. "Corban Miscellany," Vol. 1, No. 2 (January 1843), William H. Houlton and Family Papers (Minnesota Historical Society).

50. John R. Cummins Diary, June 15, 1855, John R. Cummins Papers, 1850-1916 (Minnesota Historical Society).

51. George B. Hunt and Family Papers (Minnesota Historical Society). This item is in a file containing "Children's essays and Certificates."

52. Michael Katz, *The Irony of Early American School Reform: Educational Innovation in Mid-Nineteenth Century Massachusetts* (Cambridge, Mass., 1968), pp. 118, 121, 142.

53. Jean McArthur, "A Lebanon Farmer in the 1830's," *Connecticut Historical Society Bulletin* 30 (January 1965), 18.

54. Espy Family Papers, 1800-1900 (Western Historical Manuscripts Collection, University of Missouri, Columbia).

55. Theron, Juliette, and Fanny Barber to Lawrence Parker, February 1, 1846, Barbour-Parker Family Letters (Collection of Regional History, Cornell University). In this letter to her son-in-law, Fanny Barber saw fit to sign the names of two of her children as well as her own.

56. Spinney-Hunt-Wildes Papers (Maine Historical Society).

57. Walter B. Foster Journal, 1841-1845, March 12, 1844 (Missouri Historical Society).

58. John B. Orton Diaries, 1845-1907, November 21, 1846 (Manuscripts Division, New York Public Library).

59. Edward Bellamy, "With the Eyes Shut," in *The Blindman's World and Other Stories* (New York, 1898), p. 347.

60. Merle Curti, *The Growth of American Thought*, 3d ed. (New York, 1964), p. 347.

61. F. N. Boney (ed.), "Southern Sojourn: A Yankee Salesman in Ante-bellum Alabama," *Alabama Review* 20 (April 1967), p. 145.

62. Elias Daggy Diary, May 8, 1850 (Minnesota Historical Society).

63. Daniel Boorstin, *The Americans: The National Experience* (New York, 1965), p. 65.

64. Ralph Henry Gabriel, *The Course of American Democratic Thought* (New York, 1956), p. 3.

65. Mildred Throne (ed.), "The California Journey of George D. Magoon, 1852-1854," *Iowa Journal of History* 54 (April 1956), 140.

66. Josiah B. Chancy Diary, September 23, 1851, Josiah B. Chaney Papers, 1792-1917 (Minnesota Historical Society).

67. Lucretia Fruit to Catharine M. Goddard, July 20, 1846, Orrin F. Smith and Family Papers, 1829-1932 (Minnesota Historical Society).

68. Kate Milner Rabb, "A Hoosier Listening Post," *Indianapolis Star*, May 25, 1930. This item in the series derived from the diary of twenty-year-old Samuel Chew Madden. I came upon this series in the Indiana Division of the Indiana State Library.

69. William R. Morgan to Mother, August 30, 1852, William R. Morgan Collection (Huntington Library).

70. Charles L. Camp (ed.), "The Journal of Benjamin Dore, One of the Argonauts," *California Historical Society Quarterly* 2 (July 1923), 128.

71. *Pierre, or, The Ambiguities*, Book XX, Part 1.

72. John Savage Diaries, February 29, March 1 and 2, 1860 (Manuscripts Division, Iowa Historical Library, Iowa Department of History and Archives.

73. Andrew Jackson Sterrett to Brother, March 1, 1859, Andrew Jackson Sterrett Papers (Minnesota Historical Society).

74. Joseph Workman to Benjamin Workman, June 16, 1844, Benjamin F. Workman Papers (State of Mississippi, Department of Archives and History).

75. Minutes of the Alder Creek Paulemic, December 23 and 30, 1840, and January 13, 1841, Jesse Corn Family Papers (Indiana Historical Society).

76. Minutes of the Mount Hope Debating Society, December 22, 1856, to April 8, 1857, Leander Crawford and Louisa (Canfield) Purdy, *Collectors*. Family Papers (Collection of Regional History, Cornell University).

77. "A Glimpse of Early Merrimac," *Wisconsin Magazine of History* 29 (September 1945), 87.

78. Henry Atwater Note Book, Plymouth, Connecticut, 1836-1846 (Connecticut State Library).

79. Carl Russell Fish, *The Rise of the Common Man, 1830-1850* (New York, 1927), pp. 19, 59.

80. Fred Lewis Pattee, *The Feminine Fifties* (New York, 1940), pp. 9, 45. Grace Adams and Edward Hutter told us of *The Mad Forties* (New York, 1942).

81. Fish, *The Rise of the Common Man*, p. 78.

82. Carrie Ward Campbell Letters, March 29, 1846 (Indiana Historical Society).

83. James McBeath Family Papers (Minnesota Historical Society).

84. Claire Warner Churchill (ed.), "The Journey to Oregon—A Pioneer Girl's Diary," *Oregon Historical Quarterly* 29 (March 1928), 78.

85. Henry Beeson Flanner Family Correspondence (Indiana Historical Society).

86. Unidentified Daily Journal kept on a voyage from New York to San Francisco in 1848, April 29, 1848 (New-York Historical Society).

87. Mrs. A. Marquam to Mrs. Mary J. Bass, February 5, 1856, Joel Crane and Eunice Fitch Family Correspondence (Indiana Historical Society).

88. Anna Brockway Gray (compiler), "Letters from the Long Ago," *Michigan History Magazine* 13 (Summer 1929), 479.

89. Nathan E. Parkhill Diaries, 1852-1901, April 2, August 11, November 4, 1856, August 11, 1857 (Vermont Historical Society).

90. Isaac S. Barr Penmanship Book, Mrs. I. S. Barr Manuscripts (Manuscripts Division, Alabama Department of Archives and History).

91. Richard Rollins, "Words as Social Control: Noah Webster and the Creation of the *American Dictionary*," *American Quarterly* 28 (Fall 1976), 417.

92. E. Douglas Branch, *The Sentimental Years, 1836-1860* (New York, 1934), p. 132.

93. "The Snow Storm." This distressing item was marked *agitato* and was done in that fashion by the Hutchinson family singers and others. See Philip D. Jordan and Lillian Kessler, *Songs of Yesterday: A Song Anthology of American Life* (Garden City, N.Y., 1941), pp. 82-86.

94. Henry W. Dean to Mrs. Henry W. Dean, June 9, 1847, Lyman Stuart *Collector*. Stampless Covers (Collection of Regional History, Cornell University).

95. Rosanna McCullough Copy Book (South Caroliniana Library, Columbia, South Carolina).

96. Francis W. Squires Diaries, January 19, 1855 (Collection of Regional History, Cornell University).

97. Henry James, "The Art of Fiction," in *Partial Portraits* (London, 1911), pp. 377-79.

98. Terence Martin, *The Instructed Vision: Scottish Common Sense Philosophy and the Origins of American Fiction* (Bloomington, Ind., 1961), p. 158.

99. Ephraim Thompson to My Very Dear Mother, June 18, 1854, in Philip L. Cantelon (ed.), "The California Gold Fields in the 1850s: Letters from Ephraim Thompson, Daviess County, Indiana," *Indiana Magazine of History* 65 (September 1969), 169.

100. Jennie Akehurst to Sylvanus Lines, July 4, 1858, Akehurst-Lines Collection (Division of Special Collections, University of Georgia Libraries).

101. Mary E. Copp Composition Book, Daniel Dennison Copp Letters (Manuscript Department, William R. Perkins Library, Duke University).

102. Alice Felt Tyler, "A New England Family on the Illinois Frontier," *Papers in Illinois History and Transactions for the Year 1942* (Springfield, Ill., 1944), p. 86.

103. M. H. Abrams, *The Mirror and the Lamp: Romantic Theory and the Critical Tradition* (New York, 1953), p. viii.

104. Constance Rourke, *American Humor: A Study of the National Character* (New York, 1931), p. 9.

105. Matthiessen, *American Renaissance*, pp. 603, 637.

106. Edmund Wilson, *Patriotic Gore: Studies in the Literature of the American Civil War*, Galaxy Paper Edition (New York, 1966), pp. 509-10.

107. James Jones to Mother, July 19, 1858, James T. Jones Papers, JTJ 61 (Huntington Library).

108. Kenneth S. Lynn, *The Comic Tradition in America* (Garden City, N.Y., 1958), p. xii.

109. Andrew Jackson Sterrett to Brother (probably Innis), March 1, 1859; Andrew Jackson Sterrett to Innis Sterrett, October 28, 1859, Andrew Jackson Sterrett Papers (Minnesota Historical Society).

110. "Mount-a-cellar February 9, 1858," William H. Houlton and Family Papers (Minnesota Historical Society).

111. Marie Ester Brandt Diary, February 5, 1850 (Indiana Historical Society).

112. Gilbert Garner to William S. Johnson, May 10, 1847, William S. Johnson Letters (South Caroliniana Library, Columbia, South Carolina).

113. Mary Daggett Lake (ed.), "A Diary of the Travels of William G. Randle, Daguerreotypist, of Henry County, Tennessee 1852," *Tennessee Historical Magazine* 9 (October 1925), 204-205.

114. "The Desisision of the Friends of J. B. Clark on a Report," John B. Clark Papers (Kentucky Historical Society).

115. D. A. Cary to Joshua Lipscomb, January 12, 1860, Lipscomb Family Papers (Southern Historical Collection, University of North Carolina).

116. Thomas Maitland Marshall (ed.), "The Journal of Henry B. Miller," *Missouri Historical Society Collections* 6 (1932), 274.

117. Bernard De Voto, *The Literary Fallacy* (Boston, 1944).

118. *Life on the Mississippi*, Chapter 3.

119. Daniel Boorstin, *The Americans: The Colonial Experience* (New York, 1958), p. 290.

120. Richard Weaver, *The Ethics of Rhetoric*, Gateway Paperback Edition (Chicago, 1953), pp. 164, 166-67, 172, 182, 185.

121. *The Complete Works of Ralph Waldo Emerson*, Concord Edition (Boston, 1903), I, 334.

122. John W. Ward, *Andrew Jackson: Symbol for an Age* (New York, 1955), p. 173.

123. Mary Conkling to Enos Conkling, —— 28, 1859, Enos Conkling Correspon-

dence, 1837-1888 (New-York Historical Society).

124. H. E. Hewes to William H. Garland, February 28, 1844, William H. Garland Papers (Southern Historical Collection, University of North Carolina).

125. George N. Wheeler Journal, July 4, 1850, HM16939 (Huntington Library).

126. *Complete Works of Ralph Waldo Emerson*, III, 45, 48-49.

127. Ibid., p. 49.

128. George E. Boaz to W. D. Boaz, October 22, 1858, William Davis Boaz Papers (Manuscripts Division, Alabama Department of Archives and History).

129. James Bell to Augusta Hallock, November 4, 1855, James Alvin Bell Collection (Huntington Library).

130. Marco G. Thorne (ed.), "Bound for the Land of Canaan, Ho! The Diary of Levi Stowell," *California Historical Society Quarterly* 27 (December 1948), 363.

131. Douglas T. Miller, *The Birth of Modern America 1820-1850*, Pegasus Paperback Edition (New York, 1970), p. 66.

132. Zuar Jameson Diaries, December 5, 1855, and January 5, 1856 (Vermont Historical Society).

133. Smith Collection (Six Vault, Georgia Department of Archives and History). This unsigned item is in a folder of miscellaneous poetry.

134. Edward D. Jervey and James E. Moss (eds.), "From Virginia to Missouri in 1846: The Journal of Elizabeth Ann Cooley," *Missouri Historical Review* 60 (January 1966), 166, 167, 168, 206.

Chapter 6

1. Allen F. Davis, "The Girl He Left Behind: The Letters of Harriet Hutchinson Salisbury," *Vermont History* 23 (January 1965), 274-75.

2. Chase Mooney (ed.), "Some Letters from Dover, Tennessee, 1814-1855," *Tennessee Historical Quarterly* 8 (June 1949), 155.

3. Oren Lee Diary and Journal, April 27 and May 2, 1832 (Connecticut State Library). The assessment of this document made by State Librarian George Godard is pasted on the front of it.

4. *The Complete Works of Ralph Waldo Emerson*, Autograph Centenary Edition (Boston, 1903), I, 143.

5. Jacques Ellul, *The Political Illusion*, Trans. Konrad Kellen (New York, 1967), p. 187.

6. Carl Russell Fish, *The Rise of the Common Man, 1830-1850* (New York, 1927), p. 163.

7. Ibid., p. 179.

8. William Spinney to Dear Sister, May 21, 1855, Spinney-Hunt-Wildes Papers (Maine Historical Society).

9. Fred Landon, "Extracts from the Diary of William C. King, A Detroit Carpenter, in 1832," *Michigan History Magazine* 19 (Winter 1935), 67.

10. H. M. Snyder to W. Moore, June 29, 1860, James F. Ballard Papers (Indiana Historical Society).

11. Rodney Loehr, "Some Sources for Northwest History: Minnesota Farmers' Diaries," *Minnesota History: A Quarterly Magazine* 18 (September 1937), 295-96.

12. William Jackson to Freegift Tuthill, March 20, 1840, Freegift Tuthill Papers (Collection of Regional History, Cornell University).

13. William and Mary Ireland to David and Maryann Ireland, June 15, 1851, James Ireland Family Correspondence (Indiana Historical Society).

14. ——— Campbell to Leander Campbell, November 14, 1860, Leander Melbourne Campbell Collection (Indiana Historical Society).

15. George Santayana, *Character and Opinion in the United States*, W. W. Norton Paperback (New York, 1967), p. 206.

16. Andrew Jackson Sterrett to Brother, March 1, 1859, Andrew Jackson Sterrett Papers (Minnesota Historical Society).

17. Minutes of the Mount Hope Debating Society, February 16, 1857, December 3, 1860, February 18, March 4, December 23, 1861, Leander Crawford and Louisa (Canfield) Purdy, *Collectors*. Family Papers (Collection of Regional History).

18. T.S.E., "Liberty" (school composition of July 4, 1835), Espy Family Papers (Western Historical Manuscripts Collection, University of Missouri, Columbia).

19. George Wurts, "Journal of a Tour to Niagara Falls, Montreal, Lake Champlain, &c.," *Proceedings of the New Jersey Historical Society* 69 (October 1951), 347.

20. Seth C. Whitehouse Journal, November 25, 1849 (Maine Historical Society).

21. *White Jacket or The World in a Man-of-War*, Chapter 56.

22. Whitehouse Journal, December 1, 9, and 23, 1849.

23. Oscar Osburn Winther and Rose Dodge Galey (eds.), "Mrs. Butler's 1853 Diary of Rogue River Valley," *Oregon Historical Quarterly* 41 (December 1940), 350.

24. *Its Practice and Purpose* (Baltimore, 1970), pp. 34-35.

25. *Clio and the Doctors: Psycho-History, Quanto-History and History* (Chicago, 1974), pp. 136-37.

26. Isaac and Lucy Carr to Caleb Carr and others, May 10, 1857, Caleb M. Carr Letters (Collection of Regional History, Cornell University).

27. John B. Orton Diaries, 1845-1907, July 4, 1845 (Manuscripts Division, New York Public Library).

28. Henry Putnam Diary and Account Book, 1836-1839, July 4, 1839 (New-York Historical Society). Internal evidence suggests that Henry Putnam was not the writer of this document.

29. Nathan Butler Diary, July 3 to July 10, 1859, Nathan Butler Papers, 1859-1923 (Minnesota Historical Society).

30. "Journal of a Tour to Niagara Falls," p. 343.

31. Howard H. Martin, "The Fourth of July Oration," *Quarterly Journal of Speech* 44 (December 1958), 393-401.

32. [George William Curtis], *Harper's New Monthly Magazine* 41 (September 1870), 616.

33. Barnet Baskerville, "19th Century Burlesque of Oratory," *American Quarterly* 20 (Winter 1968). See also Edmund Pearson, *Queer Books* (Garden City, N.Y., 1928), Chapter 2.

34. John Kouwenhoven, *The Beer Can by the Highway: Essays on What's "American" about America* (Garden City, N.Y., 1961), p. 30.

35. Arthur Ekirch, *The Idea of Progress in America, 1815-1860*, No. 511 of Columbia University Studies in History, Economics and Public Law (New York, 1944), p. 267.

36. Robert Riegel, *Young America, 1830-1840* (Norman, Okla., 1949); Merle

Curti, "'Young America,'" *American Historical Review* 32 (October 1926); Perry Miller, *The Raven and the Whale: The War of Words and Wits in the Era of Poe and Melville* (New York, 1956), Book II. See also John Stafford, *The Literary Criticism of 'Young America': A Study in the Relationship of Politics and Literature 1837-1850*, No. 3 in University of California Publications: English Studies (Berkeley, Calif., 1952).

37. Miller, *The Raven and the Whale*, p. 101.

38. John D. Black Diaries (Indiana Division of the Indiana State Library).

39. John E. Giddings to George [Francis Nourse], April 18, 1853, George Francis Nourse Collection (Huntington Library).

40. James Amsted Brown Diary, 1858-1860, January 9 and February 28, 1858 (Vermont Historical Society).

41. *Complete Works of Ralph Waldo Emerson*, I, 363.

42. *Pierre, or, The Ambiguities*, Book XVII. The daguerreotypical assertion appears in Section 3 of this book.

43. Joseph Baldwin, *The Flush Times of Alabama and Mississippi: A Series of Sketches* (New York, 1853), pp. 128-30.

44. Mortimer Thomson [Q. K. Philander Doesticks], *Pluri-bus-tah: A Song That's-By-No-Author* (New York, 1856), pp. 246, 260-61.

45. Merle Curti, "Young America," p. 55.

46. Roy F. Nichols, *The Disruption of American Democracy*, Collier Books Edition (New York, 1962), pp. 503-504.

47. David Donald, "An Excess of Democracy: The American Civil War and the Social Process," *Centennial Review* 5 (Winter 1961).

48. F. E. White to Dear L. C., July 17, 1859, Upshaw Collection (Division of Special Collections, University of Georgia Libraries).

49. Elmer Munson Hunt (ed.), "The Gold Rush Diary of Moses Cogswell of New Hampshire," *Historical New Hampshire* (December 1949), 39.

50. Abel and S. Holton to Nathan and Maryann, October 31, 1858, Haile Family Papers (Vermont Historical Society).

51. Michael Fleenan Luark Diary, 1846-1899, September 18, 1852 (University of Washington Manuscript Collection).

52. Seaborn Jones to Jeremiah Warren, October 2, 1844, Morgan D. Jones Letters (Manuscript Division, Alabama Department of Archives and History).

53. New York City Diary, 1844-1845, by an unknown clerk, October 13 to November 15, 1844 (Manuscripts Division, New York Public Library).

54. Henry A. Patterson Diaries, 1836-1849, October 10, 1837 (New-York Historical Society).

55. "Journal of Cyrus Sanders," *Iowa Journal of History and Politics* 37 (January 1939), 74, 76.

56. Thomas Maitland Marshall (ed.), "The Journal of Henry B. Miller," *Missouri Historical Society Collections* 6 (1931), 222-23, 261-65.

57. Winthrop Jordan, "Familial Politics: Thomas Paine and the Killing of the King, 1776," *Journal of American History* 60 (September 1973), 305.

58. Edwin Olmsted Diary, March 8, 1845 (Connecticut State Library).

59. Ibid., October 28, 1844.

60. J. F. Santee (ed.), "Letters of John R. Tice," *Oregon Historical Quarterly* 37 (March 1936), 28.

61. Donald, "An Excess of Democracy," p. 35.

62. John B. Orton Diaries, 1845-1907, July 4, 1845 (Manuscripts Division, New York Public Library).

63. LeRoy P. Graf (ed.), "The Journal of a Vermont Man in Ohio, 1836-1842," *Ohio State Archaeological and Historical Quarterly* 60 (April 1951), 193.

64. Robert H. Goodell (ed.), "Matthias Zahm's Diary," *Papers of the Lancaster County Historical Society* 47 (No. 4, 1943), 77.

65. Rush Welter, *The Mind of America, 1820-1860* (New York, 1975), pp. 416-17.

66. John W. Ward, "Jacksonian Democratic Thought: 'A Natural Charter of Privilege,'" in Stanley Coben and Lorman Ratner (eds.), *The Development of American Culture* (Englewood Cliffs, N.J., 1970), p. 50.

67. Welter, *The Mind of America*, pp. 185-87, 409, 419.

68. Ibid., pp. 185, 206, 216.

69. Graf (ed.), "Journal of a Vermont Man," p. 197.

70. John Barber to Lawrence Parker, June 15, 1844, Barbour-Parker Family Letters (Collection of Regional History, Cornell University).

71. Welter, *The Mind of America*, p. 232.

72. Mary Daggett Lake (ed.), "A Diary of the Travels of William G. Randle, Daguerreotypist, of Henry County, Tennessee, 1852," *Tennessee Historical Magazine* 9 (October 1925), 198.

73. Andrew Jackson Sterrett to Dear Brother, November 25, 1856, Andrew Jackson Sterrett Papers (Minnesota Historical Society).

74. Goodell (ed.), "Matthias Zahm's Diary," p. 77.

75. Thomas Jefferson Ingersoll to Richard Ingersoll, August 18, 1843, and Thomas Jefferson Ingersoll to Mrs. Ann Ingersoll (Richard's wife), August 1844, Thomas Jefferson Ingersoll Letters (Collection of Regional History, Cornell University).

76. Donald, "An Excess of Democracy," p. 35.

77. Goodell (ed.), "Matthias Zahm's Diary," pp. 76-91.

78. Thomas Jefferson Ingersoll to Richard Ingersoll, August 18, 1843, Thomas Jefferson Ingersoll Letters (Collection of Regional History, Cornell University).

79. Mooney (ed.), "Some Letters from Dover, Tennessee," p. 357.

80. Horatio N. Chandler Account Book, October 19, November 29, December 14 and 15, 1840, and February 3 and 27 and March 4, 1841 (New Hampshire Historical Society).

81. Walter S. Merrell Journal, January 7 and February 9, 1847 (Connecticut State Library).

82. George Sidney Camp, *Democracy* (New York, 1859), p. 180.

83. Lois W. Banner, "Religious Benevolence as Social Control: A Critique of an Interpretation," *Journal of American History* 60 (June 1973).

84. William H. Houlton and Family Papers (Minnesota Historical Society).

85. *An Essay on Man*, Epistle II, line 266.

86. Carl Degler, *Out of Our Past: The Forces That Shaped Modern America* (New York, 1959), p. 153.

87. Archibald B. Knode Diary, April 16, 1834, Archibald B. Knode Papers, Diaries and Account Books (Indiana Historical Society).

88. Mary Paul to Bela Paul, September 13, 1845; November 20, 1845; December 21, 1845; April 12, 1846; November 5, 1848; November 7, 1852; November 27, 1853;

December 18, 1853; May 7, 1854; October 2, 1854; March 3, 1855; April 15, 1855; December 27, 1857 and March 29, 1858, Mary Paul Letters (Vermont Historical Society).

89. John R. Cummins Diary, February 1, 1855, John R. Cummins Papers, 1850-1916 (Minnesota Historical Society).

90. Andrew Jackson Sterrett Diary, July 31, 1856, Andrew Jackson Sterrett Papers (Minnesota Historical Society).

91. Mary Paul Guild to Bela Paul, March 6, 1859, Mary Paul Letters (Vermont Historical Society).

92. Ira Coolidge to Bela Paul, September 22, 1844, Mary Paul Letters (Vermont Historical Society).

93. Minutes of a meeting of the Daughters of Temperance, March 8, 1852; Selina Hervey's committee report of the efforts to secure new curtains for the "Division room" of the "Economy Union of the Daughters of Temperance," May 7, 1852; Hannah Coffin and Adaline Wright Address to "Dear Sisters," probably 1852, Thomas Marshall Family Correspondence (Indiana Historical Society).

94. Donald E. Baker (ed.), "The Conine Family Letters, 1852-1863; 'Just Think How We Are Scattered,'" *Indiana Magazine of History* 70 (June, 1974), 168.

95. Jackson Thomason Diary, April 13, 1849 (State of Mississippi, Department of Archives and History).

96. Henry Putnam Diary and Account Book, 1836-1839, September 30 and December 31, 1839 (New-York Historical Society).

97. Baker (ed.), "The Conine Family Letters," p. 124.

98. Thomas Jefferson Ingersoll to Richard Ingersoll, November 25, 1847, Thomas Jefferson Ingersoll Letters (Collection of Regional History, Cornell University).

99. William Hoffman Diary, 1847-1850, March 20 and July 7, 1848 (New-York Historical Society).

100. James Amsted Brown Diary, 1858-1860, April 30, 1858 (Vermont Historical Society).

101. Augusta Hallock to James Bell, April 3, 1856, James Alvin Bell Collection (Huntington Library).

102. Martha B. Caldwell (ed.), "The Diary of George H. Hildt, June to December, 1857: Pioneer of Johnson County," *Kansas Historical Quarterly* 10 (August 1941).

103. "The Diary of James R. Stewart, Pioneer of Osage County," Part II, *Kansas Historical Quarterly* 17 (May 1949), 151-52. This diary appears in the February, May, August, and November 1949 issues of the *Kansas Historical Quarterly*.

104. Edgar Langsdorf (ed.), "The Letters of Joseph H. Trego, 1857-1864, Linn County Pioneer," *Kansas Historical Quarterly* 19 (May 1951), 120.

105. Andrew Jackson Sterrett to Dear Brother, November 25, 1856, Andrew Jackson Sterrett Papers (Minnesota Historical Society).

106. Howard Mitcham (ed.), "A Mississippian in the Gold Fields: The Letters of John Paul Dart, 1849-1856," *California Historical Society Quarterly* 35 (September, 1956), 208-209.

107. Langsdorf (ed.), "Letters of Joseph H. Trego," p. 127.

108. John Kinkade to James Kinkade, September 23, 1860, John Thompson Kinkade Collection, KI 74 (Huntington Library).

109. Carl I. Wheat (ed.), "'California's Bantam Cock': The Journals of Charles E. DeLong, 1854-1863," *California Historical Society Quarterly* 8 (September 1929), 202.

110. Francis W. Squires Diaries, August 4, 1860 (Collection of Regional History, Cornell University).

111. "Chippings with a Chisel," *Twice-Told Tales*, Vol. II, Old Manse Edition (Boston, 1900), 240-41.

112. Frances P. Warren to Mrs. Mary A. Espy, April 18, 1841, Espy Family Papers, 1800-1900 (Western Historical Manuscripts Collection, University of Missouri, Columbia).

113. Margaret M. Laird to Miss Lucretia Fruit, n.d., Orrin F. Smith and Family Papers, 1829-1932 (Minnesota Historical Society).

114. Archibald B. Knode Diary, August 5 and October 16, 1834, Archibald B. Knode Papers, Diaries and Account Books (Indiana Historical Society).

115. Edward F. Travis Diary, 1843-1847, June 24, 1845 (Manuscripts Division, New York Public Library).

116. Mary Covey Hale to Mrs. L. A. Peck, May 9, 1841, Peck Family Letters (Collection of Regional History).

117. Act II, Scene 1, lines 11-12.

118. Francis W. Squires Diaries, October 26, 1852 (Collection of Regional History, Cornell University). In the October 26 entry (two days after Webster's death), Squires noted his passing. The quoted passage specifying the time was written at the top of the page, perhaps later than the 26th.

119. "Rochester," *Complete Works of Nathaniel Hawthorne*, Riverside Edition, 12 (Boston, 1883), 17-18.

120. Louise Fogle (ed.), "Journal of Ebenezer Mattoon Chamberlain," *Indiana Magazine of History*, 15 (September 1919), 236.

121. "Sam Patch, Jumping Hero," *New York Folklore Quarterly*, 1 (1945), 150.

122. Benjamin Hodge to Lyman Hodge, November 5, 1852, Benjamin Hodge Papers (Huntington Library).

123. Irving Bartlett, "Daniel Webster as a Symbolic Hero," *New England Quarterly: A Historical Review of New England Life and Letters* 45 (December 1972), 507.

124. *Macbeth*, Act. I, Scene iv, lines 7-8.

125. Michael Fleenan Luark Diary, 1846-1899, December 27 and 31, 1860, and January 1, 1861 (University of Washington Manuscript Collection).

126. Quoted in William R. Taylor, *Cavalier and Yankee: The Old South and American National Character* (London, 1963), p. 238. See also Jay B. Hubbell, *The South in American Literature, 1607-1900* (Durham, N.C., 1954), pp. 375-85, and Clement Eaton, *The Mind of the Old South*, revised edition (Baton Rouge, La., 1967), pp. 65-67.

127. M. Gladden to J. Cassil, July 21, 1837, John Thompson Kinkade Collection, KI 17 (Huntington Library).

128. Garrit Striker Mott to S. C. Mott, December 24, 1835; L. Mott to G.(arrit) S.(triker) Mott, April 7, 1836 and —— to My Dear Son (Garrit Striker Mott), May 19, 1836, Mott Family Papers (New-York Historical Society).

129. Joseph Workman to Benjamin Workman, June 16, 1844, Benjamin F. Workman Papers (State of Mississippi, Department of Archives and History).

130. Jennie Akehurst to Mr. Lines, February 17, 1858, Akehurst-Lines Collection

(Division of Special Collections, University of Georgia Libraries).

131. Fanny Barber to Lawrence Parker, October 30, 1834, January 1, 1835, and May 7, 1836; and Lawrence Parker to Fanny Barber, August 30, 1835, Barbour-Parker Family Letters (Collection of Regional History, Cornell University).

132. Walter B. Foster Journal, 1841-1845, December 26, 1841 (Missouri Historical Society).

133. Ronald G. Walters, "The Erotic South: Civilization and Sexuality in American Abolitionism," *American Quarterly* 25 (May 1973), 200.

134. Ibid., p. 195.

135. Ibid., p. 182.

136. C. M. and A. S. Goddard to Lucretia Fruit, February 10, 1847, Orrin F. Smith and Family Papers, 1829-1932 (Minnesota Historical Society).

137. James A. Padgett (ed.), "A Yankee School Teacher in Louisiana, 1835-1837: The Diary of Caroline B. Poole," *Louisiana Historical Quarterly* 20 (July 1937), 655-56.

138. Fanny Barber to Lawrence Parker, December 25, 1836, and February 4, 1837, and Lawrence Parker to Fanny Barber, January 14, 1837, Barbour-Parker Family Letters (Collection of Regional History, Cornell University).

139. Sister Emma to My Dear Brother (probably December 1, 1856), Sherman-Safford Papers (Vermont Historical Society).

140. Jennie Akehurst to Mr. Lines, February 17, 1858, Akehurst-Lines Collection (Division of Special Collections, University of Georgia Libraries).

141. Marshall (ed.), "Journal of Henry B. Miller," p. 286.

142. Jonathan and Fanny L. Waterbury to Respected Brother and Sister, September 11, 1854, Berry Collection (Collection of Regional History, Cornell University).

143. Joseph Williams to Destamona Williams, December 28, 1851, Robert Williams Collection (Division of Special Collections, University of Georgia Libraries).

144. Andrew Jackson Sterrett to Innis, September 29, 1857, Andrew Jackson Sterrett Papers (Minnesota Historical Society).

145. Robert C. Toll, *Blacking Up: The Minstrel Show in Nineteenth-Century America* (New York, 1974), pp. 86-87.

146. Andrew Jackson Sterrett to Innis, September 4, 1858, Andrew Jackson Sterrett Papers (Minnesota Historical Society).

147. Mrs. Lucy Furber Diary, December 4, 1855, Pierce F. Furber and Family Papers (Minnesota Historical Society).

148. John Eagle to wife, March 12, 1853 and John Eagle and —— to Mrs. Eagle and ——, May 27, 1853, John H. Eagle Correspondence, EGL 18 and 23 (Huntington Library).

149. John R. Cummins Diary, December 29, 1856, John R. Cummins Papers, 1850-1916 (Minnesota Historical Society).

150. Louis Hartz, *The Liberal Tradition in America* (New York, 1955), p. 40. In Hartz's work, that was not an informing precept, as it has been in the present study.

151. Sidney Glazer (ed.), "In Old Detroit (1831-1836)," *Michigan History Magazine* 26 (Spring 1942), 206-207.

152. Sarah Woolsey Johnson Diaries, November 2, 6, and December 18, 1860 (New-York Historical Society).

153. Pauline H. Stratton Diary, 1841-1870, November 29 and December 27 to 31, 1860 (Western Historical Manuscripts Collection, University of Missouri, Columbia).

The letter containing the acceptance of marriage proposal—Pauline ——— to Thomas L. Stratton, December 15, 1841—is filed as part of the diary.

Chapter 7

1. Ira McCall to John M. and Polly Hanford, February 3, 1841, Hanford Family Letters (Collection of Regional History, Cornell University).
2. Marjorie Hope Nicolson, *Mountain Gloom and Mountain Glory: The Development of the Aesthetics of the Infinite* (Ithaca, N.Y., 1959), p. 95.
3. *An Essay on Man*, Epistle I, lines 289-92.
4. Ibid., Epistle IV, line 331.
5. Hattie Kendall to Cousin Willie, March 15, 1857, William H. Houlton and Family Papers (Minnesota Historical Society).
6. Part II, line 98.
7. James M. Day (ed.), "Diary of James A. Glasscock, Mier Man," *Texana* 1 (Spring 1963), 94.
8. Henry Starr Diary, June 21, 1850 (Indiana Division of the Indiana State Library).
9. Thomas Reber Diaries, June 20, 1854 (Collection of Regional History, Cornell University).
10. Ibid., August 12, 1854.
11. Chapter II, Section 1.
12. William Hoffman Diary, 1847-1850, March 19, 1848 (New-York Historical Society).
13. J. M. Wampler to Jefferson Martenet, August 30, 1852, Jefferson Martenet Collection (Huntington Library).
14. Samuel Nichols to Wife and Sons, March 28, 1850, Samuel Nichols Collection (Huntington Library).
15. Michael Fleenan Luark Diary, 1846-1899, May 31, 1860 (University of Washington Manuscript Collection).
16. Charlotte Whipple to Dear Mary Ann, November 9, 1852, Charlotte L. Whipple Diaries (Manuscripts Division, New York Public Library).
17. Charlotte L. Whipple Diaries, April 30 and May 2 and 3, 1847 (Manuscripts Division, New York Public Library).
18. E.A.B. Phelps to Samuel W. Phelps, April 3, 1847, and February 20, 1848, Edward Ashley Bowen Phelps Letters and Diary, 1847-1848 (Manuscripts Division, New York Public Library).
19. Diary of a journey from Catskill, N.Y. to New York, thence by water to Mobil and Portland, Alabama, November 4, 1840 (Manuscripts Division, New York Public Library). The diarist's surname was DuBois, and it is catalogued accordingly.
20. Charles Rich to Albina Rich, September 26, 1854, Rich Family Papers (Maine Historical Society).
21. "Children's essays and certificates," George B. Hunt and Family Papers (Minnesota Historical Society).
22. Elias Daggy Diary, May 22 and 23 and June 10, 1850 (Minnesota Historical Society).

23. "Journal of A. W. Harlan While Crossing the Plains in 1850," *Annals of Iowa*, Third Series, 11 (April 1913), 33-34.

24. Roderick Nash, *Wilderness and the American Mind* (New Haven, Conn., 1967), p. 1.

25. Ibid., pp. 24, 29.

26. Lewis Mumford, *The Golden Day: A Study in American Experience and Culture* (New York, 1926), p. 56. This comes from the chapter titled "The Romanticism of the Pioneer."

27. *The Confidence-Man: His Masquerade*, Chapter 21.

28. "Fate," *The Complete Works of Ralph Waldo Emerson* (Cambridge, Mass., 1904), VI, 6-8.

29. John W. Ward, *Andrew Jackson: Symbol for an Age* (New York, 1955), p. 33.

30. Leo Marx, *The Machine in the Garden: Technology and the Pastoral Ideal in America* (New York, 1964), pp. 11-16.

31. Zuar Jameson Diaries (1855-1865), September 17, 1855 (Vermont Historical Society). This lengthy entry describing the trip apparently was written after the return to Irasburgh.

32. Peter Beaver to Aaron C. Nevius, February 17, 1845, Orrin F. Smith and Family Papers, 1829-1932 (Minnesota Historical Society).

33. Milo Holcomb to Nahum Holcomb and Nahum Holcomb, Jr., January 29, 1831, Holcomb Family Letters (Connecticut State Library). It is evident that the cited portion of the letter was addressed to Milo's younger brother, Nahum, Jr.

34. Ibid.

35. Chapter III, Verse 1.

36. Mary E. Copp Composition Book, Daniel Dennison Copp Letters (Manuscript Division, William R. Perkins Library, Duke University). The context indicates that this composition was written in either 1847 or 1848.

37. Fanny Fryatt School Notebook (Collection of Regional History, Cornell University). These items were composed in 1854 and 1855.

38. Seth C. Whitehouse Journal, January 9, 1850 (Maine Historical Society).

39. Lines 612-13.

40. Josiah B. Chaney Diary, September 13, 1845, Josiah B. Chaney Papers, 1792-1917 (Minnesota Historical Society).

41. J. B. Bury, *The Idea of Progress: An Inquiry into Its Origins and Growth* (London, 1924), pp. 2, 5.

42. W. Warren Wagar, "Modern Views of the Origins of the Idea of Progress," *Journal of the History of Ideas* 28 (January-March 1967), 60, 62.

43. Isaac S. Metcalf to "Dear Ettie," July 12, 1855, Isaac S. Metcalf Letters (Minnesota Historical Society).

44. Charles Rich to Albina Rich, December 10, 1853, Rich Family Papers (Maine Historical Society).

45. Papers of Abiathar Hubbard Watkins and Emily Lewis Watkins, 1836-1894 (Manuscripts Division, New York Public Library).

46. Michael Fleenan Luark Diary, 1846-1899, May 31, 1860 (University of Washington Manuscript Collection).

47. Marco G. Thorne (ed.), "Bound for the Land of Canaan, Ho! The Diary of Levi Stowell," *California Historical Society Quarterly* 27 (December 1948), 364. This diary appears in five segments, running from March 1948 through March 1949.

48. James T. King (ed.), "'I Take This Opportunity to Inform You . . .': The Gold Rush Letters of Andrew Cairns," *California Historical Society Quarterly* 46 (September 1967), 214.

49. Papers of Abiathar Hubbard Watkins and Emily Lewis Watkins, 1836-1894 (Manuscripts Division, New York Public Library).

50. M. B. (Maria Barnett) to George H. Barnett, July 1858, Thoma-Barnett Letters (Indiana Division of the Indiana State Library).

51. Oliver Pelton to Julia Pelton, July 23, 1854, Oliver Pelton Correspondence (Connecticut State Library).

52. Nash, *Wilderness and the American Mind*, p. 3.

53. William Hoffman Diary, 1847-1850, June 29, 1850 (New-York Historical Society).

54. Victor L. Dowdell and Helen C. Everett (eds.), "California Diary of John French, 1850-51," *Michigan History Magazine* 38 (March 1954), 34.

55. Elam Slagle to Wife, April 22, 1854, Elam Slagle Papers (Southern Historical Collection, University of North Carolina).

56. Mother to My Dear Child, November 28, 1848, Newcomb-Johnson Collection (Huntington Library).

57. Perry Miller, "The Romantic Dilemma in American Nationalism and the Concept of Nature," in *Nature's Nation* (Cambridge, Mass., 1967), p. 198. This essay was originally published in the *Harvard Theological Quarterly* 48 (October 1955), 239-53; it also appears in *Errand into the Wilderness*, Harper Torchbacks (New York, 1956), pp. 205-16, as "Nature and the National Ego."

58. Miller, "The Romantic Dilemma," pp. 199, 202.

59. James A. Padgett (ed.), "A Yankee School Teacher in Louisiana, 1835-1837: The Diary of Caroline B. Poole," *Louisiana Historical Quarterly* 20 (July 1937), 658-60.

60. Miller, "The Romantic Dilemma," p. 198.

61. Daniel H. Hunt Diary, 1854-1859, July 9 and November 4, 1857 (Minnesota Historical Society).

62. "Overland Journey to California by Platte River Route and South Pass in 1850, By Fancher Stimson," *Annals of Iowa*, Third Series, 13 (October 1922), 423.

63. Miller, "The Romantic Dilemma," p. 207.

64. Ibid.

65. Augusta Hallock to James Bell, March 1, 1857, James Alvin Bell Collection (Huntington Library).

66. See, for example, Leslie Fiedler, *The Return of the Vanishing American*, Stein and Day Paperbacks (New York, 1969), pp. 114-15.

67. *The Complete Works of Nathaniel Hawthorne*, Riverside Edition (Boston, 1882), II, 279.

68. John A. Tarr (ed.), "Philo Thompson's Diary of a Journey on the Main Line Canal," *Pennsylvania History* 32 (July 1965), 298.

69. Henry Summer Diary, February 5, 1837 (South Caroliniana Library, Columbia, South Carolina).

70. Ralph Henry Gabriel, *The Course of American Democratic Thought*, 2d ed. (New York, 1956), pp. 9-10.

71. A. F. Niles Diary, 1850, June 24, 1850 (Vermont Historical Society).

72. Manuscript Journal of a young man of Burlington (Vt.) who in 1839 journeyed to Va. and other places, June 14, 1839 (Vermont Historical Society).

73. Minutes of the Alder Creek Paulemic, December 23, 1840, Jesse Corn Family Papers (Indiana Historical Society).

74. Roland Van Zandt, *The Catskill Mountain House* (New Brunswick, N.J., 1966), p. 195.

75. Nash, *Wilderness and the American Mind*, p. 45.

76. *Lectures on Rhetoric and Belles Lettres* (London, 1806), I, 99.

77. Douglas Cole and Maria Tippett, "Pleasing Diversity and Sublime Desolation: The 18th-Century British Perception of the Northwest Coast," *Pacific Northwest Quarterly* 65 (January 1974), 2.

78. Roland Van Zandt, "The Scotch School of Aesthetic Theory and the Natural Description of *The Oregon Trail*," *The Southwestern Journal* 4 (1949), 170-71.

79. Wilbur Jacobs, "Francis Parkman's Oration 'Romance in America,'" *American Historical Review* 68 (April 1963), 696.

80. John R. Cummins Diary, June 5, 1856, John R. Cummins Papers 1850-1916 (Minnesota Historical Society).

81. Elias Daggy Diary, June 18, 1850 (Minnesota Historical Society).

82. Unidentified Daily Journal kept on a voyage from New York to San Francisco in 1848, May 27, 1848 (New-York Historical Society).

83. J. E. Chamberlin, *The Harrowing of Eden: White Attitudes Toward Native Americans* (New York, 1975), pp. 49-50.

84. "Influence of Missions on the Temporal Conditions of the Heathen," *Baptist Missionary Magazine* 29 (April 1849), 105.

85. Van Zandt, *Catskill Mountain House*, Chapters 8 and 9.

86. Lumberman's Diary, June 13, 1855 (Minnesota Historical Society).

87. John R. Cummins Diary, November 14, 1856, John R. Cummins Papers 1850-1916 (Minnesota Historical Society).

88. Orville Nixon Journal, July 9 and 16, 1855, HM17012 (Huntington Library). This item is, in fact, two separate journals, the internal evidence of which indicates that only one was written by Orville Nixon. The material cited was not, I surmise, written by Nixon.

89. William Gilpin, *Remarks on Forest Scenery, and Other Woodland Views, (Related Chiefly to Picturesque Beauty) Illustrated by the Scenes of New-Forest in Hampshire* (London, 1794), I, 262.

90. George McCowen Journal, May 20 and 28 and June 5, 1854, HM18756 (Huntington Library).

91. Van Zandt, *Catskill Mountain House*, p. 191.

92. Vincent Hoover Diary, 1849-1850, May 25 and June 22, 1849, HM27628 (Huntington Library).

93. George Boas, "In Search of the Age of Reason," in Earl R. Wasserman (ed.), *Aspects of the Eighteenth Century* (Baltimore, 1965), pp. 10-11.

94. Lines 17-20.

95. James Armstrong to Mary Nelson, May 8, 1841, John Milton Armstrong and Family Papers (Minnesota Historical Society).

96. Robert Beeching Journal, June 5, 1849, HM17430 (Huntington Library).

97. Ted and Caryl Hinckley (eds.), "Overland from St. Louis to the California Gold Field in 1849: The Diary of Joseph Waring Berrien," *Indiana Magazine of History* 56 (December, 1960), 279.

98. Alcina Baldwin to N. E. Mallory, May 24, 1840, Lyman Stuart *Collector.* Stampless Covers (Collection of Regional History, Cornell University).

99. Van Zandt, *Catskill Mountain House*, p. 200.

100. A. F. Niles Diary, July 11, 1850 (Vermont Historical Society).

101. Elias Daggy Diary, June 18, 1850 (Minnesota Historical Society).

102. Van Zandt, *Catskill Mountain House*, p. 200.

103. Edmund Burke, *A Philosophical Inquiry into the Origin of Our Ideas of the Sublime and the Beautiful*, Part I, Section 7.

104. "Mrs. Hemans's Poems," *American Quarterly Review* 1 (March 1827), 154. Italics mine.

105. Diary and Sketch Book of William Williams, May 21, 1849 (?) (Manuscripts Division, Iowa Historical Library, Iowa State Department of History and Archives).

106. Edward F. Travis Diary, 1843-1847, July 19, 1845 (Manuscripts Division, New York Public Library).

107. John Kinkade to James Kinkade and Family, November 4, 1852, John Thompson Kinkade Collection, KI45 (Huntington Library).

108. Hiram Fairchild Diary, January 25, 1837 (Connecticut State Library).

109. Levi Countryman Diary, August 1, 1858, Levi N. Countryman Papers (Minnesota Historical Society).

110. "Journal of a Trip from Brooklyn to Niagara Falls in June 1841, John Read Barrows," *New York History* 23 (April 1942), 198-99.

111. Milo Holcomb to Starr Holcomb, September 29, probably 1831, Holcomb Family Letters (Connecticut State Library).

112. "On the death of Ephraim Beeson who died in Iowa territory of the Chills and Fever in the fall of 1843," Henry Beeson Flanner Coorespondence (Indiana Historical Society).

Chapter 8

1. Howard L. Scamehorn (ed.), *The Buckeye Rovers in the Gold Rush: An Edition of Two Diaries* (Athens, Ohio, 1965), pp. xix, 10.

2. "Divinity School Address," *The Complete Works of Ralph Waldo Emerson*, Autograph Centenary Edition (Boston, 1903), I, 143.

3. William Mudd to K. Jamison, April 9, 1852, Missouri History Papers (Missouri Historical Society).

4. B. F. Drew to Sister, June 6, 1858, James M. Drew and Family Papers (Minnesota Historical Society).

5. Rowland Berthoff, *An Unsettled People: Social Order and Disorder in American History* (New York, 1971), p. 175.

6. Peter and Eliza Nevius to Aaron C. Nevius, October 30, 1856, Orrin F. Smith and Family Papers, 1829-1932 (Minnesota Historical Society).

7. Walter Lippmann, *A Preface to Morals*, Beacon Press paperback (Boston, 1960), p. 7.

8. David Morris Potter (ed.), *Trail to California: The Overland Journal of Vincent Geiger and Wakeman Bryarly* (New Haven, Conn., 1945), pp. viii-ix.

9. Loren Baritz, "The Idea of the West," *American Historical Review* 66 (April, 1961), 639.

10. Ibid.

11. Harold F. Taggart (ed.), "The Journal of David Jackson Staples," *California Historical Society Quarterly* 22 (June 1943), 119.

12. "Epistle. To Robert Earl of Oxford, and Earl Mortimer," line 26.

13. Taggart (ed.), "The Journal of Staples," 127.

14. Henry Seidel Canby, *Thoreau* (Boston, 1939), p. 206.

15. George N. Wheeler Journal, September 9, 1850, HM16939 (Huntington Library).

16. Jackson Thomason Diary, April 1, 1849 (State of Mississippi, Department of Archives and History).

17. James M. Fulkerson to T. J. Hayter, May 11, 1853, Coleman-Hayter Letters, 1840-1900 (Western Historical Manuscripts Collection, University of Missouri, Columbia).

18. Ellen Charles to Malvina Charles, November 23, 1852; Same to Same, April 2, 1853; Same to Same, July 24, 1853; Tom C. Charles to Sister, December 19, 1852; Tom C. Charles to Emma C. Crutcher, January 13, 1853; and Tom C. Charles to Father, December 28, 1854, Charles-Crutcher-McRaven Papers (State of Mississippi, Department of Archives and History).

19. "Letters of Richard Emerson Ela," *Wisconsin Magazine of History* 19 (June 1936), 432-35. This series of letters was continued in the September 1936 issue.

20. Noah Webster, *An American Dictionary of the English Language . . .* Revised and enlarged (Springfield, Mass., 1855), p. 595.

21. "Letters of Ela," pp. 434, 447-48.

22. John Kinkade to James Kinkade, September 25, 1844, John Thompson Kinkade Collection KI28 (Huntington Library).

23. Elisha D. Perkins Diary, June 16, 1849, HM1547 (Huntington Library).

24. Ruth Seymour Burmester (Intro.), "Silas J. Seymour Letters," *Wisconsin Magazine of History* 32 (December 1948), 190. This series of letters was continued in the March 1949 and June 1949 issues.

25. James Harvey Young (ed.), "Land Hunting in 1836," *Journal of the Illinois State Historical Society* 45 (Autumn 1952), 246.

26. Ambrose Bierce, "The Eyes of the Panther," in *In the Midst of Life and Other Tales*, Signet Classic paperback (New York, 1961), p. 190.

27. Blake McKelvey (ed.), "The Autobiography of Asher Freeman. Written by a Frugal Pioneer of Niagara County in 1852," *New York History* 25 (April 1944), 216.

28. Burmester (Intro.), "Seymour Letters," pp. 190, 197.

29. George Winston Smith and Charles Judah (eds.), *Chronicles of the Gringos: The U.S. Army in the Mexican War, 1846-48: Accounts of Eyewitnesses and Combatants* (Albuquerque, N. Mex., 1968), p. 398.

30. Burmester (Intro.), "Seymour Letters," p. 197.

31. "Letters of Ela," p. 436.

32. Charles Sanford, *The Quest for Paradise: Europe and the American Moral Imagination* (Urbana, Ill., 1961), p. vi.

33. George H. Williams, *Wilderness and Paradise in Christian Thought: The Biblical Experience of the Desert in the History of Christianity & the Paradise Theme in the Theological Idea of the University* (New York, 1962), pp. 129-30.

34. Klaus J. Hansen, "The Millenium, the West, and Race in the Antebellum

American Mind," *Western Historical Quarterly* 3 (October 1972), 374-75. The last two sentences of this quote come from an explanatory footnote on p. 375.

35. "Journal of A. W. Harlan While Crossing the Plains in 1850," *Annals of Iowa*, Third Series, 11 (April 1913), 41.

36. "Letters of Ela," p. 436.

37. John R. Cummins Diary, June 14 and July 1, 1856, and May 26 and 28, 1857, John R. Cummins Papers, 1850-1916 (Minnesota Historical Society).

38. Joseph Houlton to Samuel Houlton, July 11, 1852, William H. Houlton and Family Papers (Minnesota Historical Society).

39. John W. Shepperd to David Ireland, February 18, 1852, James Ireland Family Correspondence (Indiana Historical Society).

40. Margaret Burr Des Champs (ed.), "Some Mississippi Letters to Robert Fraser, 1841-1844," *Journal of Mississippi History* 15 (July 1953), 183-86.

41. Catherine Woods to Willie, November 12, 1854; Same to Same, June 21, 1855; Same to Same, October 14, 1855; Sidney Smith to Uncle, December 18, 1855; and Catherine Woods to Willie, March 15, 1858, William H. Houlton and Family Papers (Minnesota Historical Society).

42. "A Letter of 1832," *Indiana Magazine of History* 25 (September 1929), 244.

43. Frederick Jackson Turner, "The Significance of the Frontier in American History," in *The Frontier in American History* (New York, 1920), p. 38.

44. Young (ed.), "Land Hunting in 1836," p. 251.

45. M. J. and E. M. Taylor to William D. Boaz, July 19, 1849, William Davis Boaz Papers (Manuscripts Division, Alabama Department of Archives and History).

46. David W. Humphrey to friends, June 20, 1855, David W. Humphrey Papers (Minnesota Historical Society).

47. "Rochester," *Complete Works of Nathaniel Hawthorne*, Riverside Edition, XII (Boston, 1883).

48. John Eagle to wife, June 13, 1852 and September 26, 1852, John H. Eagle Correspondence, EGL 4 (Huntington Library).

49. Robert W. Lovett, "Augustus Roundy's Cincinnati Sojourn," *Historical and Philosophical Society of Ohio Bulletin* 19 (October 1961), 257.

50. Victor L. Dowdell and Helen C. Everett (eds.), "California Diary of John French, 1850-51," *Michigan History Magazine* 38 (March 1954), 40.

51. James Bryce, *The American Commonwealth*, 3d ed. (New York, 1895), II, 833.

52. Daniel Boorstin, *The Americans: The National Experience* (New York, 1965), pp. 296-98.

53. LeRoy P. Graf (ed.), "The Journal of a Vermont Man in Ohio, 1836-1842," *Ohio State Archaeological and Historical Quarterly* 60 (April 1951), 187.

54. Andrew Jackson Sterrett to Dear Jim, October 17, 1853; Andrew Jackson Sterrett Diary, May 21 and November 25, 1856, Andrew Jackson Sterrett Papers (Minnesota Historical Society).

55. Isaac S. Metcalf to Wife, July 7, 1855, Isaac S. Metcalf Letters (Minnesota Historical Society).

56. James T. Jones to Mother, March 4, 1858; Same to Same, May 4, 1858; and Same to Same, May 19, 1858, James T. Jones Papers, JTJ 55, 57, 58 (Huntington Library).

57. Janet Coe Sanborn (ed.), "By Road, Rail, Canal and Lake—From Massachu-

setts to Michigan in 1836," *Inland Seas* 16 (Fall 1960), 224-29.

58. Thomas Maitland Marshall (ed.), "The Journal of Henry B. Miller," *Missouri Historical Society Collections* 6 (1931), 224-26. "Ancient Babylon and Ninevah would have been no circumstance to them. . . ."

59. D.B.H. (ed.), "A Young Yankee in the New West," *Year Book of the Society of Indiana Pioneers* (1960), p. 23.

60. Gertrude Stein, *Everybody's Autobiography* (New York, 1937), p. 233.

61. "Diary of a Journey to Wisconsin in 1840," *Wisconsin Magazine of History* 6 (December 1922), 212. This journal of Frederick J. Starin was published in the September 1922, December 1922, and March 1923 issues.

62. *Mardi: And a Voyage Thither*, Chapter 166.

63. David Brion Davis, *Homicide in American Fiction, 1798-1860: A Study in Social Values* (Ithaca, N.Y., 1957), pp. 204-205.

64. Sigmund Spaeth, *A History of Popular Music in America* (New York, 1948), p. 594.

65. "California Diary of Charles M. Tuttle, 1859," *Wisconsin Magazine of History* 15 (September 1931), 71. This diary was continued in the December 1931 issue.

66. John P. Bannan Diary, 1858-1862, September 26-29, 1858 (New-York Historical Society).

67. Solomon Gorgas Diary, May 27, 1850, HM651 (Huntington Library).

68. "Journal of A. W. Harland," p. 49.

69. David L. Hieb (ed.), "An 1850 Gold Rush Letter from Fort Laramie by A. C. Sponsler, A Thayer County Pioneer," *Nebraska History* 32 (June 1951), 137.

70. Charlotte Whipple to Mary Ann, November 9, 1852, Charlotte L. Whipple Diaries (Manuscripts Division, New York Public Library).

71. James T. Jones to Mother, May 4, 1858, James T. Jones Papers, JTJ57 (Huntington Library).

72. Obadiah Ethelbert Baker Collection (Huntington Library).

73. Louise Fogle (ed.), "Journal of Ebenezer Mattoon Chamberlain," *Indiana Magazine of History* 15 (September 1919), 242.

74. "California Letters of William Goodridge of Beverly: Experiences of One of the Forty-niners from Essex County," *Essex Institute Historical Collections* 78 (October 1942), 386.

75. John Eagle to Margaret H. Eagle, January 17, 1852; and Same to Same, November 28, 1852, John H. Eagle Correspondence, EGL1, 11 (Huntington Library).

76. James T. Jones to Mother, January 19, 1858, James T. Jones Papers, JTJ53 (Huntington Library).

77. Isaac and Lucy Carr to Caleb Carr and family, May 10, 1857; Same to Same, June 21, 1857; and Lucy Carr to Caleb Carr and family, July 1857, Caleb M. Carr Letters (Collection of Regional History, Cornell University).

78. Richard Slotkin, *Regeneration Through Violence: The Mythology of the American Frontier, 1600-1860* (Middletown, Conn., 1973), pp. 7, 19, 558, 564.

79. Prudence Kelley to Joseph Kelley, March 12, 1856, Prudence Kelley Letters (Vermont Historical Society).

80. David W. Humphrey to friends, May 26 and July 20, 1855, David W. Humphrey Papers (Minnesota Historical Society).

81. Philip L. Cantelon (ed.), "The California Gold Fields in the 1850's: Letters from

Ephraim Thompson, Daviess County, Indiana," *Indiana Magazine of History* 65 (September 1969), 165.

82. Elias Daggy Diary, June 8, 1850 (Minnesota Historical Society).

83. E. B. Comstock to Amasa Comstock, September 23, 1850, John Comstock Papers in the James A. Andrews and Family Papers (Minnesota Historical Society).

84. Davis ——— to Sister, July 29, 1849, Abby Abbe Fuller Papers (Minnesota Historical Society). A young man from Maine recently arrived in New Orleans employed the same designation of his native area—"the land of steady habits." His is an interesting variant because he very clearly brought South and West into close proximity, if not identity, on his attitudinal compass. Walter B. Foster Journal, 1841-1845, January 13, 1842 (Missouri Historical Society).

85. Elias Daggy Diary, May 6, 1850 (Minnesota Historical Society).

86. Cantelon (ed.), "Gold Fields in the 1850's," p. 167.

87. Jackson Thomason Diary, September 20, 1849 (State of Mississippi, Department of Archives and History).

88. Mary Stuart Bailey Journal, June 25, 1852, HM2018 (Huntington Library).

89. Francis Jennings, *The Invasion of America: Indians, Colonialism, and the Cant of Conquest* (Chapel Hill, N.C., 1975), pp. 10-11.

90. John P. Bannan Diary, 1858-1862, May 15, 1862 (New-York Historical Society).

91. "Locating a New Home," *Annals of Iowa*, Third Series, 23 (October 1941), 138.

92. Howard Mitcham (ed.), "A Mississippian in the Gold Fields: The Letters of John Paul Dart, 1849-1856," *California Historical Society Quarterly* 35 (September 1956), 216.

93. George F. Kent Journal, February 18, 1849, HM524 (Huntington Library).

94. Taggart (ed.), "The Journal of Staples," p. 138.

95. See, for example, Raymond D. Gastil, *Cultural Regions of the United States* (Seattle, Wash., 1975), pp. 104-05.

96. Alden T. Vaughan (ed.), *The Puritan Tradition in America 1620-1730*, Harper & Row paperback (New York, 1972), p. 308.

97. William A. Clebsch, *From Sacred to Profane America: The Role of Religion in American History* (New York, 1968), pp. 1-2, 63.

98. Horatio Houlton to Brother, January 17, 1856, William H. Houlton and Family Papers (Minnesota Historical Society).

99. Horatio Houlton to Brother, October 7, 1855, William H. Houlton and Family Papers (Minnesota Historical Society).

100. Zuar Jameson Diaries, March 4, 1856 (Vermont Historical Society).

101. William Dickinson to Mrs. Mary Ann Cowles, June, 1842, Dickinson-Cowles-Hart Family Letters (Connecticut State Library).

102. Milo Holcomb to Nahum Holcomb, July 27, 1835, Holcomb Family Letters (Connecticut State Library).

103. Thomas J. Hayter to Sarah Hayter, February 4, 1855, Coleman-Hayter Letters, 1840-1900 (Western Historical Manuscripts Collection, University of Missouri, Columbia).

104. Lydia and Erastus Bingham to Nathaniel Adams, November 3, 1831, Phinehas Adams Papers, 1759-1892 (Huntington Library).

105. Laura A. Case to Mr. and Mrs. Luke Crittenden, November 14, 1832, Laura Case Letter (Collection of Regional History, Cornell University).

106. Donald H. Welsh (ed.), "Martha J. Woods Visits Missouri in 1857," *Missouri Historical Review* 55 (January 1961), 121.

107. S. L. Wheeler to Jeremiah Simons, July 12 and 15, 1846, Lyman Stuart *Collector*. Stampless Covers (Collection of Regional History, Cornell University).

108. Donald E. Baker (ed.), "The Conine Family Letters, 1849-1851: Employed in Honest Business and Doing the Best We Can," *Indiana Magazine of History* 69 (December 1973), 338.

109. G. Cassil to James Kinkade (probably early 1850), John Thompson Kinkade Collection KI4 (Huntington Library).

110. "Thomas C. Duggins Views Northwest Missouri in 1840," *Missouri Historical Review* 55 (January 1961), 126.

111. Donald Carmony (ed.), "Frontier Life: Loneliness and Hope," *Indiana Magazine of History* 61 (March 1965), 54.

112. Sacvan Bercovitch, *The Puritan Origins of the American Self* (New Haven, Conn., 1975), p. 186.

113. George F. Kent Journal, March 4, 1849, HM524 (Huntington Library).

114. Andrew Jackson Sterrett to Brother, November 25, 1856, Andrew Jackson Sterrett Papers (Minnesota Historical Society).

115. *Israel Potter: His Fifty Years of Exile*, Chapters 21-22.

116. Michael Fleenan Luark Diary, 1846-1899, May 8, 1853 (University of Washington Manuscript Collection).

117. Elizabeth and James Olin to Brother and Sister, July 6, 1851, Peck Family Letters (Collection of Regional History, Cornell University).

118. Donald E. Baker (ed.), "The Conine Family Letters, 1852-1863; 'Just Think How We Are Scattered,'" *Indiana Magazine of History* 70 (June 1974), 152, 156.

119. Edward D. Jervey and James E. Moss (eds.), "From Virginia to Missouri in 1846: The Journal of Elizabeth Ann Cooley," *Missouri Historical Review* 60 (January 1966), 170, 183, 202, 206.

120. Ibid., pp. 175, 177.

121. Taggart (ed.), "The Journal of Staples," p. 129.

122. Bernard DeVoto, *The Year of Decision: 1846* (Boston, 1943), p. 4.

123. Taggart (ed.), "The Journal of Staples," p. 129.

124. Sarah C. Buckingham to Sarah Hayter, January 3, 1852, Coleman-Hayter Letters, 1840-1900 (Western Historical Manuscripts Collection, University of Missouri, Columbia).

Appendix

1. John Higham, "Intellectual History and Its Neighbors," *Journal of the History of Ideas* 15 (June 1954), 340.

2. John Higham, "Introduction," in John Higham and Paul K. Conkin (eds.), *New Directions in American Intellectual History* (Baltimore, 1979), p. xv. Several of the essays in the volume give attention to the genre called collective mentalities.

3. H. Stuart Hughes, *Consciousness and Society: The Reorientation of European Social Thought, 1890-1930*, Vintage Books Paperback (New York, 1958), p. 3.

4. Jesse Lemisch, "The American Revolution Seen from the Bottom Up," in Bar-

ton J. Bernstein (ed.), *Towards a New Past: Dissenting Essays in American History* (New York, 1968), p. 6.

5. Merrill Jensen, "The American People and the American Revolution," *Journal of American History* 57 (June 1970), 8-9.

6. George Boas, *Vox Populi: Essays in the History of an Idea*, The Johns Hopkins Press paperback (Baltimore, 1969), p. 215.

7. The sometimes illuminating discussion of those fellows in their late eighteenth-century setting appeared as follows, Jesse Lemisch, "Jack Tar in the Streets: Merchant Seamen in the Politics of Revolutionary America," *William and Mary Quarterly: A Magazine of Early American History*, Third Series, 25 (July 1968), 371-407; James H. Hutson, "An Investigation of the Inarticulate: Philadelphia's White Oaks," *William and Mary Quarterly: A Magazine of Early American History*, Third Series, 28 (January 1971), 3-25; and Jesse Lemisch and John K. Alexander, "The White Oaks, Jack Tar, and the Concept of the 'Inarticulate'" and Simeon J. Crowther, "A Note on the Economic Position of Philadelphia's White Oaks; With a Rebuttal by James H. Hutson," *William and Mary Quarterly: A Magazine of Early American History*, Third Series, 29 (January 1972), 109-42.

8. Lemisch, "The American Revolution Seen from the Bottom Up," pp. 6, 24.

9. Crane Brinton, *Ideas and Men: The Story of Western Thought*, 2d ed. (Englewood Cliffs, N.J., 1963), p. 6.

10. Henry Seidel Canby, *Thoreau* (Boston, 1939), p. 450.

11. Carl Bode, *The Anatomy of American Popular Culture, 1840-1861* (Berkeley, Calif., 1960), pp. 205-207.

12. C. Robert Cole, "Intellectual History and the Common Man," *Rocky Mountain Social Science Journal* 9 (October 1972), 47.

13. *The Complete Works of Ralph Waldo Emerson*, Autograph Centenary Edition (Cambridge, Mass., 1903), IV, 29.

14. Bode, *Anatomy of American Popular Culture*, pp. ix-x.

15. Ibid., p. x.

16. Roderick Nash, *The Nervous Generation: American Thought, 1917-1930* (Chicago, 1970), Chapter 4.

17. Richard Mosier, *Making the American Mind: Social and Moral Ideas in the McGuffey Readers* (New York, 1947), p. 166.

18. Ruth Miller Elson, *Guardians of Tradition: American Schoolbooks of the Nineteenth Century* (Lincoln, Nebr., 1964), pp. vii-ix.

19. David Grimsted, *Melodrama Unveiled: American Theater and Culture, 1800-1850* (Chicago, 1968), p. ix.

20. Robert C. Toll, *Blacking Up: The Minstrel Show in Nineteenth-Century America* (New York, 1974), p. vi.

21. Ibid., pp. 281-82.

22. Brinton, *Ideas and Men*, p. 6.

23. Higham, "Intellectual History and Its Neighbors," p. 340.

24. Hughes, *Consciousness and Society*, pp. 9-10.

25. R. Richard Wohl, "Intellectual History: An Historian's View," *The Historian* 16 (Autumn 1953), 63-64.

26. *Annual Report of the American Historical Association, 1900*, I, 47.

27. Jensen, "The American People and the American Revolution," p. 9.

28. Ralph Henry Gabriel, "Remarks by the Chairman," in William E. Lingelbach (ed.), *Approaches to American Social History* (New York, 1937), pp. 8-9. Gabriel presided at a general session of the annual meeting of the American Historical Association which met in Providence, Rhode Island, in December 1936.

29. Philip Jordan, "Social History: A Nation Announcing Itself," *Ohio Historical Quarterly* 66 (July 1957), 222.

30. Jesse Lemisch, "Listening to the 'Inarticulate': William Widger's Dream and the Loyalties of American Revolutionary Seamen in British Prisons," *Journal of Social History* 3 (Fall 1969), 1-3, 28-29.

31. Hughes, *Consciousness and Society*, p. 10.

32. Solon Buck, "Some Materials for the Social History of the Mississippi Valley in the Nineteenth Century," *Proceedings of the Mississippi Valley Historical Association* 4 (1910-1911), 139.

33. Louis Pelzer, "History Made by Plain Men," *Iowa Journal of History and Politics* 11 (1913), 322.

34. Jordan, "Social History," 232-33.

35. Henrietta Memler, "Virgin Fields of History," *Papers in Illinois History and Transactions for the Year 1937* (Springfield, Ill., 1938), pp. 44-46.

36. Wilbur Cortez Abbott, "Some 'New' History and Historians," *Proceedings of the Massachusetts Historical Society* 64 (October 1930-June 1932), 298.

37. David Grimsted, "Melodrama as Echo of the Historically Voiceless," in Tamara K. Hareven (ed.), *Anonymous Americans: Explorations in Nineteenth-Century Social History*, Prentice-Hall Paperback (Englewood Cliffs, N.J., 1971), p. 95.

38. Toll, *Blacking Up*, p. 282.

39. William A. Clebsch, *From Sacred to Profane America: The Role of Religion in American History* (New York, 1968).

40. Stewart Holbrook, *The Yankee Exodus: An Account of Migration from New England* (New York, 1950).

41. *See* bibliography.

42. Lemisch, "Listening to the 'Inarticulate,'" p. 6.

43. Gene Wise, *American Historical Explanations: A Strategy for Grounded Inquiry* (Homewood, Ill., 1973), p. vii.

44. Jacques Barzun, *Clio and the Doctors: Psycho-History, Quanto-History and History* (Chicago, 1974), p. 89.

45. Wise, *American Historical Explanations*, p. vii.

46. Barzun, *Clio and the Doctors*, p. 90.

47. F. O. Matthiessen, *American Renaissance: Art and Expression in the Age of Emerson and Whitman* (New York, 1941), p. xiii.

48. *Hawthorne*, Collier Books Paperback (New York, 1966), p. 125.

49. Samuel Rezneck, "A Schoolboy of 1830," *New York History* 17 (April 1936), 135.

50. J. H. Bankhead, Jr., to Thomas M. Owen, December 30, 1904, J. W. Triplet Letters (Manuscripts Division, Alabama Department of Archives and History).

51. Earl S. Pomeroy (ed.), "Wisconsin in 1847: Notes of John Q. Roods," *Wisconsin Magazine of History* 33 (December 1949), 217.

52. Frank O. Spinney, "A New Hampshire Schoolmaster Views Kentucky: Three Letters, 1847-1848," *New England Quarterly* 17 (March 1944), 87.

53. John W. Caughey (ed.), "Life in California in 1849, As Described in the 'Journal' of George F. Kent," *California Historical Society Quarterly* 20 (March 1941), 26.

54. Ibid.

55. "With Pen in Hand: Letters of a Missouri Frontier Family," *Missouri Historical Society Bulletin* 15 (October 1958), 29.

56. "Middlebury College Mourns," *Vermont History* 24 (October 1956), 296. This issue had various features commemorative of Peach who had died on July 21. Some of his poetry appeared, and one piece, printed as "Requiem" inside the back cover of the issue, closed this way:

> On paths that backward turn,
> Where home lights softly burn,
> Feet haste, no more to roam, —
> And the heart goes home.

57. Arthur Wallace Peach (ed.), "Memoirs: The Reverend Benjamin Wooster," *Proceedings of the Vermont Historical Society*, New Series, 4 (December 1936), 215.

58. Arthur Wallace Peach (ed.), "The Autobiography of John Whittemore, 1796-1885," *Proceedings of the Vermont Historical Society*, New Series, 6 (December 1938), 317.

59. Wilmond Parker, "Lympus and Lilliesville in 1855," *Proceedings of the Vermont Historical Society*, New Series, 9 (June 1941), 69.

60. Norman K. Risjord, "How the 'Common Man' Voted in Jefferson's Virginia," in John B. Boles (ed.), *America: The Middle Period: Essays in the Honor of Bernard Mayo* (Charlottesville, Va., 1973), p. 36.

61. Donald E. Baker (ed.), "The Conine Family Letters, 1849-1851: Employed in Honest Business and Doing the Best We Can," *Indiana Magazine of History* 69 (December 1973), 320. This and the continuation of the letters in the June 1974 issue of the same periodical is an exceptionally fine editing of a full and illustrative set of family letters. For a readily accessible specimen, one could hardly do better.

62. Review of Richard Albert Edward Brooks (ed.), *The Diary of Michael Floy Jr. Bowery Village 1833-1837* (New Haven, Conn., 1941) in *New York History* 23 (April 1942), 200-201.

63. "The Goodale Letters," *Connecticut Historical Society Bulletin* 20 (July 1955), 85. One tends toward the realistic conclusion that an inverse ratio obtains between the availability of traditional historical riches and the inclination of repositories to collect or accept the sorts of sources used in this book.

64. "Explanations in Everyday Life, in Science, and in History," *History and Theory: Studies in the Philosophy of History*, 2 (Number 2, 1962), 118-23.

65. Chard Powers Smith, *Yankees and God* (New York, 1954); John Hope Franklin, *The Militant South, 1800-1861* (Cambridge, Mass., 1956); and David Bertelson, *The Lazy South* (New York, 1967).

66. William R. Taylor, *Cavalier and Yankee: The Old South and American National Character* (London, 1963).

67. Smith, *Yankees and God*, p. 5.

68. Edmund S. Morgan, "The Puritan Ethic and the American Revolution," *William and Mary Quarterly*, Third Series, 24 (January 1967).

69. C. Vann Woodward, "The Southern Ethic in a Puritan World," *William and Mary Quarterly*, Third Series, 25 (July 1968).

70. Robert E. Corlew, review of Frank Lawrence Owsley, *Plain Folk of the Old South* (Baton Rouge, La., 1949) in *Tennessee Historical Quarterly* 9 (March 1950), 84-85.

71. Domingo Sarmiento, *Travels in the United States in 1847*, Translation and Introductory Essay by Michael Aaron Rockland (Princeton, N.J., 1970), pp. 197-99, 205.

72. In "The History of Ideas in America: An Essay in Redefinition," *Journal of American History* 51 (March 1965), Rush Welter contends, among other things, that the historian who studies popular ideas must treat them as he would sophisticated ideas. He must do more than measure their "irrational or emotional components," and he must also appreciate their "intellectual content" (p. 610).

73. S. M. Baker to ———, June 7, 1858, S. M. Baker Papers (Minnesota Historical Society).

74. Arthur Homer Hayes (ed.), "Diary of Taylor N. Snow, Hoosier Fifty-niner," *Indiana Magazine of History* 28 (September 1932), 194.

75. Henry Stevens Letters, 1851-1853 (Vermont Historical Society).

76. Arthur P. Thompson to Daniel C. Cargile, April 2, 1846, Arthur P. Thompson Letter (Kentucky Historical Society).

77. "Journal of Cyrus Sanders," *Iowa Journal of History and Politics* 37 (January 1939), 87.

78. Diary of an Unidentified Bostonian (Massachusetts Historical Society).

79. Thomas Gray, "Elegy Written in a Country Church Yard," line 76.

80. Henry Putnam Diary and Account Book, 1836-1839 (New-York Historical Society). The name Henry Putnam was written inside one cover, but internal evidence indicates that he was not the author.

81. Nathan Butler Diary and Account Book, July 21, 1852, Nathan Butler Papers, 1859-1923 (Minnesota Historical Society).

82. Orville Nixon Journal, HM17012 (Huntington Library).

83. Diary Record of Farm Labor (Connecticut State Library).

84. Monroe Sullivan Letter (Kentucky Historical Society).

85. Francis W. Squires Diaries, September 11, 1850 (Collection of Regional History, Cornell University).

86. Sarah R. Espy Diary, June 12, 1860 (Manuscripts Division, Alabama Department of Archives and History).

87. Stephen Thernstrom, *Poverty and Progress: Social Mobility in a Nineteenth-Century City*, Atheneum Paperback (New York, 1970), pp. 260-61.

88. The 1830 and 1840 schedules sometimes help in placing and identifying people, but they offer very little by way of description. There were, of course, territorial and state censuses that came at other than the ten-year intervals.

89. C. V. Wedgwood, *The Common Man in the Great Civil War* (Leicester, England, 1957), p. 3.

BIBLIOGRAPHY

I. Primary Material

A. POPULAR SOURCES

1. Manuscripts

Aborn, Mary J., Collection. Indiana Division of the Indiana State Library. Indianapolis, Indiana.

Adams, Andrew W. and Family, Papers. Minnesota Historical Society. Saint Paul, Minnesota.

Adams, Elizabeth, Letters. Kentucky Historical Society. Frankfort, Kentucky.

Adams, Mrs. M. S., Letters. Manuscripts Division. Alabama Department of Archives and History. Montgomery, Alabama.

Adams, Phinehas, Papers, 1759-1892. Henry E. Huntington Library and Art Gallery, San Marino, California.

Adams, Mrs. William, Papers. State of Mississippi. Department of Archives and History. Jackson, Mississippi.

Aiton, John Felix, Papers, 1835-1888. Minnesota Historical Society. Saint Paul, Minnesota.

Akehurst-Lines Collection. University of Georgia Libraries. Division of Special Collections. Athens, Georgia.

Amsden, Lysander H., Letters. Southern Historical Collection. University of North Carolina. Chapel Hill, North Carolina.

Anderson, Robert, Letter. South Caroliniana Library. University of South Carolina. Columbia, South Carolina.

Andrews, Rapin, Diary of. Indiana Division of the Indiana State Library. Indianapolis, Indiana.

Armstrong, John Milton and Family, Papers. Minnesota Historical Society. Saint Paul, Minnesota.

Arnold, Ellenor, Papers. South Caroliniana Library. University of South Carolina. Columbia, South Carolina.

Atwater, Henry, Note Book, Plymouth, Connecticut, 1836-1846. Connecticut State Library. Hartford, Connecticut.

Bacon Family Letters. Kentucky Historical Society. Frankfort, Kentucky.

Bailey, Mary Stuart, Journal, HM2018. Henry E. Huntington Library and Art Gallery. San Marino, California.

Baker, Obadiah Ethelbert, Collection. Henry E. Huntington Library and Art Gallery. San Marino, California.

Baker, S. M., Papers. Minnesota Historical Society. Saint Paul, Minnesota.

Ballard, James F., Papers. Indiana Historical Society. Indianapolis, Indiana.

Bannan, John P., Diary, 1858-1862. New-York Historical Society. New York, New York.

Barbour-Parker Family Letters. Collection of Regional History. Cornell University. Ithaca, New York.

Barker, A. B., Letter. South Caroliniana Library. University of South Carolina. Columbia, South Carolina.

Barr, Mrs. I. S., Manuscripts. Manuscripts Division. Alabama Department of Archives and History. Montgomery, Alabama.

[Bassett, William], Diary Record of Farm Labor. Connecticut State Library. Hartford, Connecticut.

Beal Family Letters. Collection of Regional History. Cornell University. Ithaca, New York.

Beard, C. S., Letter. Manuscripts Division. Alabama Department of Archives and History. Montgomery, Alabama.

Beeching, Robert, Journal, HM17430. Henry E. Huntington Library and Art Gallery. San Marino, California.

Beeler, Fielding, Diary and Account Books of. Indiana Division of the Indiana State Library. Indianapolis, Indiana.

Bell, James Alvin, Collection. Henry E. Huntington Library and Art Gallery. San Marino, California.

Berry Collection. Collection of Regional History. Cornell University. Ithaca, New York.

Bibbens Family Papers. Collection of Regional History. Cornell University. Ithaca, New York.

Black, John D., Diaries. Indiana Division of the Indiana State Library. Indianapolis, Indiana.

Blatchley Papers. Vermont Historical Society. Montpelier, Vermont.

Boatner, L. M., Diary. State of Mississippi. Department of Archives and History. Jackson, Mississippi.

Boaz, William Davis, Papers. Manuscripts Division. Alabama Department of Archives and History. Montgomery, Alabama.

Bond and Fentriss Family Papers. Southern Historical Collection. University of North Carolina. Chapel Hill, North Carolina.

Boody and Mowers Papers. Collection of Regional History. Cornell University. Ithaca, New York.

Bostwick, Alanson, Papers, 1839-1847. Minnesota Historical Society. Saint Paul, Minnesota.

Bower, John, Diary. Collection of Regional History. Cornell University. Ithaca, New York.

Brandt, Marie Ester, Diary. Indiana Historical Society. Indianapolis, Indiana.

Brewster, John, Letter. Connecticut State Library. Hartford, Connecticut.

Brophy-Beeson Papers, BB1-97. Henry E. Huntington Library and Art Gallery. San Marino, California.

Brown, Ebenezer, Papers. New Hampshire Historical Society. Concord, New Hampshire.

Brown, James Amsted, Diary, 1858-1860. Vermont Historical Society. Montpelier, Vermont.

Brown, William, Letters. South Caroliniana Library. University of South Carolina. Columbia, South Carolina.

Browne, James, Letter. Manuscripts Division. Alabama Department of Archives and History. Montgomery, Alabama.

Browning, James C., Diary. State of Mississippi. Department of Archives and History. Jackson, Mississippi.

Bunting, Mary, Letter. South Caroliniana Library. University of South Carolina. Columbia, South Carolina.

Burgess, Emsley, Papers. Southern Historical Collection. University of North Carolina. Chapel Hill, North Carolina.

Burkhart, Charlotte, Letters. Kentucky Historical Society. Frankfort, Kentucky.

Burnett Family Papers. Southern Historical Collection. University of North Carolina. Chapel Hill, North Carolina.

Burwell, George W., Letter. Connecticut State Library. Hartford, Connecticut.

Butler, Nathan, Papers, 1859-1923. Minnesota Historical Society. Saint Paul, Minnesota.

Buxton, Hannah, Diary. Maine Historical Society. Portland, Maine.

Campbell, Carrie Ward, Letters. Indiana Historical Society. Indianapolis, Indiana.

Campbell, Leander Melbourne, Collection. Indiana Historical Society. Indianapolis, Indiana.

Campbell, Lewis, Diaries. Manuscripts Division. Iowa Historical Library, Iowa State Department of History and Archives. Des Moines, Iowa.

Cantwell, John Lucas Paul, Papers. Southern Historical Collection. University of North Carolina. Chapel Hill, North Carolina.

Carr, Caleb M., Letters. Collection of Regional History. Cornell University. Ithaca, New York

Carter, Theodore G., Papers. Minnesota Historical Society. Saint Paul, Minnesota.

Case, Laura, Letter. Collection of Regional History. Cornell University. Ithaca, New York.

Chambers, Captain Franklin, Papers. Kentucky Historical Society. Frankfort, Kentucky.

Chandler, Abiel, Diary. New Hampshire Historical Society. Concord, New Hampshire.

Chandler, Horatio N., Account Book. New Hampshire Historical Society. Concord, New Hampshire.

Chandler, Sarah Ann, Diary, 1836. Western Historical Manuscripts Collection. University of Missouri. Columbia, Missouri.

Chaney, Josiah B., Papers, 1792-1917. Minnesota Historical Society. Saint Paul, Minnesota.

Chapman, A. H., Papers. Minnesota Historical Society. Saint Paul, Minnesota.

Chapman, Maud, Letters. Manuscripts Division. Alabama Department of Archives and History. Montgomery, Alabama.

Charles-Crutcher-McRaven Papers. State of Mississippi. Department of Archives and History. Jackson, Mississippi.

Chillson, Lorenzo Dow, Diary, HM4293. Henry E. Huntington Library and Art Gallery. San Marino, California.

Clark, John B. Papers. Kentucky Historical Society. Frankfort, Kentucky.

Clark, Micajah Adolphus, Journal. South Caroliniana Library. University of South Carolina. Columbia, South Carolina.

Clayton, J. E., Diary. Manuscripts Division. Alabama Department of Archives and History. Montgomery, Alabama.

Cochran, Washington Smith, Diary. South Caroliniana Library. University of South Carolina. Columbia, South Carolina.

Cochrane, John, Papers. Minnesota Historical Society. Saint Paul, Minnesota.

Coffin, Alexander H., Diary, 1830-1834. Manuscripts Division. New York Public Library. New York, New York.

Coleman-Hayter Letters, 1840-1900. Western Historical Manuscripts Collection. University of Missouri. Columbia, Missouri.

Comstock, John, Papers. James A. Andrews and Family Papers. Minnesota Historical Society. Saint Paul, Minnesota.

Conkling, Enos, Correspondence, 1837-1888. New-York Historical Society. New York, New York.

Copp, Daniel Dennison, Letters. Manuscript Department. William R. Perkins Library. Duke University. Durham, North Carolina.

Corn, Jesse, Family Papers. Indiana Historical Society. Indianapolis, Indiana.

Countryman, Levi N., Papers. Minnesota Historical Society. Saint Paul, Minnesota.

Coureton, Richard, Letter. Southern Historical Collection. University of North Carolina. Chapel Hill, North Carolina.

Crane, Joel, and Eunice Fitch, Family Correspondence. Indiana Historical Society. Indianapolis, Indiana.

Cranston Family Papers. Collection of Regional History. Cornell University. Ithaca, New York.

Crawford, Leander, and Louisa (Canfield) Purdy, *Collectors*. Family Papers. Collection of Regional History. Cornell University. Ithaca, New York.

Cummins, John R., Papers, 1850-1916. Minnesota Historical Society. Saint Paul, Minnesota.

Curtis, Samuel R., Diary, 1850-1852. Missouri Historical Society. Saint Louis, Missouri.

Daggy, Elias, Diary. Minnesota Historical Society. Saint Paul, Minnesota.

Daniell, Josiah, Almanac Diary. University of Georgia Libraries. Division of Special Collections. Athens, Georgia.

Diary kept by an unidentified student while living in Massachusetts in 1833 and 1834. Manuscripts Division. New York Public Library. New York, New York.

Diary of an unidentified Bostonian. Massachusetts Historical Society. Boston, Massachusetts.

Diary of an unidentified New Yorker covering a trip to Niagara Falls via Philadelphia, Lancaster, Williamsport, Elmira, Seneca Lake, etc. and return to New York, during June-July of 1836. Manuscripts Division. New York Public Library. New York, New York.

Dickinson-Cowles-Hart Family Letters. Connecticut State Library. Hartford, Connecticut.

Douglas, Mary, Letters. South Caroliniana Library. University of South Carolina. Columbia, South Carolina.

Drake, John, Diary. Collection of Regional History. Cornell University. Ithaca, New York.

Drew, James M. and Family, Papers. Minnesota Historical Society. Saint Paul, Minnesota.

(DuBois,   ) Diary of a journey from Catskill, N.Y. to New York, thence by water to Mobile, and Portland, Alabama. Manuscripts Division. New York Public Library. New York, New York.

Dudley, Charles W., Journal, 1856-1857, HM28925. Henry E. Huntington Library and Art Gallery. San Marino, California.

Duffe, James, Diary, 1844. New-York Historical Society. New York, New York.

Dunwell, Amelia, Correspondence, Benjamin Streeter Papers. New-York Historical Society. New York, New York.

Eagle, John H., Correspondence, EGL 1-49. Henry E. Huntington Library and Art Gallery. San Marino California.

Elsbree and Jackson Family Papers. Collection of Regional History. Cornell University. Ithaca, New York.

Ely, Edmund F., Papers. Minnesota Historical Society. Saint Paul, Minnesota.

Espy Family Papers, 1800-1900. Western Historical Manuscripts Collection. University of Missouri. Columbia, Missouri.

Espy, Sarah Rodgers, Diary. Manuscripts Division. Alabama Department of Archives and History. Montgomery, Alabama.

Fairchild, Hiram, Diary. Connecticut State Library. Hartford, Connecticut.

Farm records by an unknown writer of Rhode Island (?), hiring of men . . . annotations in almanacs for 1815, 1831, Bickerstaff's Almanac for 1838. Manuscripts Division. New York Public Library. New York, New York.

Fenn, Jeremiah, Memorandum and Family Record. Connecticut State Library. Hartford, Connecticut.

Flagg, Mary B., Papers. Minnesota Historical Society. Saint Paul, Minnesota.

Flanner, Henry Beeson, Family Correspondence. Indiana Historical Society. Indianapolis, Indiana.

Flint, Edith, Papers. Minnesota Historical Society. Saint Paul, Minnesota.

Flood, Jane Agnes, Letters. South Caroliniana Library. University of South Carolina. Columbia, South Carolina.

[Foster, John], Diary, 1856, John Harold Foster Family Papers. New Hampshire Historical Society. Concord, New Hampshire.

Foster, Walter B., Journal, 1841-1845. Missouri Historical Society. Saint Louis, Missouri.

Fryatt, Fanny, School Notebook. Collection of Regional History. Cornell University. Ithaca, New York.

Furber, Pierce F. and Family, Papers. Minnesota Historical Society. Saint Paul, Minnesota.

Garland, William Harris, Papers. Southern Historical Collection. University of North Carolina. Chapel Hill, North Carolina.

Giddings, Aranda P. and Family, Papers. Minnesota Historical Society. Saint Paul, Minnesota.

Gilbert, William W., Papers. Minnesota Historical Society. Saint Paul, Minnesota.

Gillet, George, Diary. Connecticut State Library. Hartford, Connecticut.

Givens, Spencer H., Collection, 1816-1911. Western Historical Manuscripts Collection. University of Missouri. Columbia, Missouri.

Gore, Katie W., Journal, Gore-Helfenstein Papers. Missouri Historical Society. Saint Louis, Missouri.

Gorgas, Solomon, Diary, HM651. Henry E. Huntington Library and Art Gallery. San Marino, California.

Gorgas, Solomon, Letters, HM2183-2194. Henry E. Huntington Library and Art Gallery. San Marino, California.

Graham, Henry M., Diaries. Indiana Historical Society. Indianapolis, Indiana.

Green, Edward, Diary. New-York Historical Society. New York, New York.

Griffith, Owen, Letters. Collection of Regional History. Cornell University. Ithaca, New York.

Griggs, B. B., Letters. South Caroliniana Library. University of South Carolina, Columbia, South Carolina.

Grills, Merton W., Collection. Indiana Historical Society. Indianapolis, Indiana.

Grimes Family Correspondence. New Hampshire Historical Society. Concord, New Hampshire.

Grissom, Lewis, Letters. Manuscripts Division. Alabama Department of Archives and History. Montgomery, Alabama.

Griswold, Harriet, Papers. Minnesota Historical Society. Saint Paul, Minnesota.

Haigh, William H., Papers. Southern Historical Collection. University of North Carolina. Chapel Hill, North Carolina.

Haile Family Papers. Vermont Historical Society. Montpelier, Vermont.

Hall, Lucretia Warner, Diary, 1832-1846. New-York Historical Society. New York, New York.

Hall, Mary, Diary. New Hampshire Historical Society. Concord, New Hampshire.

Hamilton, John Watts, Letters. Indiana Historical Society. Indianapolis, Indiana.

Hanford Family Letters. Collection of Regional History. Cornell University. Ithaca, New York.

Harbold, George, Letters. Kentucky Historical Society. Frankfort, Kentucky.

Harris Family Papers. Indiana Historical Society. Indianapolis, Indiana.

Havens, Charles G., Letters, 1831-1836. New-York Historical Society. New York, New York.

Hayden, Jacob S., Diary. Southern Historical Collection. University of North Carolina. Chapel Hill, North Carolina.

Haynes, Aaron, Letter. Manuscripts Division. Alabama Department of Archives and History. Montgomery Alabama.

Hendryx, Schuyler, Papers. Minnesota Historical Society. Saint Paul, Minnesota.

Herndon, Joseph F., Letter. Kentucky Historical Society. Frankfort, Kentucky.

Hickey Gift. University of Georgia Libraries. Division of Special Collections. Athens, Georgia.

Hickman-Bryan Papers. Western Historical Manuscripts Collection. University of Missouri. Columbia, Missouri.

Hickman, Josiah M., Diary. Indiana Division of the Indiana State Library. Indianapolis, Indiana.

Hill, Ivory B., Family Papers. New Hampshire Historical Society. Concord, New Hampshire.

Hill, Lewis, Correspondence, Robert Alonzo Brock Collection, BR Box 92. Henry E. Huntington Library and Art Gallery. San Marino, California.

Hodge, Benjamin, Papers. Henry E. Huntington Library and Art Gallery. San Marino, California.

Hoffman, William, Diary, 1847-1850. New-York Historical Society. New York, New York.

Holcomb Family Letters. Connecticut State Library. Hartford, Connecticut.

Hoover, Vincent, Diary, 1849-1850, HM27628. Henry E. Huntington Library and Art Gallery, San Marino, California.

Hoppin, William W., Diary, 1842, Hoppin Family Diaries. Manuscripts Division. New York Public Library. New York, New York.

Houlton, William H. and Family, Papers. Minnesota Historical Society. Saint Paul, Minnesota.

Humphrey, David W., Papers. Minnesota Historical Society. Saint Paul, Minnesota.

Humphrey, Noah Marcus and Family, Papers. Minnesota Historical Society, Saint Paul, Minnesota.

Humphreys, Thomas Keyes, Diary. Missouri Historical Society. Saint Louis, Missouri.

Hunt, Daniel H., Diary, 1854-1859. Minnesota Historical Society. Saint Paul, Minnesota.

Hunt, George B. and Family, Papers. Minnesota Historical Society. Saint Paul, Minnesota.

Hunt, Nathaniel, Letter. South Caroliniana Library. University of South Carolina. Columbia, South Carolina.

Ingersoll, Thomas Jefferson, Letters. Collection of Regional History. Cornell University. Ithaca, New York.

Ireland, James, Family Correspondence. Indiana Historical Society. Indianapolis, Indiana.

[Jackson], Algeline Ashley, Diary, HM16773. Henry E. Huntington Library and Art Gallery. San Marino, California.

Jameson, Zuar, Diaries, 1855-1865. Vermont Historical Society. Montpelier, Vermont.

Jenkins, Lewis, Letter. Manuscripts Division. Alabama Department of Archives and History. Montgomery, Alabama.

Jennings Family Diaries and Letters, 1844-1957. New-York Historical Society. New York, New York.

Johnson, Joseph H., Diary, HM19480. Henry E. Huntington Library and Art Gallery. San Marino, California.

Johnson, S., Letter. South Caroliniana Library. University of South Carolina. Columbia, South Carolina.

Johnson, Sarah Woolsey, Diaries. New-York Historical Society. New York, New York.

Johnson, William S., Letters. South Caroliniana Library. University of South Carolina. Columbia, South Carolina.

Jones, James T., Papers, JTJ 1-67. Henry E. Huntington Library and Art Gallery. San Marino, California.

Jones, Morgan D., Letters. Manuscripts Division. Alabama Department of Archives and History. Montgomery, Alabama.

Jones, Robert Marian, Letters. Manuscripts Division. Alabama Department of Archives and History. Montgomery, Alabama.

Kelley, Prudence, Letters. Vermont Historical Society. Montpelier, Vermont.

Kellogg, Martin N., Papers. Minnesota Historical Society. Saint Paul, Minnesota.

Kelly, J. W., Letter. Kentucky Historical Society. Frankfort, Kentucky.

Kent, George F., Journal, HM524. Henry E. Huntington Library and Art Gallery. San Marino, California.

Kent, Samuel, Letters. Collection of Regional History. Cornell University. Ithaca, New York.

Kinkade, John Thompson, Collection, KI 1-91. Henry E. Huntington Library and Art Gallery. San Marino, California.

Knode, Archibald B., Papers, Diaries and Account Books. Indiana Historical Society. Indianapolis, Indiana.

Kytle, Jacob, Letters. South Caroliniana Library. University of South Carolina. Columbia, South Carolina.

Laselle, Stanislaus, Diary, 1849, HM16759. Henry E. Huntington Library and Art Gallery. San Marino, California.

Lee, Oren, Diary and Journal. Connecticut State Library. Hartford, Connecticut.

Legg, John M., Diary and Memorandum. Indiana Historical Society. Indianapolis, Indiana.

Lesly, Mary G., Letter. South Caroliniana Library. University of South Carolina. Columbia, South Carolina.

Lester, Andrew, Diary, 1836-1888. New-York Historical Society. New York, New York.

Lewis, George, Diary. Connecticut State Library. Hartford, Connecticut.

Lindsay, J., Letter. Kentucky Historical Society. Frankfort, Kentucky.

Lipscomb Family Papers. Southern Historical Collection. University of North Carolina. Chapel Hill, North Carolina.

Love, Myron G., Collection. University of Georgia Libraries. Division of Special Collections. Athens, Georgia.

Lovelace, Julia Bryce, Letters. Manuscripts Division. Alabama Department of Archives and History. Montgomery, Alabama.

Lowell, Mrs. R. M., Papers. Minnesota Historical Society. Saint Paul, Minnesota.

Luark, Michael Fleenan, Diary, 1846-1899. University of Washington Manuscript Collection. Seattle, Washington.

Lull, Abram C., Papers. Minnesota Historical Society. Saint Paul, Minnesota.

Lumberman's Diary. Minnesota Historical Society. Saint Paul, Minnesota.

Lyon, T. B., Letters. Kentucky Historical Society. Frankfort, Kentucky.

McBeath, James and Family, Papers. Minnesota Historical Society. Saint Paul, Minnesota.

McBride, W. S., Journal, HM16956. Henry E. Huntington Library and Art Gallery. San Marino, California.

McCowen, George, Journal, HM16756. Henry E. Huntington Library and Art Gallery. San Marino, California.

McCullough, Rosanna, Copy Book. South Caroliniana Library. University of South Carolina. Columbia, South Carolina.

McGuire, Thomas H., Letter. Kentucky Historical Society. Frankfort, Kentucky.

McKellar, Peter and Family, Papers. Minnesota Historical Society. Saint Paul, Minnesota.

McKenzie, Benjamin, Letters. Manuscripts Division. Alabama Department of Archives and History. Montgomery, Alabama.

Mackintire, Edmund, Papers. Minnesota Historical Society. Saint Paul, Minnesota.

McLean, Ann, Letters. South Caroliniana Library. University of South Carolina. Columbia, South Carolina.

McMaster, Joseph and Family, Papers, 1848-1929. Minnesota Historical Society. Saint Paul, Minnesota.

McNeel, Allen, Letters. Manuscripts Division. Alabama Department of Archives and History. Montgomery, Alabama.

Macy, Jethro, Commonplace Book. Indiana Historical Society. Indianapolis, Indiana.

Manuscript Journal of a young man of Burlington (Vt.) who in 1839 journeyed to Va. and other places. Vermont Historical Society. Montpelier, Vermont.

Marshall, Thomas, Family Correspondence. Indiana Historical Society. Indianapolis, Indiana.

Martenet, Jefferson, Collection. Henry E. Huntington Library and Art Gallery. San Marino, California.

Mason, Albert, Diaries. New Hampshire Historical Society. Concord, New Hampshire.

Matthews, James Washington, Diary. Southern Historical Collection. University of North Carolina. Chapel Hill, North Carolina.

Maverick, Brewster, Diary, 1847. New-York Historical Society. New York, New York.

Mayberry, William, Journal, 1849-1851. Maine Historical Society. Portland, Maine.

Meredith, Samuel Caldwell, Letters. Indiana Historical Society. Indianapolis, Indiana.

Merrell, Walter S., Journal. Connecticut State Library. Hartford, Connecticut.

Mersman, Joseph I., Diary. Missouri Historical Society. Saint Louis, Missouri.

Metcalf, Isaac S., Letters. Minnesota Historical Society. Saint Paul, Minnesota.

Miller, Hiram, Diary, 1833. Manuscripts Division. New York Public Library. New York, New York.

Miller, James, Letter. South Caroliniana Library. University of South Carolina. Columbia, South Carolina.

Missouri History Papers. Missouri Historical Society. Saint Louis, Missouri.

Mitchell, Benjamin, Family Papers. Collection of Regional History. Cornell University. Ithaca, New York.

Mitchell, T. James, Papers. Minnesota Historical Society. Saint Paul, Minnesota.

Mitchell, William B. and Family, Papers, 1807-1850. Minnesota Historical Society. Saint Paul, Minnesota.

Montgomery, William, Journal, HM19474. Henry E. Huntington Library and Art Gallery. San Marino, California.

Morris, W. A., Letters. Manuscripts Division. Alabama Department of Archives and History. Montgomery, Alabama.

Mott Family Papers. New-York Historical Society. New York, New York.

Nash, William, Diary and Account Book, 1821-1841. Western Historical Manuscripts Collection. University of Missouri. Columbia, Missouri.

Nearing, Mary A., Diary, Berry Collection. Collection of Regional History. Cornell University. Ithaca, New York.

Newcomb-Johnson Collection. Henry E. Huntington Library and Art Gallery. San Marino, California.

New York City Diary, 1844-1845, by an unknown clerk. Manuscripts Division. New York Public Library. New York, New York.

Nichols, Samuel, Collection. Henry E. Huntington Library and Art Gallery. San Marino, California.

Niles, A. F., Diary, 1850. Vermont Historical Society. Montpelier, Vermont.

Nims, Brigham, Family Papers. New Hampshire Historical Society. Concord, New Hampshire.

Nixon, Orville, Journal, HM17012. Henry E. Huntington Library and Art Gallery. San Marino, California.

Norton, Cordelia, Letter. South Caroliniana Library. University of South Carolina. Columbia, South Carolina.

Nourse, George Francis, Collection. Henry E. Huntington Library and Art Gallery. San Marino, California.

Ogg, Adams Lee, Collection. Indiana Division of the Indiana State Library. Indianapolis, Indiana.

Olcott, E. M., Diaries. New-York Historical Society. New York, New York.

Oliver, W. K., Correspondence. Manuscripts Division. Alabama Department of Archives and History. Montgomery, Alabama.

Olmsted, Edwin, Diary. Connecticut State Library. Hartford, Connecticut.

Orton, John B., Diaries, 1845-1907. Manuscripts Division. New York Public Library. New York, New York.

Ostrander, John, Family Papers. Collection of Regional History. Cornell University. Ithaca, New york.

Parker, Lucien, Correspondence. Henry E. Huntington Library and Art Gallery. San Marino, California.

Parkhill, Nathan E., Diaries, 1852-1901. Vermont Historical Society. Montpelier, Vermont.

Parks, George, Letter. South Caroliniana Library. University of South Carolina. Columbia, South Carolina.

Patterson, Henry A., Diaries, 1836-1849. New-York Historical Society. New York, New York.

Patterson, Joseph, Letter. Kentucky Historical Society. Frankfort, Kentucky.

Paul, Mary, Letters. Vermont Historical Society. Montpelier, Vermont.

Peck Family Papers. Collection of Regional History. Cornell University. Ithaca, New York.

Peck, Hiram, Diary, 1830-1834. New-York Historical Society. New York, New York.

Pelton, Oliver, Correspondence. Connecticut State Library. Hartford, Connecticut.

Pelton, Oliver, Journals and Account Books. Connecticut State Library. Hartford, Connecticut.

Perkins, Elisha D., Diary, HM1547, Henry E. Huntington Library and Art Gallery. San Marino, California.

Phelps, Edward Ashley Bowen, Letters and Diary, 1847-1848. Manuscripts Division. New York Public Library. New York, New York.

Pierson, G. C., Letter. Kentucky Historical Society. Frankfort, Kentucky.

Pond, Ananias Roger, Journal, HM19383. Henry E. Huntington Library and Art Gallery. San Marino, California.

Pounds, Reuben and Elizabeth, Correspondence. Manuscripts Division. Alabama Department of Archives and History. Montgomery, Alabama.

Powell, William S., Papers. Southern Historical Collection. University of North Carolina. Chapel Hill, North Carolina.

Putnam, Henry, Diary and Account Book, 1836-1839. New-York Historical Society. New York, New York.

Reber, Thomas, Diaries. Collection of Regional History. Cornell University. Ithaca, New York.

Rhodes, H. N., Diary. Vermont Historical Society. Montpelier, Vermont.

Rich Family Papers. Maine Historical Society. Portland, Maine.

Ricketts, John, Letter. Kentucky Historical Society. Frankfort, Kentucky.

Riddick, Charles C., Papers, Southern Historical Collection. University of North Carolina. Chapel Hill, North Carolina.

Rider, Fred Jr., *Collector*. Family Papers, 1784-1856. Collection of Regional History. Cornell University. Ithaca, New York.

Rollins, John, Papers, 1848-1853. Minnesota Historical Society, Saint Paul, Minnesota.

Ryland, Robert and Josephine, Collection. Six Vault. Georgia Department of Archives and History. Atlanta, Georgia.

Savage, John, Diaries. Manuscripts Division. Iowa Historical Library, Iowa State Department of History and Archives. Des Moines, Iowa.

Savannah Yellow Fever Letter. University of Georgia Libraries. Division of Special Collections. Athens, Georgia.

Scott, John M., Letters. University of Georgia Libraries. Division of Special Collections. Athens, Georgia.

Scribner, Benjamin Franklin, Collection. Henry E. Huntington Library and Art Gallery. San Marino, California.

Shearman, Humphrey L., Letter. South Caroliniana Library. University of South Carolina. Columbia, South Carolina.

Sherman-Safford Papers. Vermont Historical Society. Montpelier, Vermont.

Silliman, Eliphalet, Journal. Connecticut State Library. Hartford, Connecticut.

Silliman, William, Journal. Connecticut State Library. Hartford, Connecticut.

Slagle, Elam, Papers. Southern Historical Collection. University of North Carolina. Chapel Hill, North Carolina.

Smedberg, John G., Letter. South Caroliniana Library. University of South Carolina. Columbia, South Carolina.

Smith Collection. Six Vault. Georgia Department of Archives and History. Atlanta, Georgia.

Smith, Elijah, Papers. Collection of Regional History. Cornell University. Ithaca, New York.

Smith, Lovina, Letters. Collection of Regional History. Cornell University. Ithaca, New York.

Smith, Orrin F. and Family, Papers, 1829-1932. Minnesota Historical Society. Saint Paul, Minnesota.

Smith, Timothy, Diary. Maine Historical Society. Portland, Maine.

Smith, William S., Letter. Manuscripts Division. Alabama Department of Archives and History. Montgomery, Alabama.

Spinney-Hunt-Wildes Papers. Maine Historical Society. Portland, Maine.

Sprague, William Y., Diaries. Connecticut State Library. Hartford, Connecticut.

Squires, Francis W., Diaries. Collection of Regional History. Cornell University. Ithaca, New York.

Starr, Henry, Diary. Indiana Division of the Indiana State Library. Indianapolis, Indiana.

Stebbins Letter. Collection of Regional History. Cornell University. Ithaca, New York.

Steele, John, Diary. Manuscripts Division. Alabama Department of Archives and History. Montgomery, Alabama.

Sterrett, Andrew Jackson, Papers. Minnesota Historical Society. Saint Paul, Minnesota.

Stevens, Henry, Letters, 1851-1853. Vermont Historical Society. Montpelier, Vermont.

Stratton, Pauline H., Diary, 1841-1870. Western Historical Manuscripts Collection. University of Missouri. Columbia, Missouri.

Stuart, Lyman, *Collector.* Stampless Covers. Collection of Regional History. Cornell University. Ithaca, New York.

Stuart, Lyman, Papers. Collection of Regional History. Cornell University. Ithaca, New York.

Sullivan, Joseph, Letter. South Caroliniana Library. University of South Carolina. Columbia, South Carolina.

Sullivan, Monroe, Letter. Kentucky Historical Society. Frankfort, Kentucky.

Summer, Henry, Diary. South Caroliniana Library. University of South Carolina. Columbia, South Carolina.

Talley, Jeptha, Diary of. Six Vault. Georgia Department of Archives and History. Atlanta, Georgia.

Tarble, Eli, Account Book. Vermont Historical Society. Montpelier, Vermont.

Taylor, John S., Letters. Kentucky Historical Society. Frankfort, Kentucky.

Teagarden, Barbara Ann, Letter. Kentucky Historical Society. Frankfort, Kentucky.

Templeton, W. A., Correspondence. South Caroliniana Library. University of South Carolina. Columbia, South Carolina.

Thoma-Barnett Letters. Indiana Division of the Indiana State Library. Indianapolis, Indiana.

Thomason, Jackson, Diary. State of Mississippi. Department of Archives and History. Jackson, Mississippi.

Thompson, Arthur P., Letter. Kentucky Historical Society. Frankfort, Kentucky.

Thomson, David, Letter. South Caroliniana Library. University of South Carolina. Columbia, South Carolina.

Tilton, Jeremiah, Papers. New Hampshire Historical Society. Concord, New Hampshire.

Towles, James Moore, Journal, Calvin Henderson Wiley Papers. Southern Historical Collection. University of North Carolina. Chapel Hill, North Carolina.

Travis, Edward F., Diary, 1843-1847. Manuscripts Division. New York Public Library. New York, New York.

Triplet, J. W., Letters. Manuscripts Division. Alabama Department of Archives and History. Montgomery, Alabama.

Tunnell, George H., Collection. Six Vault. Georgia Department of Archives and History. Atlanta, Georgia.

Tuten, James R., Letter. South Caroliniana Library. University of South Carolina. Columbia, South Carolina.

Tuthill, Freegift, Papers. Collection of Regional History. Cornell University. Ithaca, New York.

Tyner, Ezekiel, Correspondence. Indiana Historical Society. Indianapolis, Indiana.

Unidentified Daily Journal kept on a voyage from New York to San Francisco in 1848. New-York Historical Society. New York, New York.

Upshaw Collection. University of Georgia Libraries. Division of Special Collections. Athens, Georgia.

Van Patten, C. V., Letter. South Caroliniana Library. University of South Carolina. Columbia, South Carolina.

Vester, Elijah, Papers. Southern Historical Collection. University of North Carolina. Chapel Hill, North Carolina.

Wall, Charles, Letters. Collection of Regional History. Cornell University. Ithaca, New York.

Ward, Samuel Dexter, Diary, 1842. New-York Historical Society. New York, New York.

Warshinge, Samuel, account books, 1830-1852. New-York Historical Society. New York, New York.

Watkins, Abiathar Hubbard, and Jane Lewis, Papers, 1836-1894. Manuscripts Division. New York Public Library. New York, New York.

Wheeler, George N., Journal, HM16939. Henry E. Huntington Library and Art Gallery. San Marino, California.

Whipple, Charlotte L., Diaries. Manuscripts Division. New York Public Library. New York, New York.

Whitehouse, Seth C., Journal. Maine Historical Society. Portland, Maine.

Wilcox, Horatio, Letter. Collection of Regional History. Cornell University. Ithaca, New York.

Wilkinson, Mary A., Diaries, Harlan Papers. Missouri Historical Society. Saint Louis, Missouri.

Willard, Joseph, Diary. Massachusetts Historical Society. Boston, Massachusetts.

Willard, Seth H., Diary. Maine Historical Society. Portland, Maine.

Williams, Robert, Collection. University of Georgia Libraries. Division of Special Collections. Athens, Georgia.

Williams, William, Diary and Sketch Book. Manuscripts Division. Iowa Historical Library, Iowa State Department of History and Archives. Des Moines, Iowa.

Wilson, Mary Ann Covington, Papers. Southern Historical Collection. University of North Carolina. Chapel Hill, North Carolina.

Wilson, S., Letter. South Caroliniana Library. University of South Carolina. Columbia, South Carolina.

Wood, Joseph, Diary. Maine Historical Society. Portland, Maine.

Workman, Benjamin F., Papers. State of Mississippi. Department of Archives and History. Jackson, Mississippi.

Wright Gift. University of Georgia Libraries. Division of Special Collections. Athens, Georgia.

Young, Sheldon, Diary, JA555. Henry E. Huntington Library and Art Gallery. San Marino, California.

2. *Published Material*

Armstrong, F. H. (ed.). "A Stormy Voyage in 1850," *Inland Seas* 18 (Fall 1962), 219-24.

Atkinson, J. H. (ed.). "Travel in Pioneer Days," *Arkansas Historical Quarterly* 20 (Winter 1961), 351-54.

Baker, Donald E. (ed.). "The Conine Family Letters, 1849-1851: Employed in Honest Business and Doing the Best We Can," *Indiana Magazine of History* 69 (December 1973), 320-65.

————. "The Conine Family Letters, 1852-1863: 'Just Think How We Are Scattered,'" *Indiana Magazine of History* 70 (June 1974), 122-78.

Beeson, Lewis (ed.). "A Trip up the Menominee River in 1854: Alanson Forman Lyon," *Michigan History* 47 (December 1963), 301-11.

Boney, F. N. (ed.). "Southern Sojourn: A Yankee Salesman in Ante-Bellum Alabama," *Alabama Review* 20 (April 1967), 142-54.

Brooks, Richard Albert Edward (ed.). *The Diary of Michael Floy Jr. Bowery Village 1833-1837.* New Haven, Conn.: Yale University Press, 1941.

Bryan, Charles W., Jr. "From Marthasville to Marysville in 1850," *Missouri Historical Society Bulletin* 19 (January 1963), 115-26.

Buck, Solon J. (ed.). "Pioneer Letters of Gershom Flagg," *Transactions of the Illinois State Historical Society* (1910), 139-83.

Burmester, Ruth Seymour (Intro.). "Silas J. Seymour Letters," *Wisconsin Magazine of History* 32 (December 1948), 188-99; (March 1949), 328-38; (June 1949), 456-71.

C.W.D. (ed.). "Across the Plains in 1850," *Annals of Iowa*, Third Series, 9 (July-October 1910), 447-83.

Caldwell, Martha B. (ed.). "The Diary of George H. Hildt, June to December, 1857: Pioneer of Johnson County," *Kansas Historical Quarterly* 10 (August 1941), 260-98.

"California Diary of Charles M. Tuttle, 1859," *Wisconsin Magazine of History* 15 (September 1931), 69-85; (December 1931), 219-33.

"California Letters of William Goodridge of Beverly: Experiences of One of the Forty-niners from Essex County," *Essex Institute Historical Collections* 78 (October 1942), 376-86.

Cammack, Eleanore (ed.). "From Indiana to Iowa," *Annals of Iowa*, Third Series, 29 (July 1948), 400-405.

Camp, Charles L. (ed.). "The Journal of Benjamin Dore, One of the Argonauts," *California Historical Society Quarterly* 2 (July 1923), 87-139.

Camp, Truman (ed.). "The Journal of Joseph Camp, 1859," *Nebraska History* 46 (March 1965), 29-38.

Cantelon, Philip L. (ed.). "The California Gold Fields in the 1850's: Letters from Ephraim Thompson, Daviess County, Indiana," *Indiana Magazine of History* 65 (September 1969), 157-72.

Carmony, Donald (ed.). "Frontier Life: Loneliness and Hope," *Indiana Magazine of History* 61 (March 1965), 53-57.

Caughey, John W. (ed.). "Life in California in 1849, As Described in the 'Journal' of George F. Kent," *California Historical Society Quarterly* 20 (March 1941), 26-46.

Chadwick, Thomas W. (ed.). "The Diary of Samuel Edward Burges, 1860-1862," *South Carolina Historical and Genealogical Magazine* 48 (April 1947), 63-75; (July 1947), 141-63.

Churchill, Claire Warner (ed.). "The Journey to Oregon—A Pioneer Girl's Diary," *Oregon Historical Quarterly* 29 (March 1928), 77-98.

Clough, Wilson O. (ed.). "A Journal of Village Life in Vermont in 1848," *New England Quarterly* 1 (January 1928), 32-40.

Corbitt, D. L. (ed.). "Letters from Hugh Luckey, Raleigh Hatter, 1843," *North Carolina Historical Review* 25 (April 1948), 179-92.

Crookes, Harold F. (ed.). "Diary of John Peake," *Journal of the Illinois Historical Society* 8 (April 1915), 114-31.

D.B.H. (ed.). "A Young Yankee in the New West," *Year Book of the Society of Indiana Pioneers* (1960), 5-40.

Davis, Allen F. "The Girl He Left Behind: The Letters of Harriet Hutchinson Salisbury," *Vermont History* 23 (January 1965), 274-82.

Day, James M. (ed.). "Diary of James A. Glasscock, Mier Man," *Texana* 1 (Spring 1963), 85-119; (Summer 1963), 225-38.

Des Champs, Margaret Burr (ed.). "Some Mississippi Letters to Robert Fraser, 1841-1844," *Journal of Mississippi History* 15 (July 1953), 181-89.

"Diary of a Journey to Wisconsin in 1840," *Wisconsin Magazine of History* 6 (September 1922), 73-94; (December 1922), 207-32; (March 1923), 334-45.

"Diary of an Emigrant of 1845," *Washington Historical Quarterly* 1 (April 1907), 138-58.

"The Diary of Henry Stevens," *Proceedings of the Vermont Historical Society* 2 (September 1931), 115-28.

"The Diary of James R. Stewart, Pioneer of Osage County, April, 1855-April, 1857; May, 1858-November, 1860," *Kansas Historical Quarterly* 17 (February 1949), 1-36; (May 1949), 122-75; (August 1949); 254-95; (November 1949), 360-97.

"Diary of the Mexican War, By Thomas Bailey, Musician, Company C, Fifth Regiment, Indiana Volunteers," *Indiana Magazine of History* 14 (June 1918), 134-47.

Donald, David (ed.). "Lexington, Mississippi in 1844," *Journal of Mississippi History* 9 (October 1947), 265-67.

Dowdell, Victor L., and Helen C. Everett (eds.). "California Diary of John French, 1850-51," *Michigan History Magazine* 38 (March 1954), 33-44.

Duckett, Kenneth (ed.). "A 'Down-Easter' in Wisconsin: Sears Letters, 1849, 1854," *Wisconsin Magazine of History* 41 (Spring 1958), 204-207.

E.R.H. (ed.). "Journal of the Oregon Trail," *Annals of Iowa*, Third Series, 8 (January 1908), 304-10.

Easterby, J. H. (ed.). "South Carolina Through New England Eyes: Almira Coffin's Visit to the Low Country in 1851," *South Carolina Historical and Genealogical Magazine* 45 (July 1944), 127-36.

"An 1849 Letter from California Advising His Father of His Arrival, By Joseph Ledlie Moody," *California Historical Society Quarterly* 13 (March 1934), 84-85.

"An Emigrant's Letter in 1840," *Annals of Iowa*, Third Series, 34 (October 1958), 460-64.

Everett, Helen (ed.). "Early Michigan Letters," *Michigan History* 42 (December 1958). 414-18.

Fogle, Louise (ed.). "Journal of Ebenezer Mattoon Chamberlain," *Indiana Magazine of History* 15 (September 1919), 235-59.

"Footnotes to Vermont History: A Department," *Vermont Quarterly: A Magazine of History*, New Series, 21 (January 1953), 51-52.

Gibson, Edmund P. (ed.). "To Michigan by Water—1844," *Inland Seas* 10 (Spring 1954), 51-55.

Glazer, Sidney (ed.). "In Old Detroit (1831-1836)," *Michigan History Magazine* 26 (Spring 1942), 202-14.

"A Glimpse of Early Merrimac," *Wisconsin Magazine of History* 29 (September 1945), 85-88.

G.O.A. (ed.). "A Gold Rush Diary," *Historical Society of Southern California Quarterly* 36 (December 1954), 287-91.

Goodell, Robert H. (ed.). "Matthias Zahm's Diary," *Papers of the Lancaster County Historical Society* 47 (No. 4, 1943), 61-92.

Graf, LeRoy P. (ed.). "The Journal of a Vermont Man in Ohio, 1836-1842," *Ohio State Archaeological and Historical Quarterly* 60 (April 1951), 175-99.

Gray, Anna Brockway (comp.). "Letters from the Long Ago," *Michigan History Magazine* 13 (Summer 1929), 469-91; 15 (Summer 1931), 459-80; 18 (Spring 1934), 150-60; 20 (Spring and Summer 1936), 185-212.

Greer, James K. (ed.). "Diary of a Pennsylvania Volunteer in the Mexican War," *Western Pennsylvania Historical Magazine* 12 (July 1929), 147-54.

———. "Journal of Ammon Underwood, 1834-1838," *Southwestern Historical Quarterly* 32 (October 1928), 124-51.

Harry, Bertha S. (ed.). "Extracts from the Diary of Susan W. Yerkes," *Bulletin of the Historical Society of Montgomery County Pennsylvania* 3 (October 1942), 182-202.

Hayes, Arthur Homer (ed.). "Diary of Taylor N. Snow, Hoosier Fifty-niner," *Indiana Magazine of History* 28 (September 1932), 193-208.

Henderson, Alfred. "A Morgan County Volunteer in the Mexican War," *Journal of the Illinois State Historical Society* 41 (December 1948), 383-401.

Hendrickson, Walter B. (ed.). "The Happy Soldier: The Mexican War Letters of John Nevin King," *Journal of the Illinois State Historical Society* 46 (Spring 1953), 13-27; (Summer, 1953), 151-70.

Hieb, David L. (ed.). "An 1850 Gold Rush Letter from Fort Laramie by A. C. Sponsler, A Thayer County Pioneer," *Nebraska History* 32 (June 1951), 130-39.

Hinckley, Ted and Caryl (eds.). "Overland from St. Louis to the California Gold Field in 1849: The Diary of Joseph Waring Berrien," *Indiana Magazine of History* 56 (December 1960), 274-352.

Howell, N. R. (ed.). "Journal of a Tour from Riverhead, Long Island, to the Falls of Niagara in June 1831, By Moses C. Cleveland," *New York History* 27 (July 1946), 352-64.

Hunt, Elmer Munson (ed.). "The Gold Rush Diary of Moses Cogswell of New Hampshire, *Historical New Hampshire* (December 1949), 1-26.

Hyatt, L. Paul (ed.). "J. M. Alexander: A Gold Miner's Letter, 1852," *California Historical Society Quarterly* 49 (December 1970), 353-58.

Jenkins, John H. (ed.). "Texas Letters and Documents," *Texana* 1 (Fall 1963), 54-61; 2 (Fall 1964), 217-21.

Jervey, Edward D., and James E. Moss (eds.). "From Virginia to Missouri in 1846: The

Journal of Elizabeth Ann Cooley," *Missouri Historical Review* 60 (January 1966), 162-206.

Jones, Dorsey D. (ed.). "Two Letters by a Pioneer from Arkansas," *Oregon Historical Quarterly* 45 (September 1944), 228-37.

"Journal of a Tour to Niagara Falls, Montreal, Lake Champlain, &c.," *Proceedings of the New Jersey Historical Society* 69 (October 1951), 342-62.

"Journal of a Trip from Brooklyn to Niagara Falls in June 1841: John Read Barrows," *New York History* 23 (April 1942), 190-99.

"Journal of A. W. Harlan While Crossing the Plains in 1850," *Annals of Iowa*, Third Series, 11 (April 1913), 32-62.

"Journal of Cyrus Sanders," *Iowa Journal of History and Politics* 37 (January 1939), 52-88.

"The Journal of Jane Vorhees Lewis," *Proceedings of the New Jersey Historical Society* 65 (April 1947), 83-92.

"Journal of John T. Williams," *Indiana Magazine of History* 32 (December 1936), 393-409.

"Journal of Lewis Birdsall Harris," *Southwestern Historical Quarterly* 25 (July 1921), 63-71; (October 1975), 131-46; (January 1922), 185-97.

Kincaid, Robert L. (ed.). "Letter of John M. Crockett, 1846," *Register of the Kentucky Historical Society* 52 (October 1954), 305-309.

King, James T. (ed.). "'I Take This Opportunity to Inform You . . .': The Gold Rush Letters of Andrew Cairns," *California Historical Society Quarterly* 46 (September 1967), 206-22.

Kull, Nell W. "'I Can Never Be Happy There in Among So Many Mountains'—The Letters of Sally Rice," *Vermont History* 38 (Winter 1970), 49-57.

Lake, Mary Daggett (ed.). "A Diary of the Travels of William G. Randle, Daguerreotypist, of Henry County, Tennessee, 1852," *Tennessee Historical Magazine* 9 (October 1925), 195-208.

Landon, Fred. "Extracts from the Diary of William C. King, A Detroit Carpenter, in 1832," *Michigan History Magazine* 19 (Winter 1935), 65-70.

Langsdorf, Edgar (ed.). "The Letters of Joseph H. Trego, 1857-1864, Linn County Pioneer," *Kansas Historical Quarterly* 19 (May 1951), 113-32.

"A Letter of 1832," *Indiana Magazine of History* 25 (September 1929), 242-45.

"Letters from the Past," *Vermont Quarterly: A Magazine of History*, New Series, 20 (January 1952), 45-50; (April 1952), 125-32; (July 1952), 208-14; (October 1952), 295-303; 21 (January, 1953), 38-46.

"Letters Home from '49ers," *Journal of the Illinois State Historical Society* 42 (March 1949), 84-89.

"Letters of a Frederick County Forty-Niner," *Maryland Historical Magazine* 44 (June 1949), 130-37.

"Letters of a Pioneer Teacher," *Annals of Iowa*, Third Series, 35 (Spring 1961), 616-20.

"Letters of Hugh Moore," *Kansas Historical Quarterly* 10 (May 1941), 115-23.

"Letters of Richard Emerson Ela," *Wisconsin Magazine of History* 19 (June 1936), 431-53; (September 1936), 72-88.

Lindsey, David (ed.). "The Journal of an 1859 Pike's Peak Gold Seeker," *Kansas Historical Quarterly* 22 (Winter 1956), 321-41.

"Locating a New Home," *Annals of Iowa*, Third Series, 23 (October 1941), 138-42.

Loehr, Rodney C. (ed.). *Minnesota Farmers' Diaries: William R. Brown, 1845-46;*

Mitchell Y. Jackson, 1852-63. Saint Paul, Minn.: Minnesota Historical Society, 1939.

Lovett, Robert W. (ed.). "Augustus Roundy's Cincinnati Sojourn," *Historical and Philosophical Society of Ohio Bulletin* 19 (October 1961), 254-64.

McArthur, Jean. "A Lebanon Farmer in the 1830's," *Connecticut Historical Society Bulletin* 30 (January 1965), 18-25.

McKelvey, Blake (ed.). "The Autobiography of Asher Freeman. Written by a Frugal Pioneer of Niagara County in 1852," *New York History* 25 (April 1944), 212-25.

Marshall, Thomas Maitland (ed.). "The Journal of Henry B. Miller," *Missouri Historical Society Collections* 6 (1931), 213-87.

Martin, Mabelle Eppard (ed.). "From Texas to California in 1849: Diary of C. C. Cox," *Southwestern Historical Quarterly* 29 (July 1925), 36-50; (October 1925), 128-46; (January 1926), 201-23.

Millsap, Kenneth F. (ed.). "Romanzo Kingman's Pike's Peak Journal, 1859," *Iowa Journal of History* 48 (January 1950), 55-85.

"Minnesota as Seen by Travelers: A Pennsylvanian Visits the West in 1855," *Minnesota History* 7 (December 1926), 336-39.

Mitcham, Howard (ed.). "A Mississippian in the Gold Fields: The Letters of John Paul Dart, 1849-1856," *California Historical Society Quarterly* 35 (September 1956), 205-31.

Mooney, Chase C. (ed.). "Some Letters from Dover, Tennessee, 1814-1855," *Tennessee Historical Quarterly* 8 (June 1949), 154-84; (September, 1949), 252-83; (December 1949), 345-65; 9 (March 1950), 64-83; (June 1950), 155-70.

Moore, John Hammond (ed.). "Private Johnson Fights the Mexicans, 1847-1848," *South Carolina Historical Magazine* 7 (October 1966), 203-28.

"A New Englander in the West: Letters of Eben Weld, 1845-50," *Minnesota History: A Quarterly Magazine* 15 (September 1934), 301-308.

"An Optimistic Pioneer in a Period of Depression," *Minnesota History* 13 (June 1932), 174-78.

"Overland in 1853: William Warner's Letter to His Mother," *California Historical Society Quarterly* 5 (September 1926), 289-92.

"Overland Journey to California by Platte River Route in 1850, By Fancher Stimson," *Annals of Iowa*, Third Series, 13 (October 1922), 403-40.

Padgett, James A. (ed.). "A Yankee School Teacher in Louisiana, 1835-1837: The Diary of Caroline B. Poole," *Louisiana Historical Quarterly* 20 (July 1937), 651-79.

Palmer, Norman D. "Maine Man in California: A Record of the Gold Rush Era," *New England Quarterly* 20 (June 1947), 252-59.

Park, Helen O'Boyle (ed.). "Pepper Wife," *Essex Institute Historical Collections* 94 (April 1958), 151-55.

Parsons, John E. (ed.). "Grandfather in the Gold Rush: Isaac Annis Writes Home from the Auburn Dry Diggins," *New-York Historical Society Quarterly* 41 (January 1957), 5-23.

Peach, Arthur Wallace (ed.). "John Clark's Journal (1824-1842)," *Proceedings of the Vermont Historical Society*, New Series, 10 (December 1942), 187-213.

Perrigo, Lynn I. (ed.). "Hawley's Diary of His Trip Across the Plains in 1860," *Wisconsin Magazine of History* 19 (March 1939), 319-42.

"The 'Pleisures' of Western Traveling," *Journal of the Illinois State Historical Society* 46 (Autumn 1953), 305-308.

"Pollock Correspondence," *Indiana Magazine of History* 31 (March 1935), 50-65.

Pomeroy, Earl S. (ed.). "Wisconsin in 1847: Notes of John Q. Roods," *Wisconsin Magazine of History* 33 (December 1949), 216-20.

Rabb, Kate Milner. "A Hoosier Listening Post," *Indianapolis Star*, April 6, 1929 (Excerpts from diary of Lewis Brooks.)

———. "A Hoosier Listening Post," *Indianapolis Star*, May 5, 10, 13, 14, 16, 18, 22, 24, 25, 26, June 4, 12, 1930. (Excerpts from diary of Samuel Chew Madden.)

"The Retrospect of a Pioneer in the New Hampshire Grants," *Proceedings of the Vermont Historical Society*, New Series, 8 (September 1940), 263-81.

Rex, Millicent B. (ed.). "Three Letters of a Century Ago," *Western Pennsylvania Historical Magazine* 22 (December 1939), 263-78.

Rezneck, Samuel. "A Schoolboy of 1830," *New York History* 17 (April 1936), 135-46.

Rogers, Gladys Gage. "Seth Shaler Arnold (1788-1871): Vermonter," *Proceedings of the Vermont Historical Society*, New Series, 7 (December 1939), 217-45.

Roseboom, Eugene H. (ed.). "Charles Tinker's Journal: A Trip to California in 1849," *Ohio State Archaeological and Historical Quarterly* 61 (January 1952), 64-85.

Sanborn, Janet Coe (ed.). "By Road, Rail, Canal and Lake—From Massachusetts to Michigan in 1836," *Inland Seas* 16 (Fall 1960), 224-29.

Sanford, Charles L. "'A New Home—Who'll Follow?' Letters of a New England Emigrant Family in Ohio, 1831-1842," *Ohio Historical Quarterly* 65 (April 1956), 152-66.

Santee, J. F. (ed.). "Letters of John R. Tice," *Oregon Historical Quarterly* 37 (March 1936), 24-44.

Scamehorn, Howard L. (ed.). *The Buckeye Rovers in the Gold Rush: An Edition of Two Diaries*. Athens, Ohio: Ohio University Press, 1965.

Scribner, Benjamin Franklin. *Camp Life of a Volunteer. A Campaign in Mexico, or a Glimpse at Life in Camp. By "One Who Has Seen the Elephant."* Philadelphia: Grigg, Elliot & Co., 1847.

"Selections from the Plymouth Diary of Abigail Baldwin, 1853-4," *Vermont History* 40 (Summer 1972), 218-23.

Silliman, Sue. "Overland to Michigan in 1846," *Michigan History Magazine* 5 (July-October 1921), 424-34.

Silver, James W. (ed.). "The Wandering Westons: Some Letters of Henry and Sidney Weston," *Journal of Mississippi History* 25 (April 1963), 123-34.

Skillin, Rebecca C. (ed.). "William Cheney (1787-1875): The Life of a Vermont Woodsman and Farmer," *Vermont History* 39 (Winter 1971), 43-50.

Smith, George Winston, and Charles Judah (eds.). *Chronicles of the Gringos: The U.S. Army in the Mexican War, 1846-48. Accounts of Eyewitnesses and Combatants.* Albuquerque, N. Mex.: University of New Mexico Press, 1968.

Spellmann, L. U. (ed.). "Letters of the 'Dawson Men' from Perote Prison, Mexico, 1842-1843," *Southwestern Historical Quarterly* 38 (April 1935), 246-69.

Spinney, Frank O. "A New Hampshire Schoolmaster Views Kentucky: Three Letters, 1847-1848," *New England Quarterly* 17 (March 1944), 87-94.

Stewart, Edgar A. (ed.). "The Journal of James Mallory, 1834-1877," *Alabama Review*

14 (July 1961), 219-32.

Stokes, Durward T. (ed.). "The Wilson Letters, 1835-1849," *Missouri Historical Review* 60 (July 1966), 495-517.

Taggart, Harold F. (ed.). "The Journal of David Jackson Staples," *California Historical Society Quarterly* 22 (June 1943), 119-50.

Tanis, Robert James (ed.). "The Journal of Levi Lathrop Smith, 1847-1848," *Pacific Northwest Quarterly* 43 (October 1952), 277-301.

Tarr, John A. (ed.). "Philo Thompson's Diary of a Journey on the Main Line Canal," *Pennsylvania History* 32 (July 1965), 295-304.

"Thomas C. Duggins Views Northwest Missouri in 1840," *Missouri Historical Review* 55 (January 1961), 124-26.

Thompson, Arthur W. (ed.). "A Massachusetts Mechanic in Florida and Mexico—1847," *Florida Historical Quarterly* 33 (October 1954), 130-41.

————. "A Massachusetts Traveller on the Florida Frontier," *Florida Historical Quarterly* 38 (October 1959), 129-41.

Thorne, Marco G. (ed.). "Bound for the Land of Canaan, Ho! The Diary of Levi Stowell," *California Historical Society Quarterly* 27 (March 1948), 33-50; (June 1948), 157-64; (September 1948), 259-66; (December 1948), 361-70; 28 (March 1949), 57-68.

Throne, Mildred (ed.). "The California Journey of George D. Magoon, 1852-1854," *Iowa Journal of History* 54 (April 1956), 131-68.

Tyler, Alice Felt. "A New England Family on the Illinois Frontier," *Papers in Illinois History and Transactions for the Year 1942* (Springfield, 1944), 72-92.

"A Voyage to California in 1849," *Proceedings of the New Jersey Historical Society*, New Series, 8 (October 1923), 299-301.

Warner, Robert M. (ed.). "A Document of Michigan Pioneer Life," *Michigan History* 40 (June 1956), 215-24.

Welsh, Donald H. (ed.). "Martha J. Woods Visits Missouri in 1857," *Missouri Historical Review* 55 (January 1961), 109-23.

Wheat, Carl I. (ed.). "'California's Bantam Cock': The Journals of Charles E. De Long, 1854-1863," *California Historical Society Quarterly* 8 (September 1929), 193-213, (December 1929), 337-63; 9 (March 1930), 50-80, (June 1930), 129-81, (September 1930), 243-87; 10 (March 1931), 40-78, (June 1931), 165-201, (September 1931), 245-97, (December 1931), 355-95; 11 (March 1932), 47-64.

White, Kate (ed.). "The Diary of a '49-er'—Jacob Stuart," *Tennessee Historical Magazine*, Second Series, 1 (July 1931), 279-85.

Winther, Oscar Osburn, and Rose Dodge Galey (eds.). "Mrs. Butler's 1853 Diary of Rogue River Valley," *Oregon Historical Quarterly* 41 (December 1940), 337-66.

Winton, Harry N.M. (ed.). "William T. Newby's Diary of the Emigration of 1843," *Oregon Historical Quarterly* 40 (September 1939), 219-42.

"A Wisconsin Tour in 1841," *Proceedings of the New Jersey Historical Society*, New Series, 10 (April 1925), 171-74.

"With Pen in Hand: Letters of a Missouri Frontier Family," *Missouri Historical Society Bulletin* 15 (October 1958), 29-35.

"William Paddock Letters—1848," *Wisconsin Magazine of History* 33 (September 1949), 87-91.

Young, James Harvey (ed.). "Land Hunting in 1836," *Journal of the Illinois State Historical Society* 45 (Autumn 1952), 241-51.

B. LITERARY SOURCES

To this category belong those works, used directly in this study, which might be thought of as constituent parts of the cultural and intellectual climate of pre-Civil War America. Where Emerson, Hawthorne, and Melville are concerned, I have resorted to expedients in the large majority of citations. In the cases of Emerson and Hawthorne, I have not seen fit to assemble (or to deny others the library use of) some one complete, authoritative collected set of the works. The notes will indicate that, for Emerson, I have used the Autograph Centenary, Centenary, and Concord editions; and for Hawthorne, the Riverside and Old Manse editions. Melville's writings lent themselves to another expedient. Because his books are prodigiously segmented, I have cited these interior divisions rather than pages in my notes, thereby dispensing with full bibliographical information.

"The American Mind," *Harper's New Monthly Magazine* 15 (October 1857), 692-98.

Anderson, David D. (ed.). *The Literary Works of Abraham Lincoln*. Columbus, Ohio: Charles E. Merrill Publishing Co., 1970.

Baird, Robert. *Religion in America; or, An Account of the Origin, Progress, Relation to the State, And Present Condition of the Evangelical Churches in the United States. With Notices of the Unevangelical Denominations*. New York: Harper & Brothers, 1844.

Baldwin, Joseph Glover. *The Flush Times of Alabama and Mississippi: A Series of Sketches*. New York: Appleton, 1853.

Blair, Hugh. *Lectures on Rhetoric and Belles Lettres*. 3 vols. in 2. London: Printed T. Cadell & W. Davies, in the Strand, 1806.

Bryce, James. *The American Commonwealth*. 2 vols. 3d ed., revised. New York: Macmillan Co., 1895.

Camp, George Sidney. *Democracy*. New York: Harper & Brothers, Publishers, 1859.

[Channing, William Ellery, the Younger]. "The Friends," *The Dial: A Magazine for Literature, Philosophy, and Religion* 3 (April 1843), 509-11.

Clemens, Samuel L. [Mark Twain]. *The Adventures of Tom Sawyer*. New York: Harper & Brothers, 1938.

———. *Life on the Mississippi*. New York: Harper, 1899.

———. and Charles Dudley Warner. *The Gilded Age: A Tale of To-Day*. 2 vols. New York: Harper & Brothers Publishers, 1915.

[Curtis, George William]. "Editor's Easy Chair," *Harper's New Monthly Magazine* 41 (September 1870), 616-21.

Emerson, Ralph Waldo. "Solitude and Society," *Atlantic Monthly: A Magazine of Literature, Art and Politics* 1 (December 1857), 225-29.

Gilpin, William. *Remarks on Forest Scenery, and Other Woodland Views, (Related Chiefly to Picturesque Beauty) Illustrated by the Scenes of New-Forest in Hampshire*. 2 vols. 2d ed. London: R. Blamire, 1794.

[Hopkins, Mark]. "The Law of Progress of the Race," *United States and Democratic Review* 15 (August 1844), 195-202.

"How Ought American Mind to Be Cultivated?," *Harper's New Monthly Magazine* 15 (June 1857), 121-25.

Howells, William Dean. *The Rise of Silas Lapham*. New York: Signet Classic Paperback, 1963.

"Influence of Missions on the Temporal Conditions of the Heathen," *Baptist Missionary Magazine* 29 (April 1849), 101-105.

James, Henry. *Hawthorne*. New York: Collier Books Paperback, 1966.

[Longstreet, Augustus Baldwin]. *Georgia: Scenes, Characters, Incidents, &c. In the First Half Century of the Republic*. Augusta, Ga.: Printed at the S. R. Sentinel Office, 1835.

M'Cosh, James. *The Method of Divine Government, Physical and Moral*. New York: R. Carter & Brothers, 1852.

Marryat, Frederick. *Diary in America*. Edited by Jules Zanger. Bloomington, Ind.: Indiana University Press, 1960.

Melville, Herman. "Bartleby, the Scrivener. A Tale of Wall-Street," *Putnam's Monthly Magazine of American Literature, Science, and Art*, 2 (November 1853), 547-57; (December 1853), 609-15.

——. "Cock-A-Doodle-Do! Or, The Crowing of the Noble Cock Beneventano," *Harper's New Monthly Magazine* 8 (December 1853), 77-86.

"Mrs. Hemans's Poems," *American Quarterly Review* 1 (March 1827), 153-62.

New York Evening Post, July 3, 1839.

New York Times, July 4, 1856.

Orme, Mary. "Providence," *United States and Democratic Review* 18 (February 1846), 141.

Roehm, Marjorie Catlin. *The Letters of George Catlin and His Family: A Chronicle of the American West*. Berkeley, Calif.: University of California Press, 1966.

Sarmiento, Domingo. *Travels in the United States in 1847*. Translation and Introductory Essay by Michael Aaron Rockland. Princeton, N.J.: Princeton University Press, 1970.

Schaff, Philip. *America: A Sketch of Its Political, Social, and Religious Character*. Edited with Introductory Essay by Perry Miller. Cambridge, Mass.: Harvard University Press, 1961.

Sedgewick, Catherine. "A Memoir of Lucretia Maria Davidson," in *Lives of Sir William Phips, Israel Putnam, Lucretia Maria Davidson, and David Rittenhouse*. Vol. 7 of The Library of American Biography Conducted by Jared Sparks. New York: Harper & Brothers, Publishers, 1870.

Sigma. "Lines Written on Visiting Greenwood Cemetery," *The Knickerbocker, New-York Monthly Magazine* 36 (October 1850), 352-53.

[Smith, Charles Henry]. *Bill Arp's Scrap Book; Humor and Philosophy. Letters 'Pendente Lite,' Letters Historic, Domestic and Pastoral, with Some True Stories Added*. Atlanta, Ga.: Jas. P. Harrison & Co., Publishers and Engravers, 1884.

Thomson, Mortimer [Q.K. Philander Doesticks]. *Pluri-bus-tah: A Song That's-By-No-Author*. New York: Livermore & Rudd, 1856.

Thoreau, Henry David. *Walden*. Volume II of *The Writings of Henry David Thoreau*. Boston: Houghton, Mifflin & Co., 1906.

Tupper, Martin. *Tupper's Poetical Works: Containing 'Proverbial Philosophy,' 'A*

Thousand Lines,' Etc. With a Portrait of the Author. Auburn and Buffalo, N.Y.: John E. Beardsley, n.d.

Watts, Isaac. *The Improvement of the Mind: Or, A Supplement to the Art of Logic....* New York: Published by N. Bangs & T. Mason, 1822.

Webster, Noah. *An American Dictionary of the English Language....* Revised and Enlarged. Springfield, Mass.: George & Charles Merriam, 1855.

II. Secondary Material (Modern scholarship and modern essays)

Abbott, Wilbur Cortez. "Some 'New' History and Historians," *Proceedings of the Massachusetts Historical Society* 64 (October 1930-June 1932), 286-319.

Abrams, M. H. *The Mirror and the Lamp: Romantic Theory and the Critical Tradition.* New York: Oxford University Press, 1953.

Adams, Grace, and Edward Hutter. *The Mad Forties.* New York: Harper & Brothers Publishers, 1942.

Ahlstrom, Sidney. *A Religious History of the American People.* New Haven, Conn.: Yale University Press, 1972.

Aly, Bower. "The Gallows Speech: A Lost Genre," *The Southern Speech Journal* 34 (Spring 1969), 204-13.

Banner, Lois W. "Religious Benevolence as Social Control: A Critique of an Interpretation," *Journal of American History* 60 (June 1973), 23-41.

Baritz, Loren. "The Idea of the West," *American Historical Review* 66 (April 1961), 618-40.

Bartlett, Irving H. "Daniel Webster as a Symbolic Hero," *New England Quarterly: A Historical Review of New England Life and Letters* 45 (December 1972), 484-507.

Barzun, Jacques. *Clio and the Doctors: Psycho-History, Quanto-History and History.* Chicago: University of Chicago Press, 1974.

Baskerville, Barnet. "19th Century Burlesque of Oratory," *American Quarterly* 20 (Winter 1968), 726-43.

Beek, M. van. *An Enquiry into Puritan Vocabulary.* Groningen, Netherlands: Wolters-Noordhoff, 1969.

Bercovitch, Sacvan. *The Puritan Origins of the American Self.* New Haven, Conn.: Yale University Press, 1975.

Bertelson, David. *The Lazy South.* New York: Oxford University Press, 1967.

Berthoff, Rowland. *An Unsettled People: Social Order and Disorder in American History.* New York: Harper & Row, 1971.

Bestor, Arthur. Review of Richard Albert Edward Brooks (ed.). *The Diary of Michael Floy Jr. Bowery Village 1833-1837* (New Haven, Conn., 1941), in *New York History* 23 (April 1942), 200-201.

Bierce, Ambrose. "The Eyes of the Panther," in *In the Midst of Life and Other Tales.* New York: Signet Classic Paperback, 1961.

Billington, Ray Allen. *Protestant Crusade: A Study of the Origins of American Nativism.* New York: Macmillan Co., 1938.

Boas, George. "In Search of the Age of Reason," in Earl R. Wasserman (ed.), *Aspects of the Eighteenth Century.* Baltimore: The Johns Hopkins Press, 1965.

————. *Vox Populi: Essays in the History of an Idea.* Baltimore: The Johns Hopkins
    Press Paperback, 1969.
Bode, Carl. *The Anatomy of American Popular Culture, 1840-1861.* Berkeley, Calif.:
    University of California Press, 1960.
Bodo, John R. *The Protestant Clergy and Public Issues 1812-1848.* Princeton, N.J.:
    Princeton University Press, 1954.
Boorstin, Daniel J. *America and the Image of Europe: Reflections on American
    Thought.* New York: Meridian Book Paperback, 1960.
————. *The Americans: The Colonial Experience.* New York: Random House, 1958.
————. *The Americans: The Democratic Experience.* New York: Random House,
    1973.
————. *The Americans: The National Experience.* New York: Random House, 1965.
Branch, E. Douglas. *The Sentimental Years, 1836-1860.* New York: Hill & Wang
    Paperback, 1965.
Brinton, Crane. *Ideas and Men: The Story of Western Thought.* Englewood Cliffs, N.J.:
    Prentice-Hall, 1963.
Buck, Solon J. "Some Materials for the Social History of the Mississippi Valley in the
    Nineteenth Century," *Proceedings of the Mississippi Valley Historical Associa-
    tion* 4 (1910-1911), 139-51.
Burns, Edward McNall. *The American Idea of Mission: Concepts of National Destiny
    and Purpose.* New Brunswick, N.J.: Rutgers University Press, 1957.
Bury, J. B. *The Idea of Progress: An Inquiry into Its Origins and Growth.* London:
    Macmillan & Co., Ltd., 1924.
Callcott, George H. *History in the United States 1800-1860: Its Practice and Purpose.*
    Baltimore: The Johns Hopkins Press, 1970.
Canby, Henry Seidel. *Thoreau.* Boston: Houghton Mifflin Co., 1939.
Carter, Paul A. *The Spiritual Crisis of the Gilded Age.* DeKalb, Ill.: Northern Illinois
    University Press, 1971.
Cawelti, John G. *Apostles of the Self-Made Man.* Chicago: University of Chicago Press,
    1965.
Chamberlin, J. E. *The Harrowing of Eden: White Attitudes Toward Native Americans.*
    New York: Seabury Press, 1975.
Cherry, Conrad (comp.). *God's New Israel: Religious Interpretations of American
    Destiny.* Englewood Cliffs, N.J.: Prentice-Hall, 1971.
Clebsch, William A. *From Sacred to Profane America: The Role of Religion in Ameri-
    can History.* New York: Harper & Row, 1968.
Cole, C. Robert. "Intellectual History and the Common Man," *Rocky Mountain Social
    Science Journal* 9 (October 1972), 45-55.
Cole, Douglas, and Maria Tippett. "Pleasing Diversity and Sublime Desolation: The
    18th Century British Perception of the Northwest Coast," *Pacific Northwest
    Quarterly* 65 (January 1974), 1-7.
Corlew, Robert E. Review of Frank Lawrence Owsley, *Plain Folk of the Old South*
    (Baton Rouge, La., 1949), in *Tennessee Historical Quarterly* 9 (March 1950),
    84-85.
Covey, Cyclone. *The American Pilgrimage: The Roots of American History, Religion
    and Culture.* New York: Collier Books Paperback, 1961.

Cremin, Lawrence A. *The American Common School: An Historic Conception*. New York: Teachers College, Columbia University, 1951.

Cross, Whitney. *The Burned-over District: The Social and Intellectual History of Enthusiastic Religion in Western New York, 1800-1850*. Ithaca, N.Y.: Cornell University Press, 1950.

Crowther, Simeon J. "A Note on the Economic Position of Philadelphia's White Oaks With a Rebuttal by James H. Hutson," *William and Mary Quarterly: A Magazine of Early American History*, Third Series, 29 (January 1972), 134-36.

Curti, Merle. "The Great Mr. Locke, America's Philosopher, 1783-1861," *The Huntington Library Bulletin* 11 (April 1937), 107-51.

———. *The Growth of American Thought*. 3d ed. New York: Harper & Row, Publishers, 1964.

———. "'Young America'," *American Historical Review* 32 (October 1926), 34-55.

Dahl, Curtis. "The American School of Catastrophe," *American Quarterly* 11 (Fall 1959), 380-90.

Davis, David Brion. *Homicide in American Fiction, 1798-1860: A Study in Social Values*. Ithaca, N.Y.: Cornell University Press, 1957.

———. "Some Themes of Countersubversion: An Analysis of Anti-Masonic, Anti-Catholic, and Anti-Mormon Literature," *Mississippi Valley Historical Review* 47 (September 1960), 205-24.

Degler, Carl N. *Out of Our Past: The Forces That Shaped Modern America*. New York: Harper & Brothers, Publishers, 1959.

Delp, Robert W. "Andrew Jackson Davis: Prophet of American Spiritualism," *Journal of American History* 54 (June 1967), 43-56.

DeVoto, Bernard. *The Literary Fallacy*. Boston: Little, Brown & Co., 1944.

———. *The Year of Decision: 1846*. Boston: Little, Brown & Co., 1943.

Donald, David. "An Excess of Democracy: The American Civil War and the Social Process," *Centennial Review* 5 (Winter 1961), 21-39.

Dorson, Richard M. *Folklore: Selected Essays*. Bloomington, Ind.: Indiana University Press, 1972.

———. "Sam Patch, Jumping Hero," *New York Folklore Quarterly* 1 (1945), 133-51.

Douglas, Ann. "Heaven Our Home: Consolation Literature in the Northern United States, 1830-1880," *American Quarterly* 26 (December 1974), 496-515.

Eastman, Max. *The Sense of Humor*. New York: Charles Scribner's Sons, 1936.

Eaton, Clement. *The Mind of the Old South*. Revised ed. Baton Rouge, La.: Louisiana State University Press, 1967.

Eggleston, Edward. "The New History," *Annual Report of the American Historical Association, 1900* I, 35-47.

Ekirch, Arthur. *The Idea of Progress in America, 1815-1860*. New York: Columbia University Studies in History, Economics and Public Law, 1944.

Eliot, T. S. *American Literature and the American Language: An Address Delivered at Washington University on June 9, 1953*. Saint Louis, Mo.: Washington University Studies, 1953.

Ellul, Jacques. *The Political Illusion*. Translated by Konrad Kellen. New York: Alfred A. Knopf, 1967.

Elson, Ruth Miller. *Guardians of Tradition: American Schoolbooks of the Nineteenth*

Century. Lincoln, Nebr.: University of Nebraska Press, 1964.

Erickson, Charlotte. *Invisible Immigrants: The Adaptation of English and Scottish Immigrants in Nineteenth-Century America*. Coral Gables, Fla.: University of Miami Press, 1972.

Fiedler, Leslie A. *The Return of the Vanishing American*. New York: Stein & Day Paperbacks, 1969.

Fischer, David Hackett. *Historians' Fallacies: Toward a Logic of Historical Thought*. New York: Harper & Row, Publishers, 1970.

Fish, Carl Russell. *The Rise of the Common Man, 1830-1850*. New York: Macmillan Co., 1927.

Fitch, Robert Elliot. *Odyssey of the Self-Centered Self, or Rake's Progress in Religion*. New York: Harcourt, Brace & World, 1960, 1961.

Franklin, John Hope. *The Militant South, 1800-1861*. Cambridge, Mass.: Harvard University Press, 1956.

Fussell, Edwin. *Frontier: American Literature and the American West*. Princeton, N.J.: Princeton University Press, 1965.

Gabriel, Ralph Henry. *The Course of American Democratic Thought*. 2d ed. New York: Ronald Press Co., 1956.

————. "Evangelical Religion and Popular Romanticism in Early Nineteenth-Century America," *Church History* 19 (March 1950), 34-47.

Gastil, Raymond D. *Cultural Regions of the United States*. Seattle, Wash.: University of Washington Press, 1975.

"The Goodale Letters," *Connecticut Historical Society Bulletin* 20 (July 1955), 85-95.

Gorer, Goeffrey. "The Pornography of Death," *Encounter* 5 (October 1955), 49-52.

Greven, Philip. *The Protestant Temperament: Patterns of Child-Rearing, Religious Experience, and the Self in Early America*. New York: Alfred A. Knopf, 1977.

Grimsted, David. "Melodrama as Echo of the Historically Voiceless," in Tamara K. Hareven (ed.), *Anonymous Americans: Explorations in Nineteenth-Century Social History*. Englewood Cliffs, N.J.: Prentice-Hall, 1971.

————. *Melodrama Unveiled: American Theater and Culture, 1800-1850*. Chicago: University of Chicago Press, 1968.

Hacker, Andrew. *The End of the American Era*. New York: Atheneum, 1970.

Handlin, Oscar. *Boston's Immigrants: A Study in Acculturation*. New York: Atheneum Paperback, 1968.

Hansen, Klaus, J. "The Millenium, the West, and Race in the Antebellum American Mind," *Western Historical Quarterly* 3 (October 1972), 373-90.

Haroutunian, Joseph. *Piety Versus Moralism: The Passing of the New England Theology*. New York: Harper Torchbooks Paperback, 1970.

Hartz, Louis. *The Liberal Tradition in America*. New York: Harcourt, Brace & World, 1955.

Hastings, James (ed.). *Dictionary of the Bible*. New York: Charles Scribner's Sons, 1951.

Hay, Robert P. "Providence and the American Past," *Indiana Magazine of History* 65 (June 1969), 79-101.

Higham, John. "Another Look at Nativism," *Catholic Historical Review* 44 (July 1958), 147-58.

————. "Intellectual History and Its Neighbors," *Journal of the History of Ideas: A Quarterly Devoted to Intellectual History* 15 (June 1954), 339-47.

————, and Paul K. Conkin (eds.). *New Directions in American Intellectual History.* Baltimore: The Johns Hopkins University Press, 1979.

Holbrook, Stewart H. *The Yankee Exodus: An Account of Migration from New England.* New York: Macmillan Co., 1950.

Hubbell, Jay B. *The South in American Literature, 1607-1900.* Durham, N.C.: Duke University Press, 1954.

Hughes, H. Stuart. *Consciousness and Society: The Reorientation of European Social Thought, 1890-1930.* New York: Vintage Books Paperback, 1958.

Hutson, James H. "An Investigation of the Inarticulate: Philadelphia's White Oaks," *William and Mary Quarterly: A Magazine of Early American History,* Third Series, 28 (January 1971), 3-25.

————. "Rebuttal" of Simeon J. Crowther's "A Note on the Economic Position of the Philadelphia White Oaks," *William and Mary Quarterly: A Magazine of Early American History,* Third Series, 29 (January 1972), 136-42.

Jacobs, Wilbur. "Francis Parkman's Oration 'Romance in America,'" *American Historical Review* 68 (April 1963), 692-97.

James, Henry. "The Art of Fiction," in *Partial Portraits.* London: Macmillan & Co., Ltd., 1911.

Jamison, A. Leland. "Religions of the Christian Perimeter," in James Ward Smith and A. Leland Jamison (eds.), *The Shaping of American Religion,* I, *Religion in American Life.* Princeton, N.J.: Princeton University Press, 1961.

Jennings, Francis. *The Invasion of America: Indians, Colonialism, and the Cant of Conquest.* Chapel Hill, N.C.: University of North Carolina Press, 1975.

Jensen, Merrill. "The American People and the American Revolution," *Journal of American History* 57 (June 1970), 5-35.

Johnson, Charles Albert. *The Frontier Camp Meeting: Religion's Harvest Time.* Dallas, Tex.: Southern Methodist University Press, 1955.

Johnson, James T. "The Covenant Idea and the Puritan View of Marriage," *Journal of the History of Ideas* 32 (January-March 1971), 107-18.

————. "English Puritan Thought on the Ends of Marriage," *Church History* 38 (December 1969), 429-36.

————. *A Society Ordained by God: English Puritan Marriage Doctrine in the First Half of the Seventeenth Century.* Nashville, Tenn.: Abingdon Press, 1970.

Jordan, Philip D. "Social History: A Nation Announcing Itself," *Ohio Historical Quarterly* 66 (July 1957), 229-37.

————, and Lillian Kessler. *Songs of Yesterday: A Song Anthology of American Life.* Garden City, N.Y.: Doubleday, Doran & Co., 1941.

Jordan, Winthrop D. "Familial Politics: Thomas Paine and the Killing of the King, 1776," *Journal of American History* 60 (September 1973), 294-308.

Judah, J. Stillson. *The History and Philosophy of the Metaphysical Movements in America.* Philadelphia: Westminster Press, 1967.

Katz, Michael B. *The Irony of Early American School Reform: Educational Innovation in Mid-Nineteenth Century Massachusetts.* Cambridge, Mass.: Harvard University Press, 1968.

Kazin, Alfred, and Daniel Aaron (eds.). *Emerson: A Modern Anthology*. New York: Dell Paperback, 1958.

Kelley, Robert E., and O. M. Brack, Jr. *Samuel Johnson's Early Biographies*. Iowa City, Iowa: University of Iowa Press, 1971.

Kouwenhoven, John. *The Beer Can by the Highway: Essays on What's "American" about America*. Garden City, N.Y.: Doubleday, 1961.

Krutch, Joseph Wood (ed.). *Is the Common Man Too Common? An Informal Survey of Our Cultural Resources and What We Are Doing About Them*. Norman, Okla: University of Oklahoma Press, 1954.

————. *The Modern Temper: A Study and a Confession*. New York: Harcourt, Brace & Co., 1929.

Kuhlmann, Susan. *Knave, Fool, and Genius: The Confidence Man as He Appears in Nineteenth-Century Fiction*. Chapel Hill, N.C.: University of North Carolina Press, 1973.

Lawrence, D. H. "Model Americans," *Dial* 74 (May 1923), 503-10.

Leisy, Ernest E. "Fatalism in Moby-Dick," in *Moby-Dick Centennial Essays*. Dallas, Tex.: Southern Methodist University Press, 1953.

Lemisch, Jesse. "The American Revolution Seen from the Bottom Up," in Barton J. Bernstein (ed.), *Towards a New Past: Dissenting Essays in American History*. New York: Pantheon Books, 1968.

————. "Jack Tar in the Streets: Merchant Seamen in the Politics of Revolutionary America," *William and Mary Quarterly: A Magazine of Early American History*, Third Series, 25 (July 1968), 371-407.

————. "Listening to the 'Inarticulate': William Widger's Dream and the Loyalties of Revolutionary Seamen in British Prisons," *Journal of Social History* 3 (Fall 1969), 1-29.

————, and John K. Alexander. "The White Oaks, Jack Tar, and the Concept of the 'Inarticulate'," *William and Mary Quarterly: A Magazine of Early American History*, Third Series, 29 (January 1972), 109-34.

"Let's Keep a Diary," *Annals of Iowa*, Third Series, 23 (January 1942), 254-60.

Lingelbach, William E. (ed.). *Approaches to American Social History*. New York: D. Appleton-Century Co., 1937.

Lippmann, Walter. *A Preface to Morals*. Boston: Beacon Press Paperback, 1960.

Loehr, Rodney C. "Some Sources for Northwest History: Minnesota Farmers' Diaries," *Minnesota History: A Quarterly Magazine* 18 (September 1937), 284-97.

Lucas, F. L. *The Decline of the Romantic Ideal*. Cambridge, England: Cambridge University Press Paperback, 1963.

Lynn, Kenneth S. (ed.). *The Comic Tradition in America*. Garden City, N.Y.: Doubleday Anchor Books, 1958.

————. "Editor's Introduction," for *Uncle Tom's Cabin or, Life Among the Lowly*. Cambridge, Mass.: Harvard University Press, 1962.

Lyons, John O. *The Invention of the Self: The Hinge of Consciousness in the Eighteenth Century*. Carbondale, Ill.: Southern Illinois University Press, 1978.

McCormick, Mrs. Stewart. "Death and Adornment," *Missouri Historical Society Bulletin* 25 (April 1969), 201-206.

McCurdy, Frances Lea. *Stump, Bar, and Pulpit: Speechmaking on the Missouri Frontier*. Columbia, Mo.: University of Missouri Press, 1969.

McLaughlin, Robert W. *The Spiritual Element in History*. New York: Abingdon Press, 1926.

Maclear, J. F. "The Republic and the Millenium," in Elwyn Allen Smith (ed.), *The Religion of the Republic*. Philadelphia: Fortress Press, 1971.

Malin, James C. *The Contriving Brain and the Skillful Hand in the United States: Something About History and the Philosophy of History*. Lawrence, Kans.: Privately printed, 1955.

Martin, Howard H. "The Fourth of July Oration," *Quarterly Journal of Speech* 44 (December 1958), 393-401.

Martin, Terence. *The Instructed Vision: Scottish Common Sense Philosophy and the Origins of American Fiction*. Bloomington, Ind.: Indiana University Press, 1961.

Marty, Martin E. *Righteous Empire: The Protestant Experience in America*. New York: Dial Press, 1970.

Marx, Leo. *The Machine in the Garden: Technology and the Pastoral Ideal in America*. New York: Oxford University Press, 1964.

Matthiessen, F. O. *American Renaissance: Art and Expression in the Age of Emerson and Whitman*. New York: Oxford University Press, 1941.

Memler, Henrietta L. "Virgin Fields of History," *Papers in Illinois History and Transactions for the Year 1937*, (1938), 43-52.

Merk, Frederick. *Manifest Destiny and Mission in American History: A Reinterpretation*. New York: Alfred A. Knopf, 1963.

"Middlebury College Mourns," *Vermont History* 24 (October 1956), 29.

Miller, Douglas T. *The Birth of Modern America 1820-1850*. New York: Pegasus Paperback Edition, 1970.

Miller, Perry. *Consciousness in Concord; The Text of Thoreau's Hitherto 'Lost Journal' (1840-1841) Together with Notes and a Commentary by Perry Miller*. Boston: Houghton Mifflin, 1958.

———. *Errand into the Wilderness*. Cambridge, Mass.: Harvard University Press, 1956.

———. "From the Covenant to the Revival," in James Ward Smith and A. Leland Jamison (eds.), *The Shaping of American Religion*, I, *Religion in American Life*. Princeton, N.J.: Princeton University Press, 1961.

———. *The Life of the Mind in America from the Revolution to the Civil War*. New York: Harcourt, Brace & World, 1965.

———. *Nature's Nation*. Cambridge, Mass.: Harvard University Press, 1967.

———. *The New England Mind: The Seventeenth Century*. Cambridge, Mass.: Harvard University Press, 1963.

———. *The Raven and the Whale: The War of Words and Wits in the Era of Poe and Melville*. New York: Harcourt, Brace, 1956.

Moore, R. Laurence. "Spiritualism and Science: Reflections on the First Decade of the Spirit Rappings," *American Quarterly* 24 (October 1972), 474-500.

More, Paul Elmer. "The Solitude of Nathaniel Hawthorne," *Atlantic Monthly* 88 (November 1901), 588-99.

Morgan, Edmund S. "The Puritan Ethic and the American Revolution," *William and Mary Quarterly: A Magazine of Early American History,* Third Series, 24 (January 1967), 3-43.

Mosier, Richard D. *The American Temper: Patterns of Our Intellectual Heritage.* Berkeley, Calif.: University of California Press, 1952.

————. *Making the American Mind: Social and Moral Ideas in the McGuffey Readers.* New York: King's Crown Press, 1947.

Mumford, Lewis. *The Golden Day: A Study in American Experience and Culture.* New York: Boni & Liveright Publishers, 1926.

Murdock, Kenneth B. "William Hubbard and the Providential Interpretation of History," *Proceedings of the American Antiquarian Society* 52, Part I (April 1942), 15-37.

Nagel, Paul C. *This Sacred Trust: American Nationality 1798-1898.* New York: Oxford University Press, 1971.

Nash, Roderick. *The Nervous Generation: American Thought, 1917-1930.* Chicago: Rand McNally & Co., 1970.

————. *Wilderness and the American Mind.* New Haven, Conn.: Yale University Press, 1967.

Nichols, Roy F. *The Disruption of American Democracy.* New York: Collier Books Paperback, 1962.

Nicolson, Marjorie Hope. *Mountain Gloom and Mountain Glory: The Development of the Aesthetics of the Infinite.* Ithaca, N.Y.: Cornell University Press, 1959.

Niebuhr, H. Richard. *The Kingdom of God in America.* New York: Harper Torchback Edition, 1959.

Nock, Albert Jay. *On Doing the Right Thing: And Other Essays.* New York: Harper & Brothers, 1928.

Nye, Russel B. "The Search for the Individual: 1750-1850," *Centennial Review* 5 (Winter 1961), 1-20.

————. *This Almost Chosen People: Essays in the History of American Ideas.* East Lansing, Mich.: Michigan State University Press, 1966.

Owsley, Frank Lawrence. *Plain Folk of the Old South.* Baton Rouge, La.: Louisiana State University Press, 1949.

Parker, Wilmond W. "Lympus and Lilliesville in 1855," *Proceedings of the Vermont Historical Society,* New Series, 9 (June 1941), 69-83.

Passmore, John. "Explanations in Everyday Life, in Science, and in History," *History and Theory: Studies in the Philosophy of History* 2 (No. 2, 1962), 105-23.

Pattee, Fred Lewis. *The Feminine Fifties.* New York: D. Appleton-Century Co., 1940.

Peach, Arthur Wallace. "Requiem," *Vermont History* 24 (October 1956), inside back cover.

———— (ed.). "The Autobiography of John Whittemore, 1796-1885" *Proceedings of the Vermont Historical Society,* New Series, 6 (December, 1938), 317-51.

———— (ed.). "Memoirs: The Reverend Benjamin Wooster," *Proceedings of the Vermont Historical Society,* New Series, 4 (December 1936), 215-51.

Pearson, Edmund Lester. *Queer Books.* Garden City, N.Y.: Doubleday, Doran & Co., Inc., 1928.

Pelzer, Louis. "History Made by Plain Men," *Iowa Journal of History and Politics* 11 (1913), 307-22.

Post, Albert. *Popular Freethought in America, 1825-1850.* New York: Columbia University Press, 1943.

Potter, David M. (ed.). *Trail to California: The Overland Journal of Vincent Geiger and Wakeman Bryarly*. New Haven, Conn.: Yale University Press, 1945.

Praz, Mario. *The Romantic Agony*. Translated by Angus Davidson. London: Oxford University Press, 1951.

Riegel, Robert Edgar. *Young America, 1830-1840*. Norman, Okla.: University of Oklahoma Press, 1949.

Rinhart, Floyd and Marion. *America's Affluent Age*. New York: A. S. Barnes & Co., 1971.

Risjord, Norman K. "How the 'Common Man' Voted in Jefferson's Virginia," in John B. Boles (ed.), *America: The Middle Period: Essays in the Honor of Bernard Mayo*. Charlottesville, Va.: University Press of Virginia, 1973.

Rockland, Michael Aaron (ed.). *America in the Fifties and Sixties: Julián Marías on the United States*. Translated by Blanche De Puy and Harold C. Raley. University Park, Pa.: Pennsylvania State University Press, 1972.

Rollins, Richard M. "Words as Social Control: Noah Webster and the Creation of the *American Dictionary*," *American Quarterly* 28 (Fall 1976), 415-30.

Rotundo, Barbara. "The Rural Cemetery Movement," *Essex Institute Historical Collections* 109 (July 1973), 231-40.

Rourke, Constance. *American Humor: A Study of the National Character*. New York: Doubleday, 1931.

Sandeen, Ernest R. *The Roots of Fundamentalism: British and American Millenarianism 1800-1930*. Chicago: University of Chicago Press, 1970.

Sanford, Charles L. *The Quest for Paradise: Europe and the American Moral Imagination*. Urbana, Ill.: University of Illinois Press, 1961.

Santayana, George. *Character and Opinion in the United States*. New York: W. W. Norton & Co., Paperback, 1967.

Schlesinger, Arthur, Jr. "America: Experiment or Destiny?," *American Historical Review* 82 (June 1977), 505-22.

Skotheim, Robert Allen. *American Intellectual History and Historians*. Princeton, N.J.: Princeton University Press, 1966.

Slotkin, Richard. *Regeneration Through Violence: The Mythology of the American Frontier, 1600-1860*. Middletown, Conn.: Wesleyan University Press, 1973.

Smith, Chard Powers. *Yankees and God*. New York: Hermitage House, 1954.

Smith, David E. "Millenarian Scholarship in America," *American Quarterly* 17 (Fall 1965), 535-49.

Smith, Timothy L. *Revivalism and Social Reform in Mid-Nineteenth Century America*. New York: Abingdon Press, 1957.

Somkin, Fred. *Unquiet Eagle: Memory and Desire in the Idea of American Freedom, 1815-1860*. Ithaca, N.Y.: Cornell University Press, 1967.

Spaeth, Sigmund. *A History of Popular Music in America*. New York: Random House, 1948.

Stafford, John. *The Literary Criticism of 'Young America': A Study in the Relationship of Politics and Literature 1837-1850*. Berkeley, Calif.: University of California Publications: English Studies, 1952.

Stein, Gertrude. *Everybody's Autobiography*. New York: Random House, 1937.

Taylor, William R. *Cavalier and Yankee: The Old South and American National Char-*

acter. London: W. H. Allen, 1963.

Thernstrom, Stephen. *Poverty and Progress: Social Mobility in a Nineteenth-Century City*. New York: Atheneum Paperback, 1970.

Toll, Robert C. *Blacking Up: The Minstrel Show in Nineteenth-Century America*. New York: Oxford University Press, 1974.

Turner, Frederick Jackson. *The Frontier in American History*. New York: H. Holt & Co., 1920.

Tuveson, Ernest Lee. *Redeemer Nation: The Idea of America's Millennial Role*. Chicago: University of Chicago Press, 1968.

Tyler, Alice Felt. *Freedom's Ferment: Phases of American Social Thought to 1860*. Minneapolis: University of Minnesota Press, 1944.

———. "The Westward Movement as Reflected in Family Papers," *Minnesota History* 24 (June 1943), 111-24.

Tyler, Moses Coit. *A History of American Literature During the Colonial Period 1607-1765*. 2 vols. Revised. New York: G. P. Putnams, 1898.

Van Zandt, Roland. *The Catskill Mountain House*. New Brunswick, N.J.: Rutgers University Press, 1966.

———. "The Scotch School of Aesthetic Theory and the Natural Description of *The Oregon Trail*," *The Southwestern Journal* 4 (1949), 156-72.

Vaughan, Alden T. (ed.). *The Puritan Tradition in America 1620-1730*. New York: Harper & Row Paperback, 1972.

Wagar, W. Warren. "Modern Views of the Origins of the Idea of Progress," *Journal of the History of Ideas: A Quarterly Devoted to Cultural and Intellectual History* 28 (January-March 1967), 55-70.

Walters, Ronald G. "The Erotic South: Civilization and Sexuality in American Abolitionism," *American Quarterly* 25 (May 1973), 177-201.

Ward, John William. *Andrew Jackson: Symbol for an Age*. New York: Oxford University Press, 1955.

———. "Jacksonian Democratic Thought: 'A Natural Charter of Privilege,'" in Stanley Coben and Lorman Ratner (eds.), *The Development of American Culture*. Englewood Cliffs, N.J.: Prentice-Hall, 1970.

———. *Red, White, and Blue: Men, Books, and Ideas in American Culture*. New York: Oxford University Press, 1969.

Weaver, Raymond M. *Herman Melville: Mariner and Mystic*. New York: George H. Doran Co., 1921.

Weaver, Richard. *The Ethics of Rhetoric*. Chicago: Gateway Paperback Edition, 1953.

Wedgwood, C. V. *The Common Man in the Great Civil War*. Leicester, England: Leicester University Press, 1957.

Weinberg, Albert Katz. *Manifest Destiny: A Study of Nationalist Expansionism in American History*. Baltimore: The Johns Hopkins University Press, 1935.

Welter, Rush. "The History of Ideas in America: An Essay in Redefinition," *Journal of American History* 51 (March 1965), 599-614.

———. *The Mind of America, 1820-1860*. New York: Columbia University Press, 1975.

Williams, George H. *Wilderness and Paradise in Christian Thought: The Biblical Experience of the Desert in the History of Christianity & the Paradise Theme in the Theological Idea of the University*. New York: Harper, 1962.

Wilson, Edmund. *Patriotic Gore: Studies in the Literature of the American Civil War.* New York: Galaxy Paper Edition, 1966.

Wise, Gene. *American Historical Explanations: A Strategy for Grounded Inquiry.* Homewood, Ill.: Dorsey Press, 1973.

Wohl, R. Richard. "Intellectual History: An Historian's View," *The Historian: A Journal of History* 16 (Autumn, 1953), 62-77.

Wolfe, Tom. *Mauve Gloves & Madmen, Clutter & Vine and Other Stories, Sketches, and Essays.* New York: Farrar, Straus & Giroux, 1976.

Woodward, C. Vann. "The Southern Ethic in a Puritan World," *William and Mary Quarterly: A Magazine of Early American History*, Third Series, 25 (July 1968), 343-70.

Wylie, Philip. *Generation of Vipers*. New York: Rinehart & Co., 1942.

INDEX

About the Author

LEWIS O. SAUM is Professor of History at the University of Washington, Seattle. He is the author of *The Fur Trader and the Indian*. His articles have appeared in a variety of journals including *Civil War History, Missouri Historical Review, American Quarterly*, and *Pacific Northwest Quarterly*.